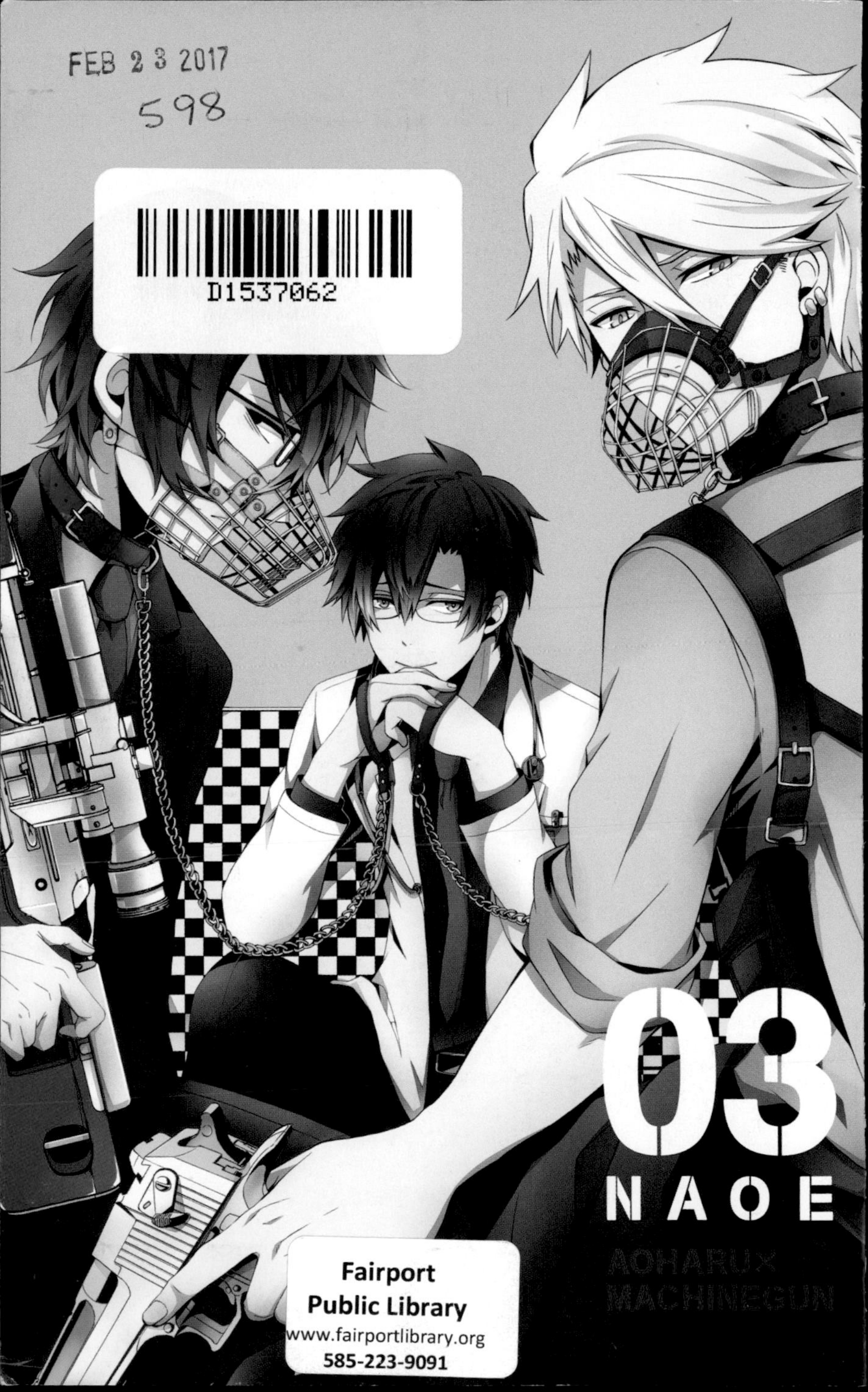
03
NAOE
AOHARUX
MACHINEGUN

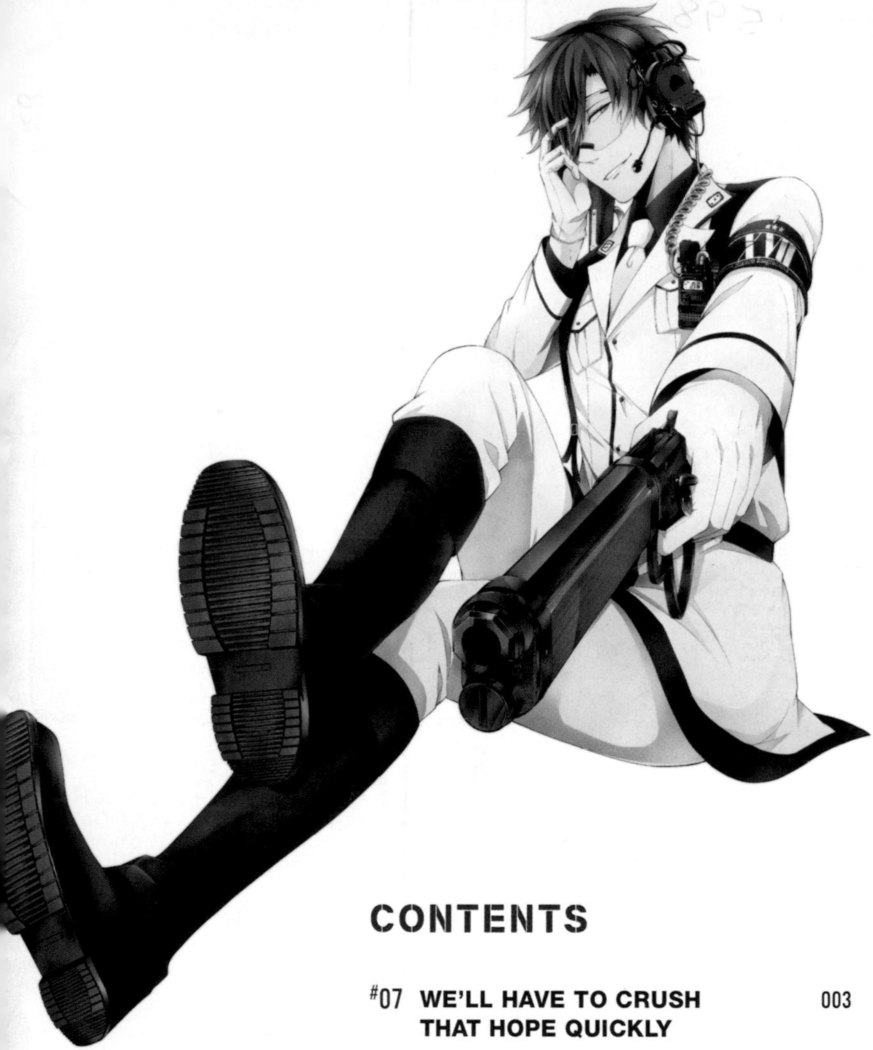

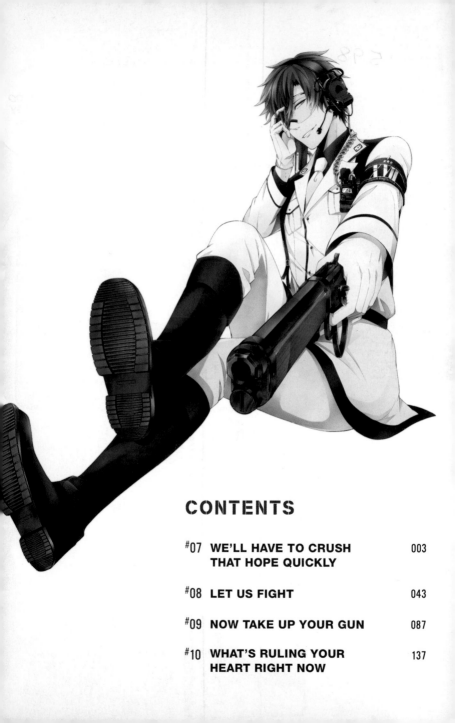

CONTENTS

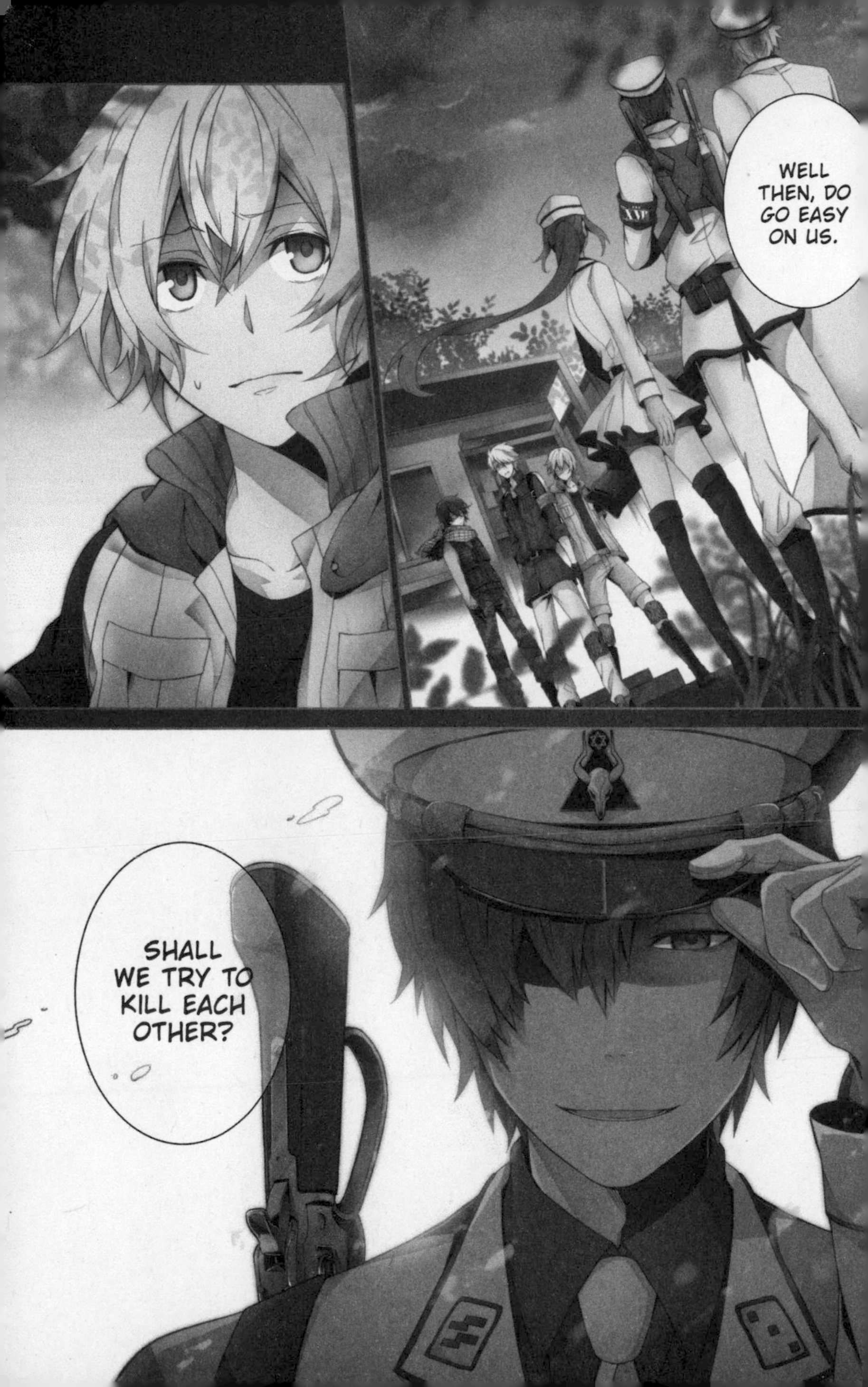
WELL THEN, DO GO EASY ON US.
SHALL WE TRY TO KILL EACH OTHER?

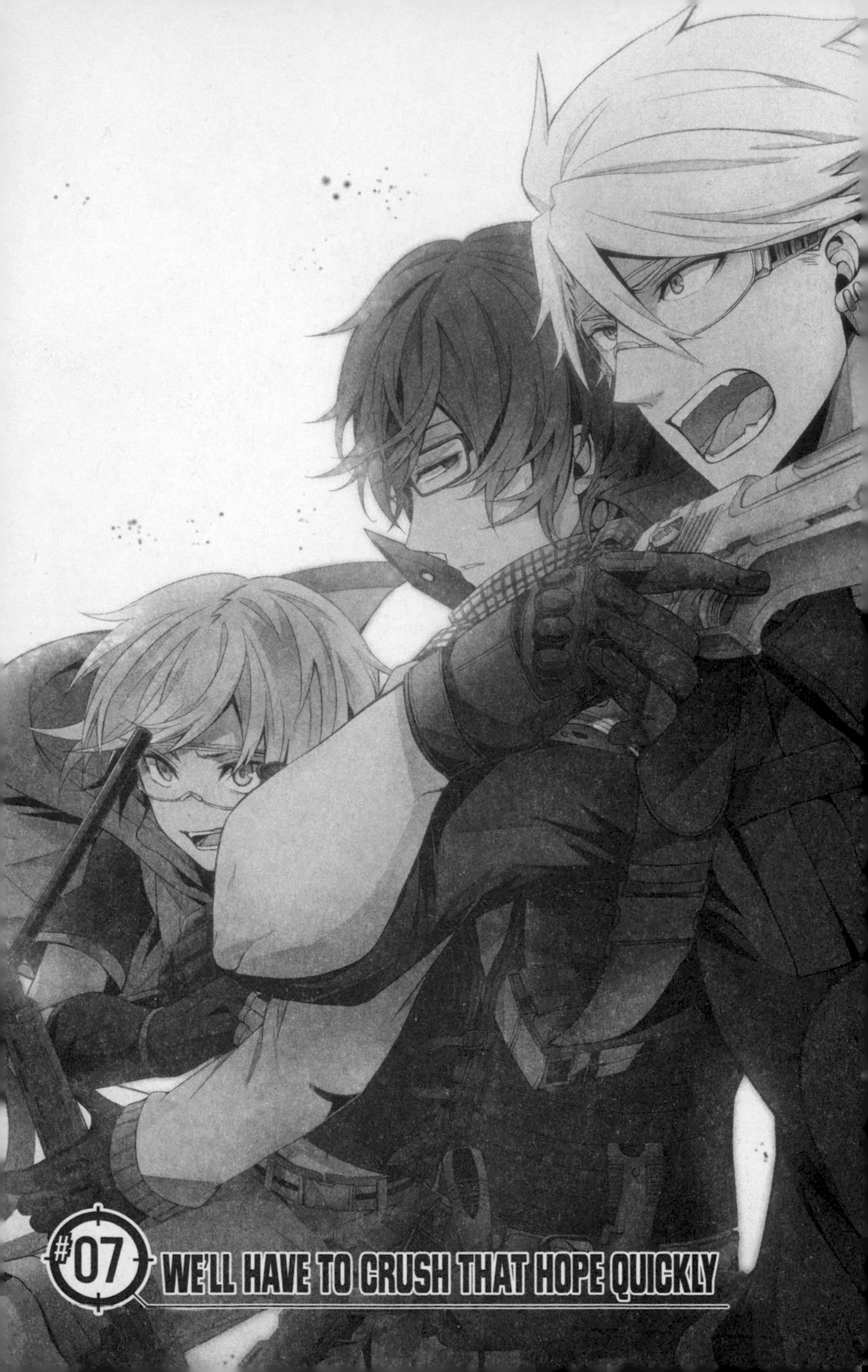
#07
WE'LL HAVE TO CRUSH THAT HOPE QUICKLY

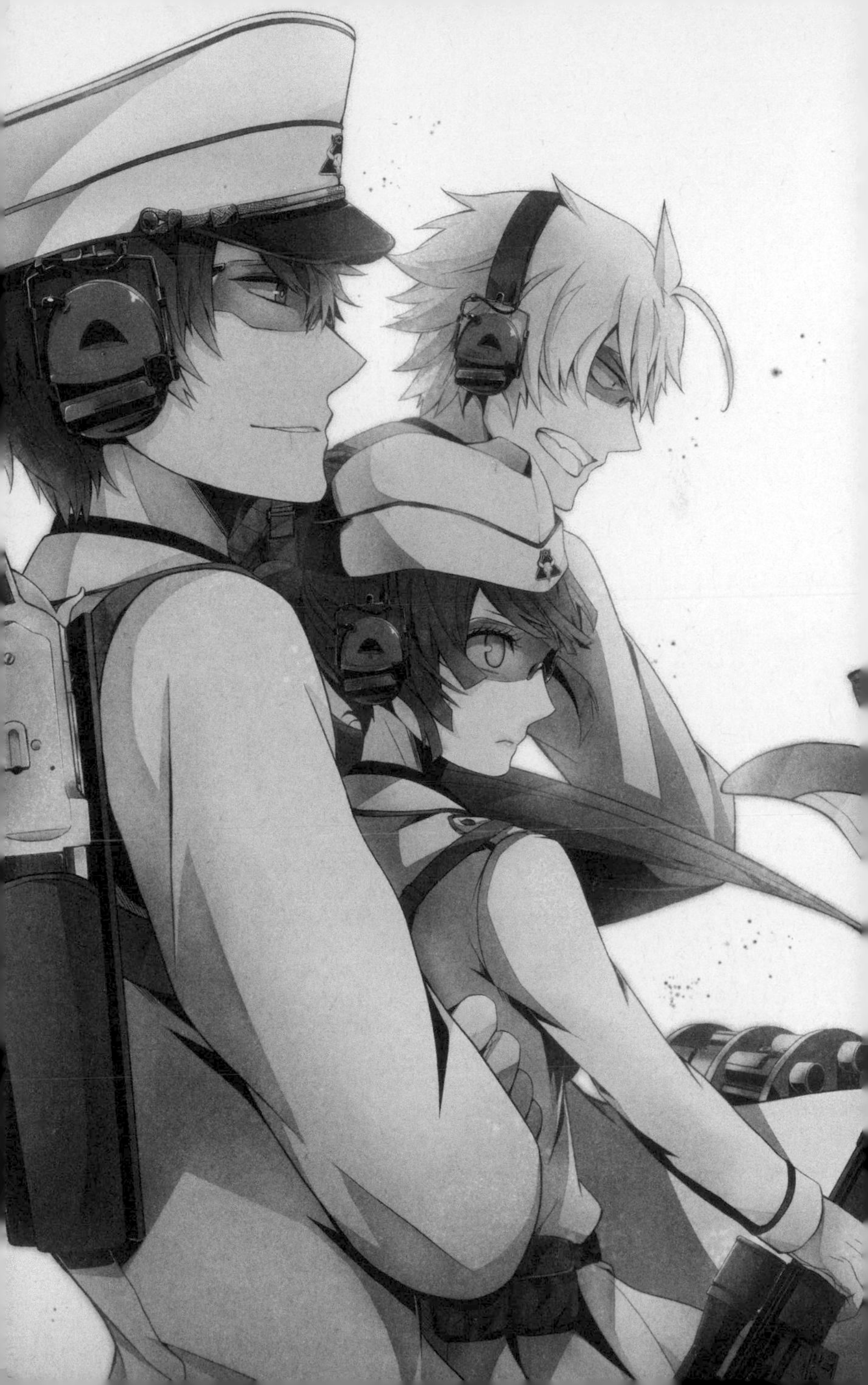

AOHARU

MACHINE GUN

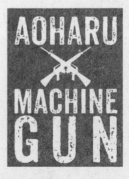

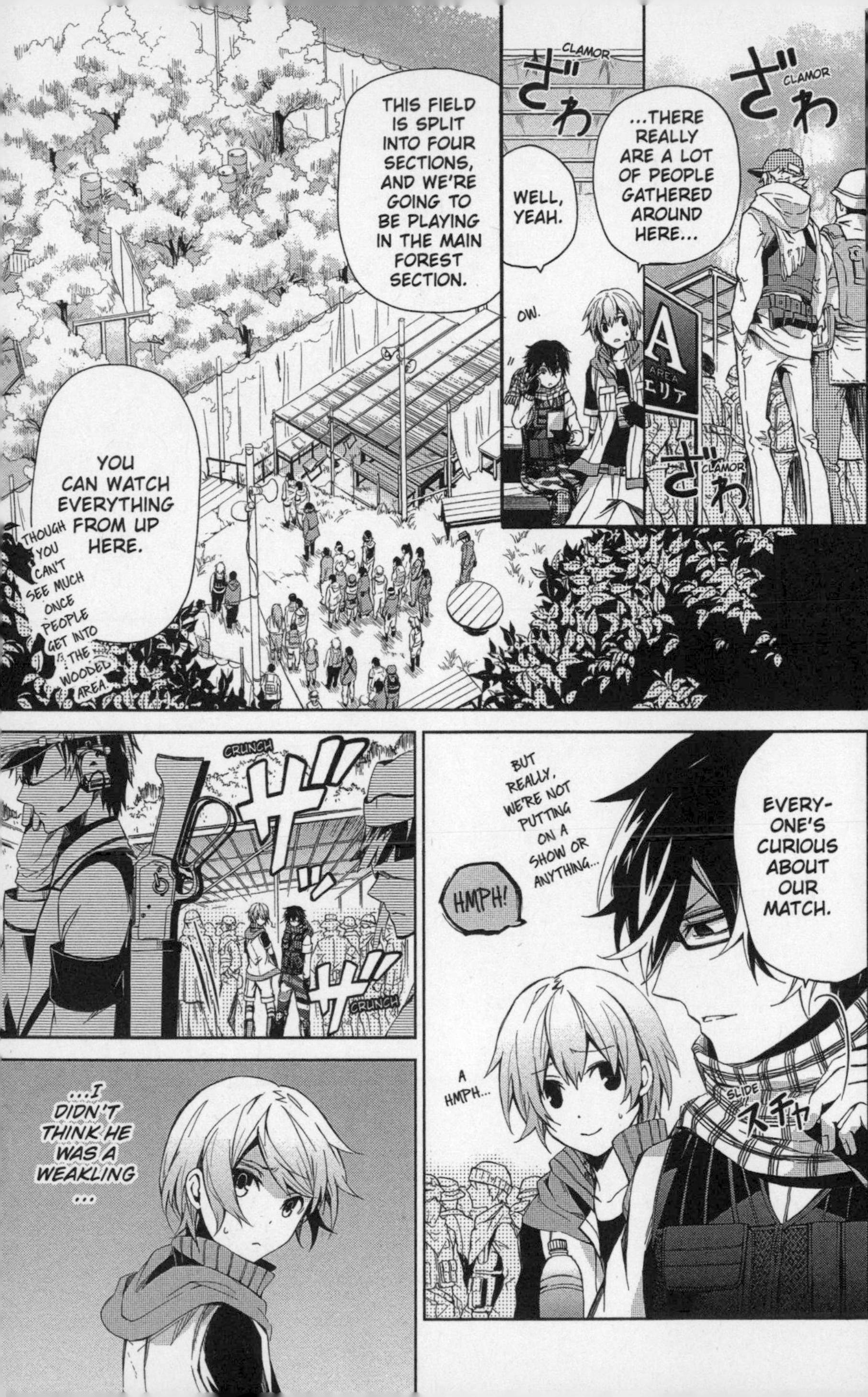

CLAMOR
ざわ
CLAMOR
ざわ
...THERE REALLY ARE A LOT OF PEOPLE GATHERED AROUND HERE...
WELL, YEAH.
OW.
A
AREA
エリア
CLAMOR
ざわ
THIS FIELD IS SPLIT INTO FOUR SECTIONS, AND WE'RE GOING TO BE PLAYING IN THE MAIN FOREST SECTION.
YOU CAN WATCH EVERYTHING FROM UP HERE.
THOUGH YOU CAN'T SEE MUCH ONCE PEOPLE GET INTO THE WOODED AREA.
EVERY-ONE'S CURIOUS ABOUT OUR MATCH.
BUT REALLY, WE'RE NOT PUTTING ON A SHOW OR ANYTHING...
HMPH!
A HMPH...
SLIDE
スチャ
CRUNCH
ザッ
ザッ
CRUNCH
...I DIDN'T THINK HE WAS A WEAKLING...

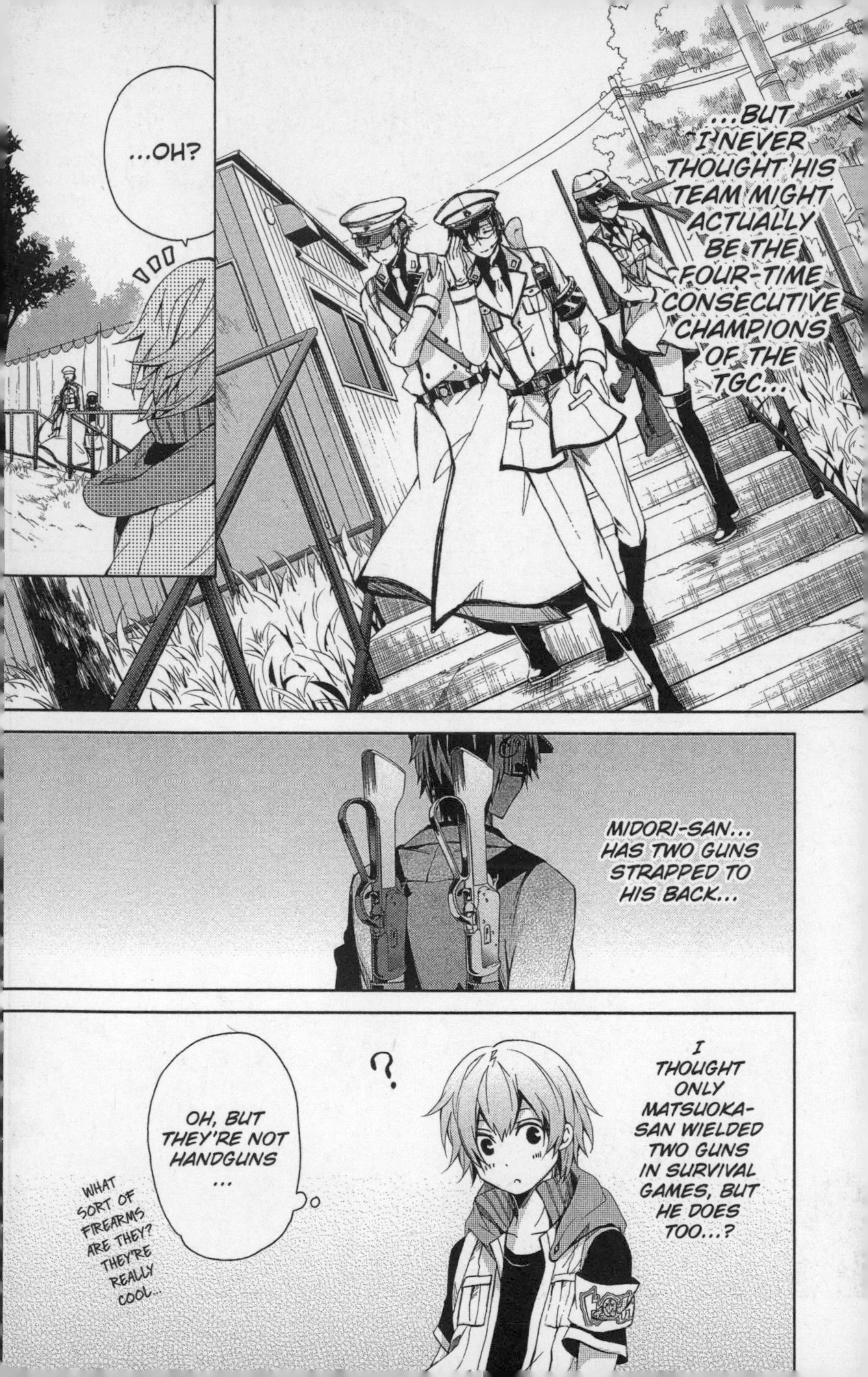
...BUT I NEVER THOUGHT HIS TEAM MIGHT ACTUALLY BE THE FOUR-TIME CONSECUTIVE CHAMPIONS OF THE TGC...
...OH?
MIDORI-SAN... HAS TWO GUNS STRAPPED TO HIS BACK...
I THOUGHT ONLY MATSUOKA-SAN WIELDED TWO GUNS IN SURVIVAL GAMES, BUT HE DOES TOO...?
OH, BUT THEY'RE NOT HANDGUNS...
WHAT SORT OF FIREARMS ARE THEY? THEY'RE REALLY COOL...

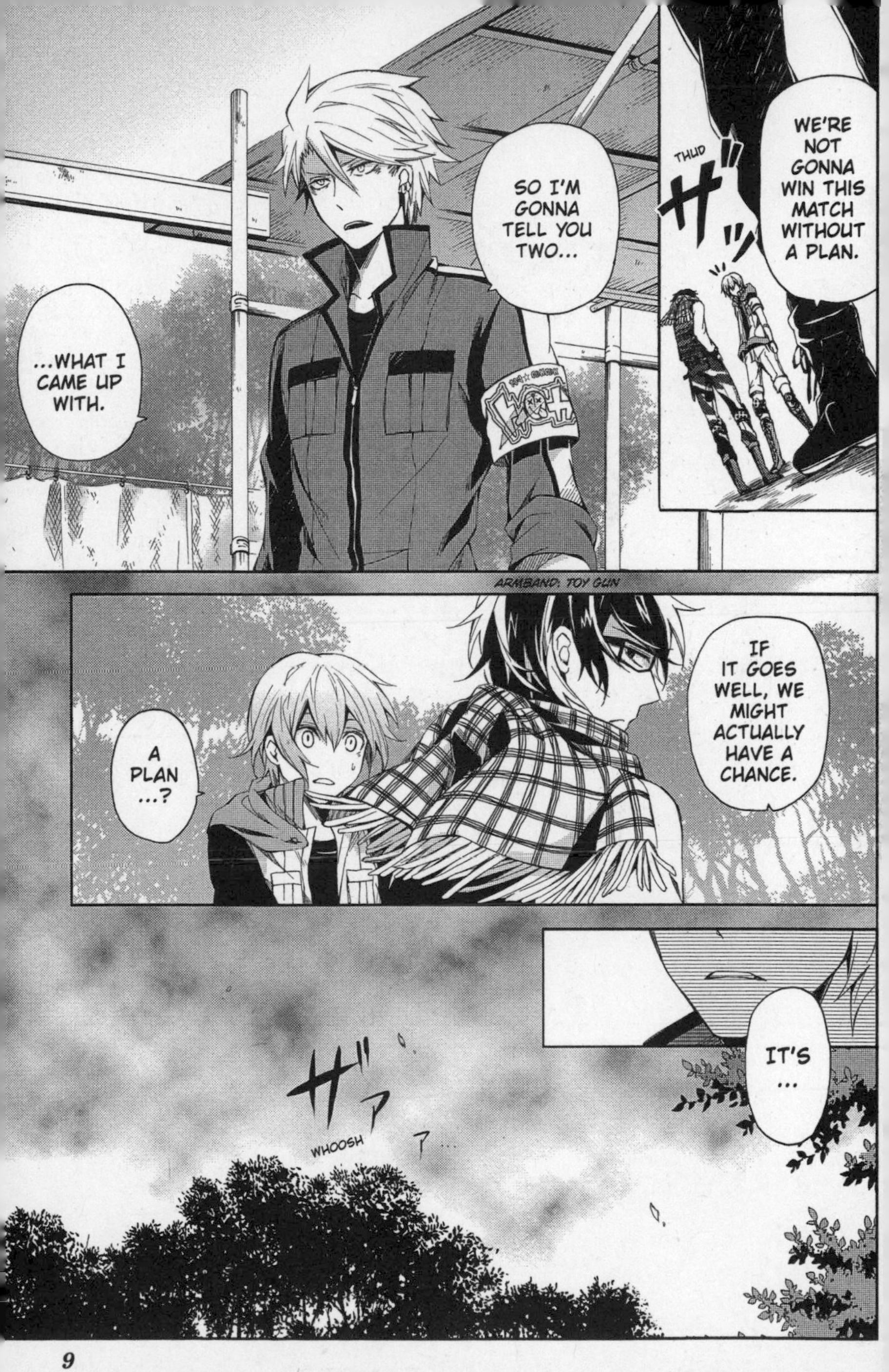
WE'RE NOT GONNA WIN THIS MATCH WITHOUT A PLAN.
THUD
ザッ
SO I'M GONNA TELL YOU TWO...
...WHAT I CAME UP WITH.
ARMBAND: TOY GUN
IF IT GOES WELL, WE MIGHT ACTUALLY HAVE A CHANCE.
A PLAN ...?
IT'S ...
ザァァ...
WHOOSH

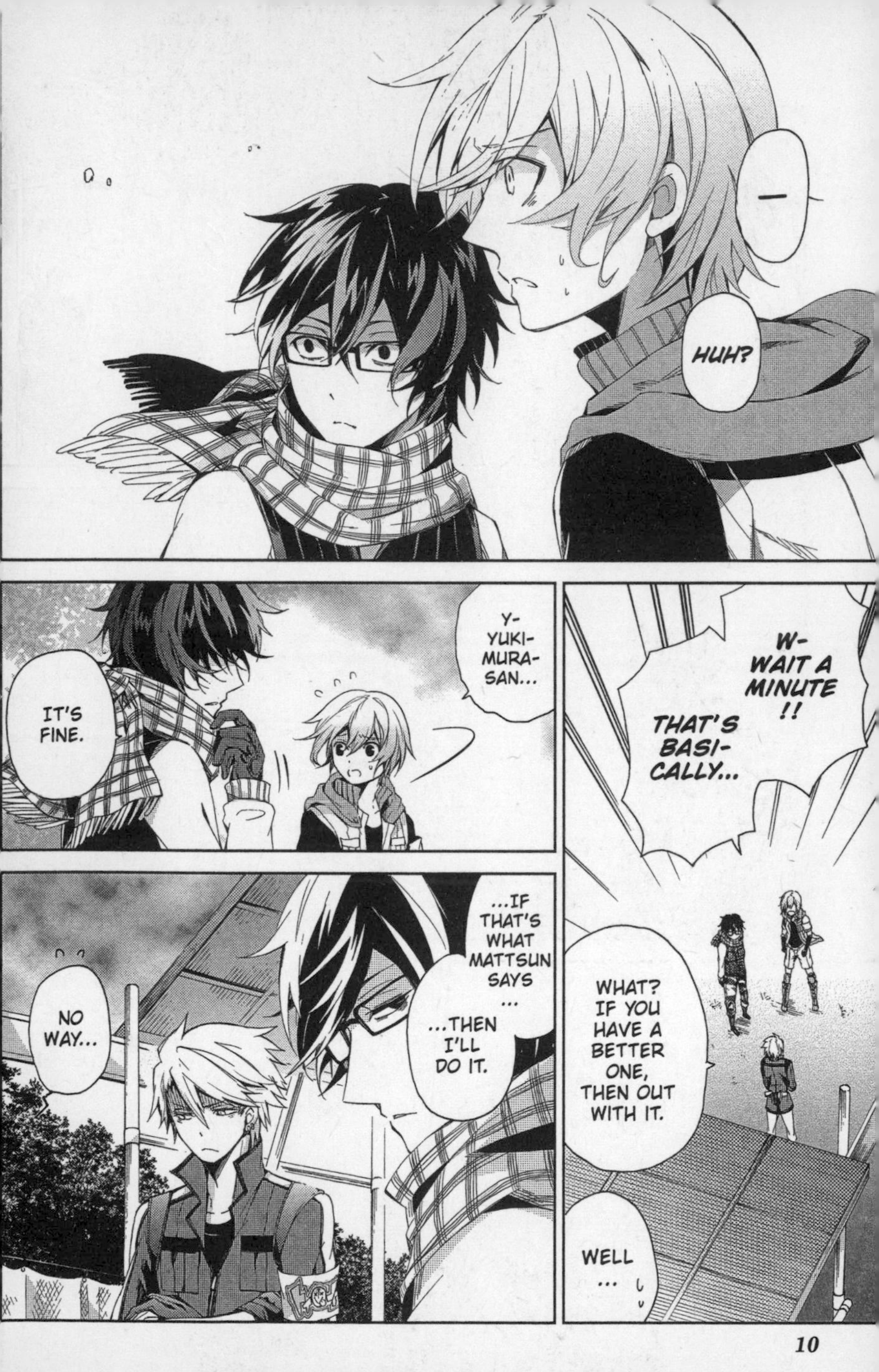
HUH?
W-
WAIT A MINUTE!!
THAT'S BASICALLY...
WHAT? IF YOU HAVE A BETTER ONE, THEN OUT WITH IT.
WELL...
Y-YUKIMURA-SAN...
IT'S FINE.
...IF THAT'S WHAT MATTSUN SAYS...
...THEN I'LL DO IT.
NO WAY...

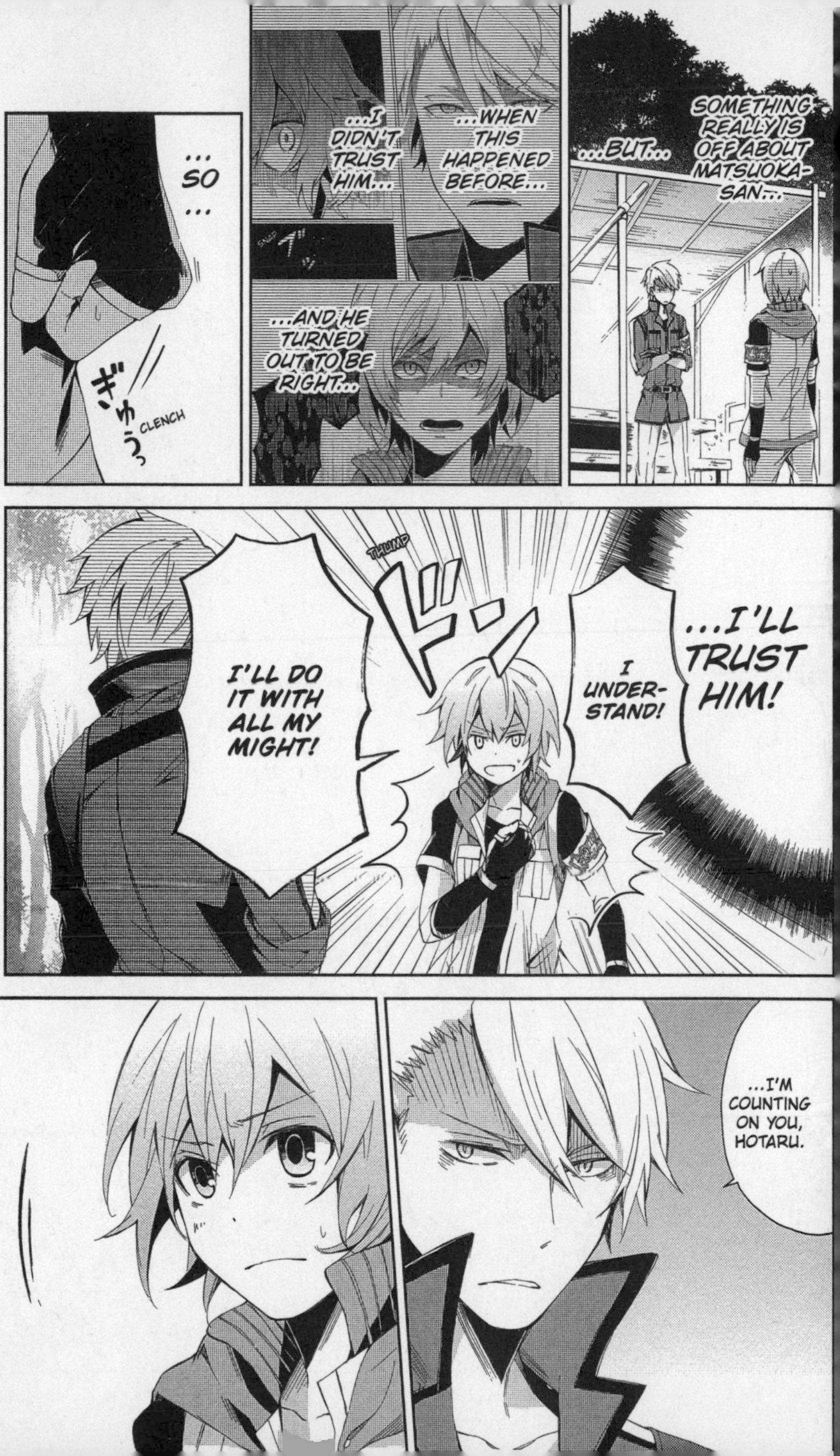

SOMETHING REALLY IS OFF ABOUT MATSUOKA-SAN...
...BUT...
...WHEN THIS HAPPENED BEFORE...
...I DIDN'T TRUST HIM...
SNAP
...AND HE TURNED OUT TO BE RIGHT...
...SO...
CLENCH
...I'LL TRUST HIM!
I UNDERSTAND!
THUMP
I'LL DO IT WITH ALL MY MIGHT!
...I'M COUNTING ON YOU, HOTARU.

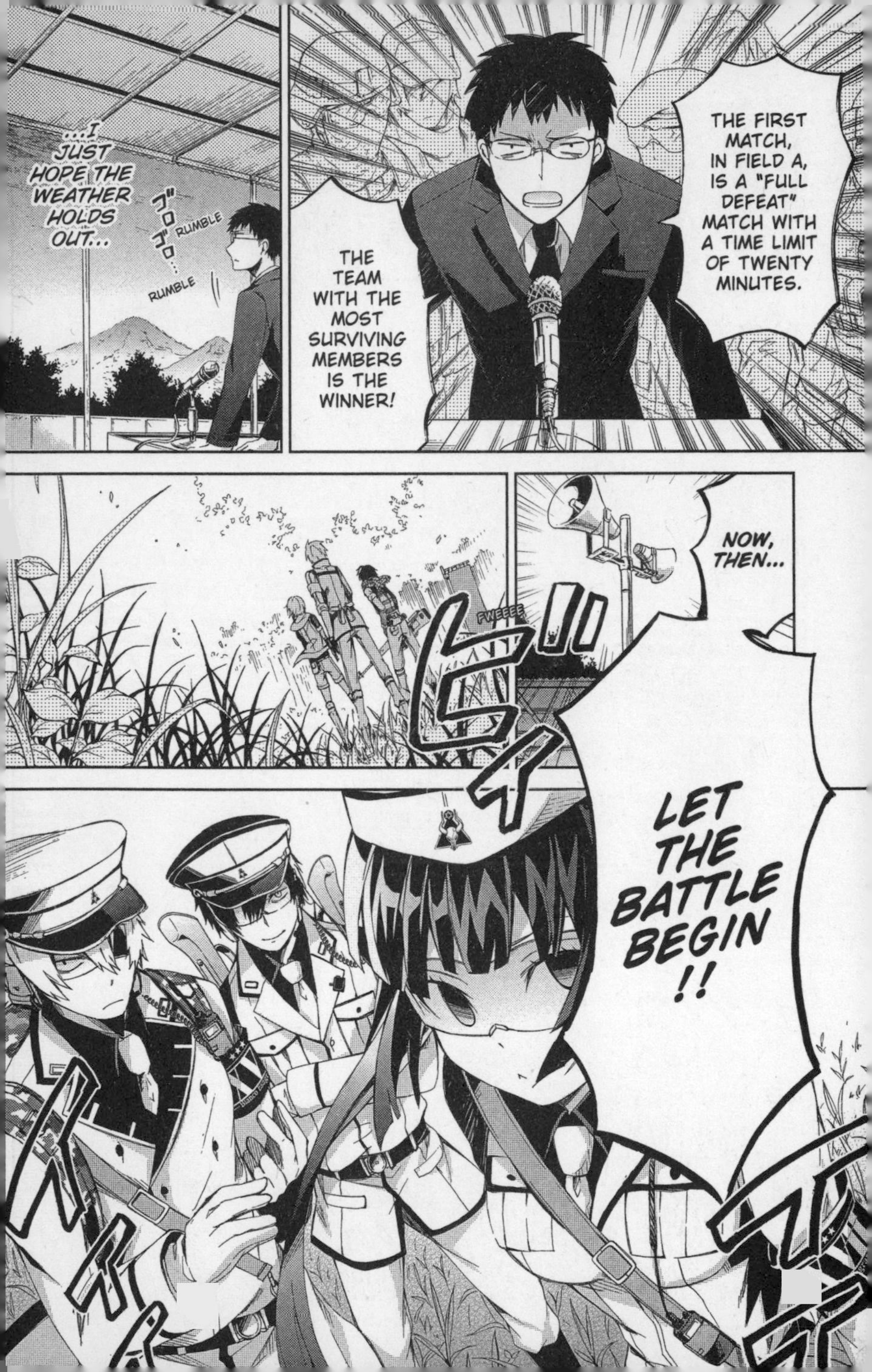
THE FIRST MATCH, IN FIELD A, IS A "FULL DEFEAT" MATCH WITH A TIME LIMIT OF TWENTY MINUTES.
THE TEAM WITH THE MOST SURVIVING MEMBERS IS THE WINNER!
...I JUST HOPE THE WEATHER HOLDS OUT...
ゴロゴロ...
RUMBLE
RUMBLE
NOW, THEN...
ピィ
FWEEEE
LET THE BATTLE BEGIN!!

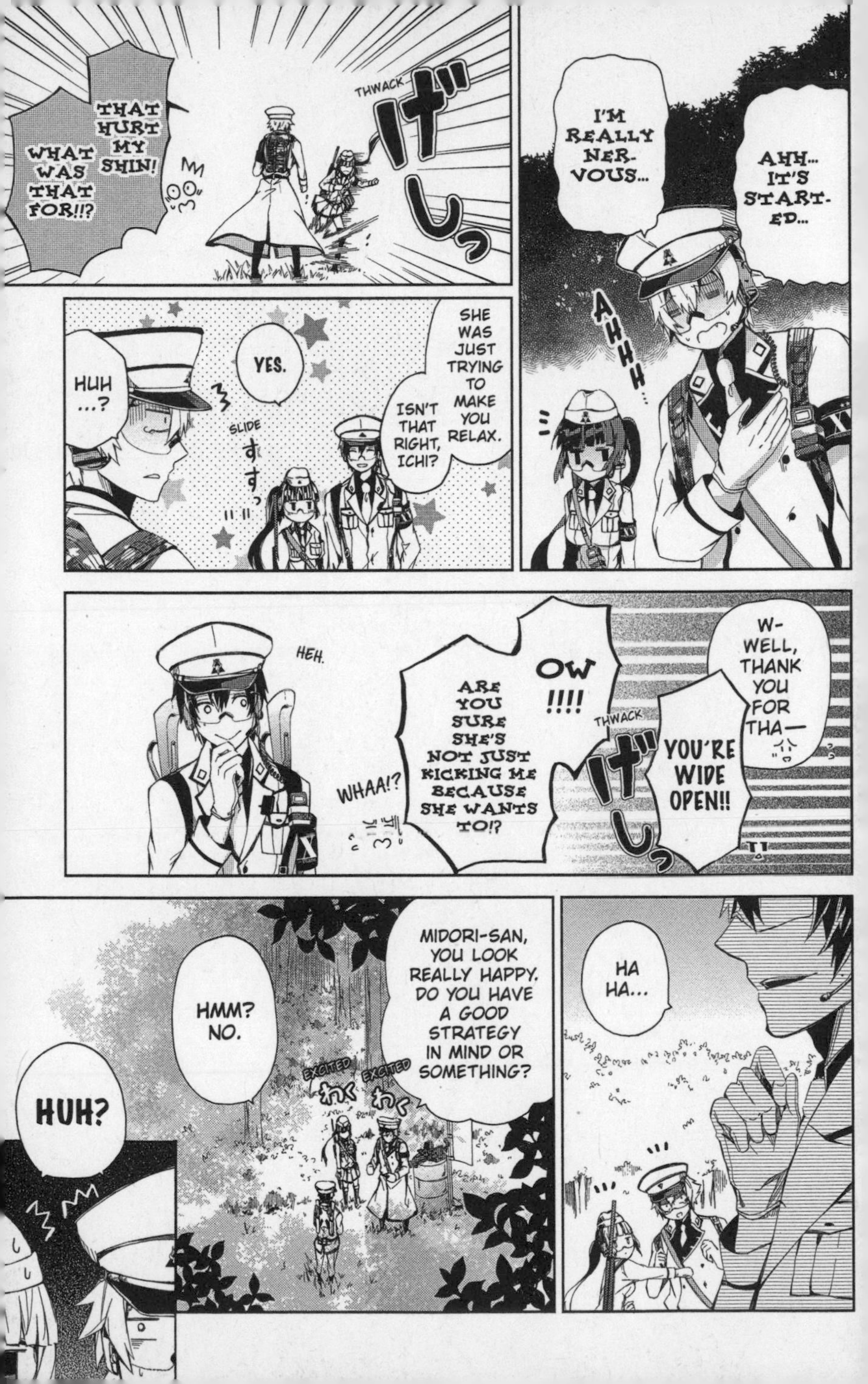
AHH... IT'S START-ED...
I'M REALLY NER-VOUS...
AHHH...
THWACK
THAT HURT MY SHIN!
WHAT WAS THAT FOR!!?
SHE WAS JUST TRYING TO MAKE YOU RELAX.
ISN'T THAT RIGHT, ICHI?
YES.
SLIDE
HUH ...?
W-WELL, THANK YOU FOR THA—
YOU'RE WIDE OPEN!!
THWACK
OW !!!!
ARE YOU SURE SHE'S NOT JUST KICKING ME BECAUSE SHE WANTS TO!?
WHAA!?
HEH.
HA HA...
MIDORI-SAN, YOU LOOK REALLY HAPPY. DO YOU HAVE A GOOD STRATEGY IN MIND OR SOMETHING?
HMM? NO.
EXCITED
EXCITED
HUH?

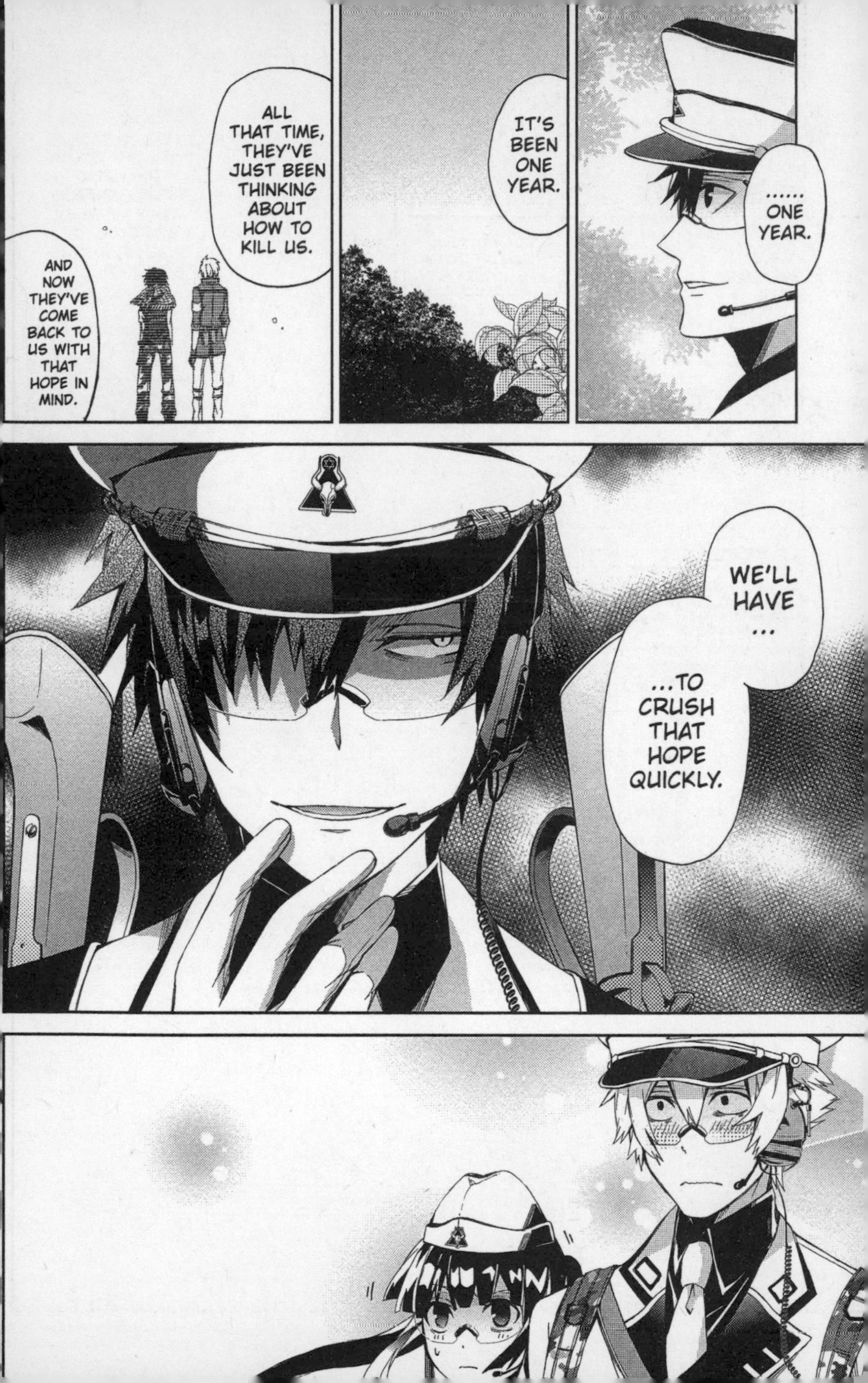
...... ONE YEAR.
IT'S BEEN ONE YEAR.
ALL THAT TIME, THEY'VE JUST BEEN THINKING ABOUT HOW TO KILL US.
AND NOW THEY'VE COME BACK TO US WITH THAT HOPE IN MIND.
WE'LL HAVE ...
...TO CRUSH THAT HOPE QUICKLY.

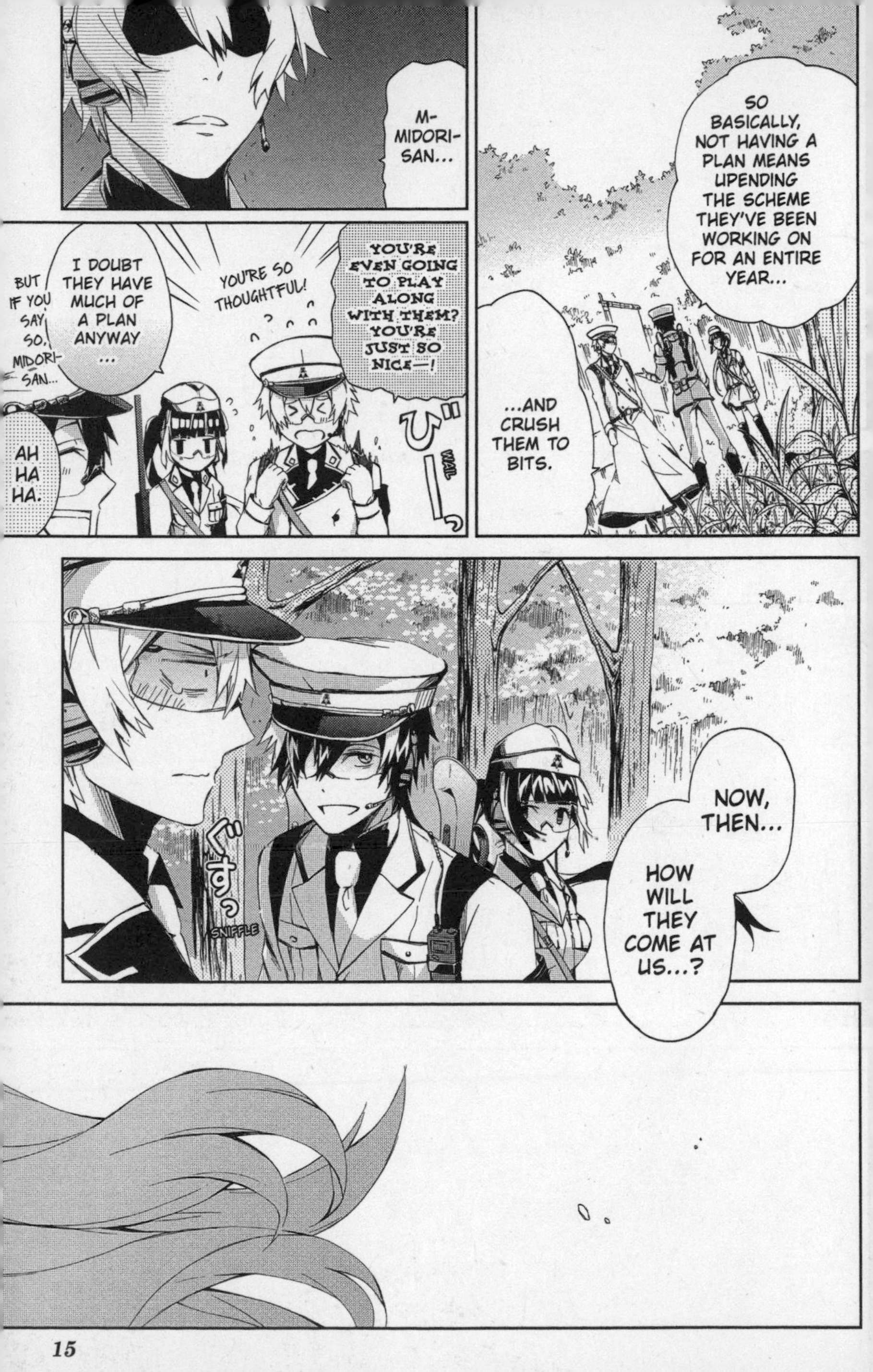

SO BASICALLY, NOT HAVING A PLAN MEANS UPENDING THE SCHEME THEY'VE BEEN WORKING ON FOR AN ENTIRE YEAR...
...AND CRUSH THEM TO BITS.
M-MIDORI-SAN...
YOU'RE EVEN GOING TO PLAY ALONG WITH THEM? YOU'RE JUST SO NICE—!
YOU'RE SO THOUGHTFUL!
うーっ
WAIL
I DOUBT THEY HAVE MUCH OF A PLAN ANYWAY...
BUT IF YOU SAY SO, MIDORI-SAN...
AH HA HA.
NOW, THEN...
HOW WILL THEY COME AT US...?
ぐすっ
SNIFFLE

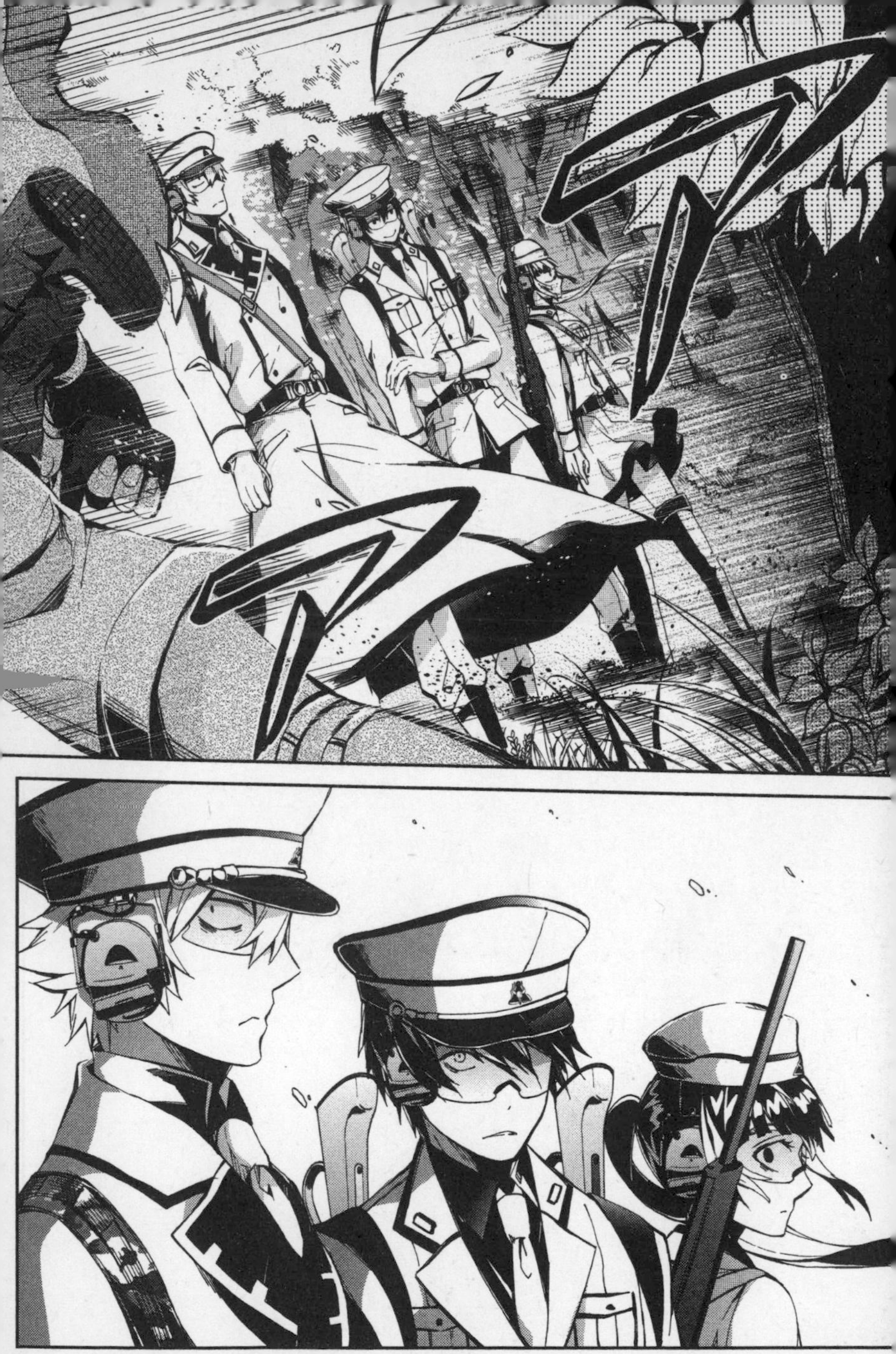

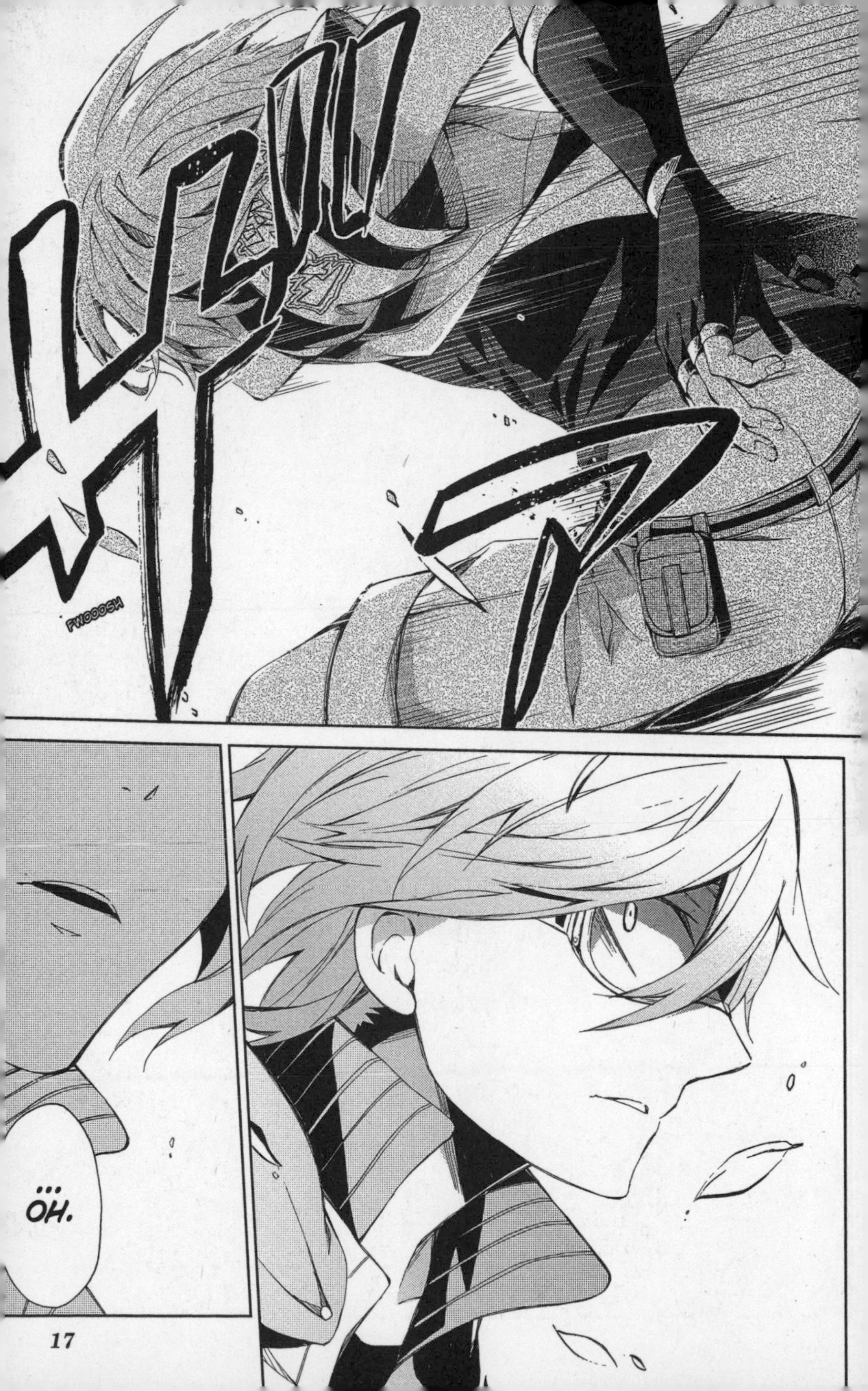
FWOOOSH
...OH.

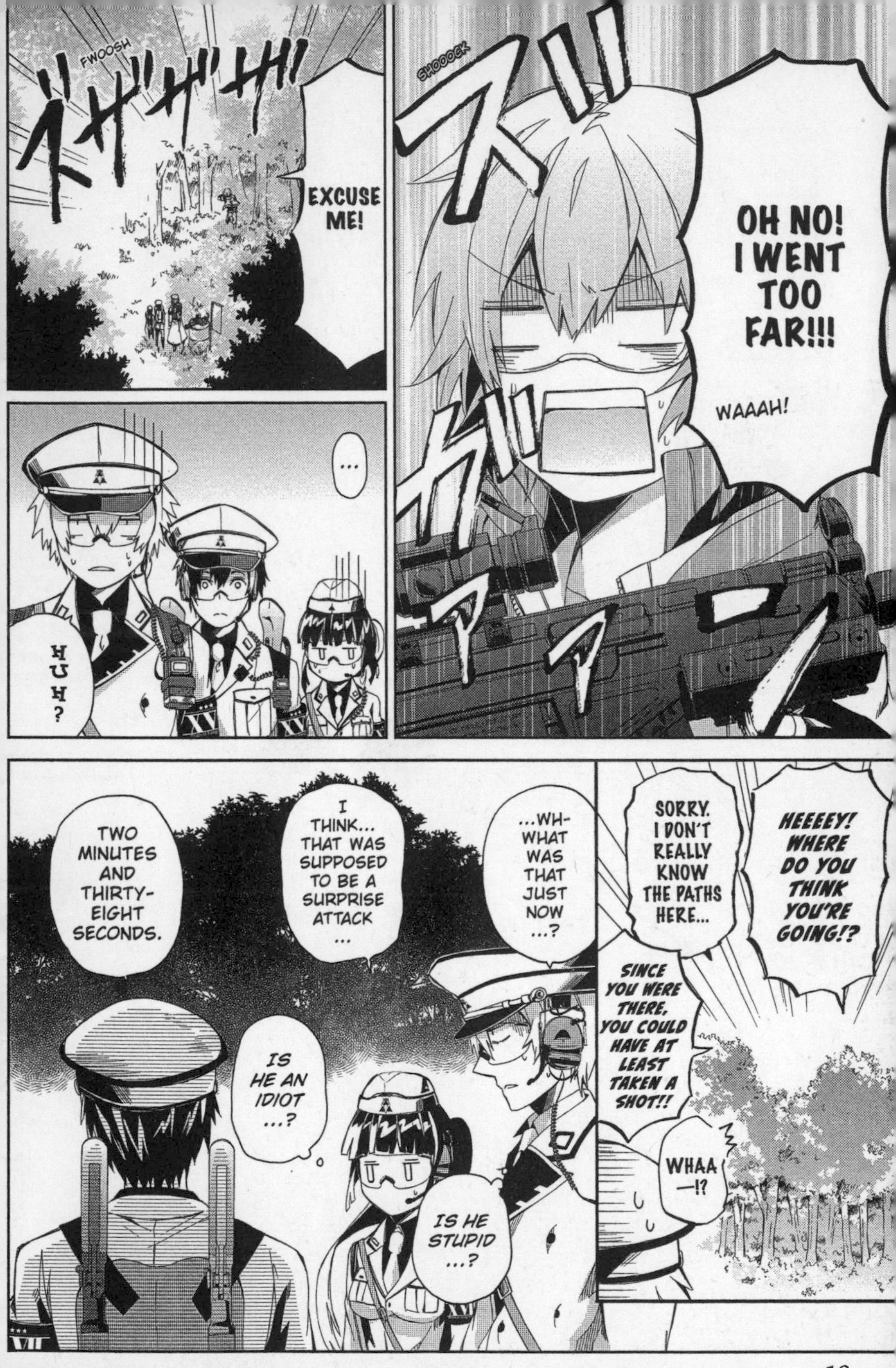
FWOOSH
EXCUSE ME!
SHOOOCK
OH NO! I WENT TOO FAR!!!
WAAAH!
...
HUH?
HEEEEY! WHERE DO YOU THINK YOU'RE GOING!?
SORRY. I DON'T REALLY KNOW THE PATHS HERE...
SINCE YOU WERE THERE, YOU COULD HAVE AT LEAST TAKEN A SHOT!!
WHAA—!?
...WH-WHAT WAS THAT JUST NOW ...?
I THINK... THAT WAS SUPPOSED TO BE A SURPRISE ATTACK ...
TWO MINUTES AND THIRTY-EIGHT SECONDS.
IS HE AN IDIOT ...?
IS HE STUPID ...?

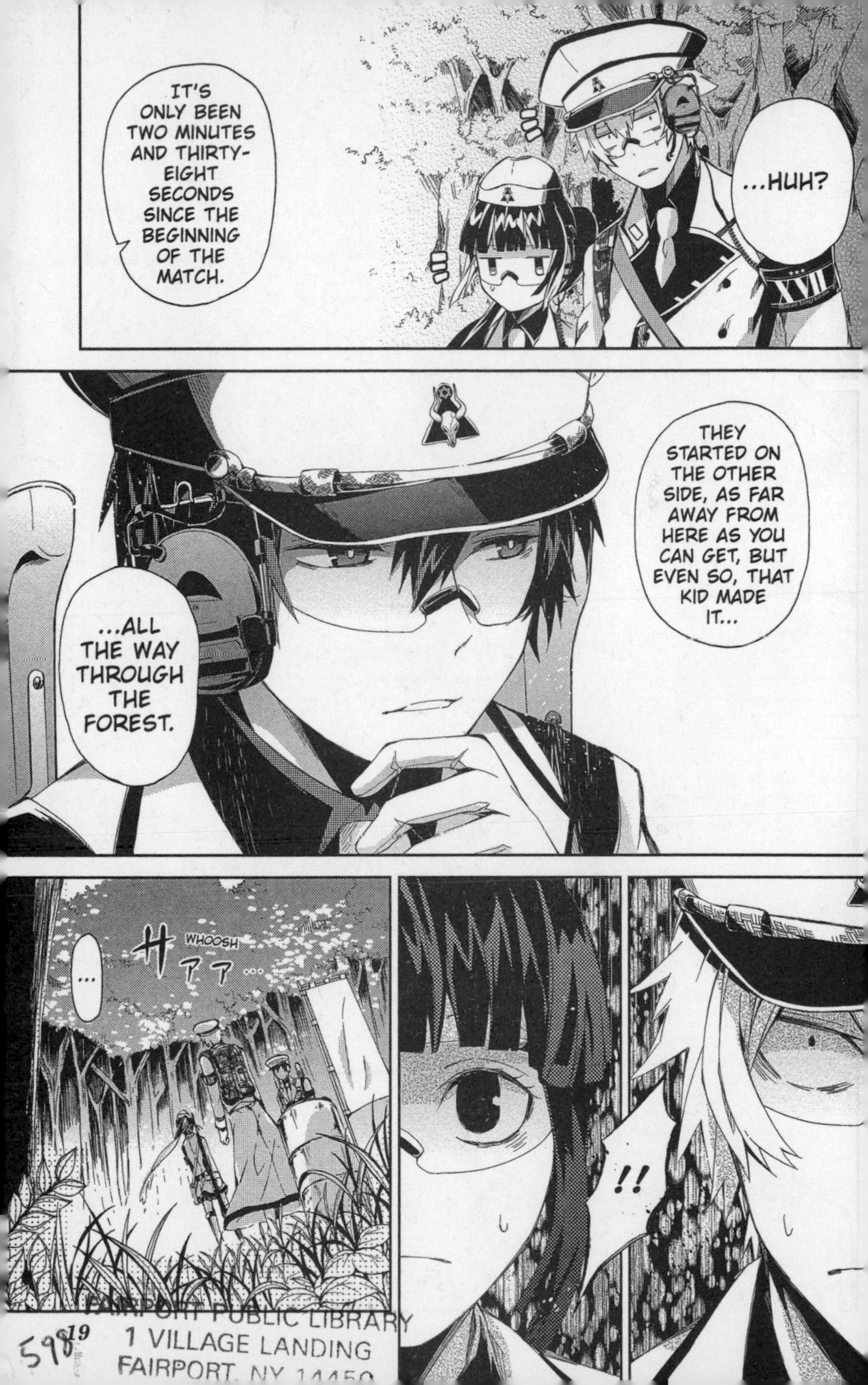
...HUH?
IT'S ONLY BEEN TWO MINUTES AND THIRTY-EIGHT SECONDS SINCE THE BEGINNING OF THE MATCH.
THEY STARTED ON THE OTHER SIDE, AS FAR AWAY FROM HERE AS YOU CAN GET, BUT EVEN SO, THAT KID MADE IT...
...ALL THE WAY THROUGH THE FOREST.
!!
...
WHOOSH

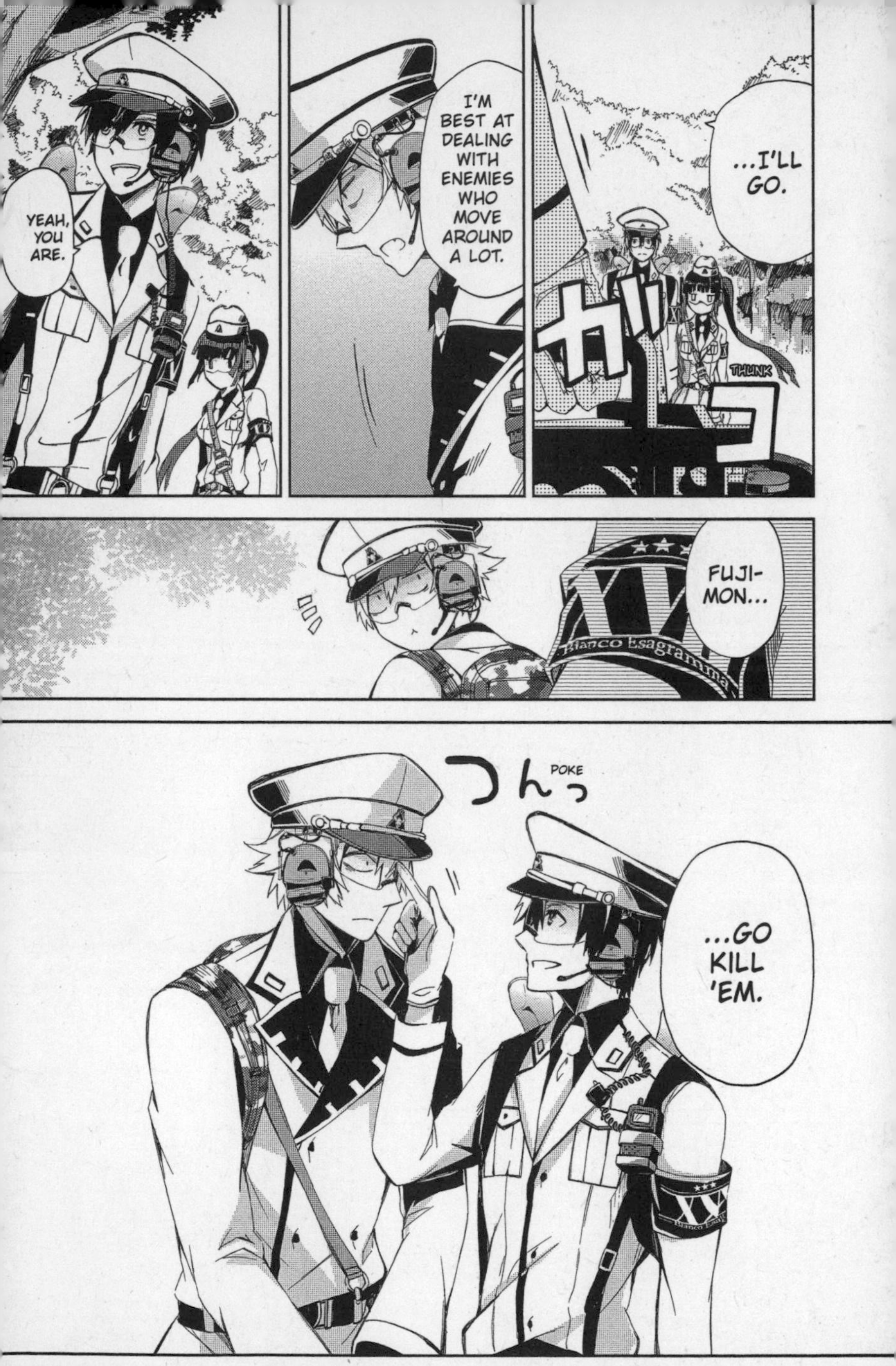
...I'LL GO.
THUNK
I'M BEST AT DEALING WITH ENEMIES WHO MOVE AROUND A LOT.
YEAH, YOU ARE.
FUJI-MON...
Blanco Esagramma
POKE
...GO KILL 'EM.

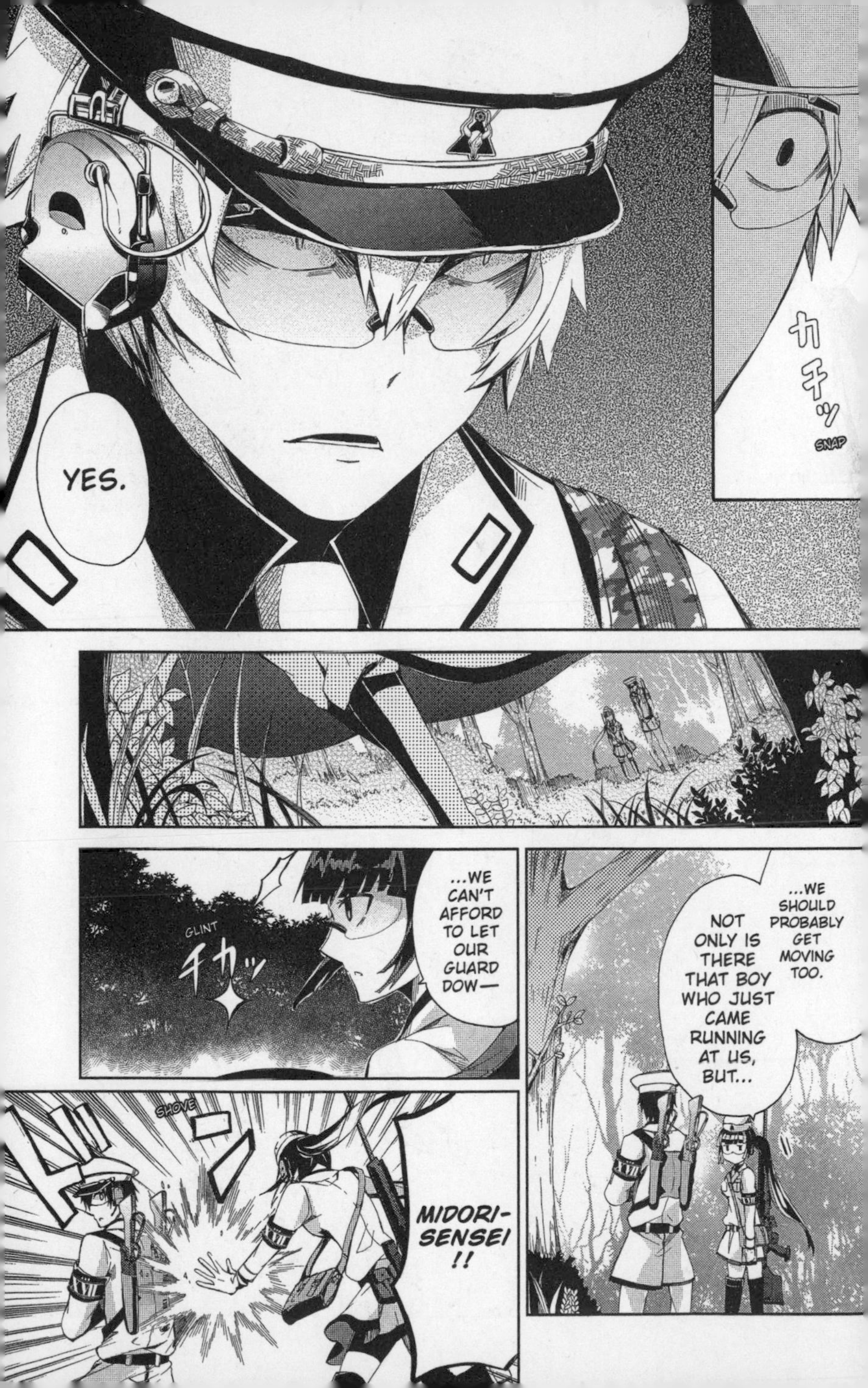
カチッ
SNAP
YES.
...WE SHOULD PROBABLY GET MOVING TOO.
NOT ONLY IS THERE THAT BOY WHO JUST CAME RUNNING AT US, BUT...
...WE CAN'T AFFORD TO LET OUR GUARD DOW—
GLINT
チカッ
SHOVE
MIDORI-SENSEI!!

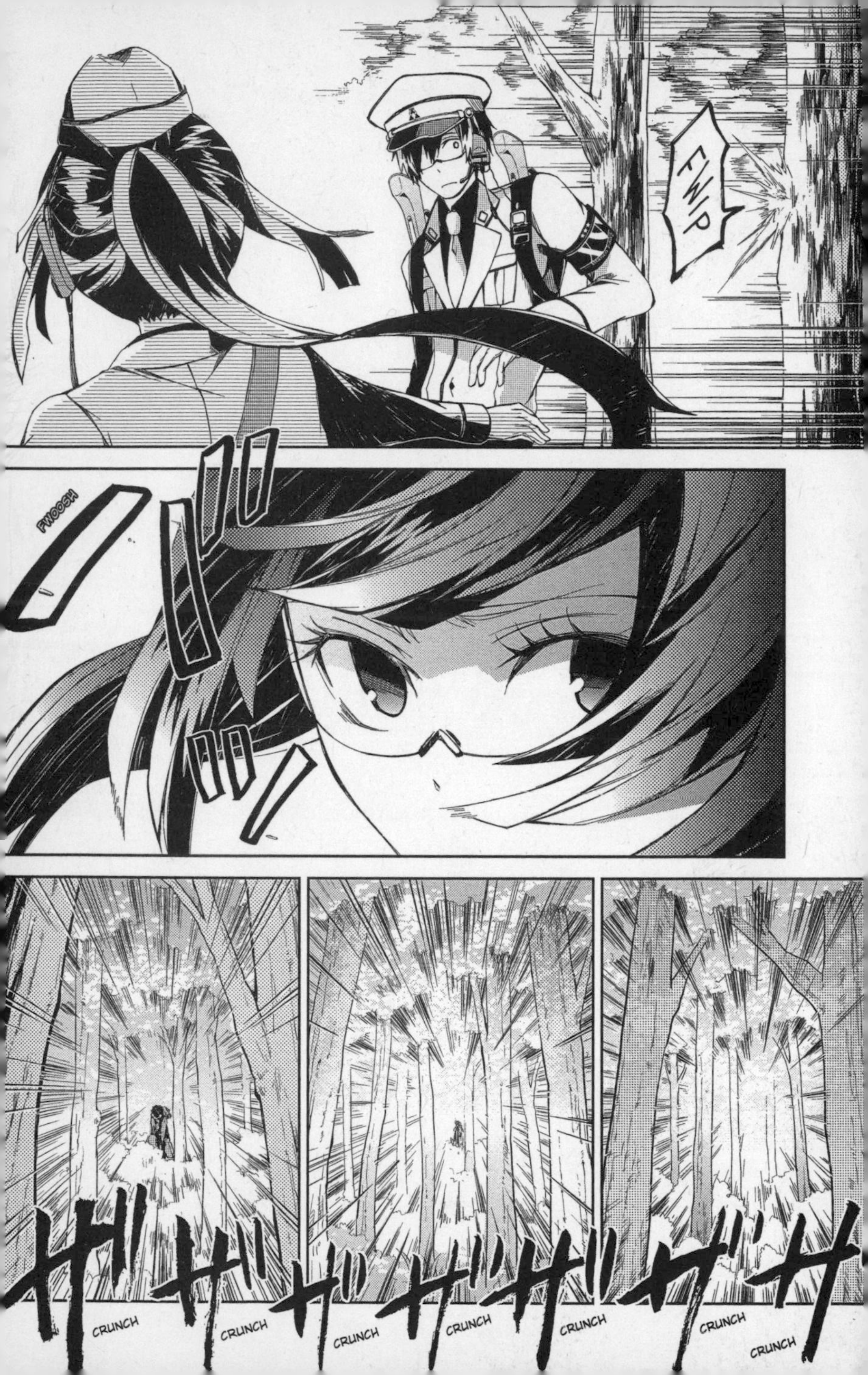

FWIP
FWOOSH
ザザザザザザザザ
CRUNCH
CRUNCH
CRUNCH
CRUNCH
CRUNCH
CRUNCH
CRUNCH

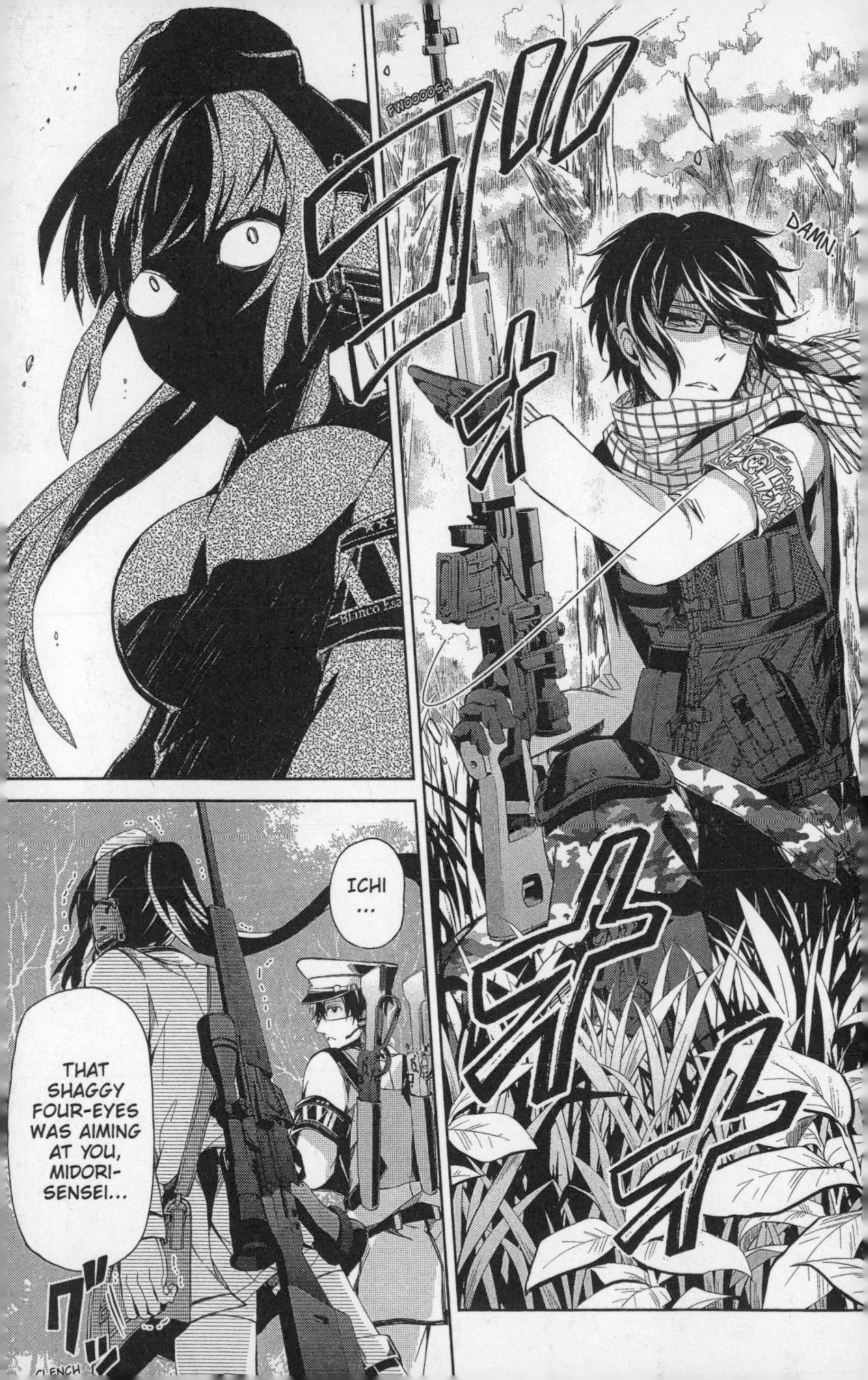
FWOOOOSH
DAMN.
ICHI ...
THAT SHAGGY FOUR-EYES WAS AIMING AT YOU, MIDORI-SENSEI...
CLENCH

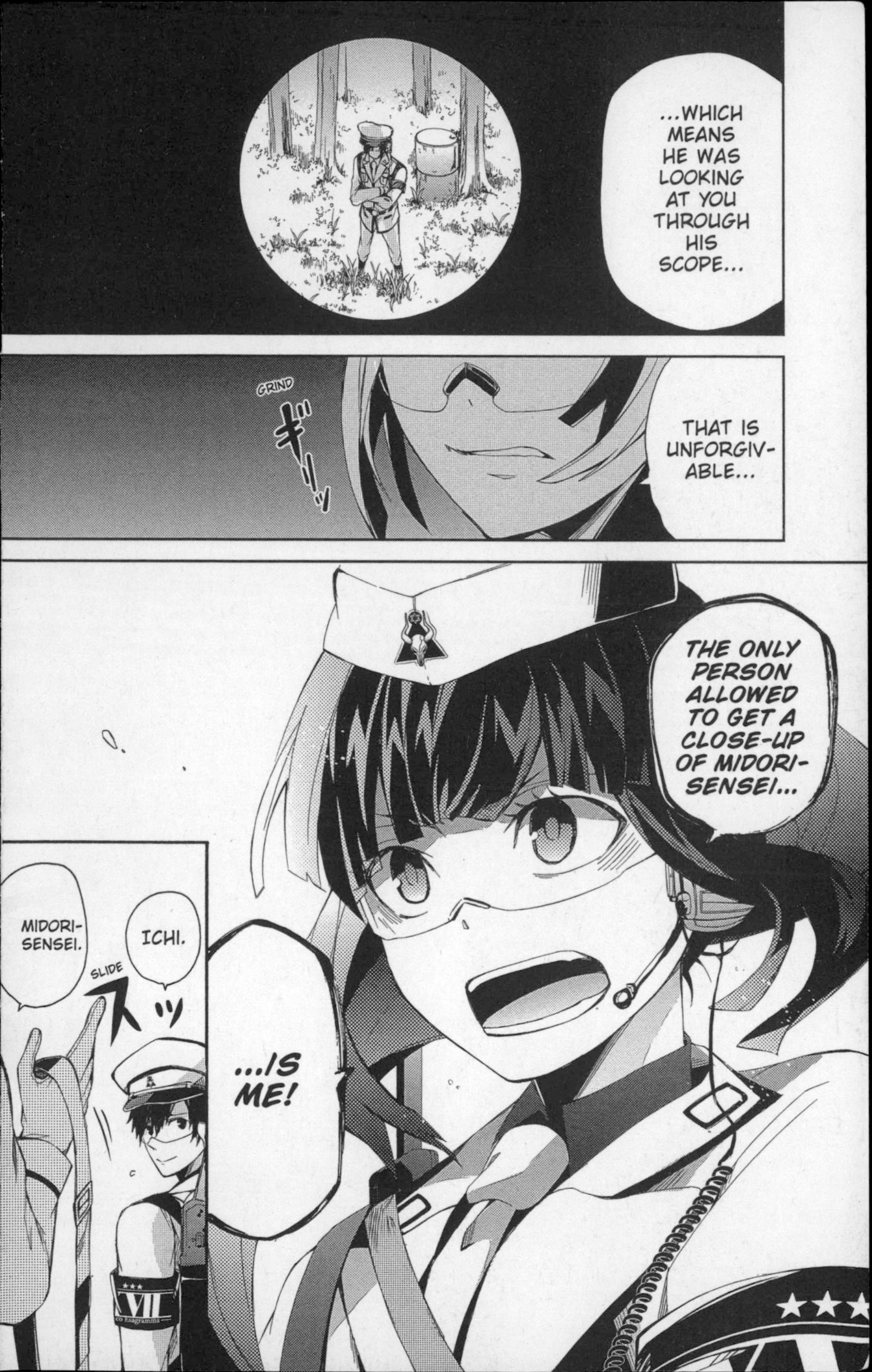
...WHICH MEANS HE WAS LOOKING AT YOU THROUGH HIS SCOPE...
GRIND
THAT IS UNFORGIV-ABLE...
THE ONLY PERSON ALLOWED TO GET A CLOSE-UP OF MIDORI-SENSEI...
...IS ME!
ICHI.
MIDORI-SENSEI.
SLIDE
VII

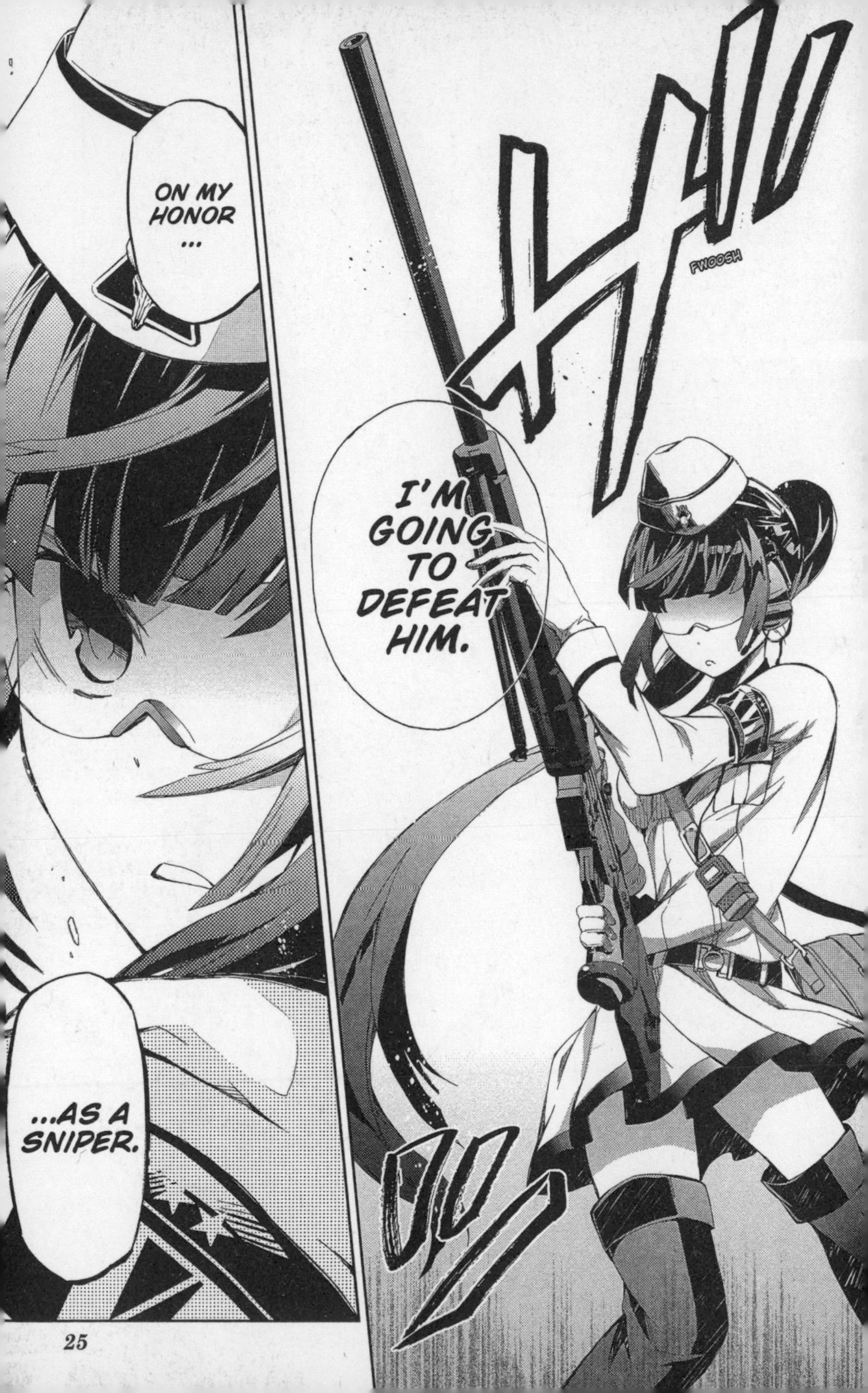
FWOOSH
I'M GOING TO DEFEAT HIM.
ON MY HONOR ...
...AS A SNIPER.

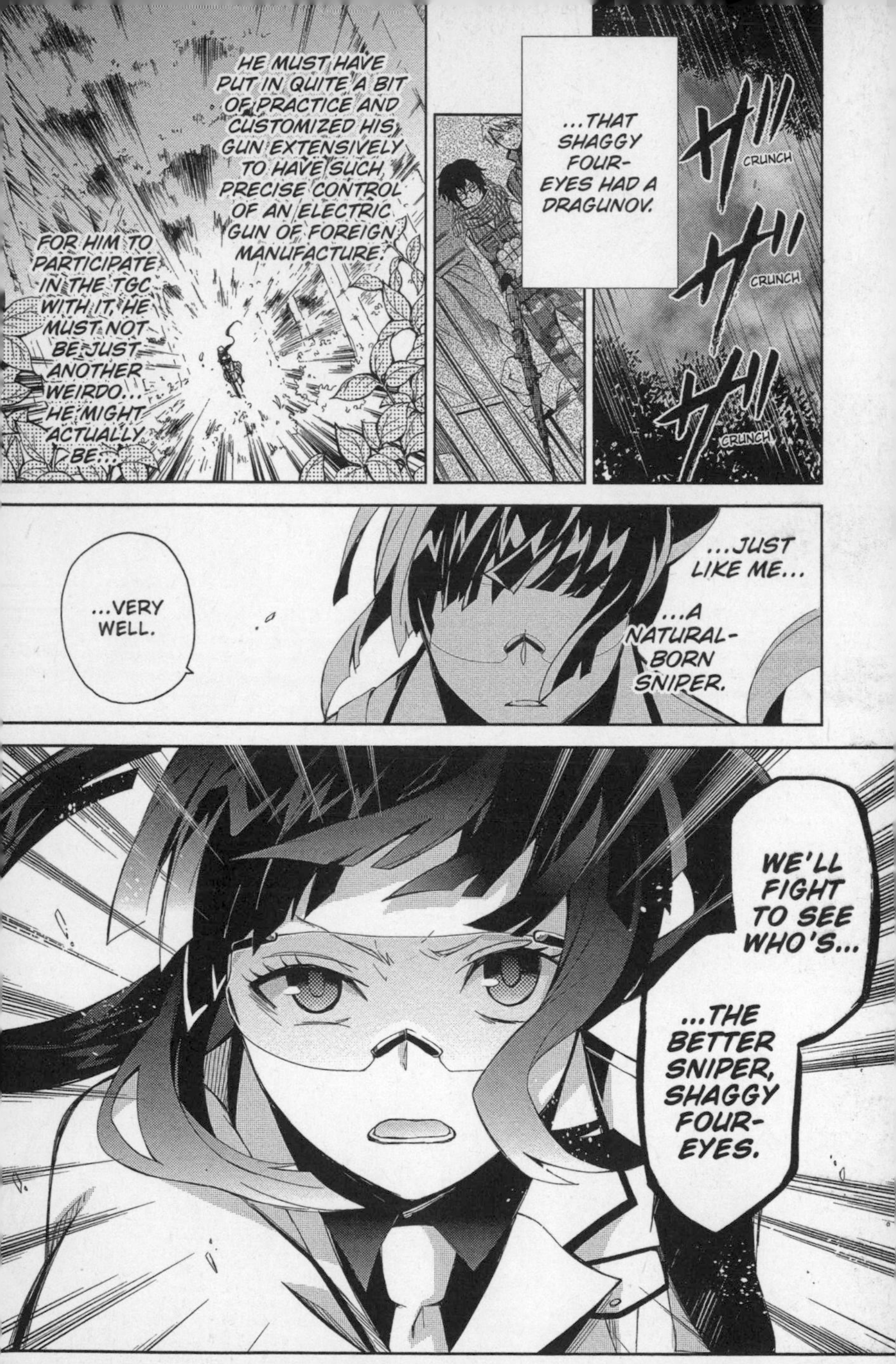

CRUNCH
CRUNCH
CRUNCH
...THAT SHAGGY FOUR-EYES HAD A DRAGUNOV.
HE MUST HAVE PUT IN QUITE A BIT OF PRACTICE AND CUSTOMIZED HIS GUN EXTENSIVELY TO HAVE SUCH PRECISE CONTROL OF AN ELECTRIC GUN OF FOREIGN MANUFACTURE.
FOR HIM TO PARTICIPATE IN THE TGC WITH IT, HE MUST NOT BE JUST ANOTHER WEIRDO... HE MIGHT ACTUALLY BE...
...JUST LIKE ME...
...A NATURAL-BORN SNIPER.
...VERY WELL.
WE'LL FIGHT TO SEE WHO'S...
...THE BETTER SNIPER, SHAGGY FOUR-EYES.

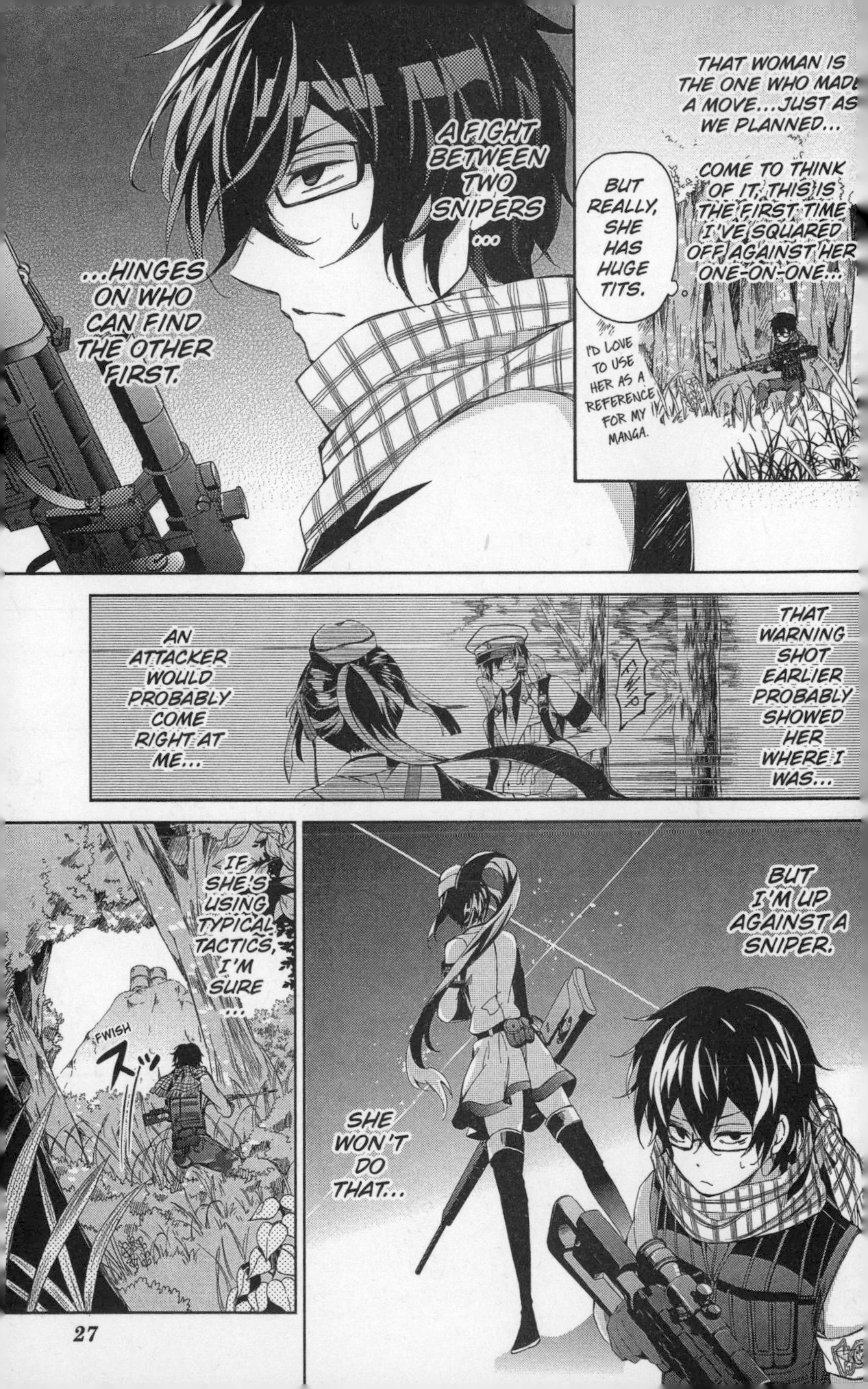
THAT WOMAN IS THE ONE WHO MADE A MOVE...JUST AS WE PLANNED...
COME TO THINK OF IT, THIS IS THE FIRST TIME I'VE SQUARED OFF AGAINST HER ONE-ON-ONE...
BUT REALLY, SHE HAS HUGE TITS.
I'D LOVE TO USE HER AS A REFERENCE FOR MY MANGA.
A FIGHT BETWEEN TWO SNIPERS...
...HINGES ON WHO CAN FIND THE OTHER FIRST.
THAT WARNING SHOT EARLIER PROBABLY SHOWED HER WHERE I WAS...
FWIP
AN ATTACKER WOULD PROBABLY COME RIGHT AT ME...
BUT I'M UP AGAINST A SNIPER.
SHE WON'T DO THAT...
IF SHE'S USING TYPICAL TACTICS, I'M SURE...
FWISH

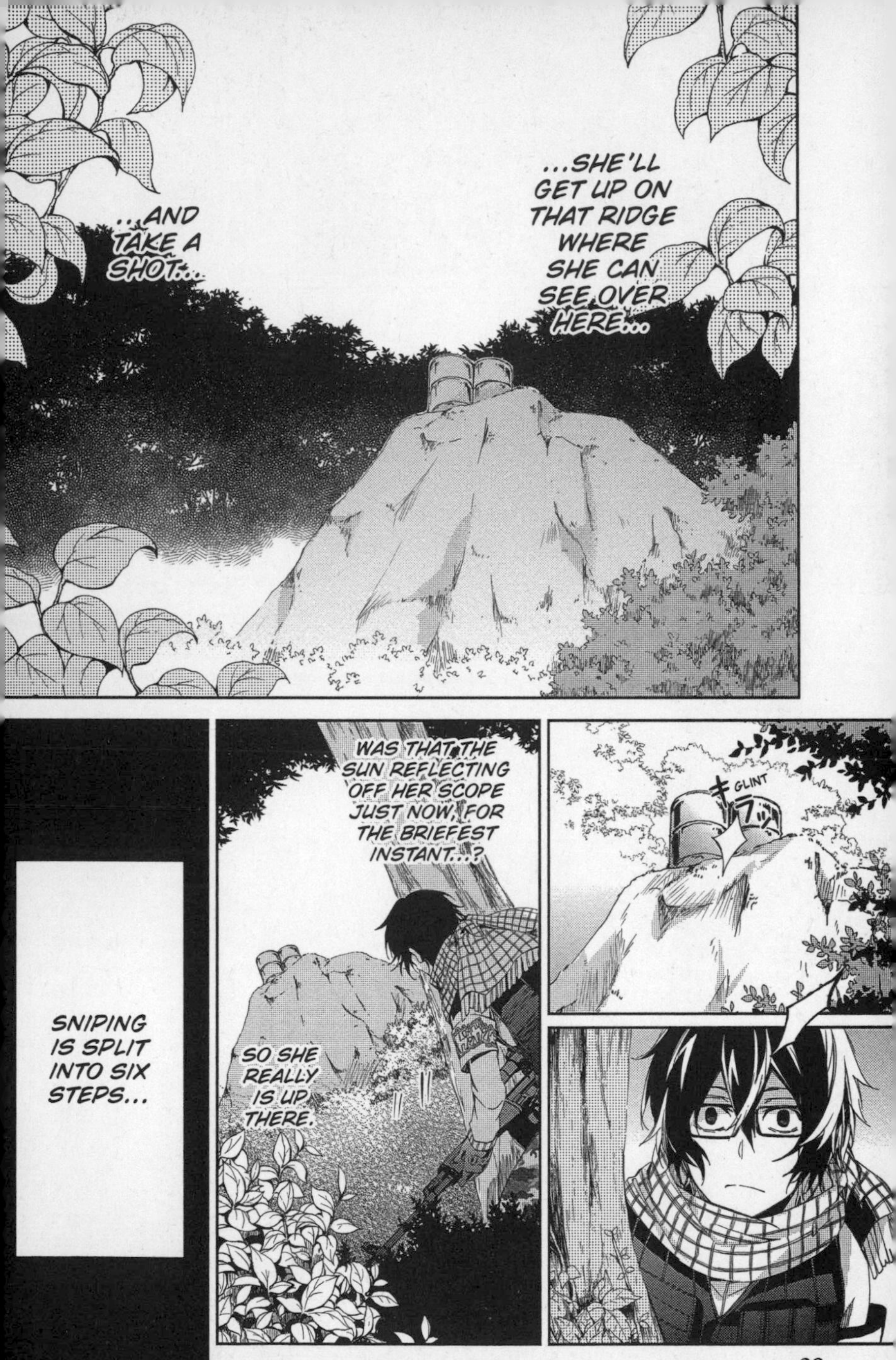
...SHE'LL GET UP ON THAT RIDGE WHERE SHE CAN SEE OVER HERE...
...AND TAKE A SHOT...
GLINT
WAS THAT THE SUN REFLECTING OFF HER SCOPE JUST NOW, FOR THE BRIEFEST INSTANT...?
SO SHE REALLY IS UP THERE.
SNIPING IS SPLIT INTO SIX STEPS...

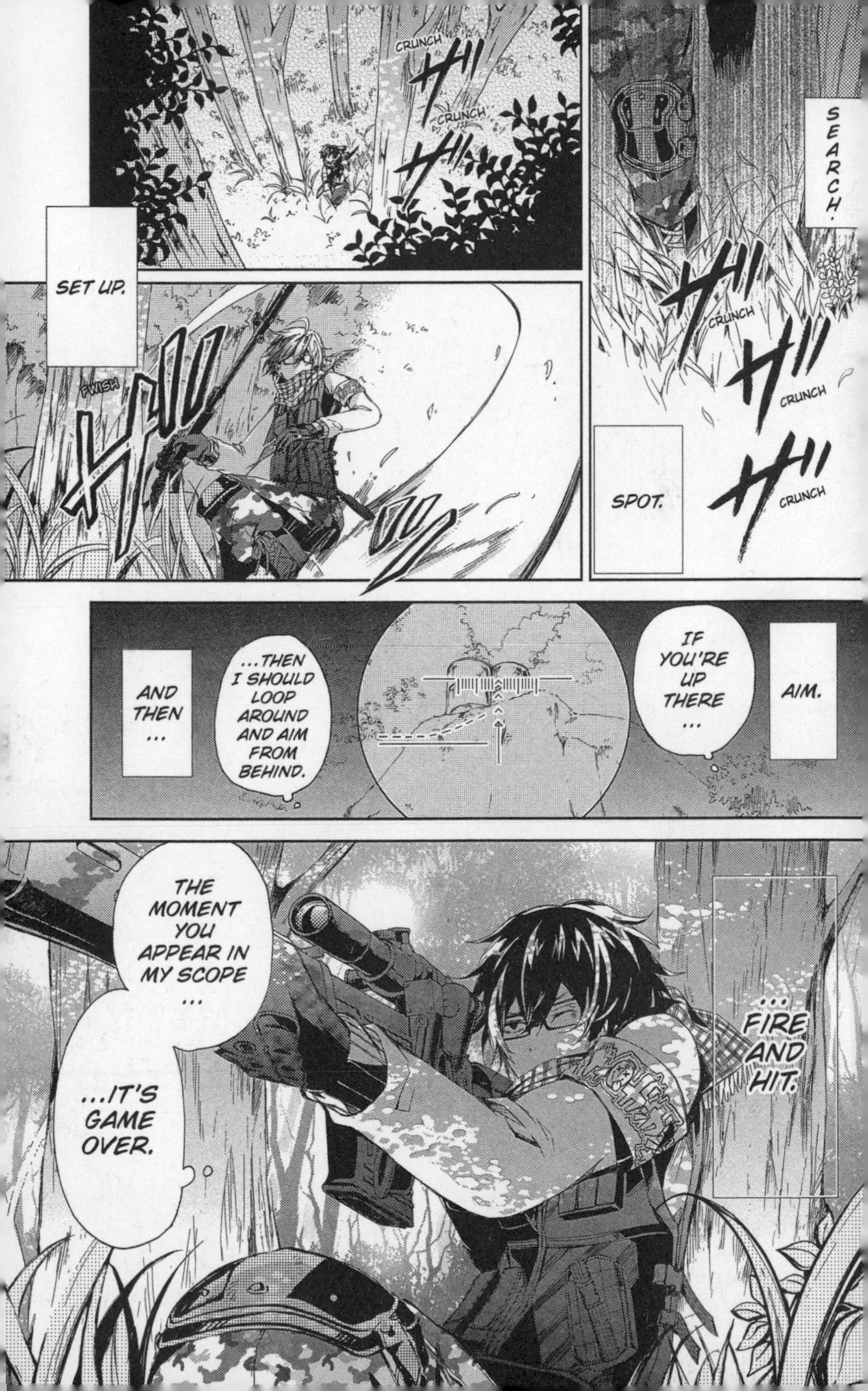
SEARCH.
CRUNCH
CRUNCH
CRUNCH
SPOT.
CRUNCH
CRUNCH
SET UP.
FWISH
AIM.
IF YOU'RE UP THERE ...
...THEN I SHOULD LOOP AROUND AND AIM FROM BEHIND.
AND THEN ...
...FIRE AND HIT.
THE MOMENT YOU APPEAR IN MY SCOPE ...
...IT'S GAME OVER.

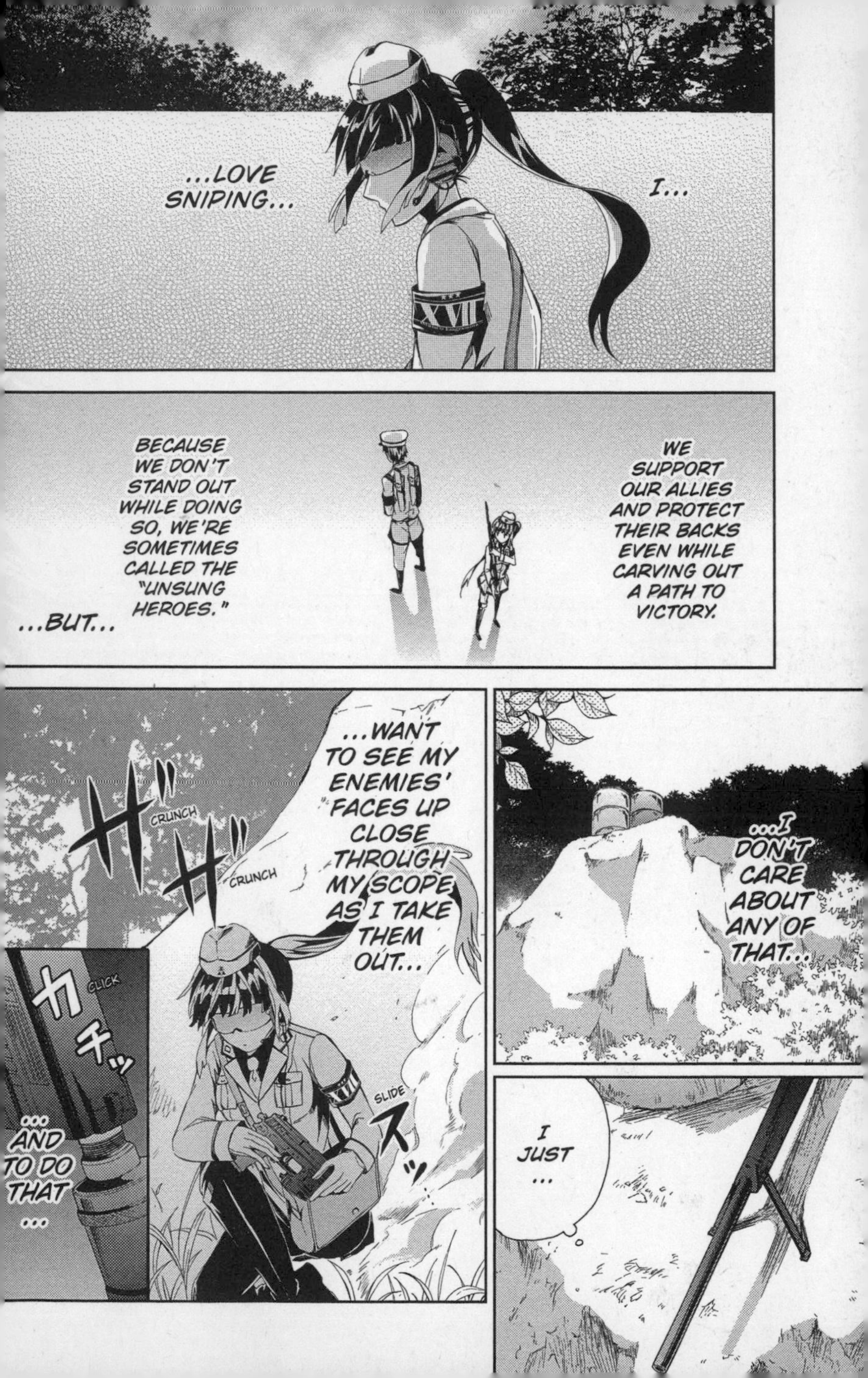
I...
...LOVE SNIPING...
WE SUPPORT OUR ALLIES AND PROTECT THEIR BACKS EVEN WHILE CARVING OUT A PATH TO VICTORY.
BECAUSE WE DON'T STAND OUT WHILE DOING SO, WE'RE SOMETIMES CALLED THE "UNSUNG HEROES."
...BUT...
...I DON'T CARE ABOUT ANY OF THAT...
...WANT TO SEE MY ENEMIES' FACES UP CLOSE THROUGH MY SCOPE AS I TAKE THEM OUT...
CRUNCH
CRUNCH
I JUST ...
SLIDE
CLICK
...AND TO DO THAT ...

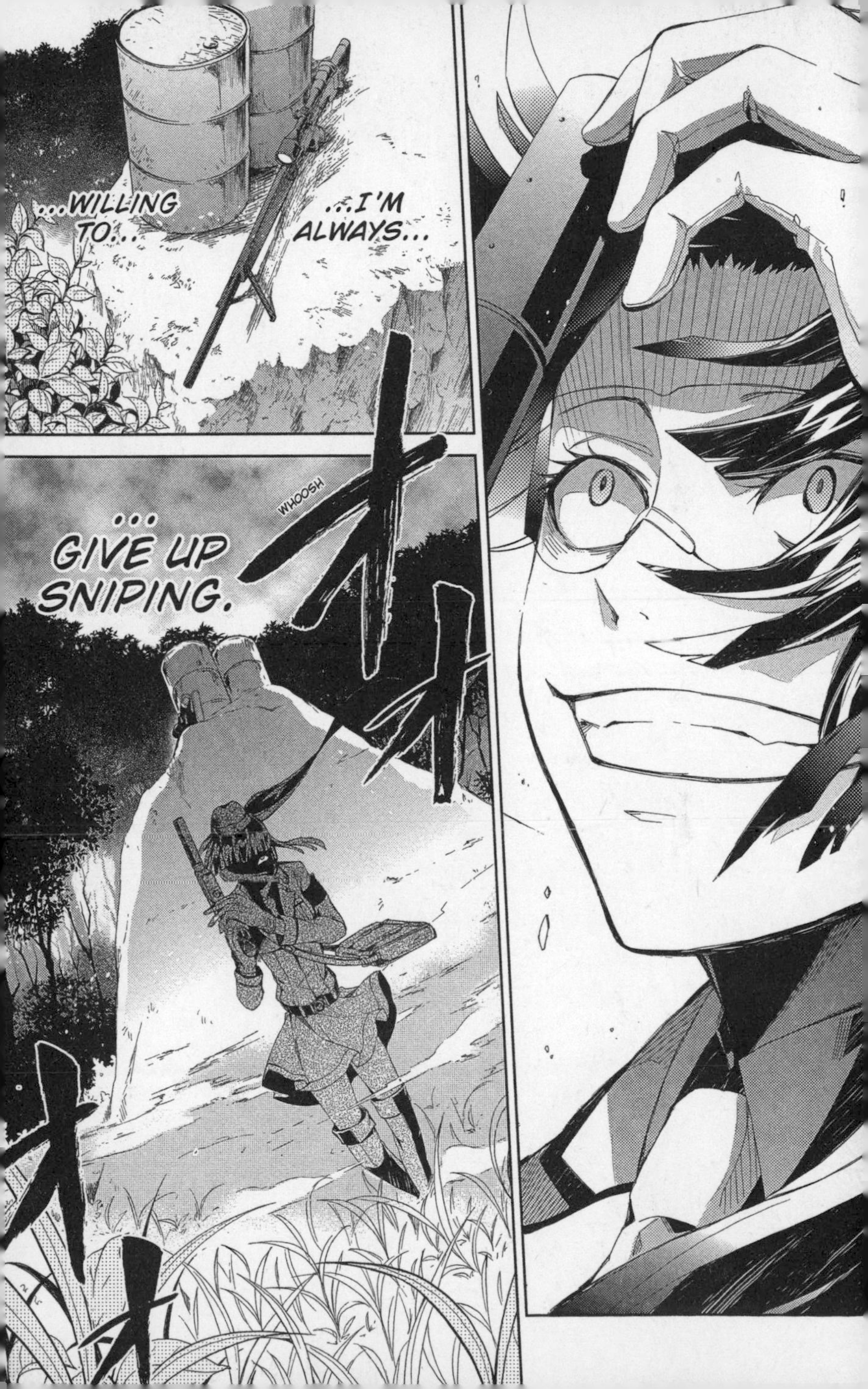
...I'M ALWAYS...
...WILLING TO...
WHOOSH
... GIVE UP SNIPING.

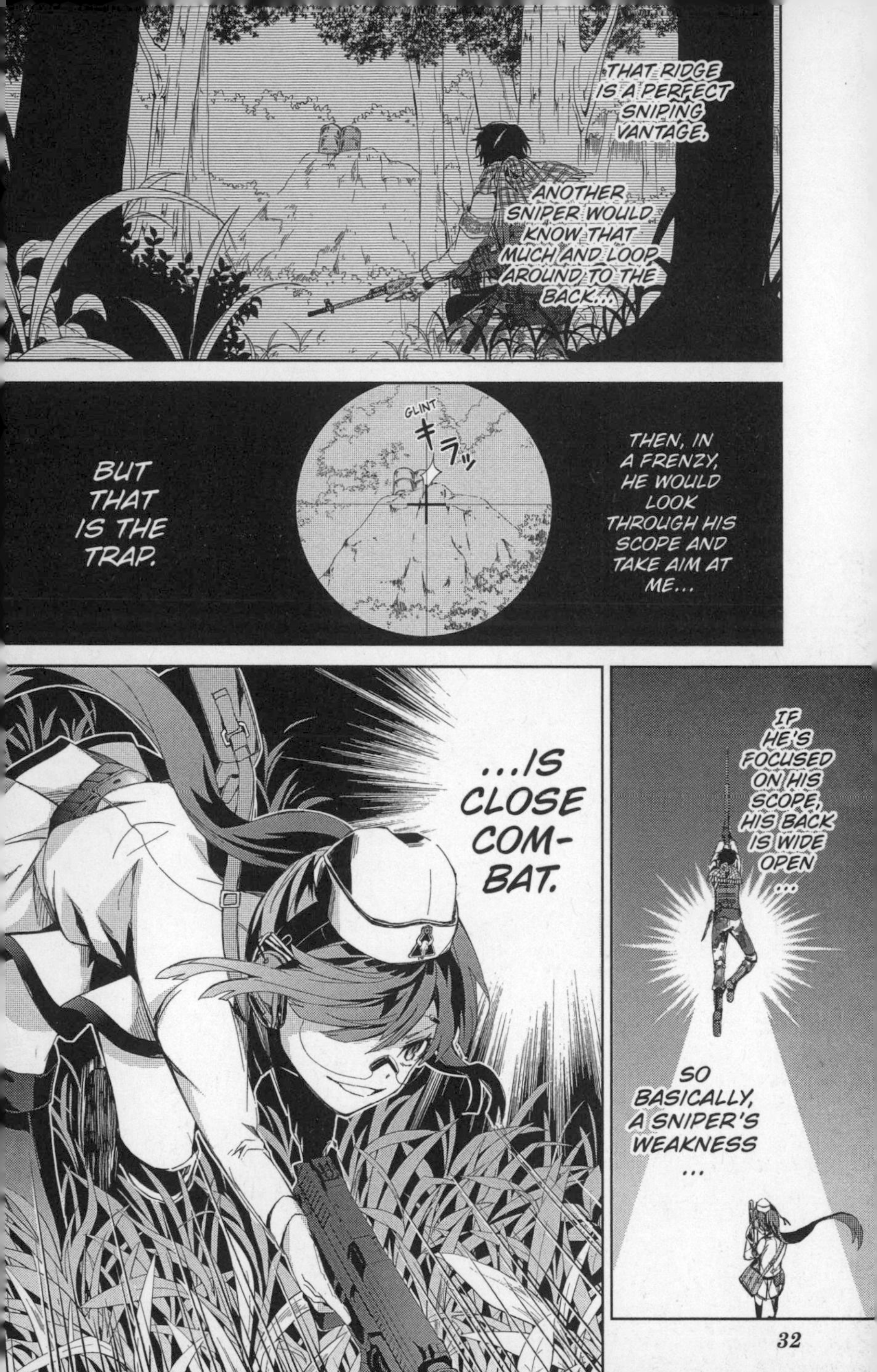

THAT RIDGE IS A PERFECT SNIPING VANTAGE.
ANOTHER SNIPER WOULD KNOW THAT MUCH AND LOOP AROUND TO THE BACK...
THEN, IN A FRENZY, HE WOULD LOOK THROUGH HIS SCOPE AND TAKE AIM AT ME...
GLINT
キラッ
BUT THAT IS THE TRAP.
IF HE'S FOCUSED ON HIS SCOPE, HIS BACK IS WIDE OPEN ...
SO BASICALLY, A SNIPER'S WEAKNESS ...
...IS CLOSE COM-BAT.

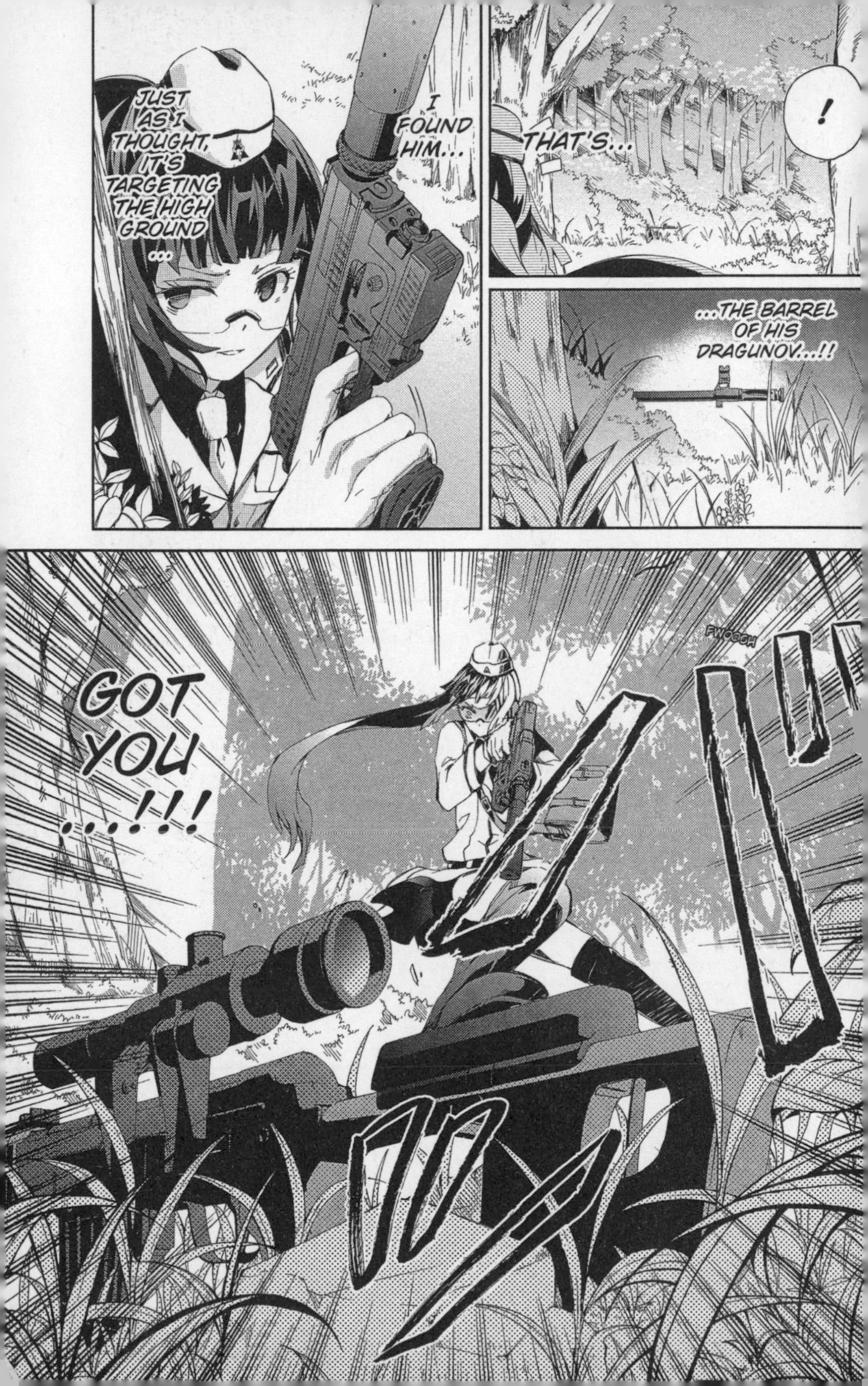
!
THAT'S...
...THE BARREL OF HIS DRAGUNOV...!!
I FOUND HIM...
JUST AS I THOUGHT, IT'S TARGETING THE HIGH GROUND...
FWOOSH
GOT YOU...!!!

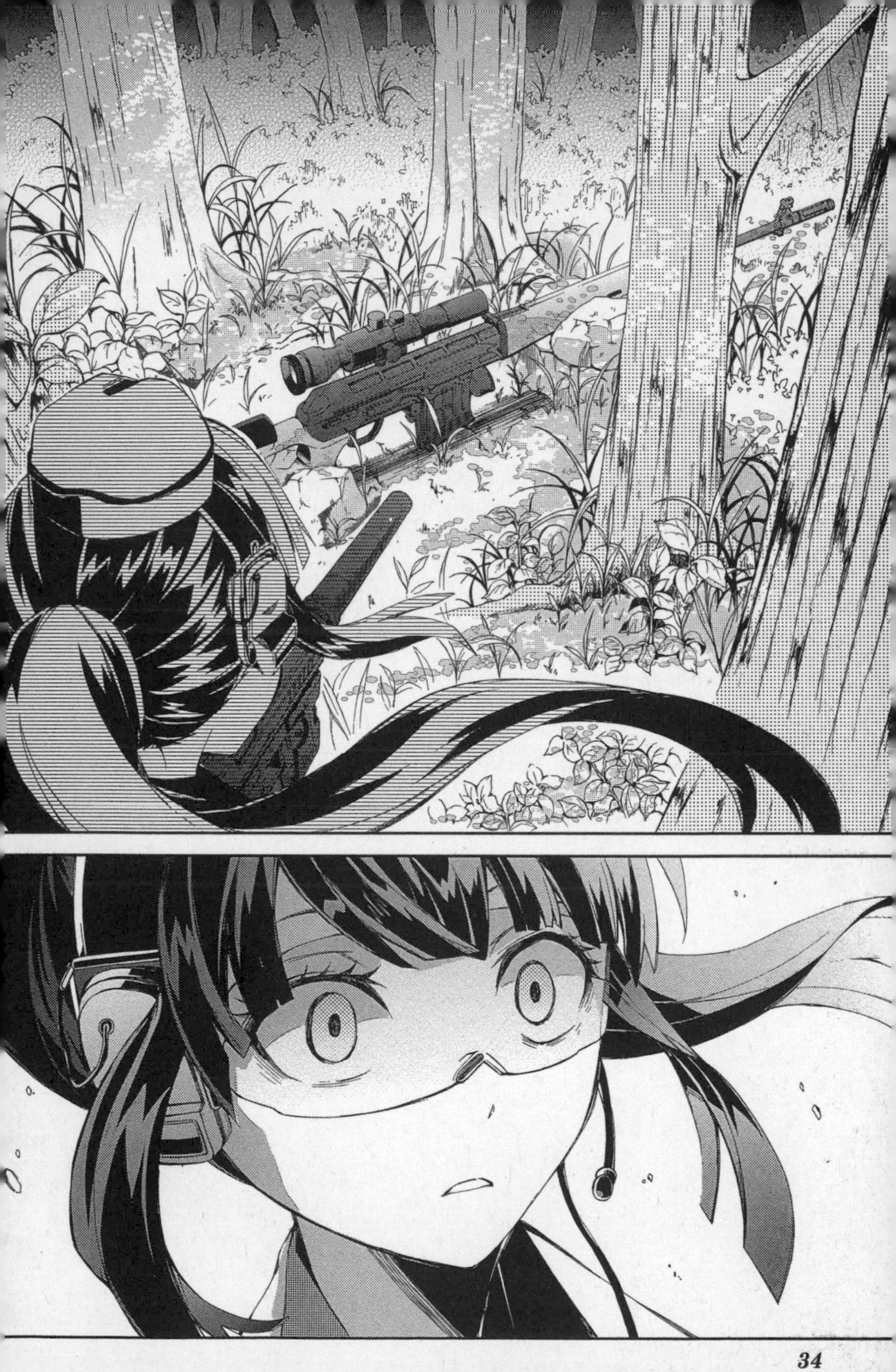

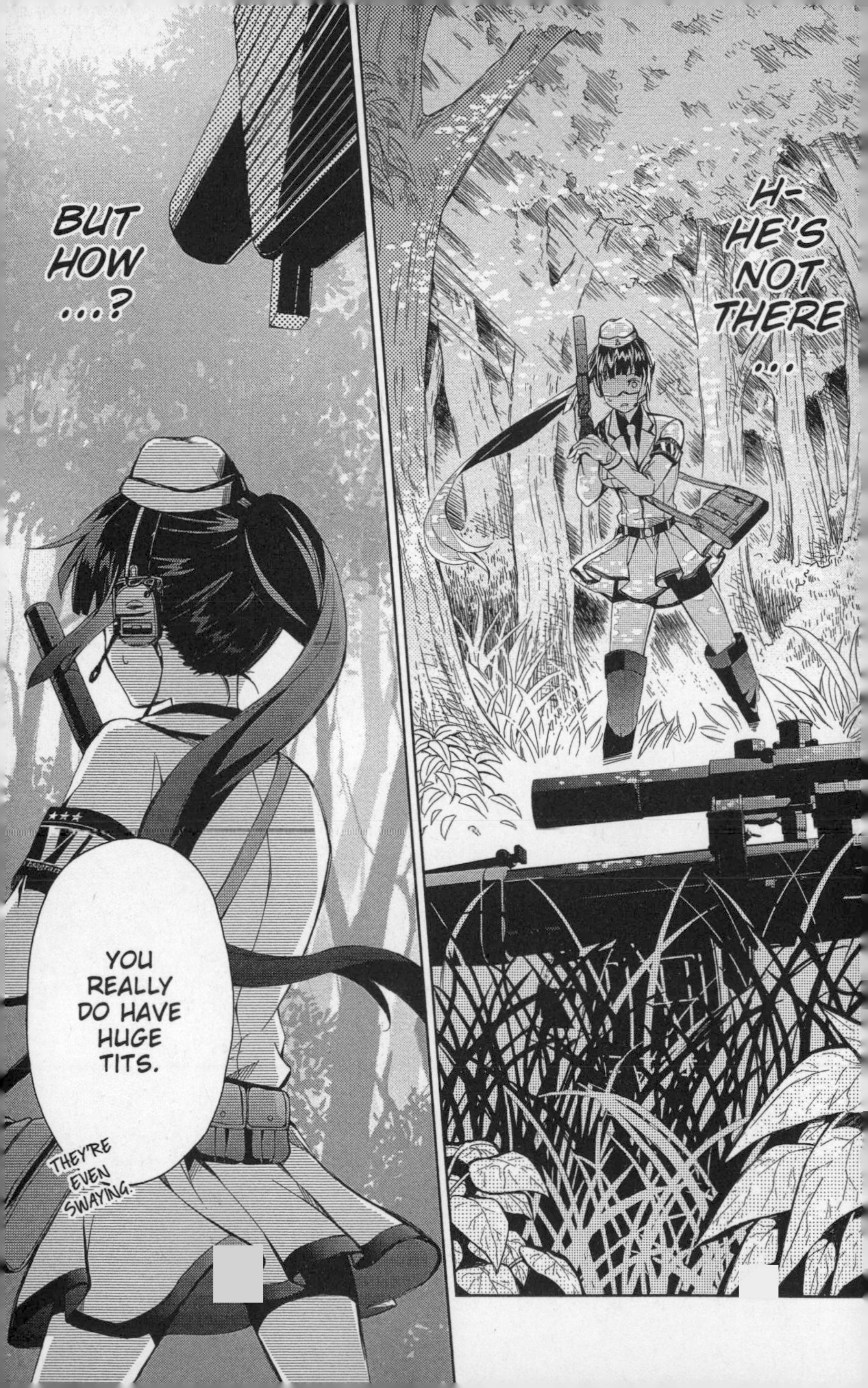
H-HE'S NOT THERE...
BUT HOW...?
YOU REALLY DO HAVE HUGE TITS.
THEY'RE EVEN SWAYING.

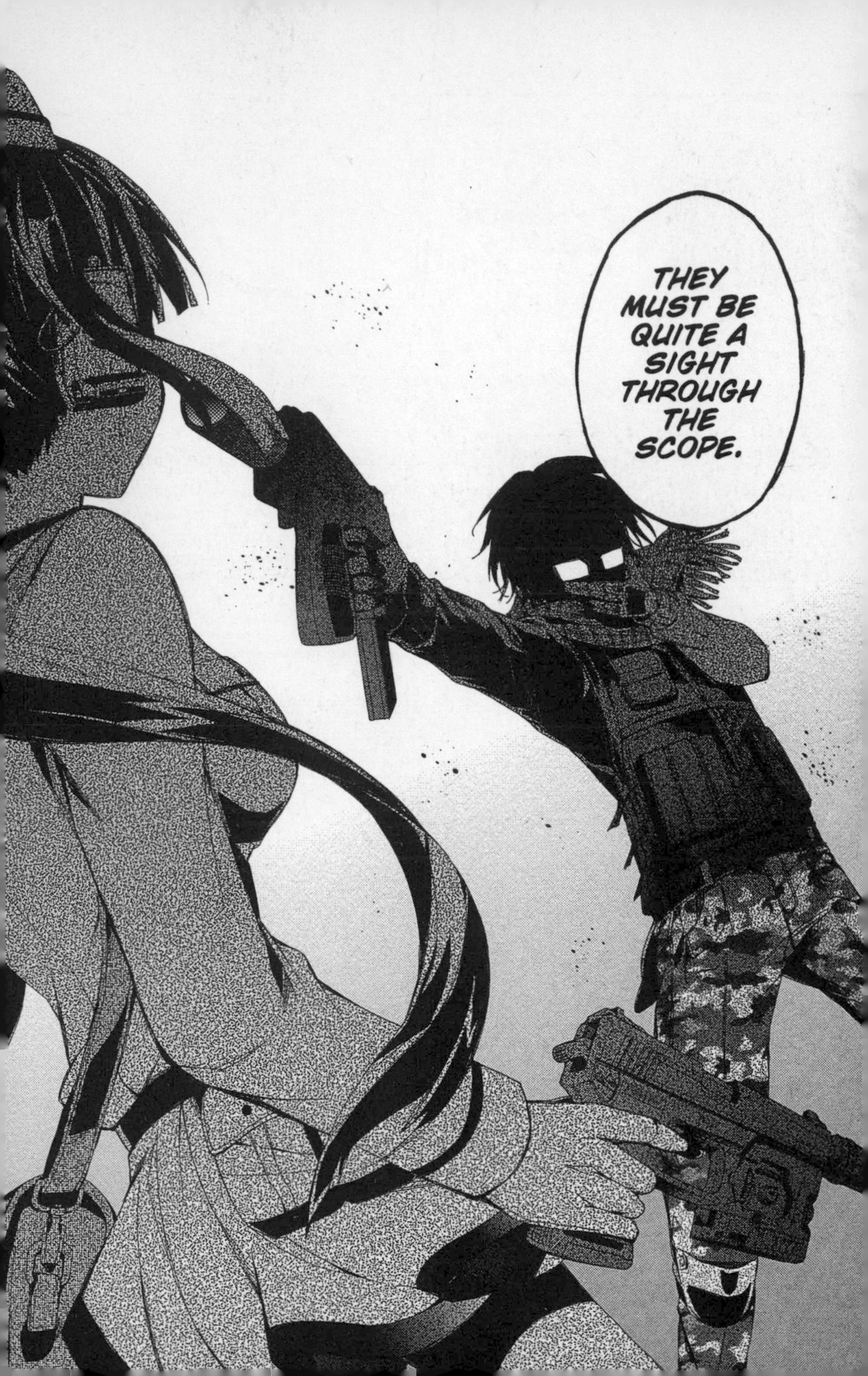
THEY MUST BE QUITE A SIGHT THROUGH THE SCOPE.

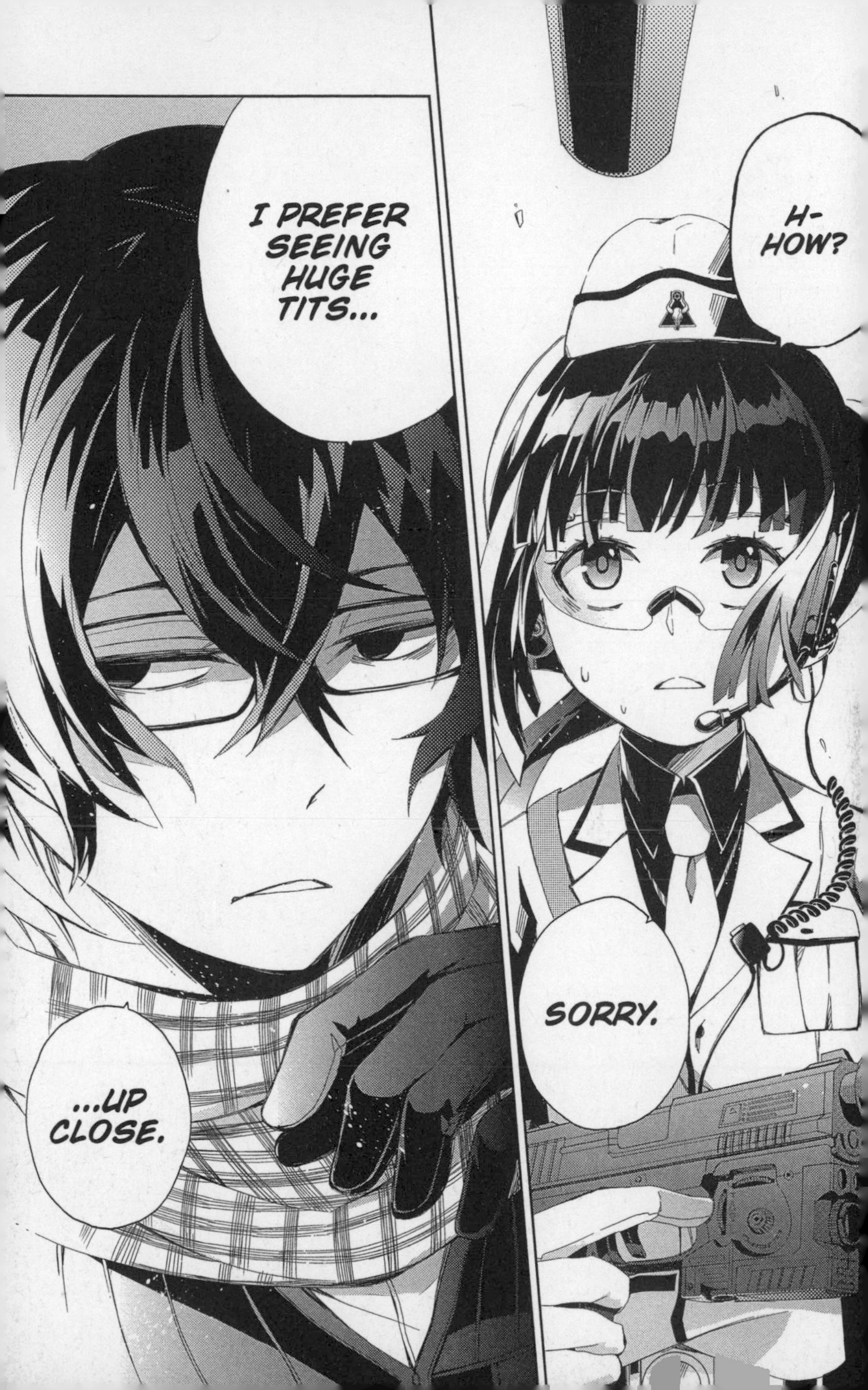
H-HOW?
SORRY.
I PREFER SEEING HUGE TITS...
...UP CLOSE.

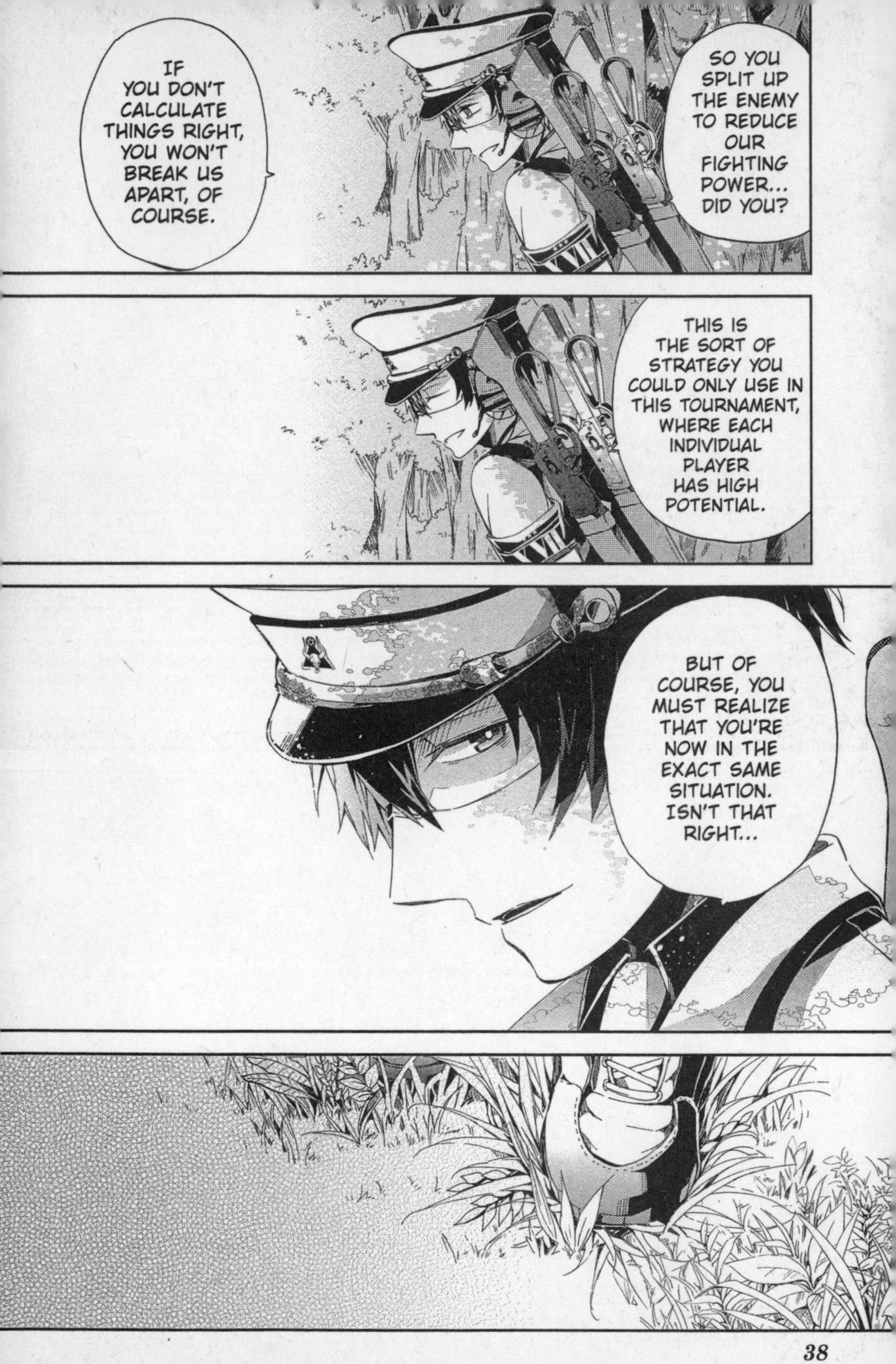
SO YOU SPLIT UP THE ENEMY TO REDUCE OUR FIGHTING POWER... DID YOU?
IF YOU DON'T CALCULATE THINGS RIGHT, YOU WON'T BREAK US APART, OF COURSE.
THIS IS THE SORT OF STRATEGY YOU COULD ONLY USE IN THIS TOURNAMENT, WHERE EACH INDIVIDUAL PLAYER HAS HIGH POTENTIAL.
BUT OF COURSE, YOU MUST REALIZE THAT YOU'RE NOW IN THE EXACT SAME SITUATION. ISN'T THAT RIGHT...

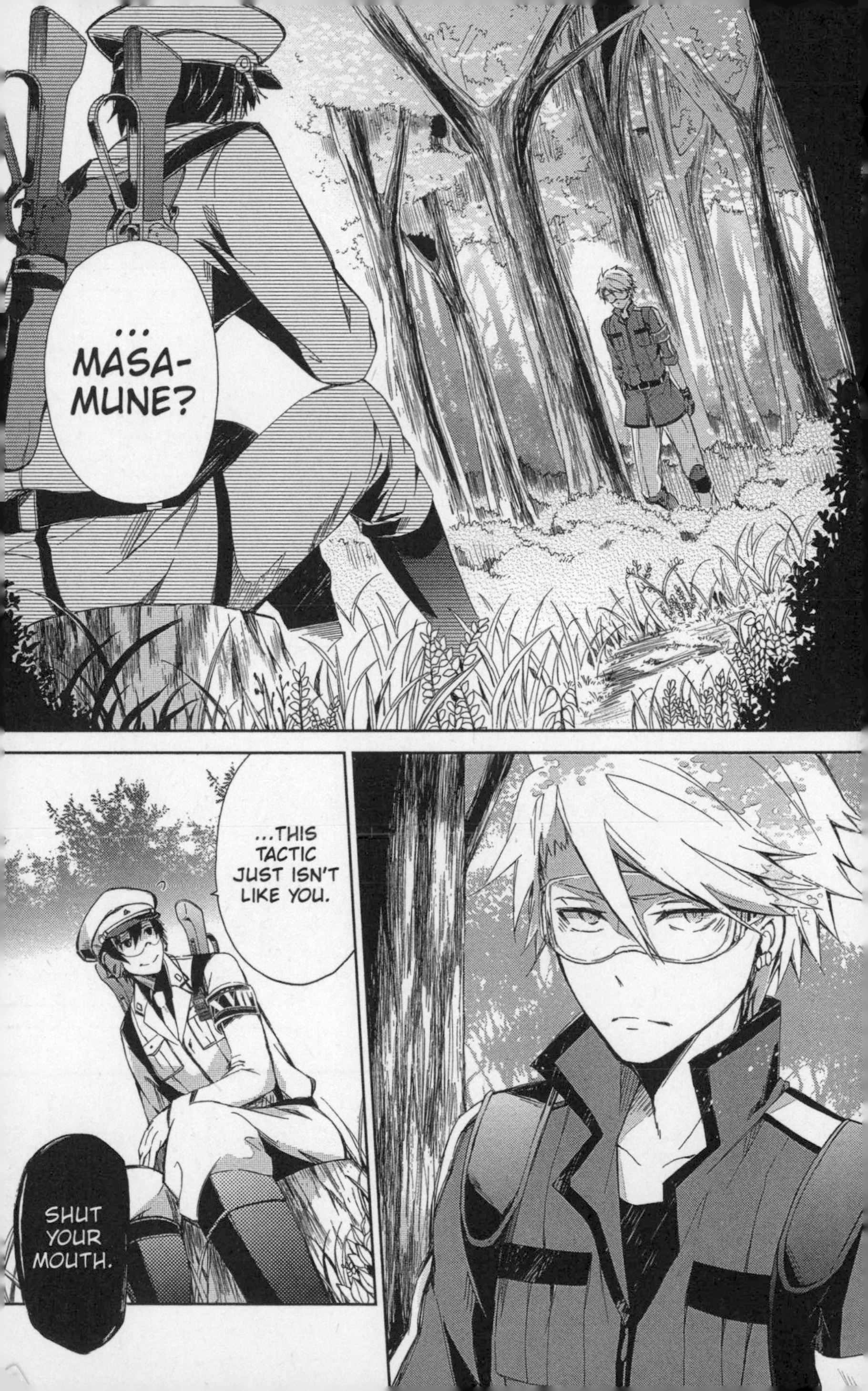
...MASA-MUNE?
...THIS TACTIC JUST ISN'T LIKE YOU.
SHUT YOUR MOUTH.

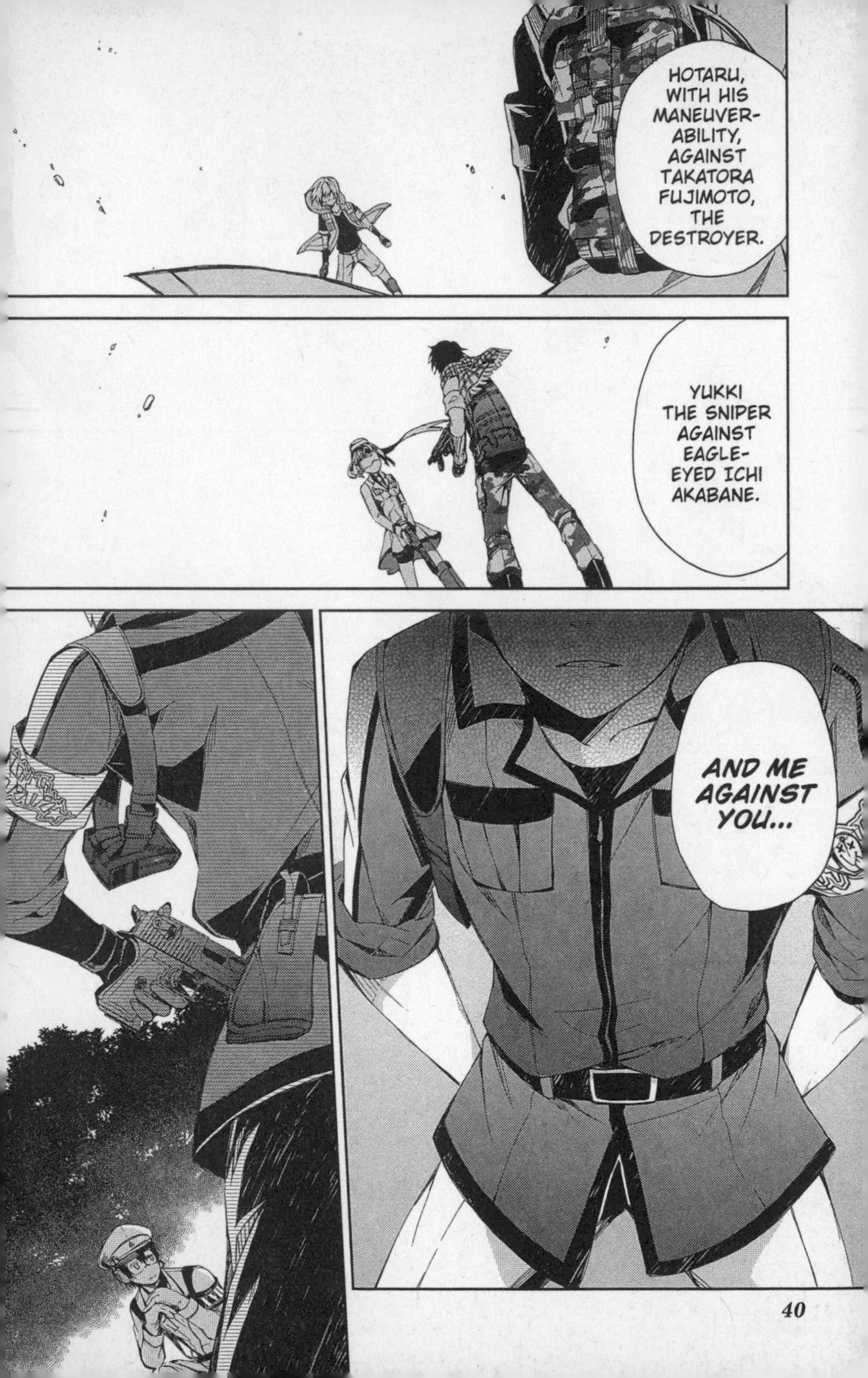
HOTARU, WITH HIS MANEUVER-ABILITY, AGAINST TAKATORA FUJIMOTO, THE DESTROYER.
YUKKI THE SNIPER AGAINST EAGLE-EYED ICHI AKABANE.
AND ME AGAINST YOU...

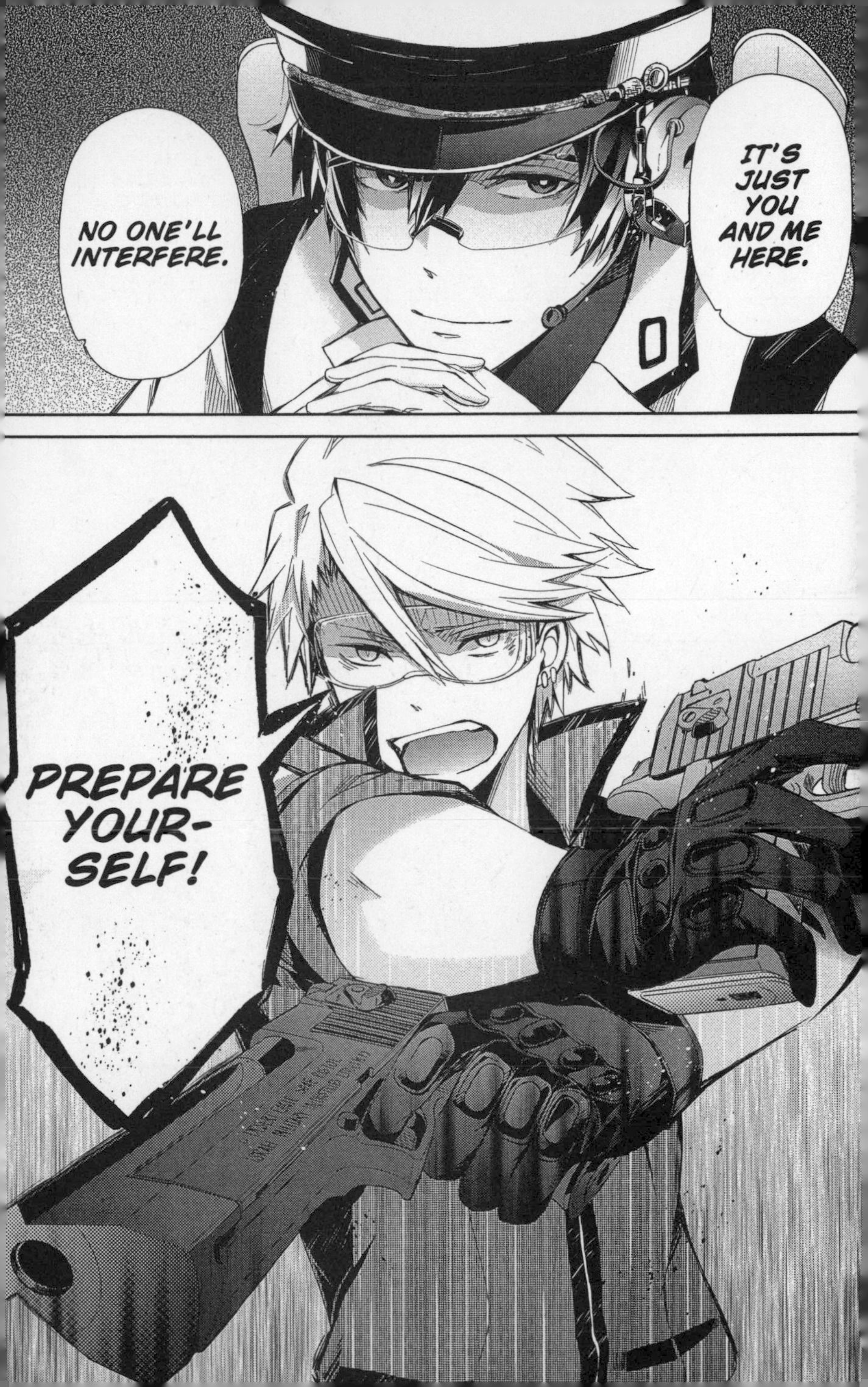
IT'S JUST YOU AND ME HERE.
NO ONE'LL INTERFERE.
PREPARE YOUR-SELF!

AOHARU
MACHINE
GUN

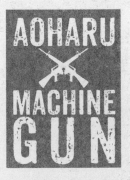

#08 LET US FIGHT

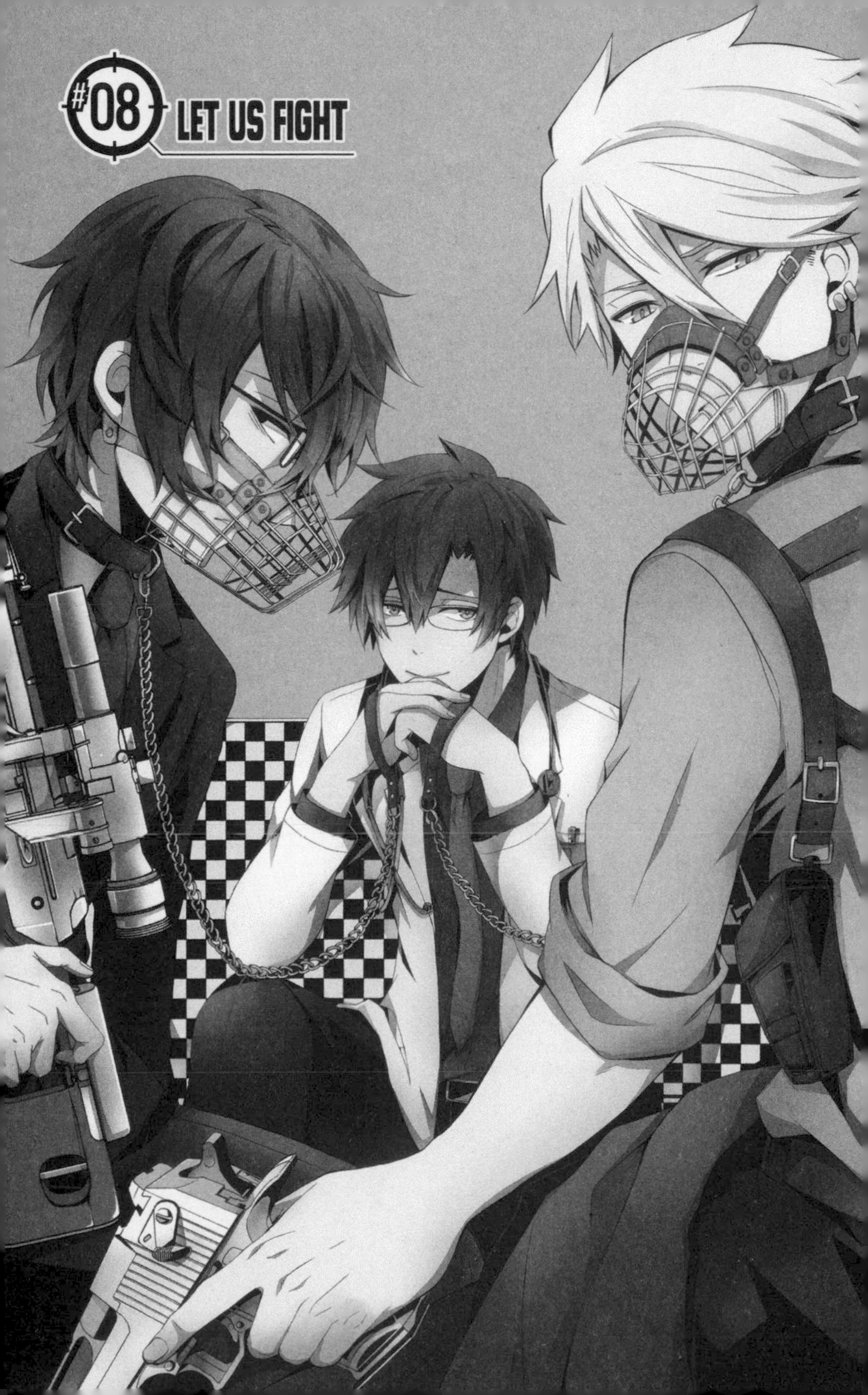

AOHARU×MACHINEGUN

IF THEY WERE DOGS

MI-DORI
HEY, WE'RE GOING FOR A WALK, MASA-MUNE~!
COME ON, YUKIMURA-KUN. NO TRYING TO RUN AWAY!
PUUUULL
むぎぎ
AH HA HA.
MASAMUNE
TREMBLE
ぷるぷる
ぷる
TREMBLE
TREMBLE
たしたし
SCRABBLE SCRABBLE

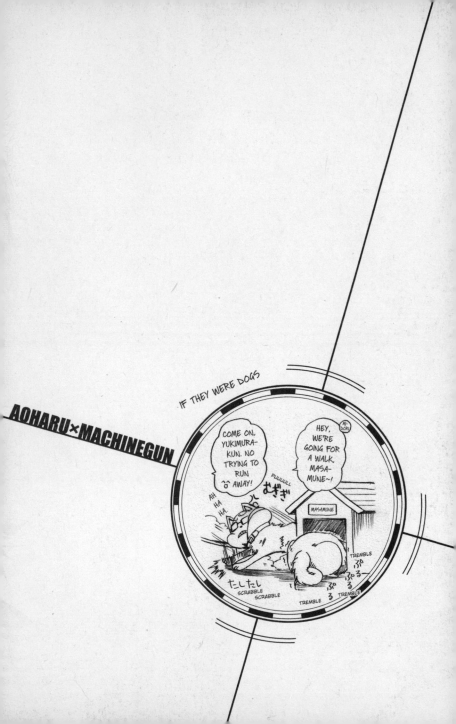

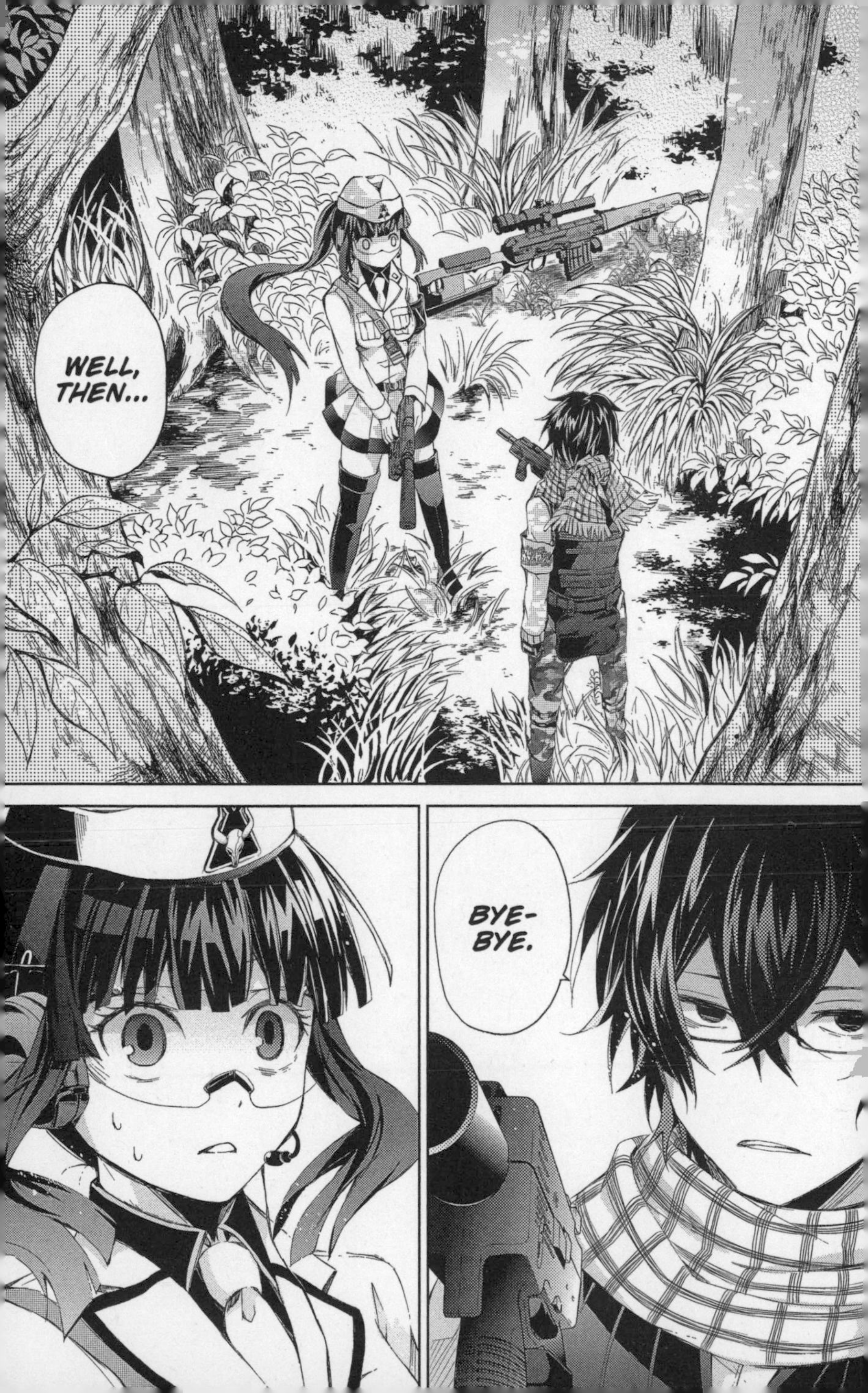
WELL, THEN...
BYE-BYE.

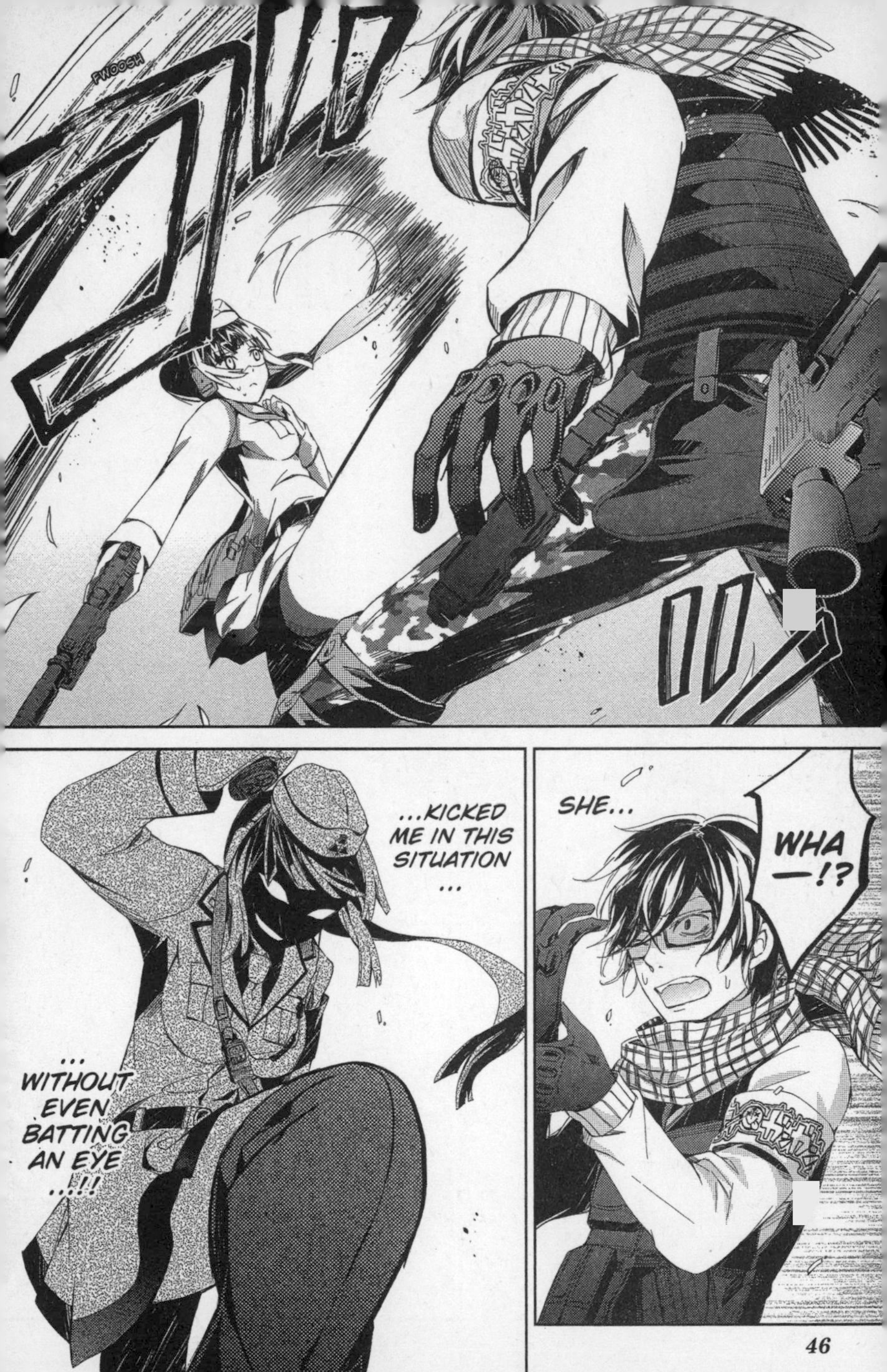
FWOOSH
WHA—!?
SHE...
...KICKED ME IN THIS SITUATION ...
... WITHOUT EVEN BATTING AN EYE ...!!

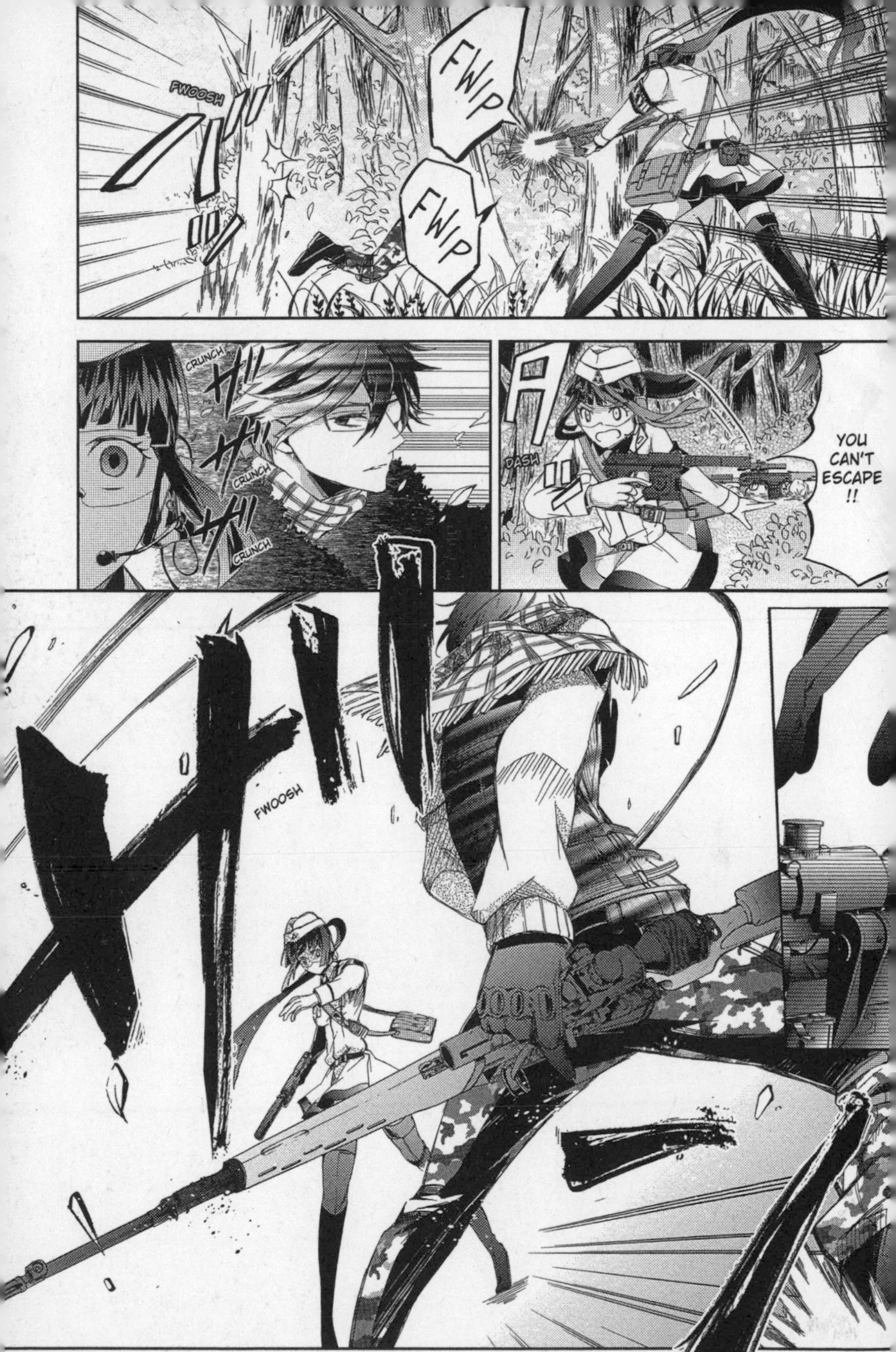
FWIP
FWIP
FWOOSH
YOU CAN'T ESCAPE !!
DASH
CRUNCH
CRUNCH
CRUNCH
FWOOSH

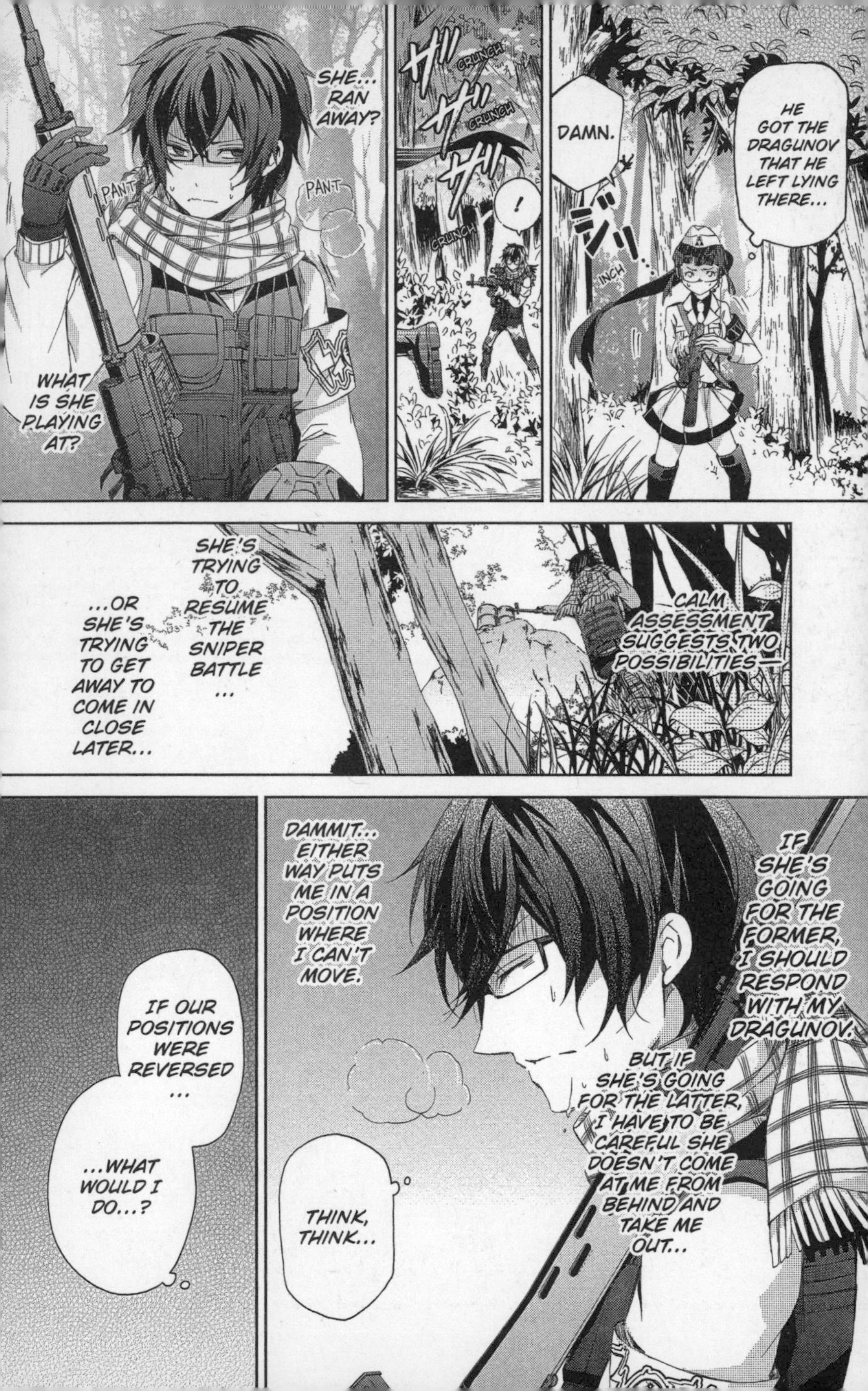
HE GOT THE DRAGUNOV THAT HE LEFT LYING THERE...
DAMN.
INCH
CRUNCH
CRUNCH
!
CRUNCH
SHE... RAN AWAY?
PANT
PANT
WHAT IS SHE PLAYING AT?
CALM ASSESSMENT SUGGESTS TWO POSSIBILITIES—
SHE'S TRYING TO RESUME THE SNIPER BATTLE...
...OR SHE'S TRYING TO GET AWAY TO COME IN CLOSE LATER...
IF SHE'S GOING FOR THE FORMER, I SHOULD RESPOND WITH MY DRAGUNOV.
BUT IF SHE'S GOING FOR THE LATTER, I HAVE TO BE CAREFUL SHE DOESN'T COME AT ME FROM BEHIND AND TAKE ME OUT...
DAMMIT... EITHER WAY PUTS ME IN A POSITION WHERE I CAN'T MOVE.
THINK, THINK...
IF OUR POSITIONS WERE REVERSED...
...WHAT WOULD I DO...?

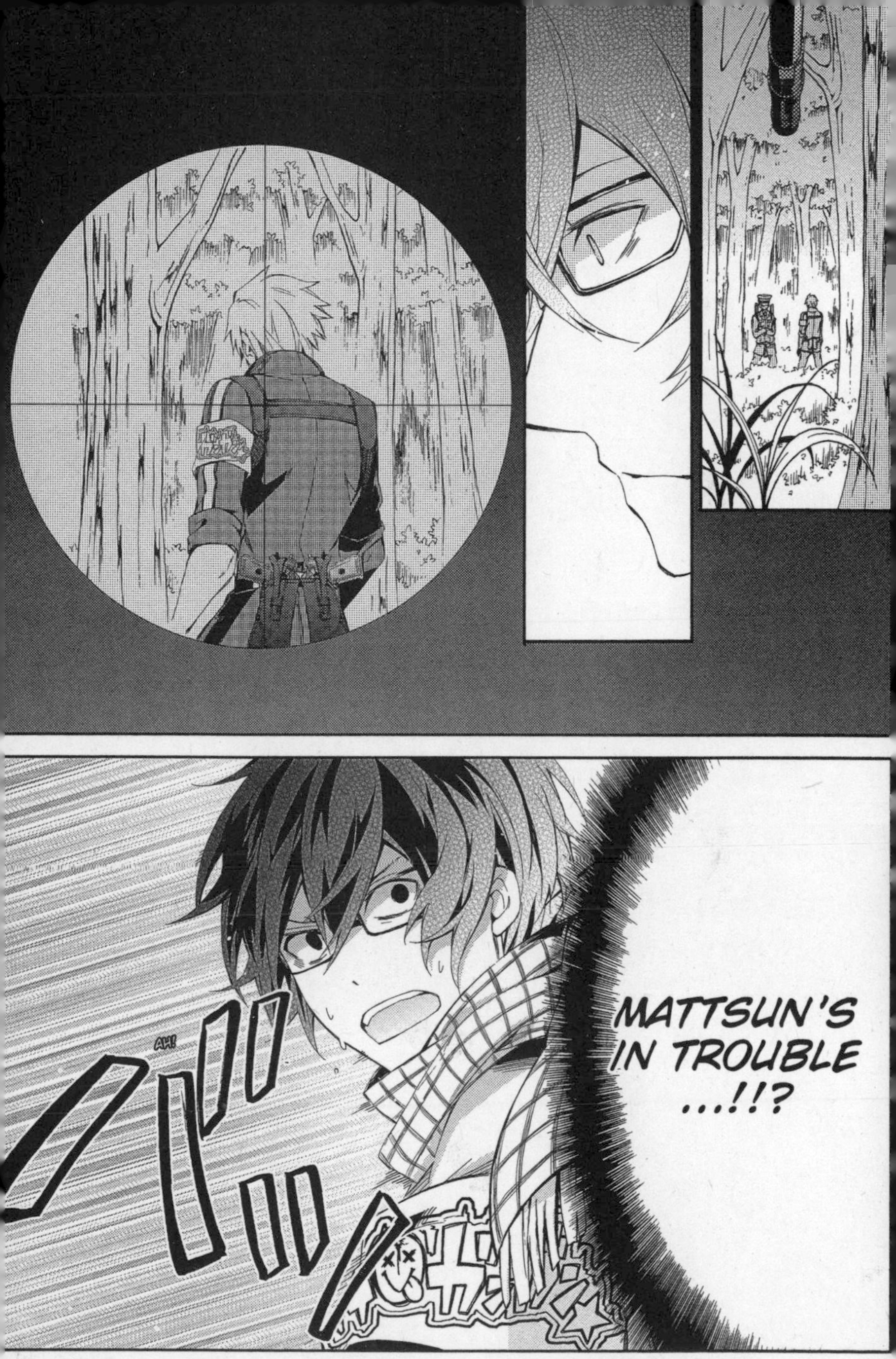
AH!
MATTSUN'S IN TROUBLE ...!!?

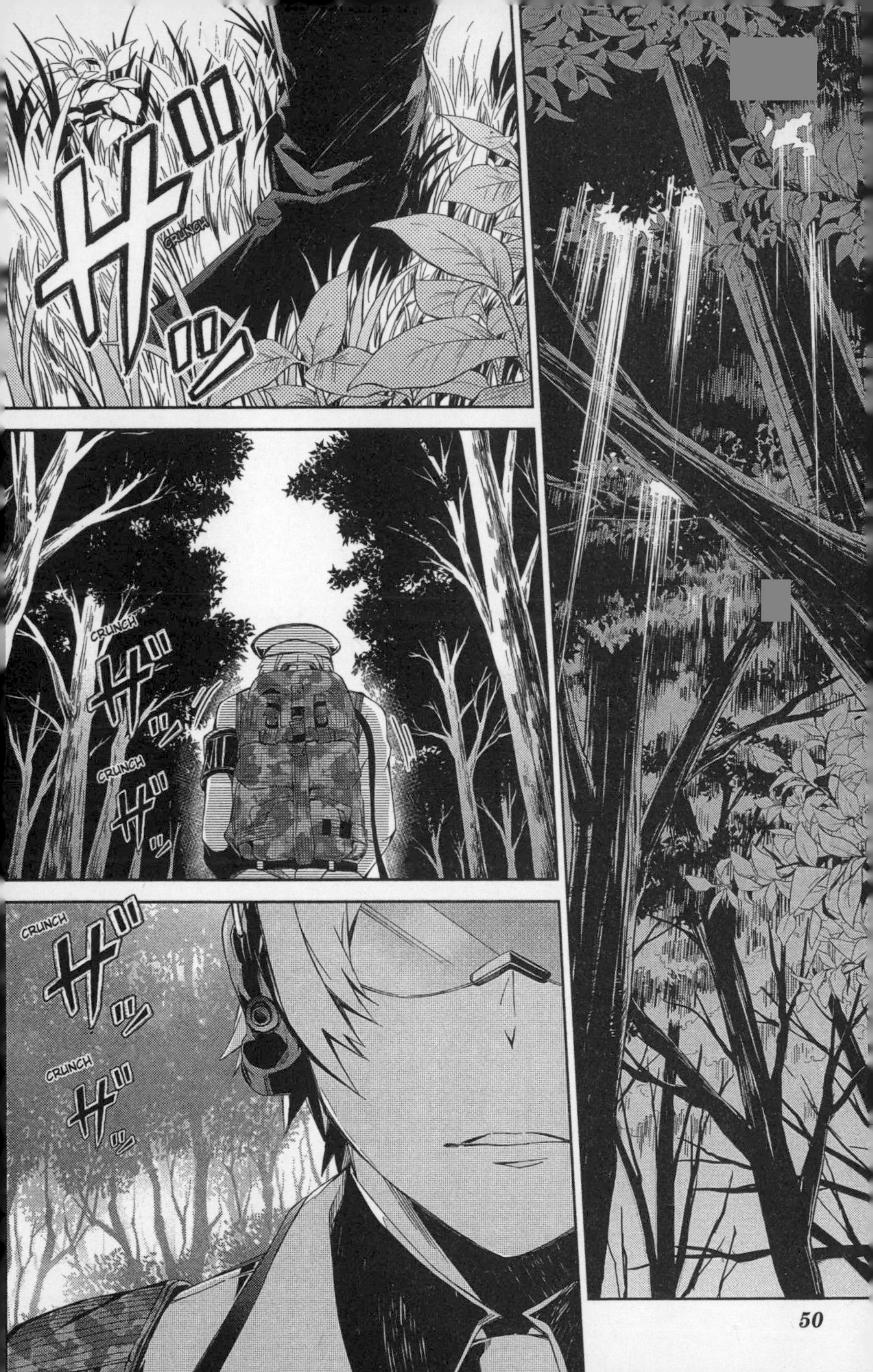
ザッ
CRUNCH
ザッ
CRUNCH
ザッ
CRUNCH
ザッ
CRUNCH
ザッ
CRUNCH
ザッ

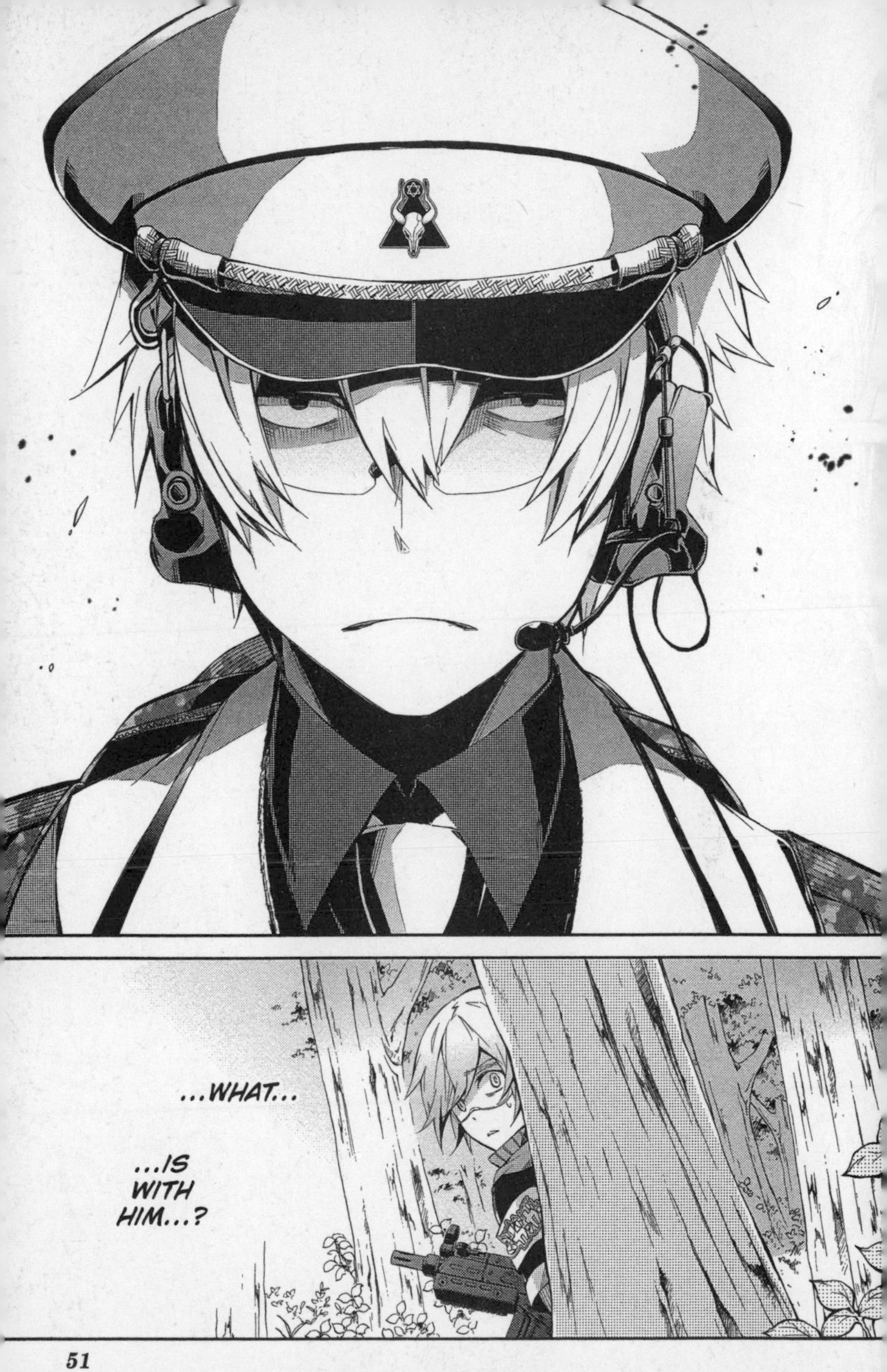
...WHAT...
...IS WITH HIM...?

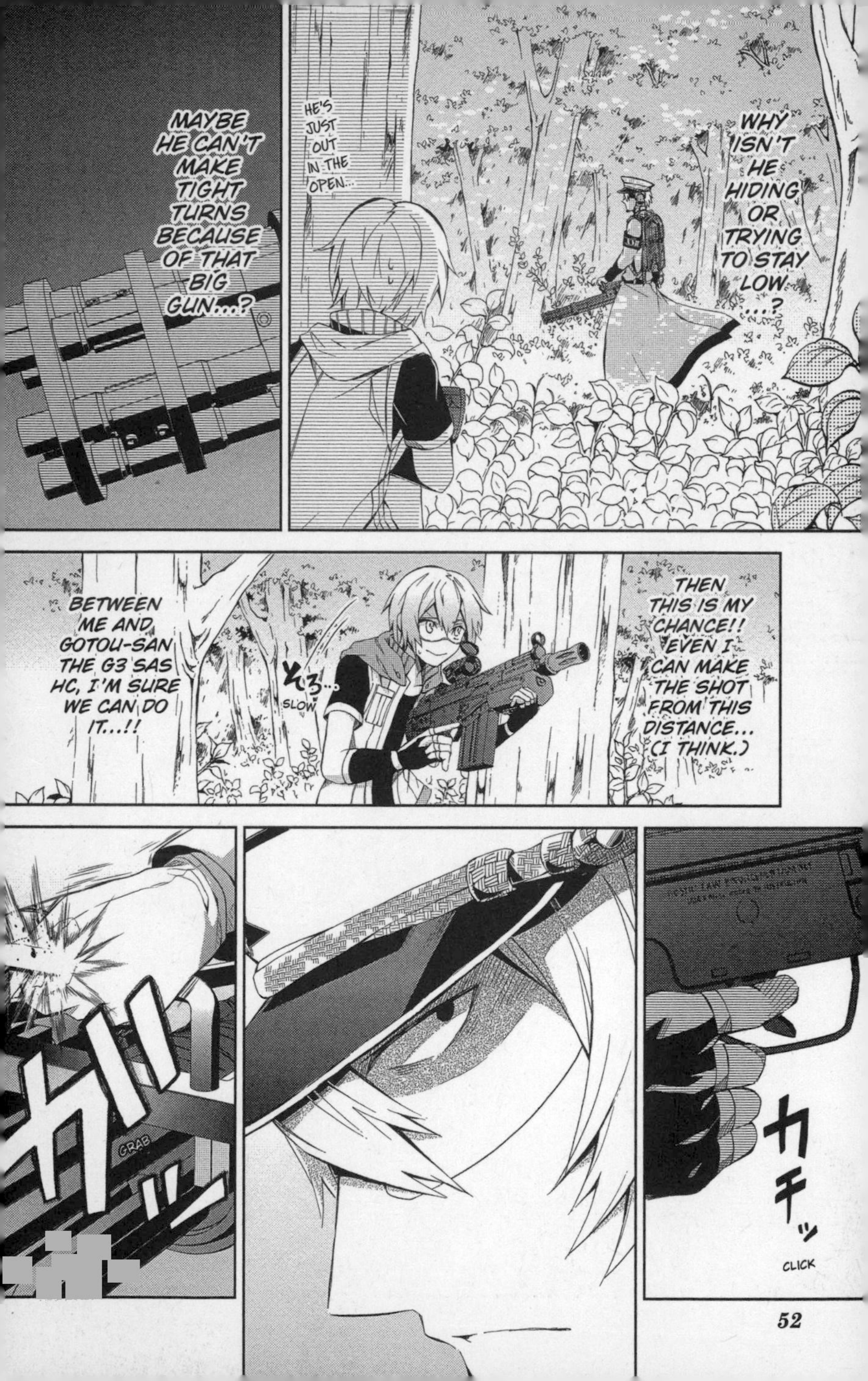
WHY ISN'T HE HIDING OR TRYING TO STAY LOW...?
HE'S JUST OUT IN THE OPEN...
MAYBE HE CAN'T MAKE TIGHT TURNS BECAUSE OF THAT BIG GUN...?
THEN THIS IS MY CHANCE!! EVEN I CAN MAKE THE SHOT FROM THIS DISTANCE... (I THINK.)
そろ...
SLOW
BETWEEN ME AND GOTOU-SAN THE G3 SAS HC, I'M SURE WE CAN DO IT...!!
カチッ
CLICK
ガッ
GRAB

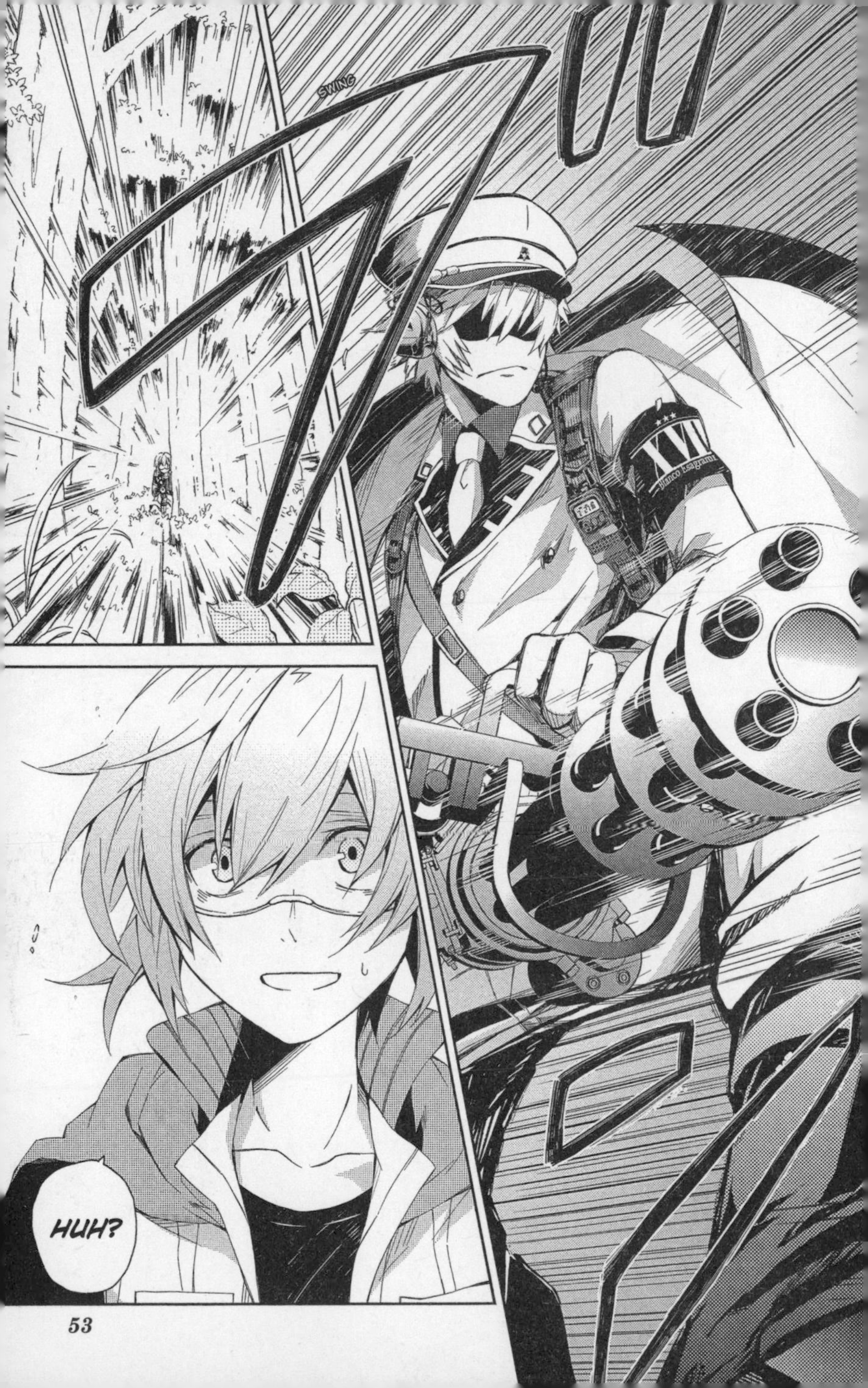
SWING
HUH?

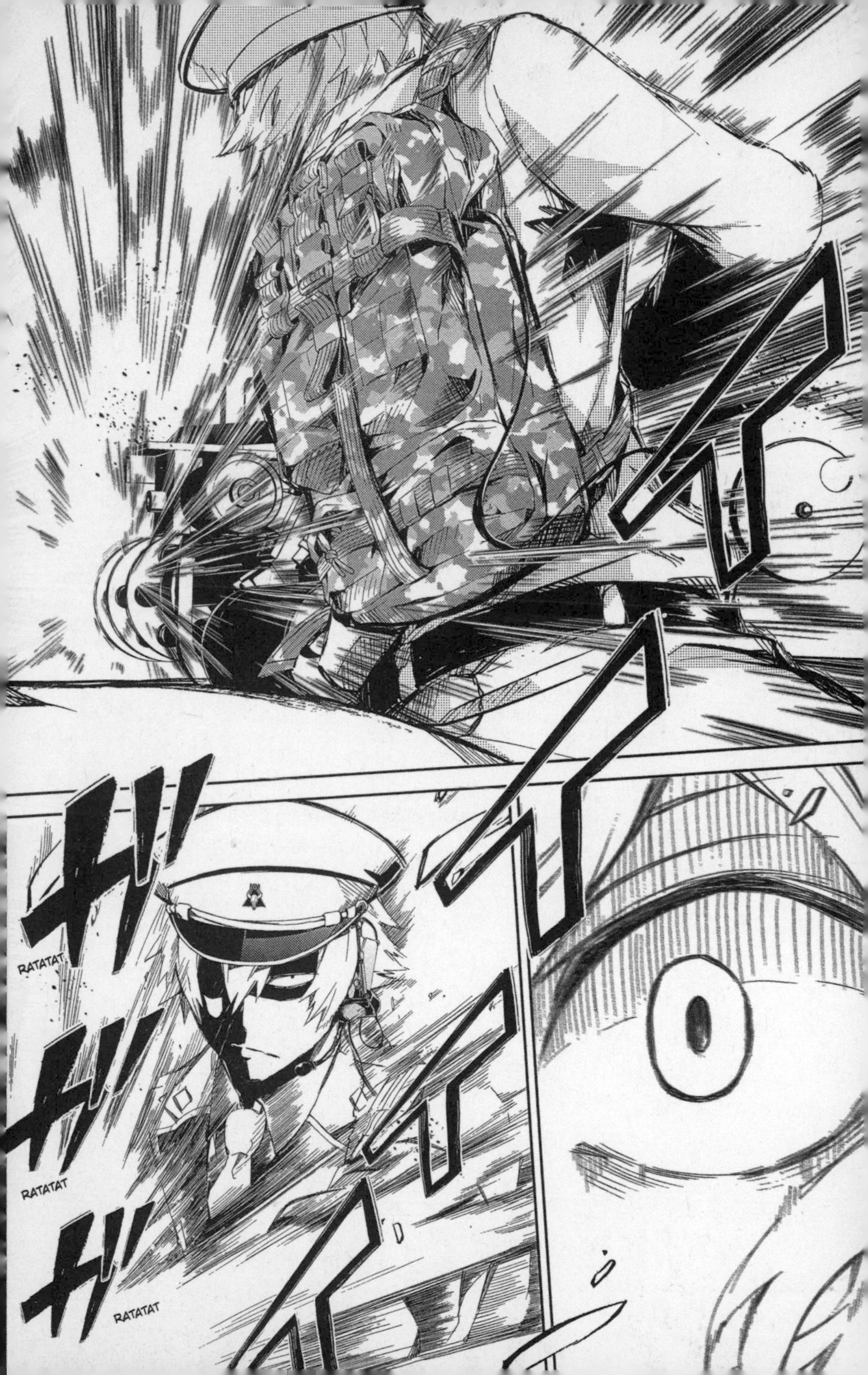

RATATAT
RATATAT
RATATAT

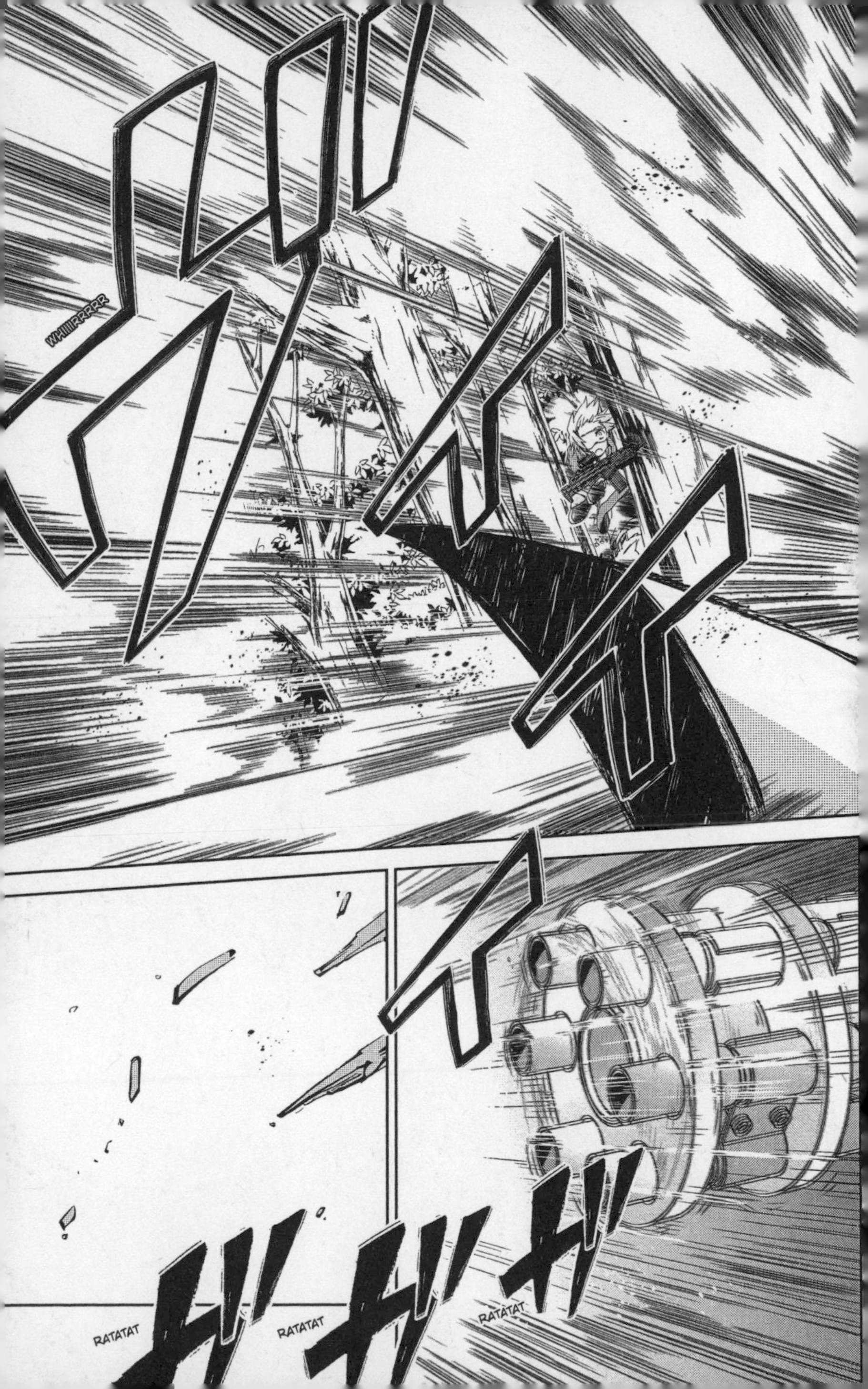
WHIIIIIRRRRR
RATATAT
RATATAT
RATATAT

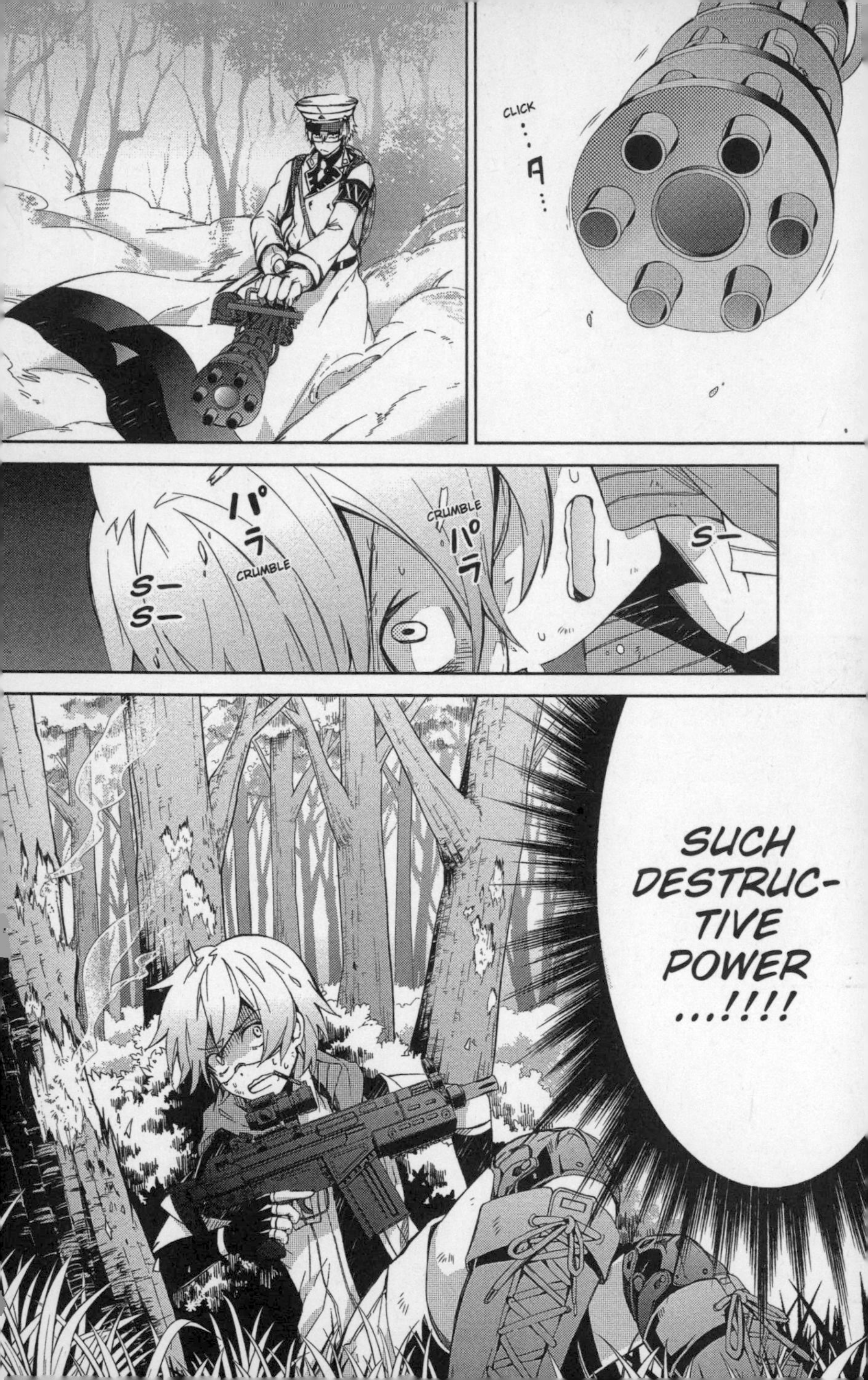
CLICK
…ガ…
パラ
CRUMBLE
パラ
CRUMBLE
S—
S—
S—
SUCH DESTRUC-TIVE POWER …!!!!

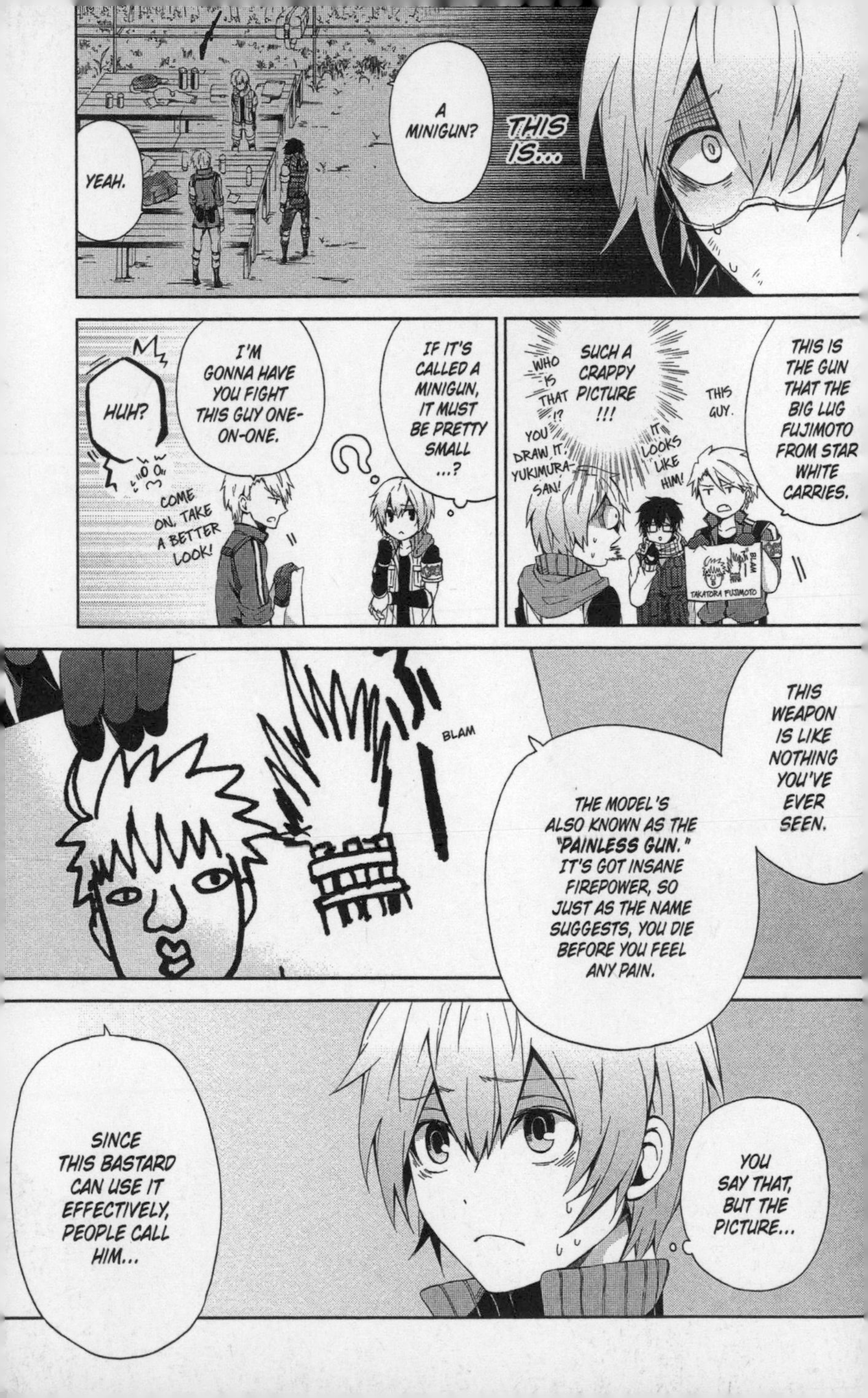
THIS IS...
A MINIGUN?
YEAH.
THIS IS THE GUN THAT THE BIG LUG FUJIMOTO FROM STAR WHITE CARRIES.
THIS GUY.
SUCH A CRAPPY PICTURE!!!
WHO IS THAT!?
YOU DRAW IT, YUKIMURA-SAN!
IT LOOKS LIKE HIM!
TAKATORA FUJIMOTO
BLAM
IF IT'S CALLED A MINIGUN, IT MUST BE PRETTY SMALL...?
I'M GONNA HAVE YOU FIGHT THIS GUY ONE-ON-ONE.
HUH?
COME ON, TAKE A BETTER LOOK!
THIS WEAPON IS LIKE NOTHING YOU'VE EVER SEEN.
THE MODEL'S ALSO KNOWN AS THE "PAINLESS GUN." IT'S GOT INSANE FIREPOWER, SO JUST AS THE NAME SUGGESTS, YOU DIE BEFORE YOU FEEL ANY PAIN.
BLAM
YOU SAY THAT, BUT THE PICTURE...
SINCE THIS BASTARD CAN USE IT EFFECTIVELY, PEOPLE CALL HIM...

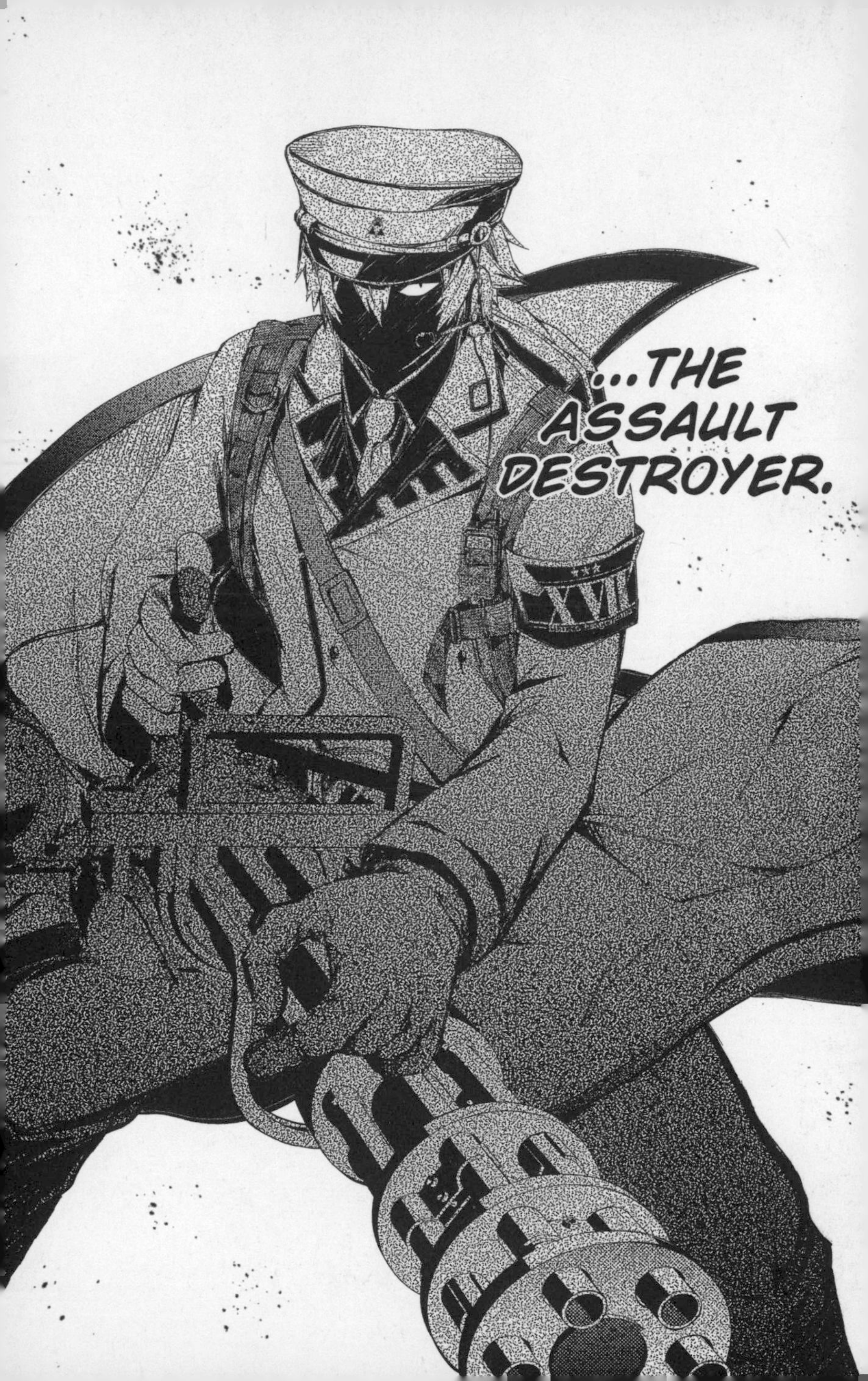
...THE ASSAULT DESTROYER.

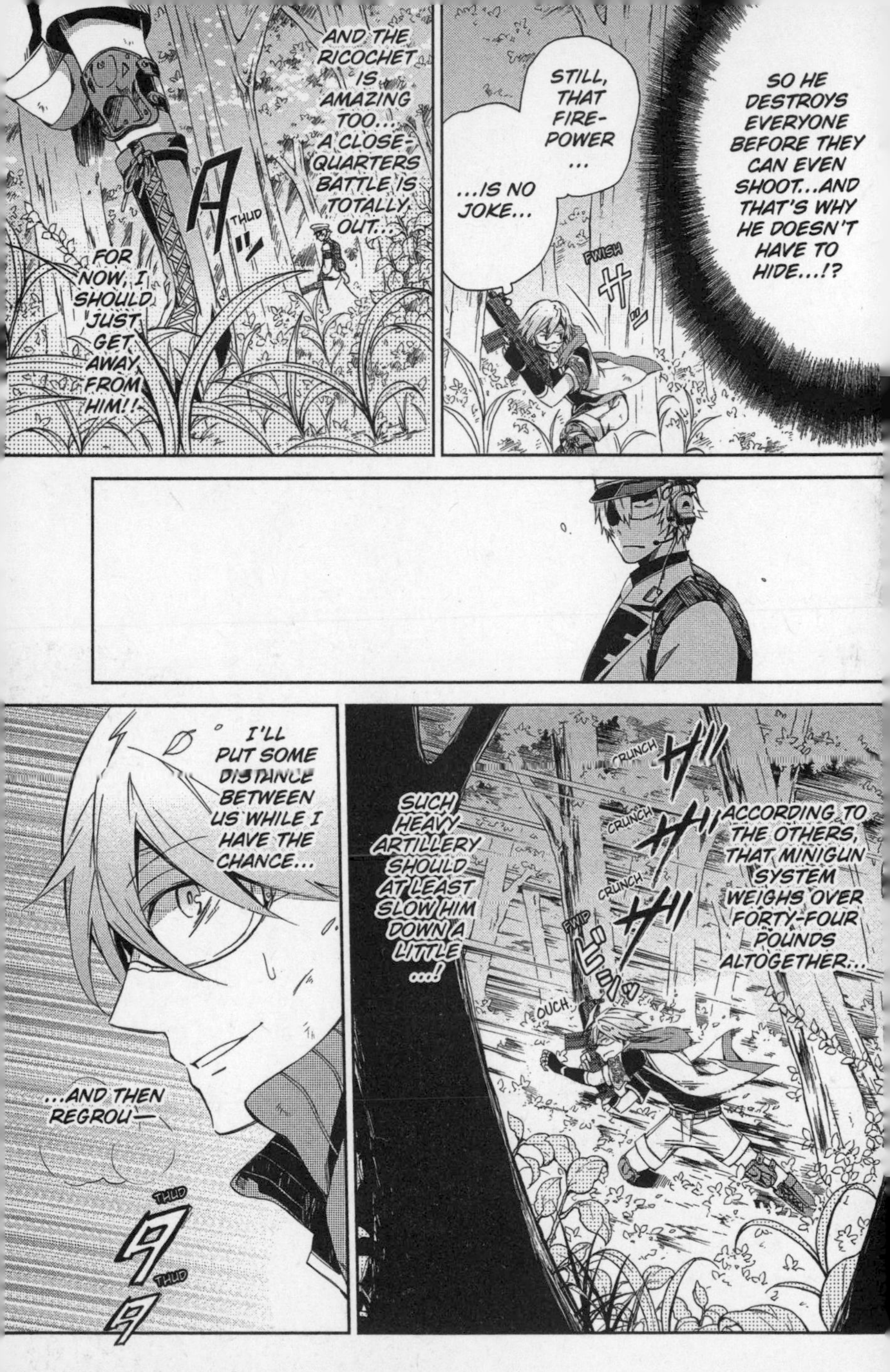
SO HE DESTROYS EVERYONE BEFORE THEY CAN EVEN SHOOT...AND THAT'S WHY HE DOESN'T HAVE TO HIDE...!?
STILL, THAT FIRE-POWER...
...IS NO JOKE...
FWISH
AND THE RICOCHET IS AMAZING TOO... A CLOSE-QUARTERS BATTLE IS TOTALLY OUT...
THUD
FOR NOW, I SHOULD JUST GET AWAY FROM HIM!!
CRUNCH
CRUNCH
CRUNCH
ACCORDING TO THE OTHERS, THAT MINIGUN SYSTEM WEIGHS OVER FORTY-FOUR POUNDS ALTOGETHER...
SUCH HEAVY ARTILLERY SHOULD AT LEAST SLOW HIM DOWN A LITTLE...!
FWIP
OUCH
I'LL PUT SOME DISTANCE BETWEEN US WHILE I HAVE THE CHANCE...
...AND THEN REGROU—
THUD
THUD

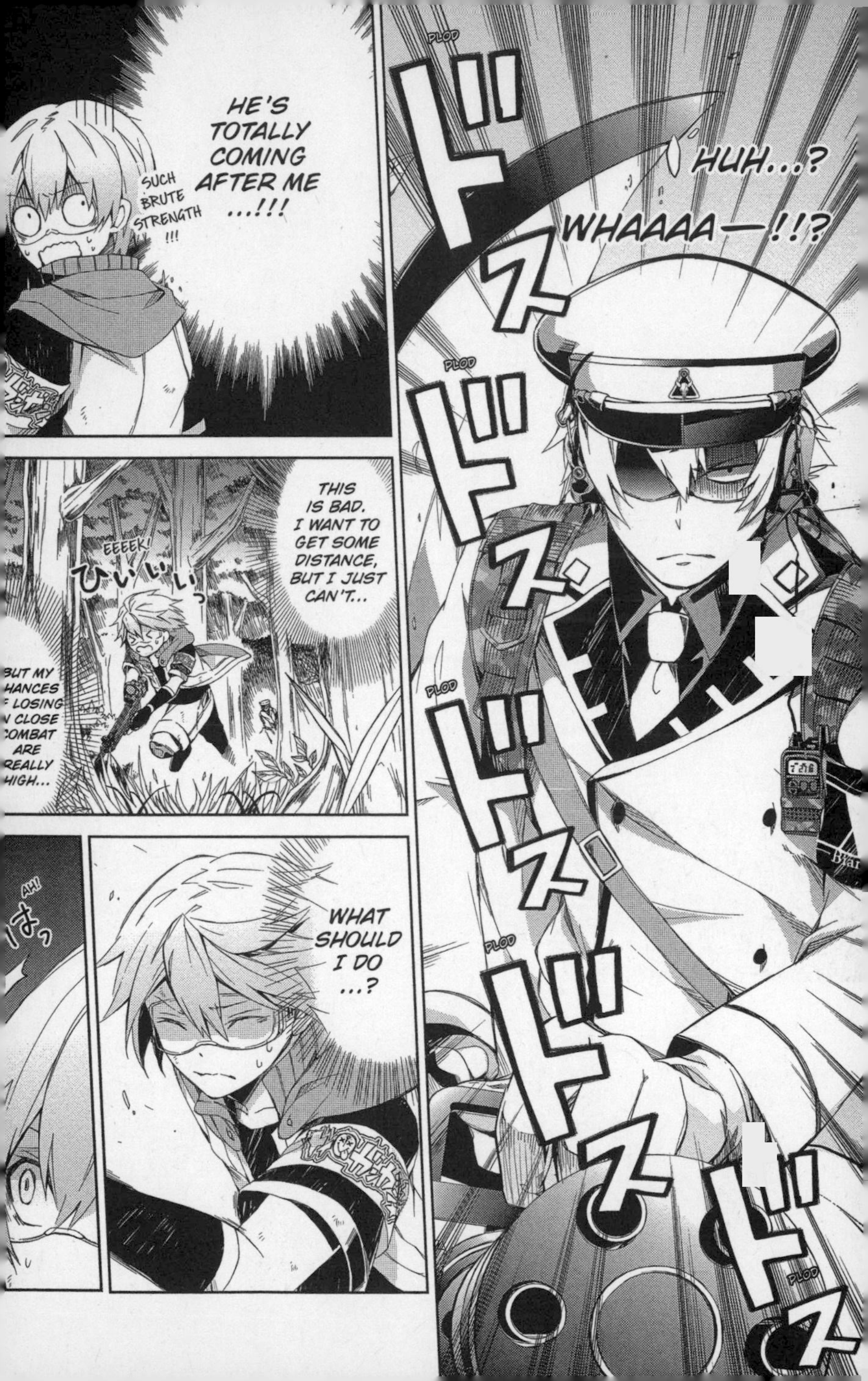
PLOD
HUH...?
WHAAAA—!!?
PLOD
PLOD
PLOD
PLOD
HE'S TOTALLY COMING AFTER ME ...!!!
SUCH BRUTE STRENGTH !!!
THIS IS BAD. I WANT TO GET SOME DISTANCE, BUT I JUST CAN'T...
EEEEK!
ひぃぃぃっ
BUT MY HANCES F LOSING N CLOSE COMBAT ARE REALLY HIGH...
WHAT SHOULD I DO ...?
AH!
はっ

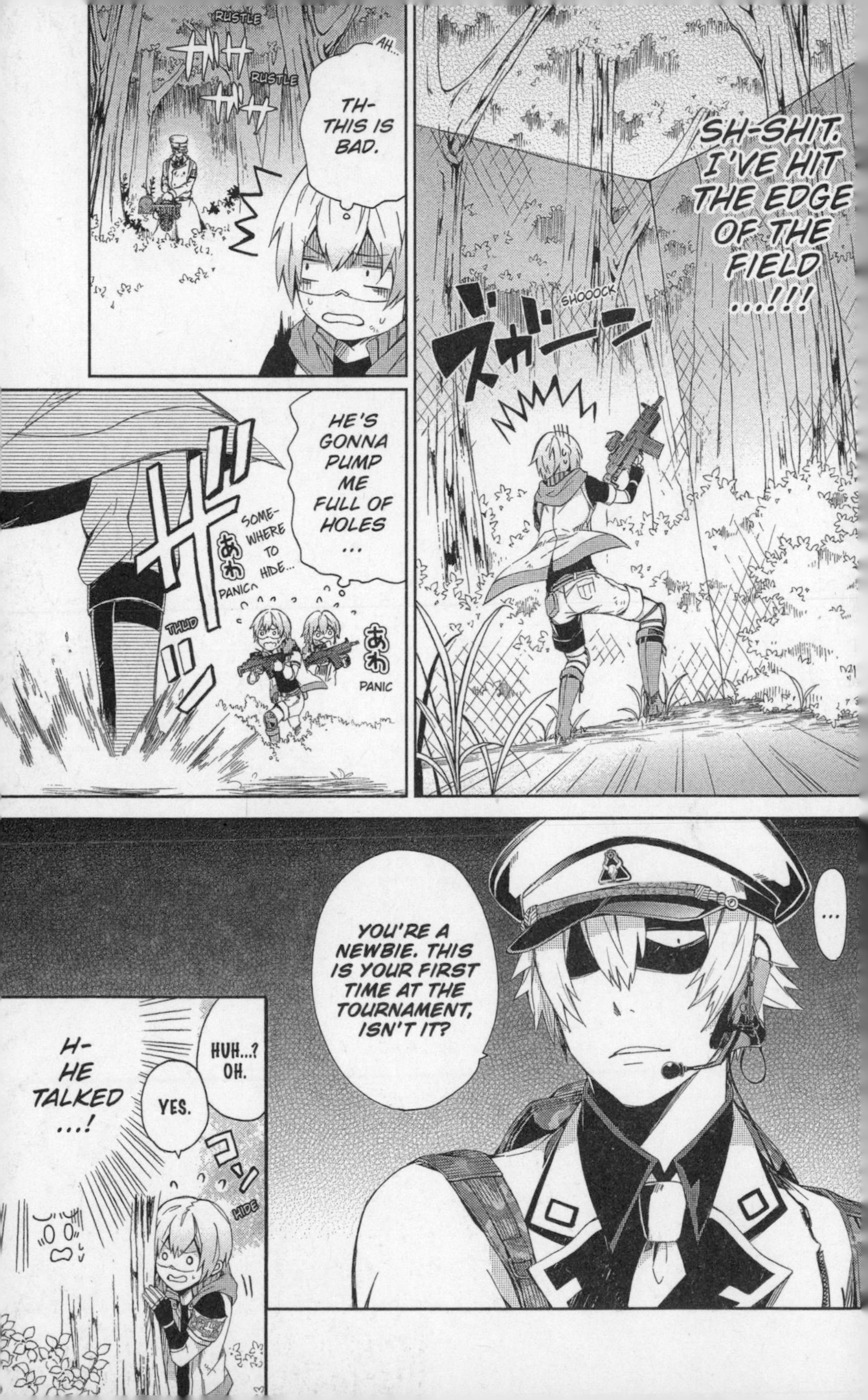
SHOOOCK
SH-SHIT. I'VE HIT THE EDGE OF THE FIELD...!!!
RUSTLE
RUSTLE
AH...
TH-THIS IS BAD.
HE'S GONNA PUMP ME FULL OF HOLES...
SOME-WHERE TO HIDE...
あわ
PANIC
あわ
PANIC
THUD
...
YOU'RE A NEWBIE. THIS IS YOUR FIRST TIME AT THE TOURNAMENT, ISN'T IT?
HUH...? OH.
YES.
H-HE TALKED...!
HIDE

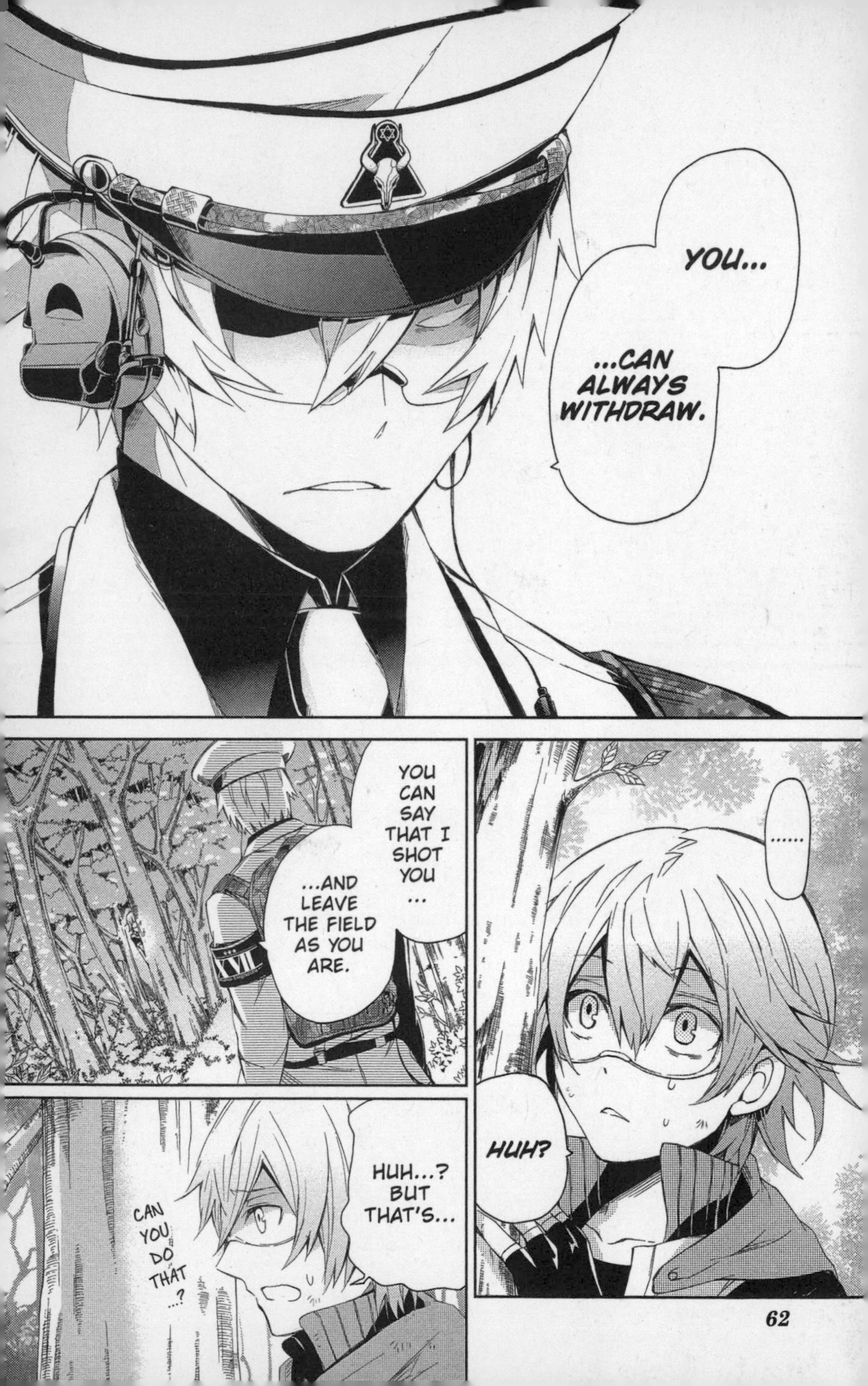
YOU...
...CAN ALWAYS WITHDRAW.
......
YOU CAN SAY THAT I SHOT YOU ...
...AND LEAVE THE FIELD AS YOU ARE.
HUH?
HUH...? BUT THAT'S...
CAN YOU DO THAT ...?

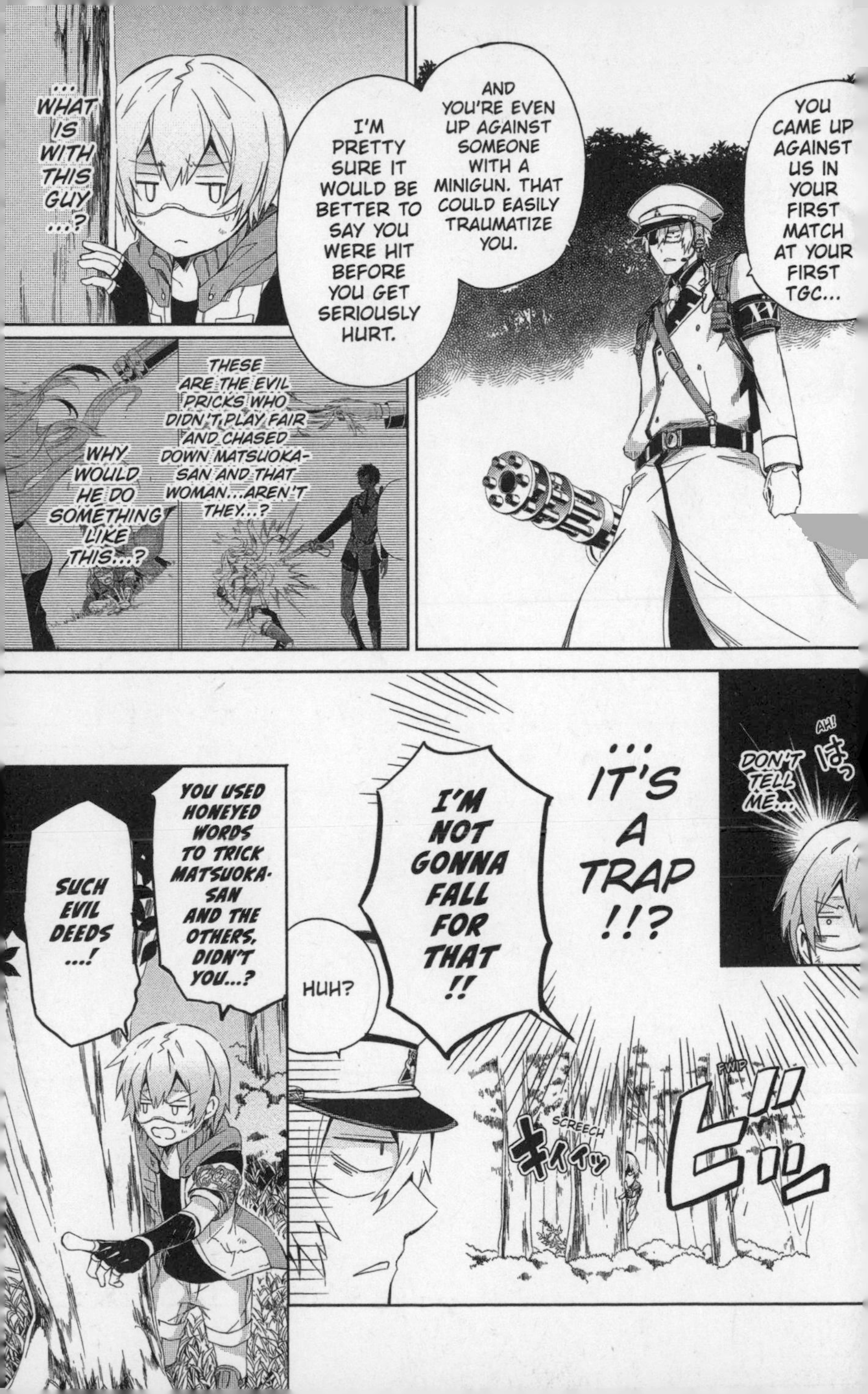
YOU CAME UP AGAINST US IN YOUR FIRST MATCH AT YOUR FIRST TGC...
AND YOU'RE EVEN UP AGAINST SOMEONE WITH A MINIGUN. THAT COULD EASILY TRAUMATIZE YOU.
I'M PRETTY SURE IT WOULD BE BETTER TO SAY YOU WERE HIT BEFORE YOU GET SERIOUSLY HURT.
...WHAT IS WITH THIS GUY...?
THESE ARE THE EVIL PRICKS WHO DIDN'T PLAY FAIR AND CHASED DOWN MATSUOKA-SAN AND THAT WOMAN...AREN'T THEY...?
WHY WOULD HE DO SOMETHING LIKE THIS...?
AH!
はっ
DON'T TELL ME...
...IT'S A TRAP!!?
FWIP
ビッ
SCREECH
キィイッ
I'M NOT GONNA FALL FOR THAT!!
HUH?
YOU USED HONEYED WORDS TO TRICK MATSUOKA-SAN AND THE OTHERS, DIDN'T YOU...?
SUCH EVIL DEEDS...!

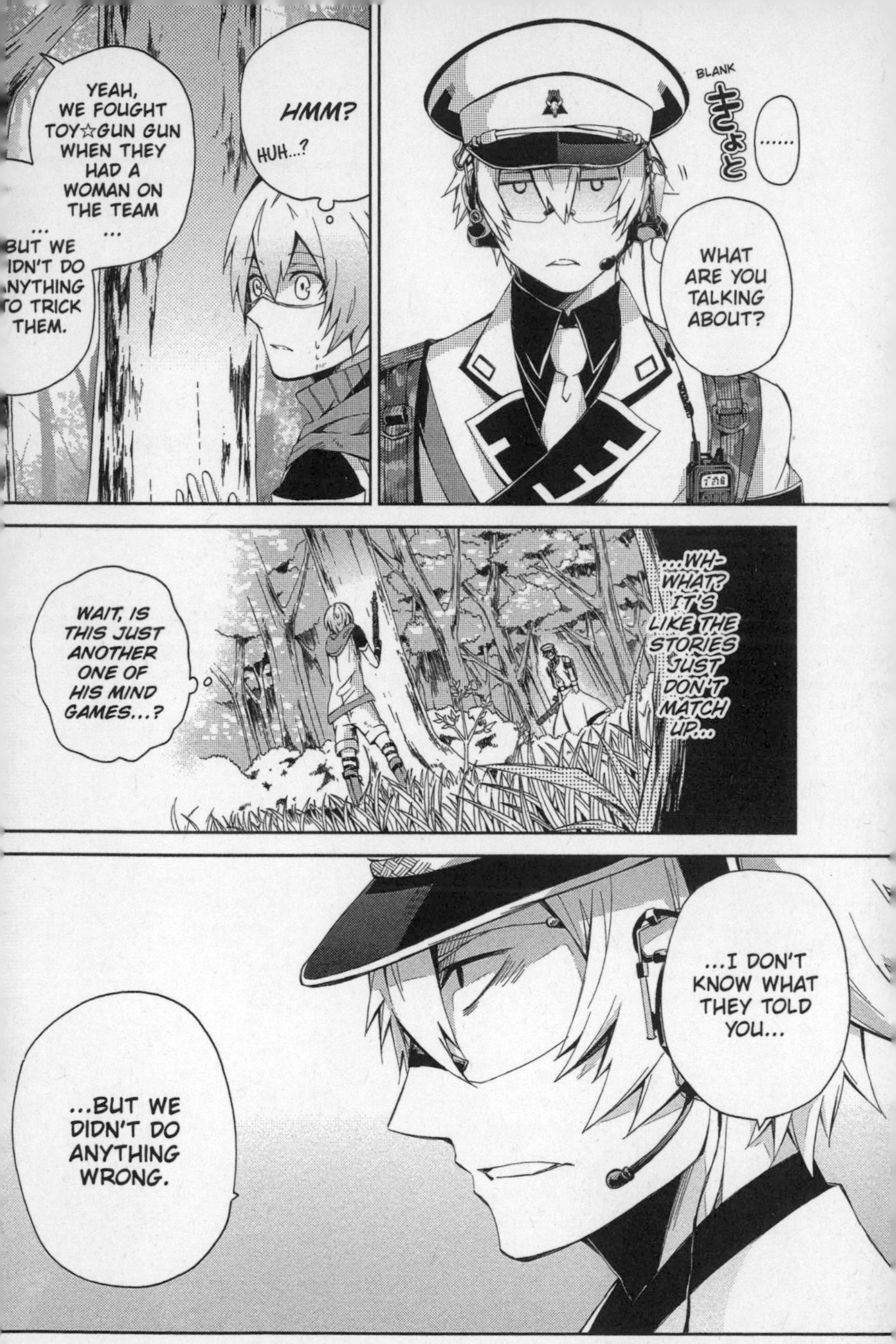
BLANK
きょと
......
WHAT ARE YOU TALKING ABOUT?
HMM?
HUH...?
YEAH, WE FOUGHT TOY☆GUN GUN WHEN THEY HAD A WOMAN ON THE TEAM ... ... BUT WE IDN'T DO NYTHING TO TRICK THEM.
...WH-WHAT? IT'S LIKE THE STORIES JUST DON'T MATCH UP...
WAIT, IS THIS JUST ANOTHER ONE OF HIS MIND GAMES...?
...I DON'T KNOW WHAT THEY TOLD YOU...
...BUT WE DIDN'T DO ANYTHING WRONG.

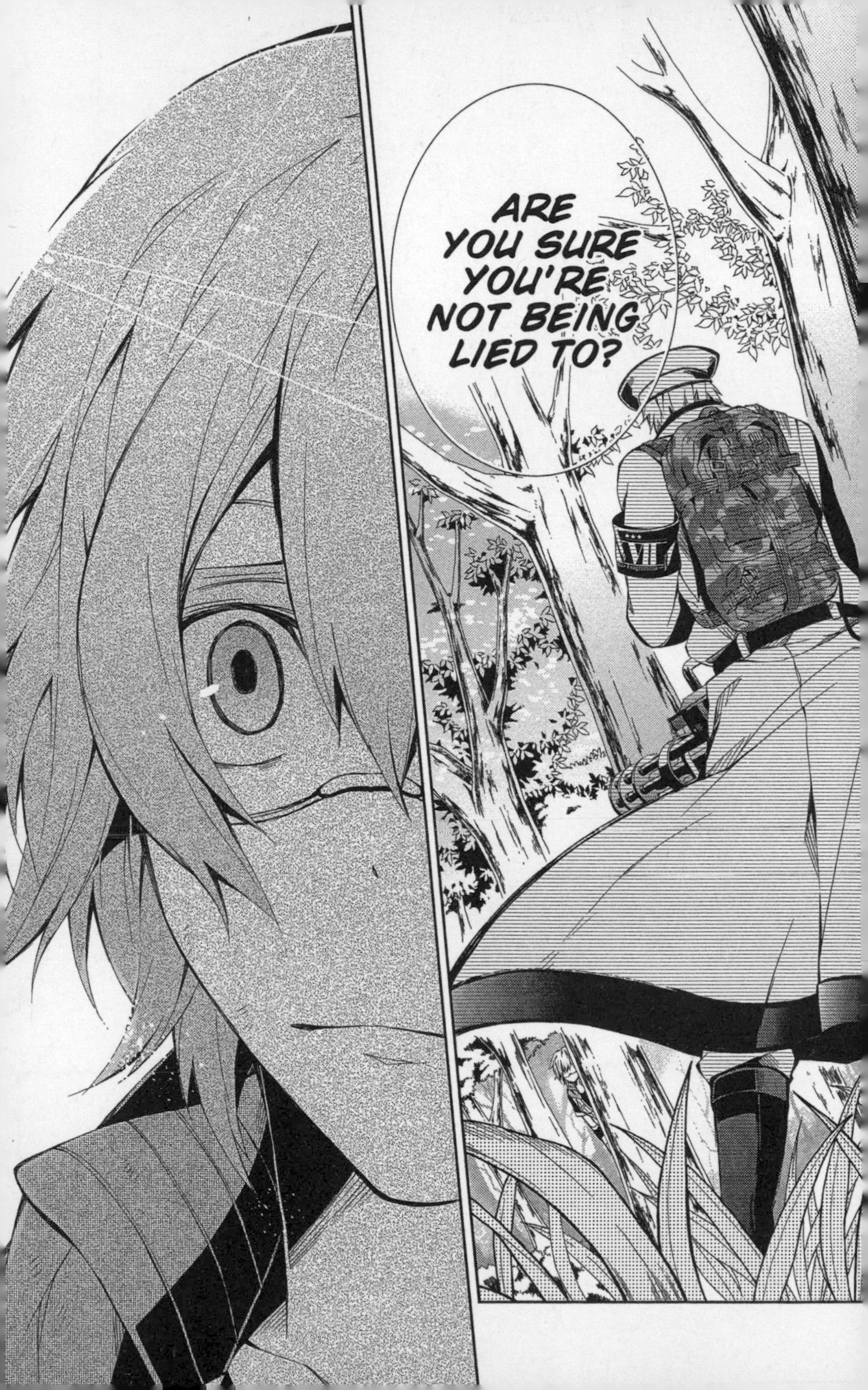
ARE YOU SURE YOU'RE NOT BEING LIED TO?

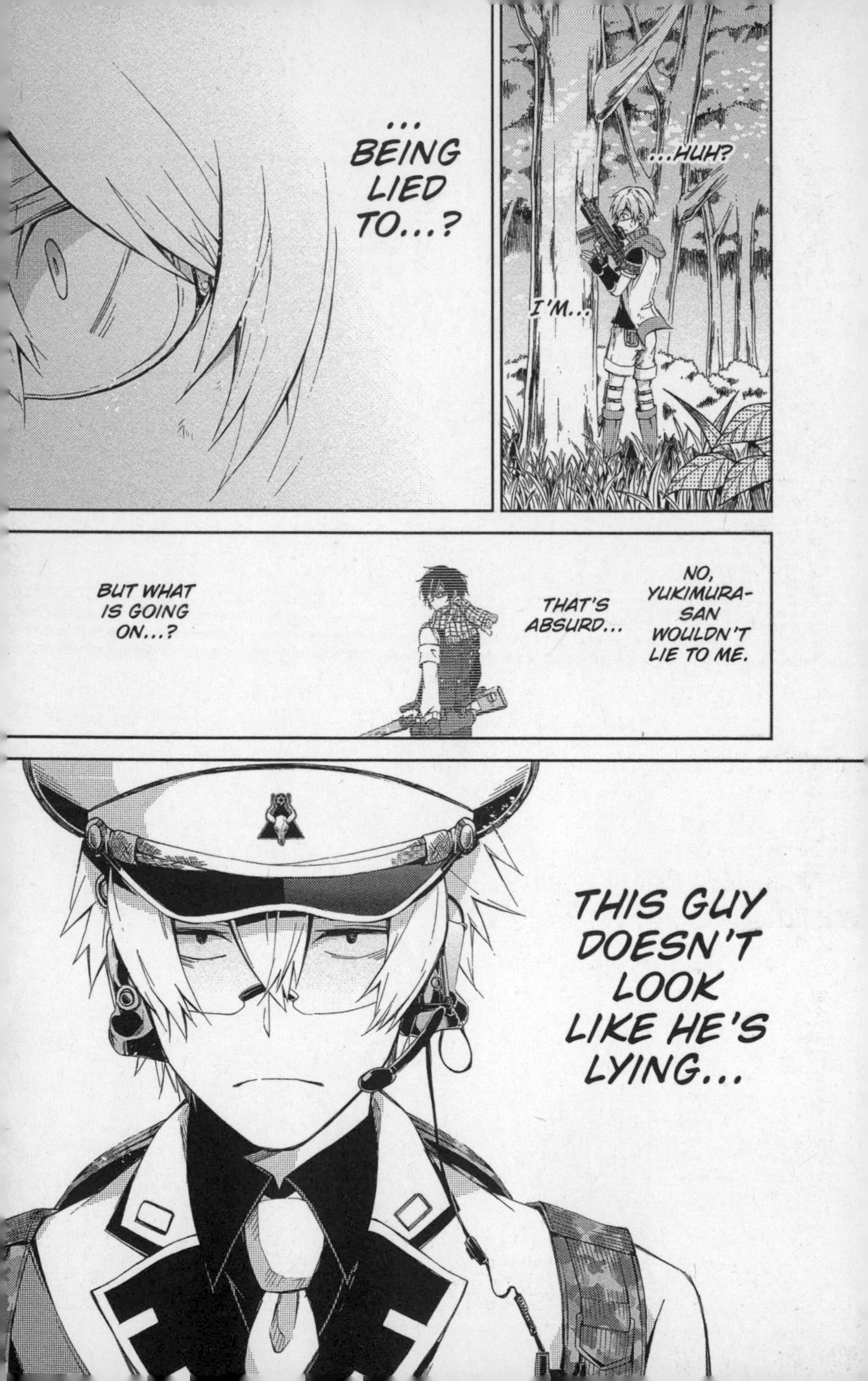
...HUH?
I'M...
...BEING LIED TO...?
NO, YUKIMURA-SAN WOULDN'T LIE TO ME.
THAT'S ABSURD...
BUT WHAT IS GOING ON...?
THIS GUY DOESN'T LOOK LIKE HE'S LYING...

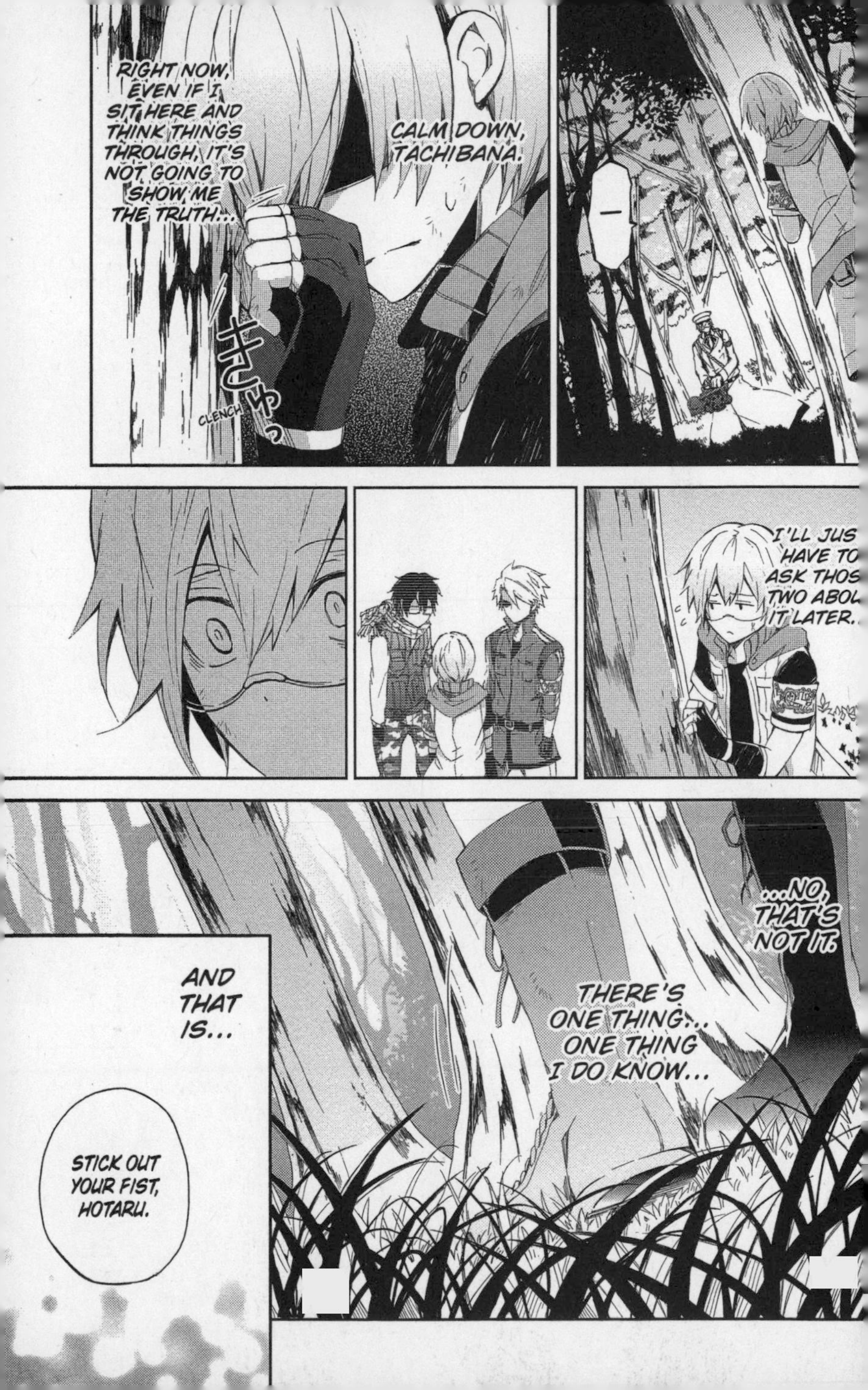
—
CALM DOWN, TACHIBANA.
RIGHT NOW, EVEN IF I SIT HERE AND THINK THINGS THROUGH, IT'S NOT GOING TO SHOW ME THE TRUTH...
CLENCH
I'LL JUS HAVE TO ASK THOS TWO ABOU IT LATER..
...NO, THAT'S NOT IT.
THERE'S ONE THING... ONE THING I DO KNOW...
AND THAT IS...
STICK OUT YOUR FIST, HOTARU.

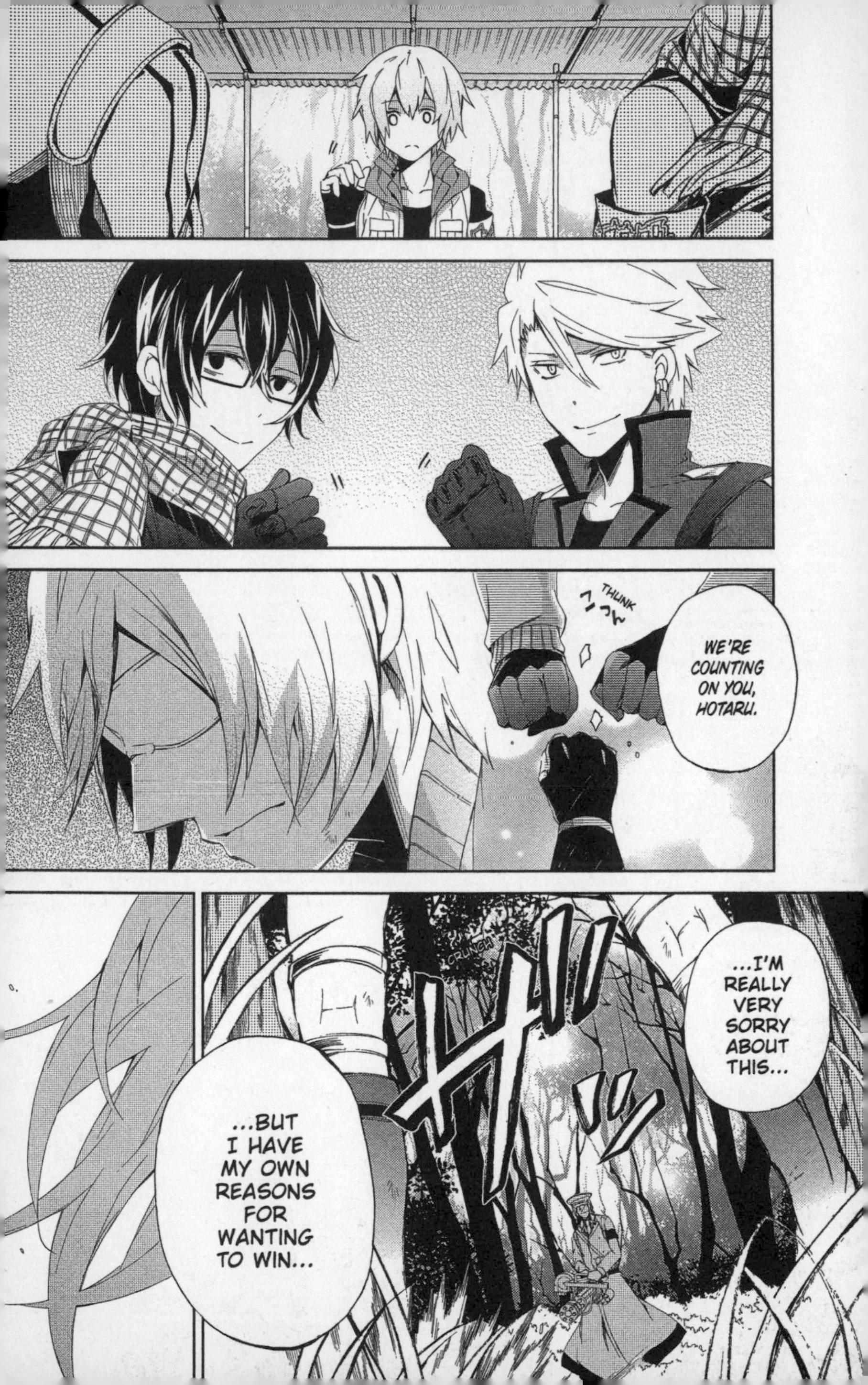
THUNK
WE'RE COUNTING ON YOU, HOTARU.
...I'M REALLY VERY SORRY ABOUT THIS...
CRUNCH
...BUT I HAVE MY OWN REASONS FOR WANTING TO WIN...

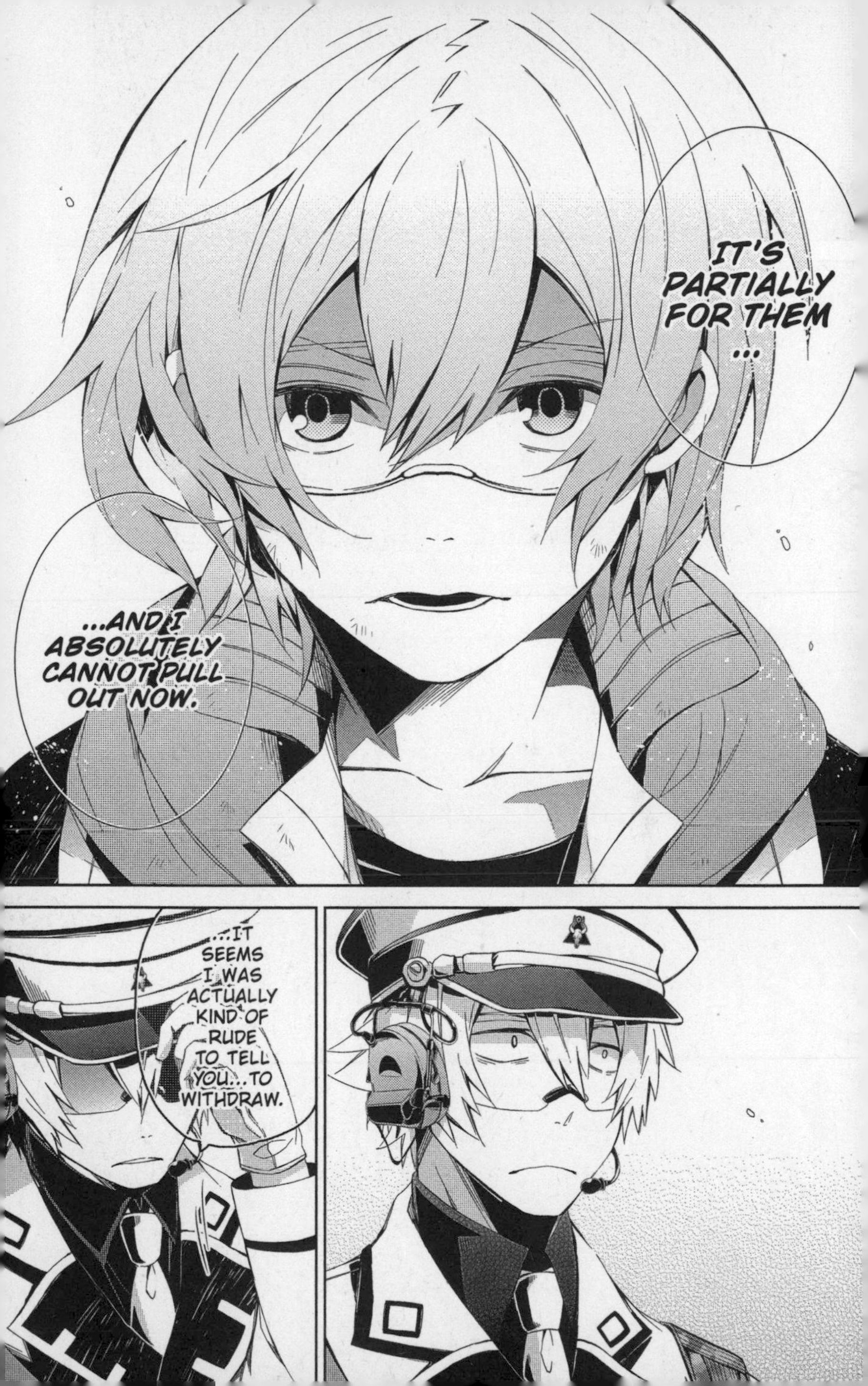
IT'S PARTIALLY FOR THEM ...
...AND I ABSOLUTELY CANNOT PULL OUT NOW.
...IT SEEMS I WAS ACTUALLY KIND OF RUDE TO TELL YOU...TO WITHDRAW.

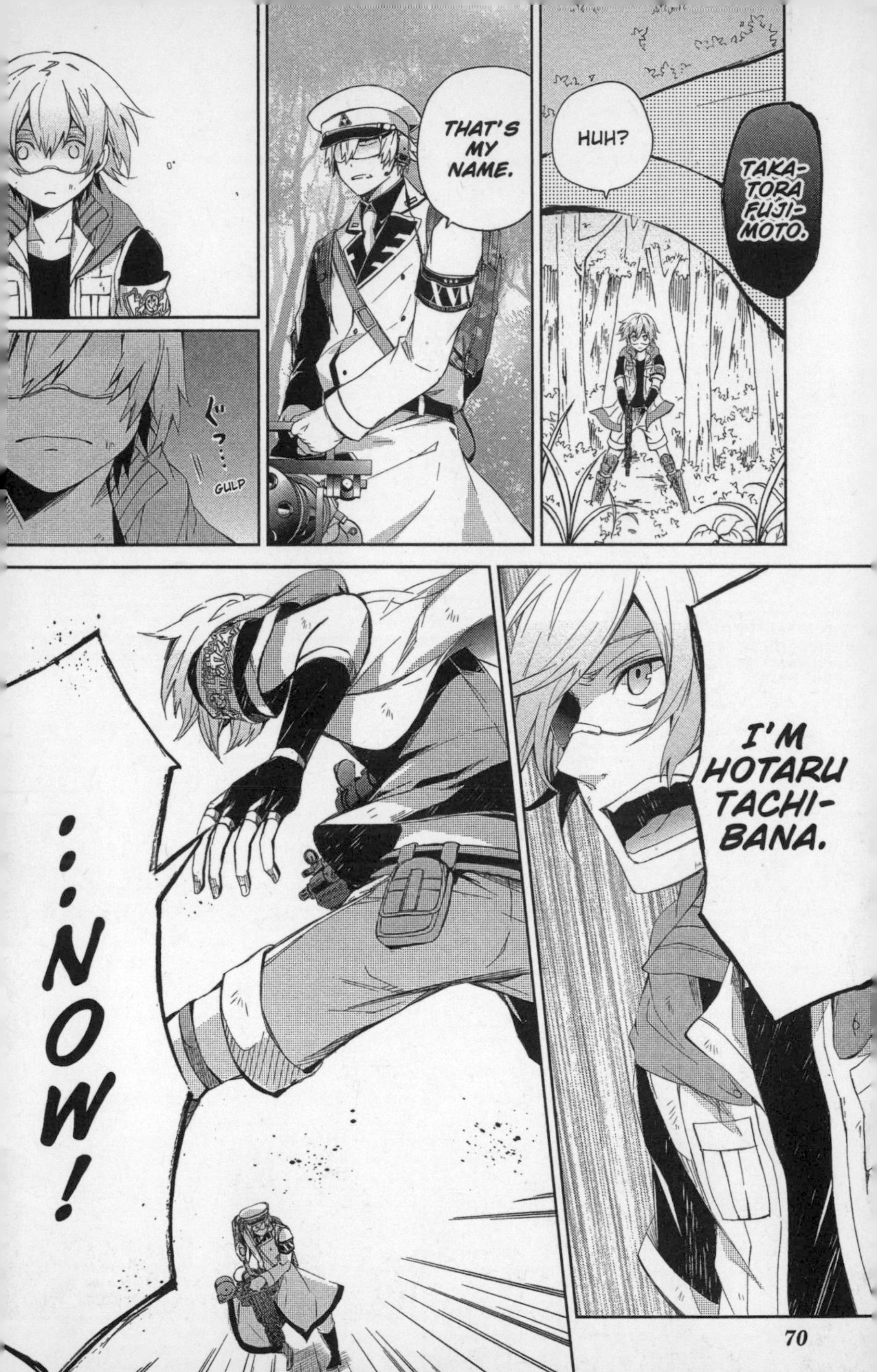
TAKA-TORA FUJI-MOTO.
HUH?
THAT'S MY NAME.
ぐっ…
GULP
I'M HOTARU TACHI-BANA.
...NOW!

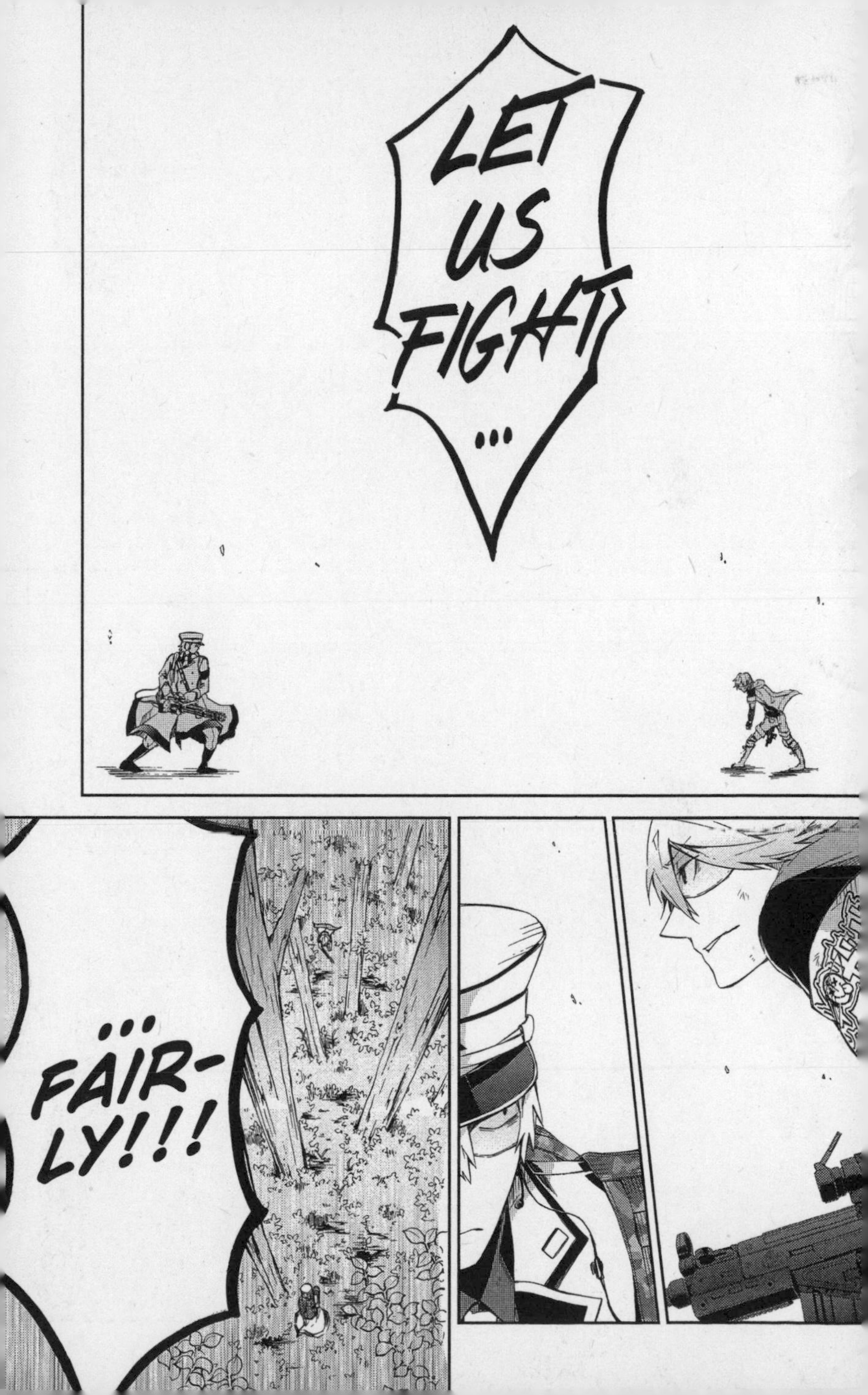
LET US FIGHT...
...FAIR-LY!!!

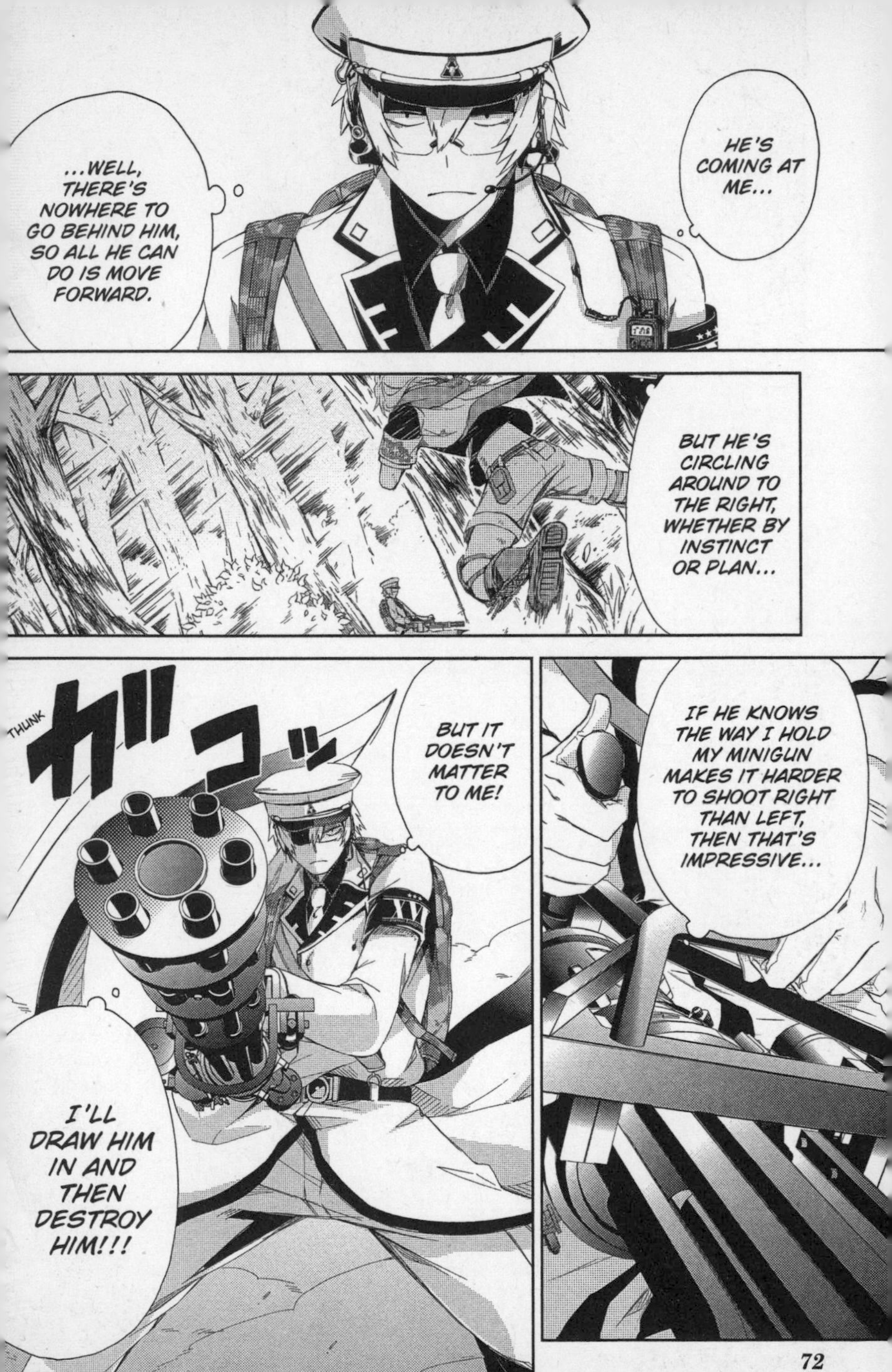
HE'S COMING AT ME...
...WELL, THERE'S NOWHERE TO GO BEHIND HIM, SO ALL HE CAN DO IS MOVE FORWARD.
BUT HE'S CIRCLING AROUND TO THE RIGHT, WHETHER BY INSTINCT OR PLAN...
IF HE KNOWS THE WAY I HOLD MY MINIGUN MAKES IT HARDER TO SHOOT RIGHT THAN LEFT, THEN THAT'S IMPRESSIVE...
BUT IT DOESN'T MATTER TO ME!
THUNK
I'LL DRAW HIM IN AND THEN DESTROY HIM!!!

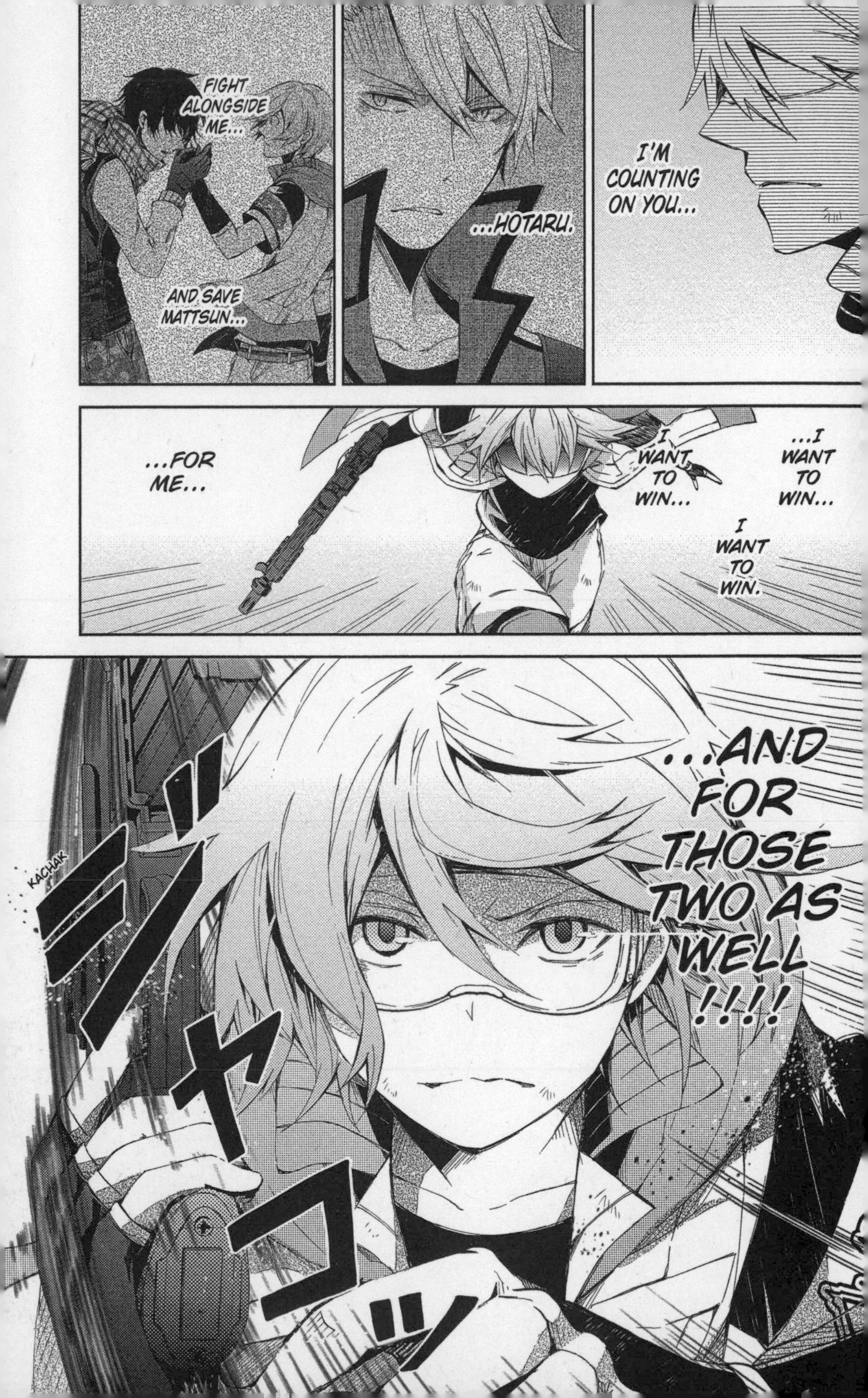
I'M COUNTING ON YOU...
...HOTARU.
FIGHT ALONGSIDE ME...
AND SAVE MATTSUN...
...I WANT TO WIN...
I WANT TO WIN...
I WANT TO WIN.
...FOR ME...
...AND FOR THOSE TWO AS WELL!!!!
ジャコッ
KACHAK

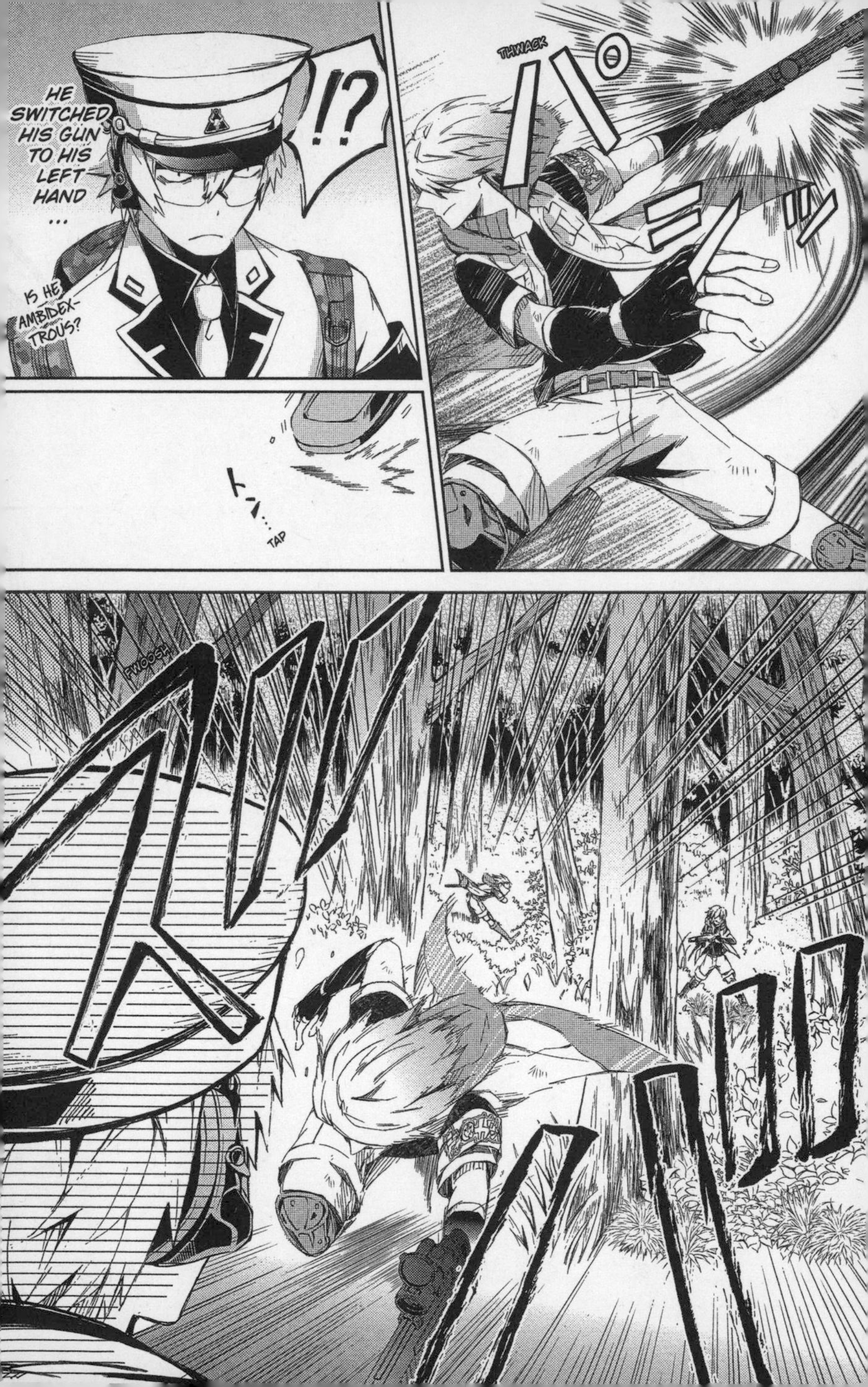

THWACK
!?
HE SWITCHED HIS GUN TO HIS LEFT HAND...
IS HE AMBIDEXTROUS?
TAP
FWOOSH

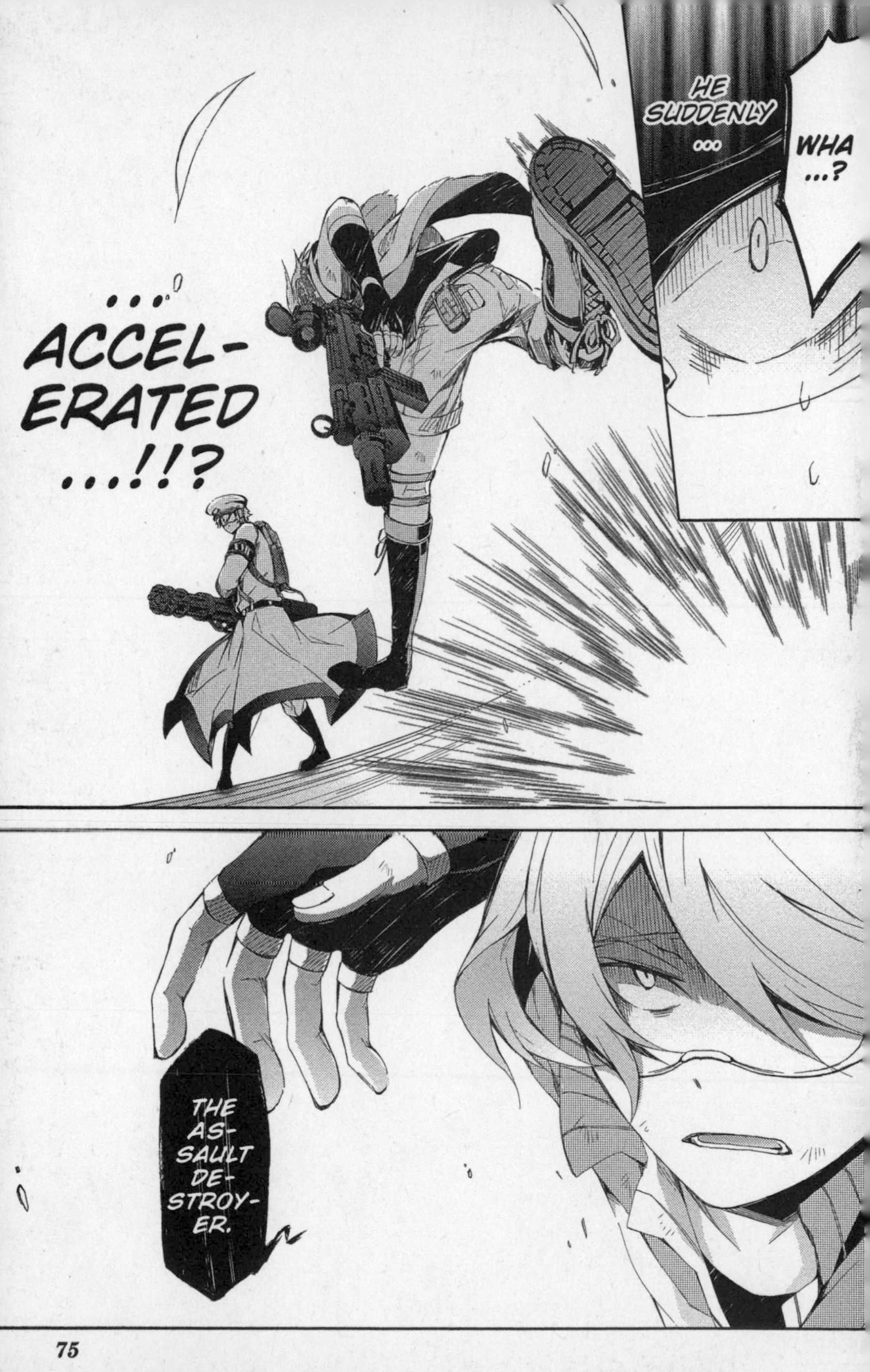
WHA ...?
HE SUDDENLY ...
...ACCEL-ERATED ...!!?
THE AS-SAULT DE-STROY-ER.

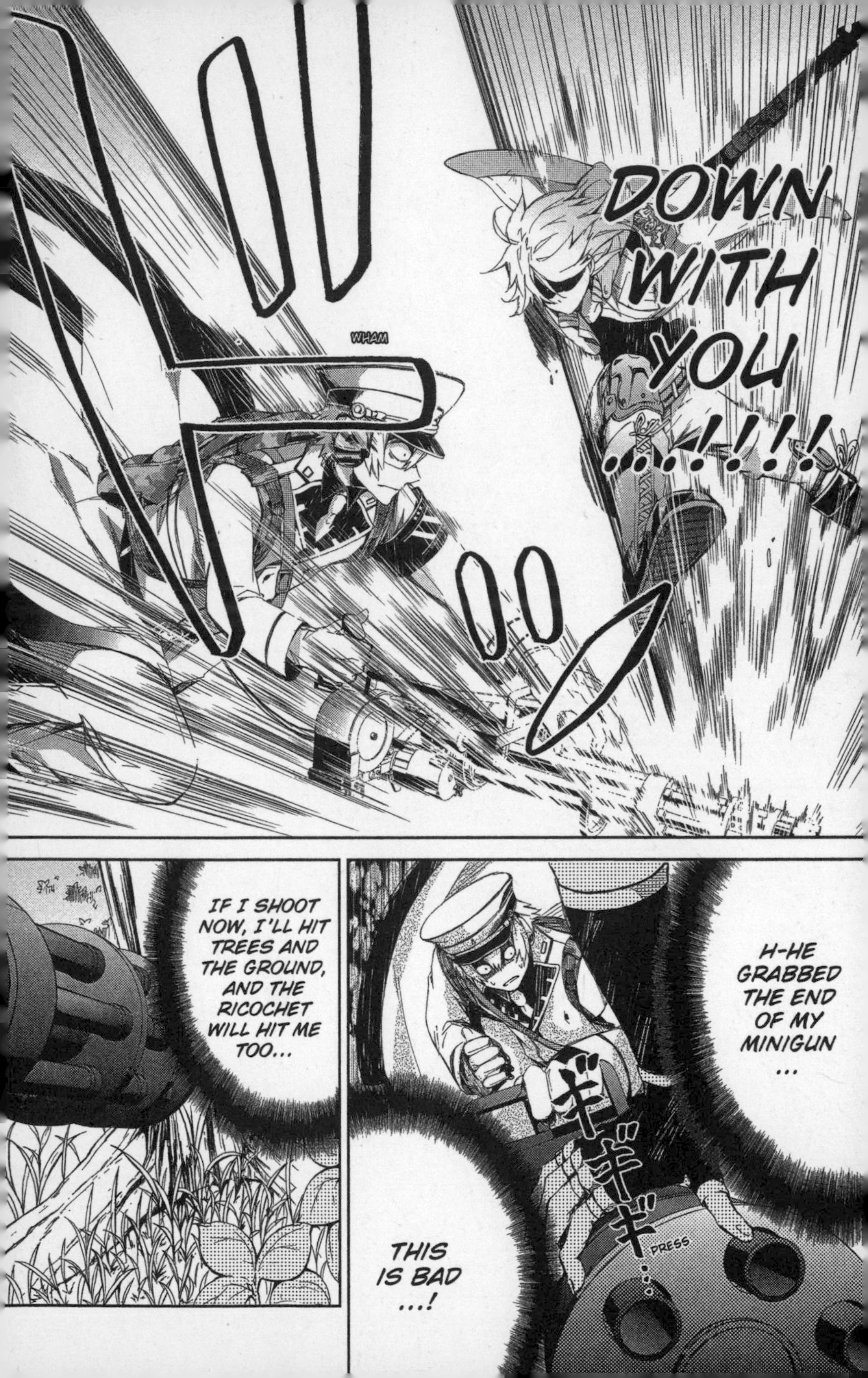

DOWN WITH YOU ...!!!!!
WHAM
H-HE GRABBED THE END OF MY MINIGUN ...
IF I SHOOT NOW, I'LL HIT TREES AND THE GROUND, AND THE RICOCHET WILL HIT ME TOO...
PRESS
THIS IS BAD ...!

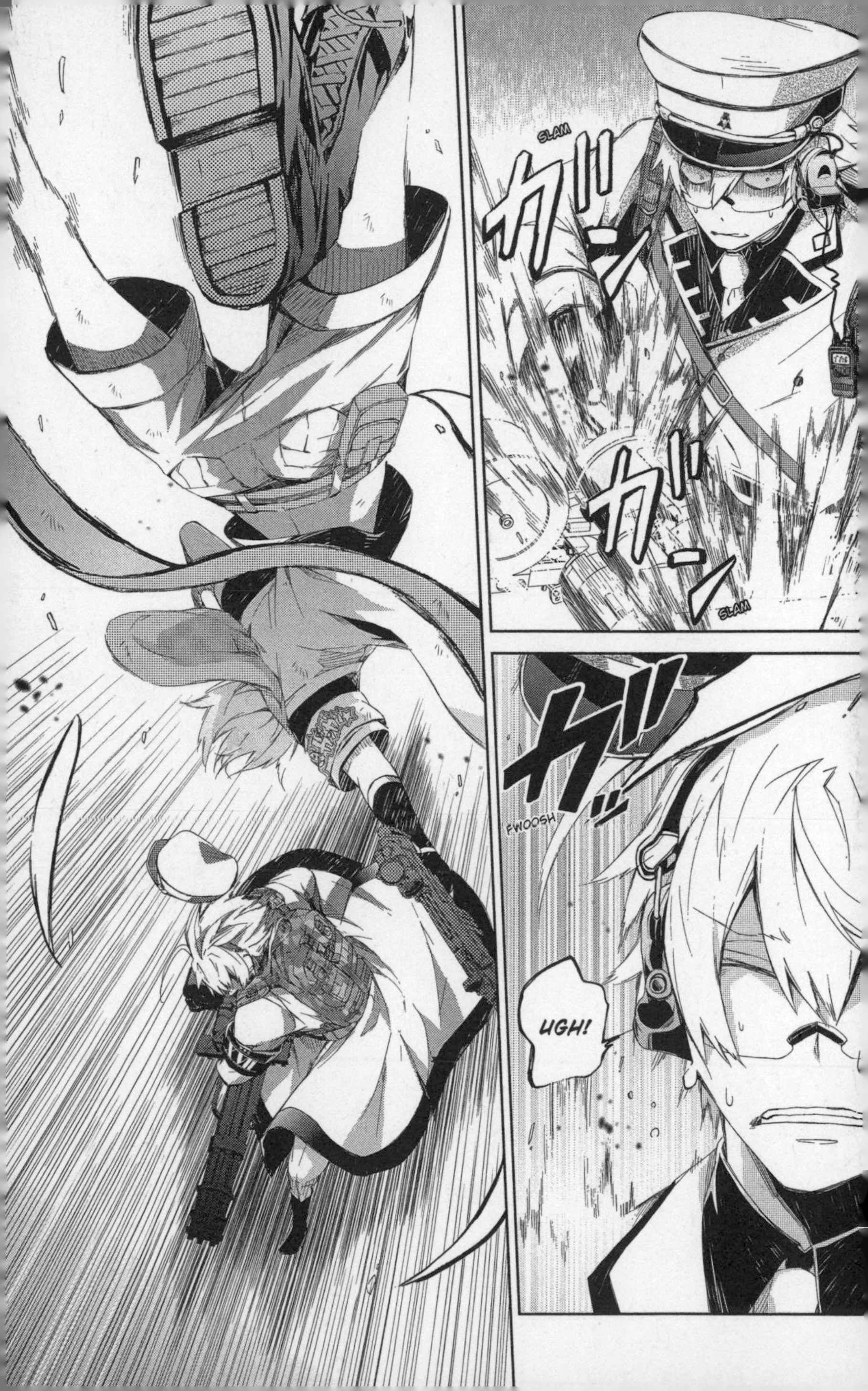
SLAM
ガッ
ガン
SLAM
グッ
FWOOSH
UGH!

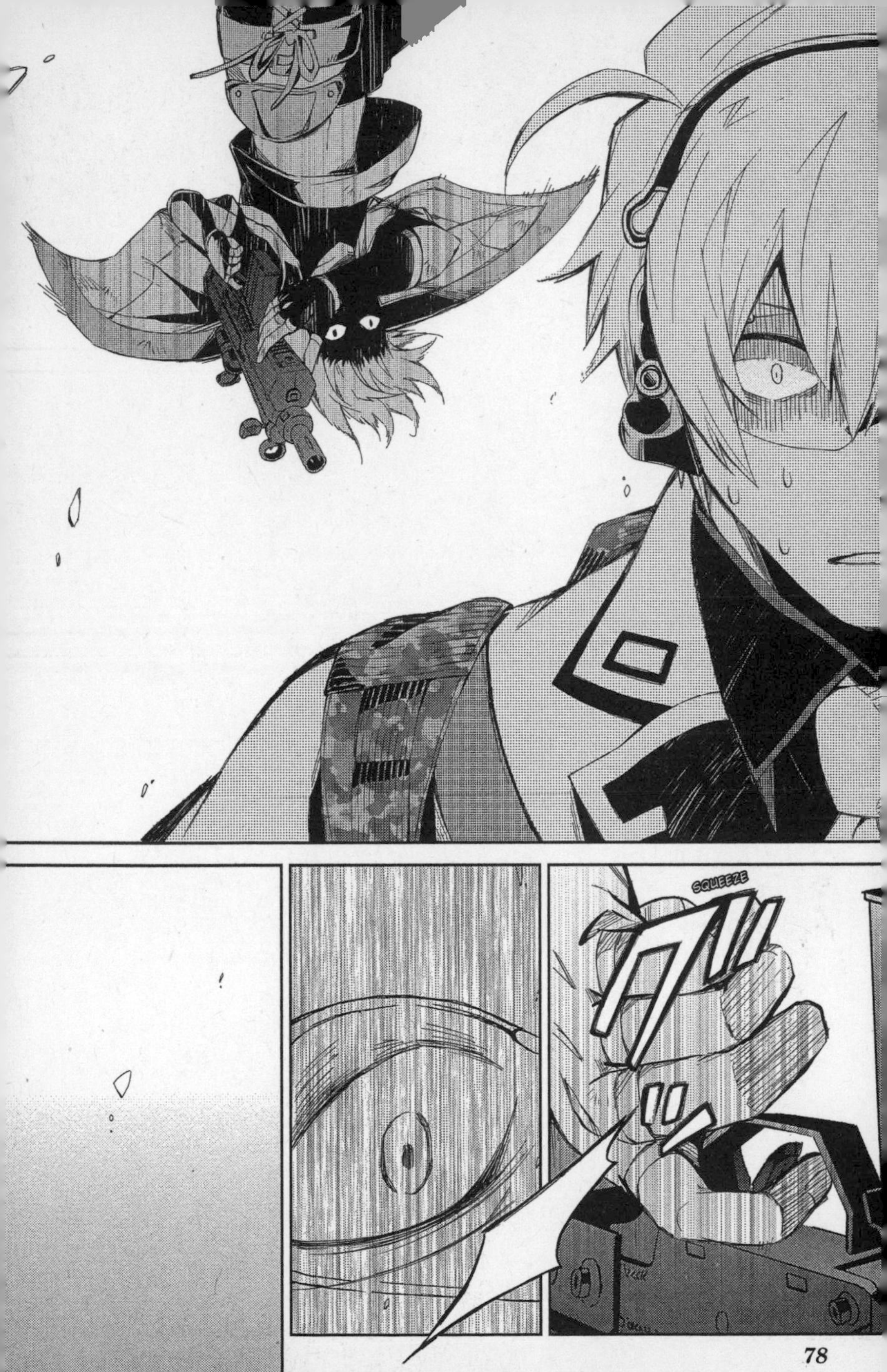
SQUEEZE

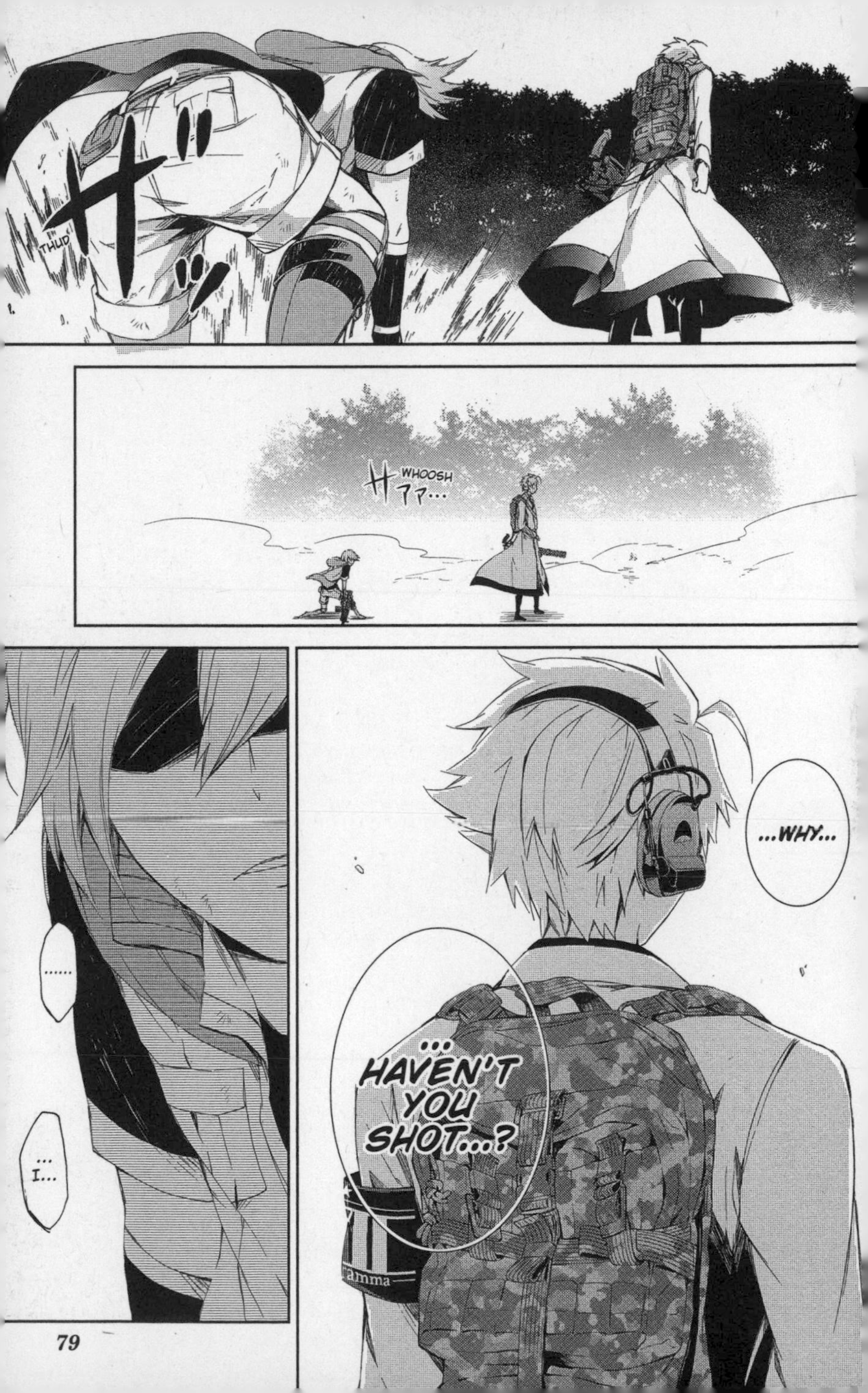
THUD
WHOOSH
...WHY...
...HAVEN'T YOU SHOT...?
......
... I...

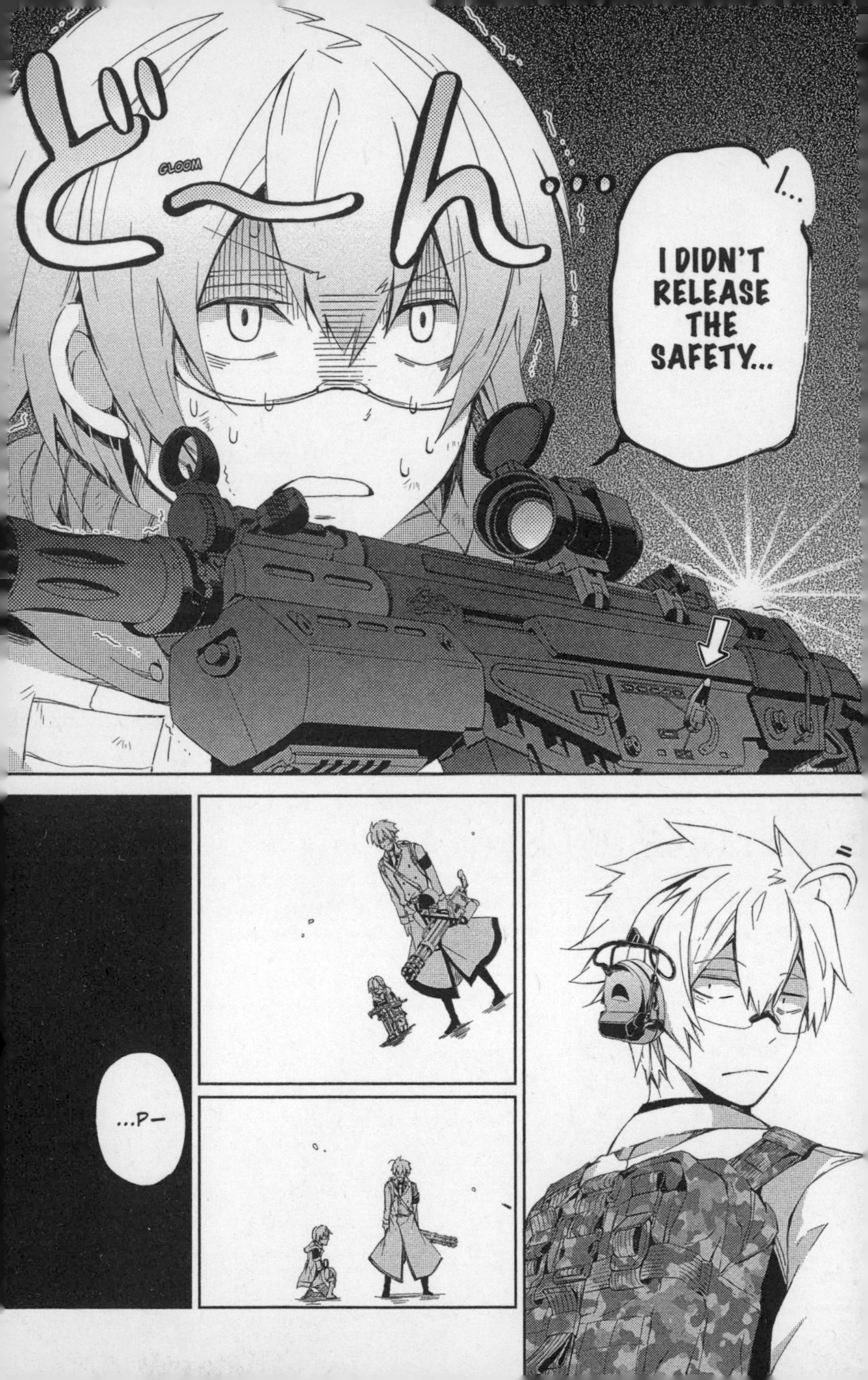

ど〜ん…
GLOOM
I...
I DIDN'T RELEASE THE SAFETY...
...P—

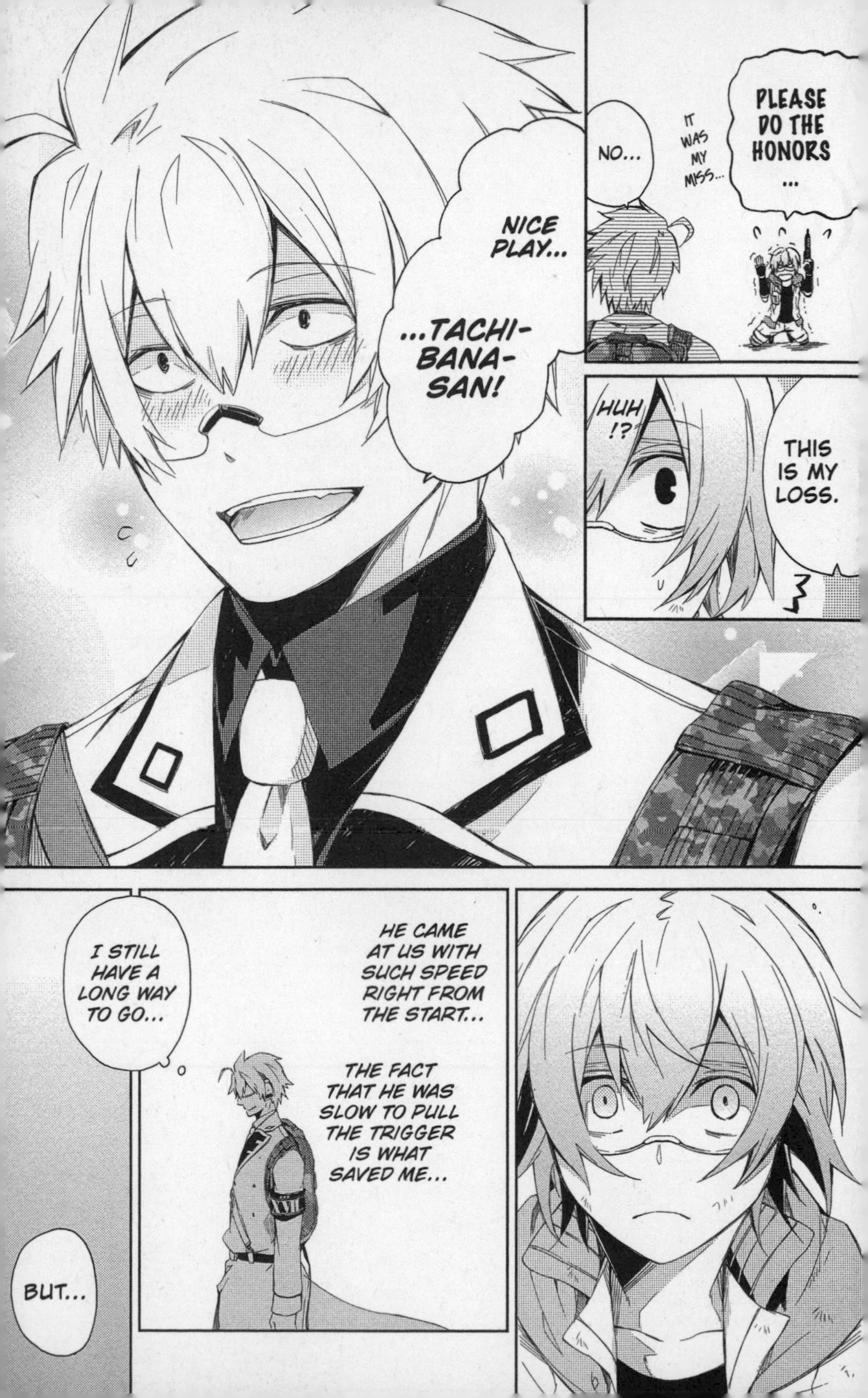
PLEASE DO THE HONORS ...
IT WAS MY MISS...
NO...
NICE PLAY...
...TACHI-BANA-SAN!
THIS IS MY LOSS.
HUH!?
HE CAME AT US WITH SUCH SPEED RIGHT FROM THE START...
THE FACT THAT HE WAS SLOW TO PULL THE TRIGGER IS WHAT SAVED ME...
I STILL HAVE A LONG WAY TO GO...
BUT...

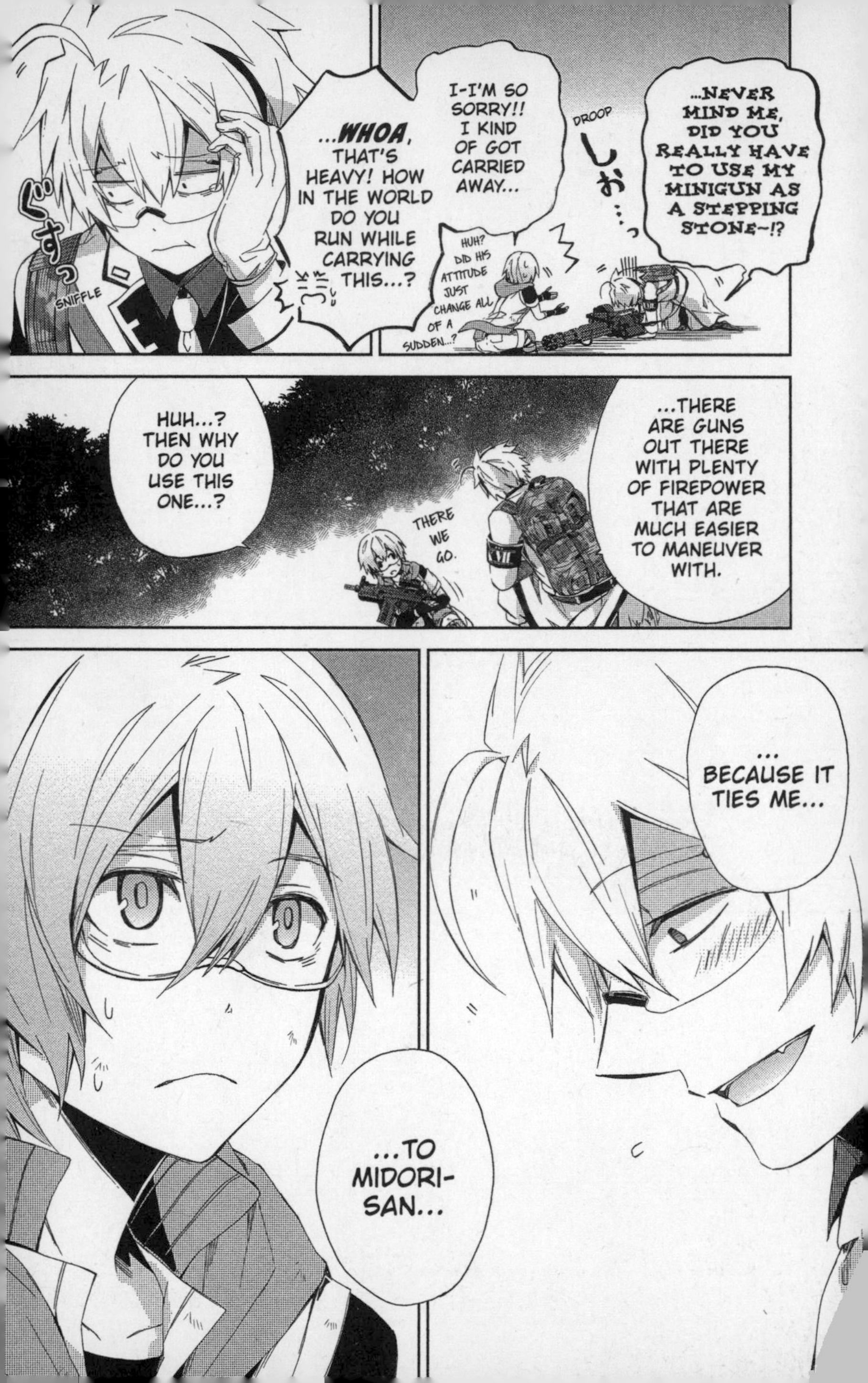

...NEVER MIND ME, DID YOU REALLY HAVE TO USE MY MINIGUN AS A STEPPING STONE~!?
しお…っ
DROOP
I-I'M SO SORRY!! I KIND OF GOT CARRIED AWAY...
HUH? DID HIS ATTITUDE JUST CHANGE ALL OF A SUDDEN...?
...**WHOA**, THAT'S HEAVY! HOW IN THE WORLD DO YOU RUN WHILE CARRYING THIS...?
ぐすっ
SNIFFLE
...THERE ARE GUNS OUT THERE WITH PLENTY OF FIREPOWER THAT ARE MUCH EASIER TO MANEUVER WITH.
THERE WE GO.
HUH...? THEN WHY DO YOU USE THIS ONE...?
... BECAUSE IT TIES ME...
...TO MIDORI-SAN...

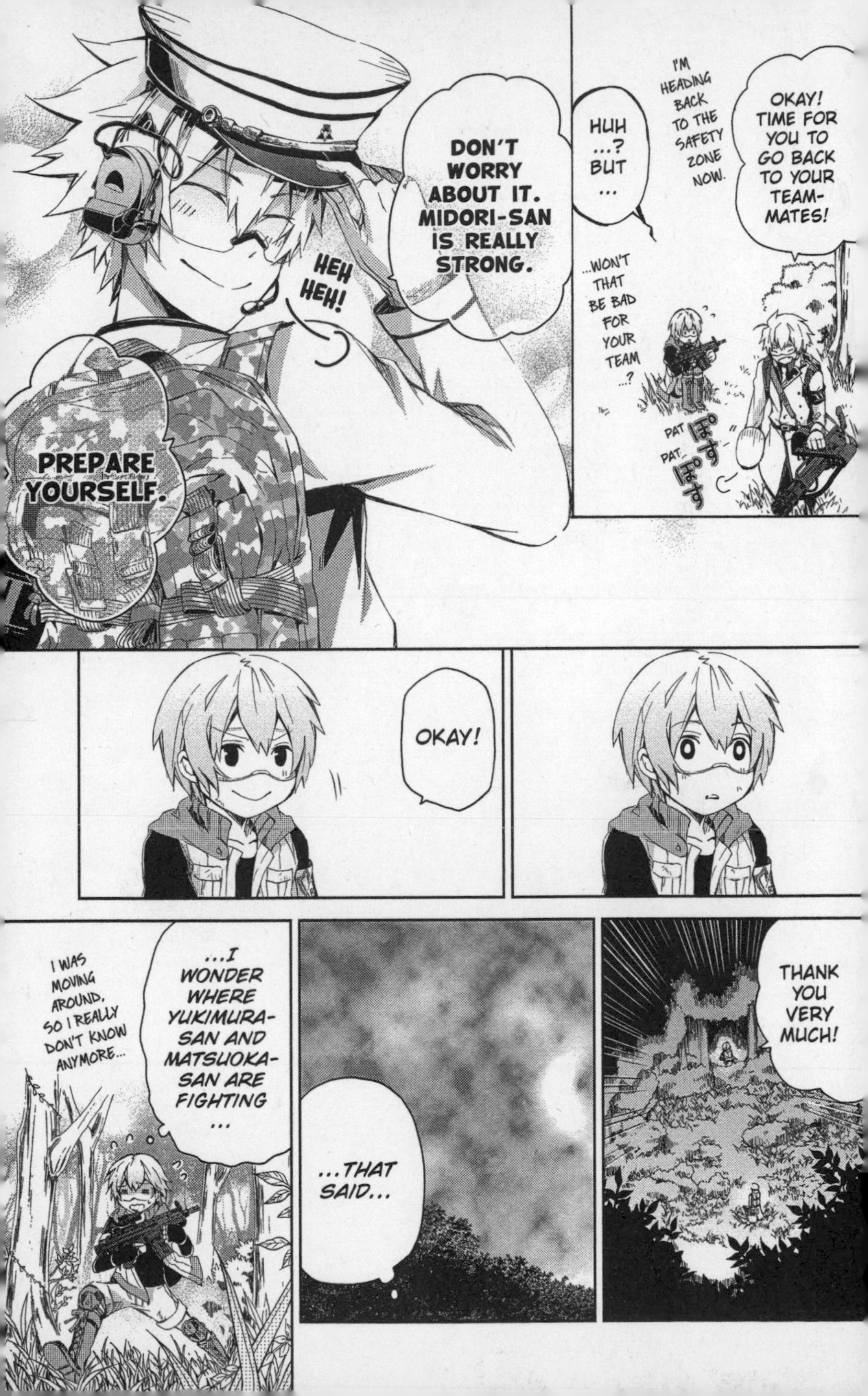
OKAY! TIME FOR YOU TO GO BACK TO YOUR TEAM-MATES!
I'M HEADING BACK TO THE SAFETY ZONE NOW.
HUH ...? BUT ...
...WON'T THAT BE BAD FOR YOUR TEAM ...?
PAT PAT
ぽすぽす
DON'T WORRY ABOUT IT. MIDORI-SAN IS REALLY STRONG.
HEH HEH!
PREPARE YOURSELF.
OKAY!
THANK YOU VERY MUCH!
...THAT SAID...
...I WONDER WHERE YUKIMURA-SAN AND MATSUOKA-SAN ARE FIGHTING ...
I WAS MOVING AROUND, SO I REALLY DON'T KNOW ANYMORE...

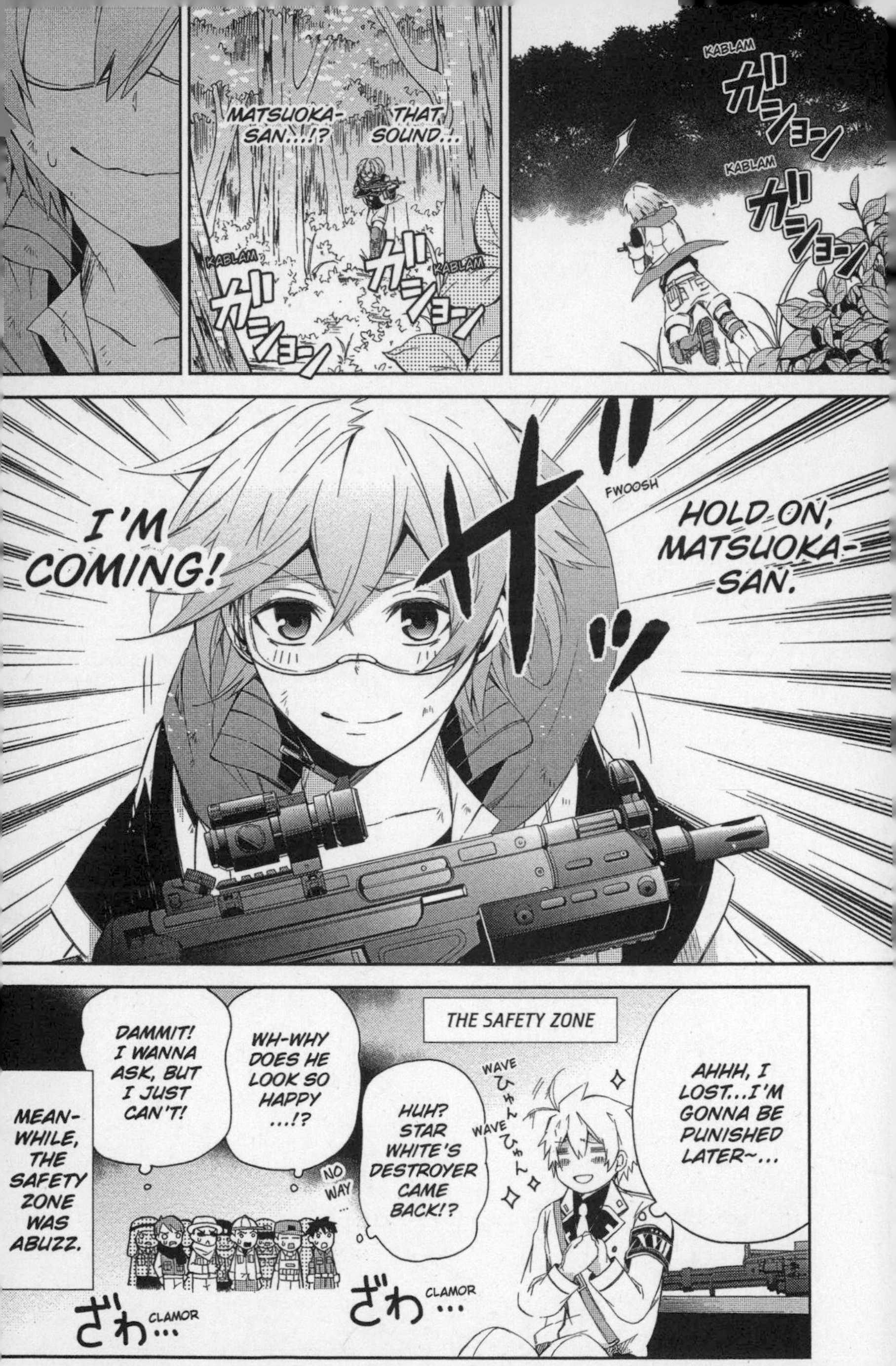
KABLAM
ガショーン
KABLAM
ガショーン
THAT SOUND...
MATSUOKA-SAN...!?
KABLAM
ガショーン
KABLAM
ガショーン
FWOOSH
HOLD ON, MATSUOKA-SAN.
I'M COMING!
THE SAFETY ZONE
AHHH, I LOST...I'M GONNA BE PUNISHED LATER~...
WAVE
ひゅん
WAVE
ひゅん
HUH? STAR WHITE'S DESTROYER CAME BACK!?
NO WAY...
WH-WHY DOES HE LOOK SO HAPPY ...!?
DAMMIT! I WANNA ASK, BUT I JUST CAN'T!
MEAN-WHILE, THE SAFETY ZONE WAS ABUZZ.
ざわ... CLAMOR
ざわ... CLAMOR

AOHARU×MACHINEGUN

IS IT DONE YET? IS IT DONE YET...?
HE'S A DOG...
HE'S A DOG...
FWOOSH
FWOOSH

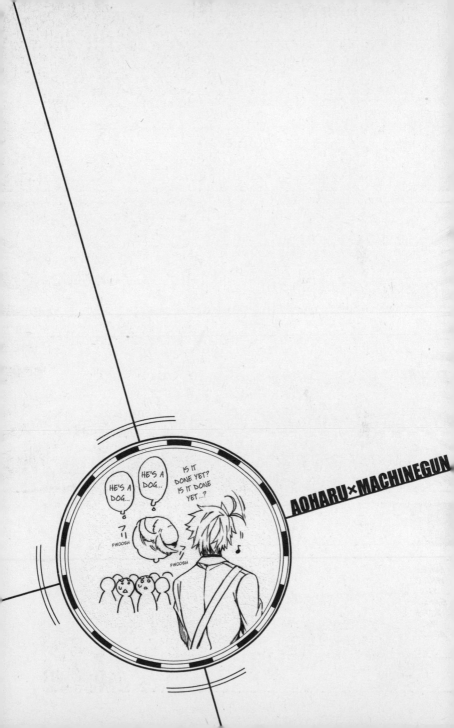

AOHARU
MACHINE
GUN

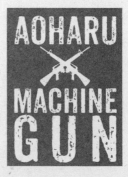

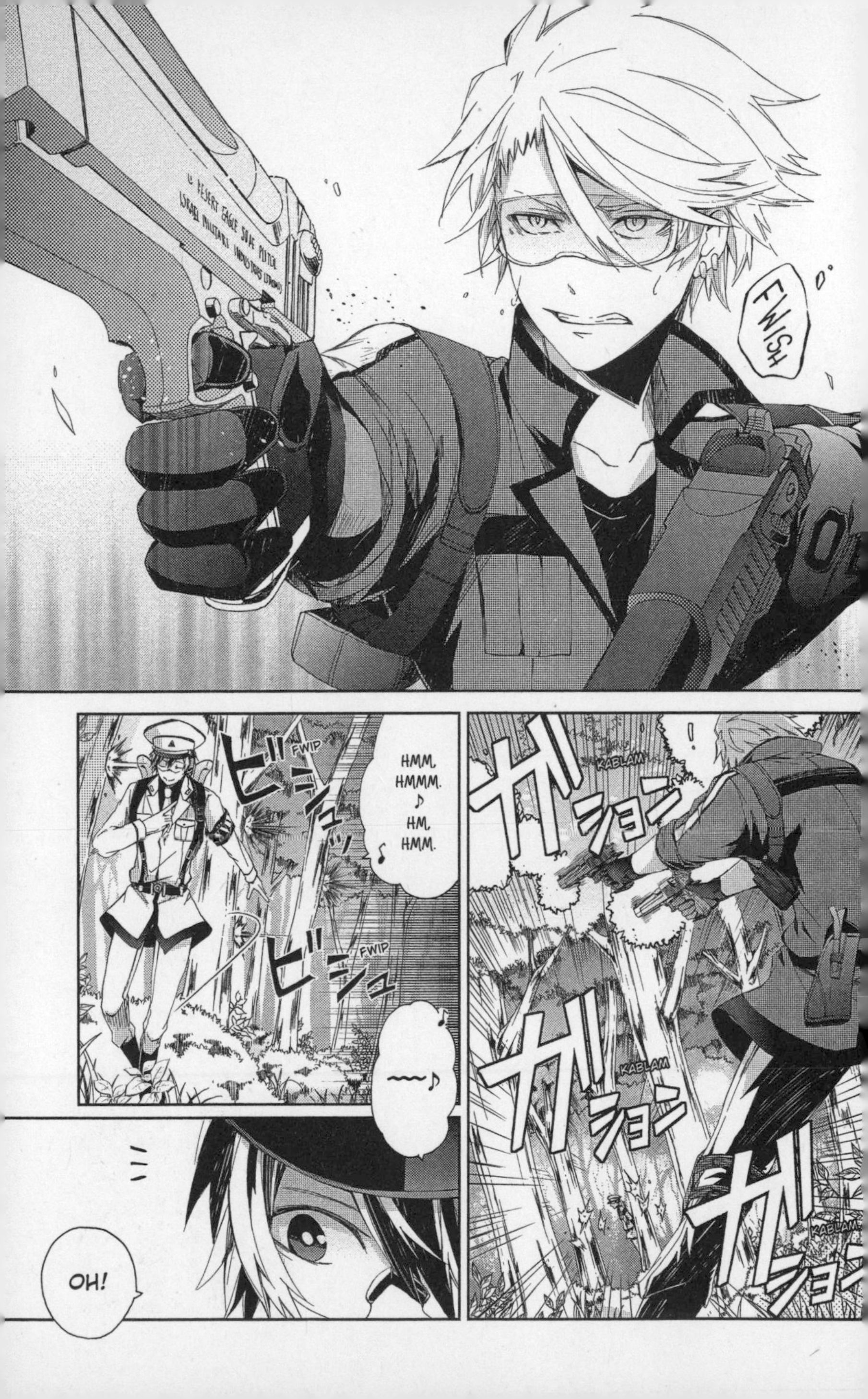
FWISH
KABLAM
KABLAM
KABLAM
FWIP
HMM, HMMM. ♪ HM, HMM.
FWIP
~~~♪
OH!
~~~

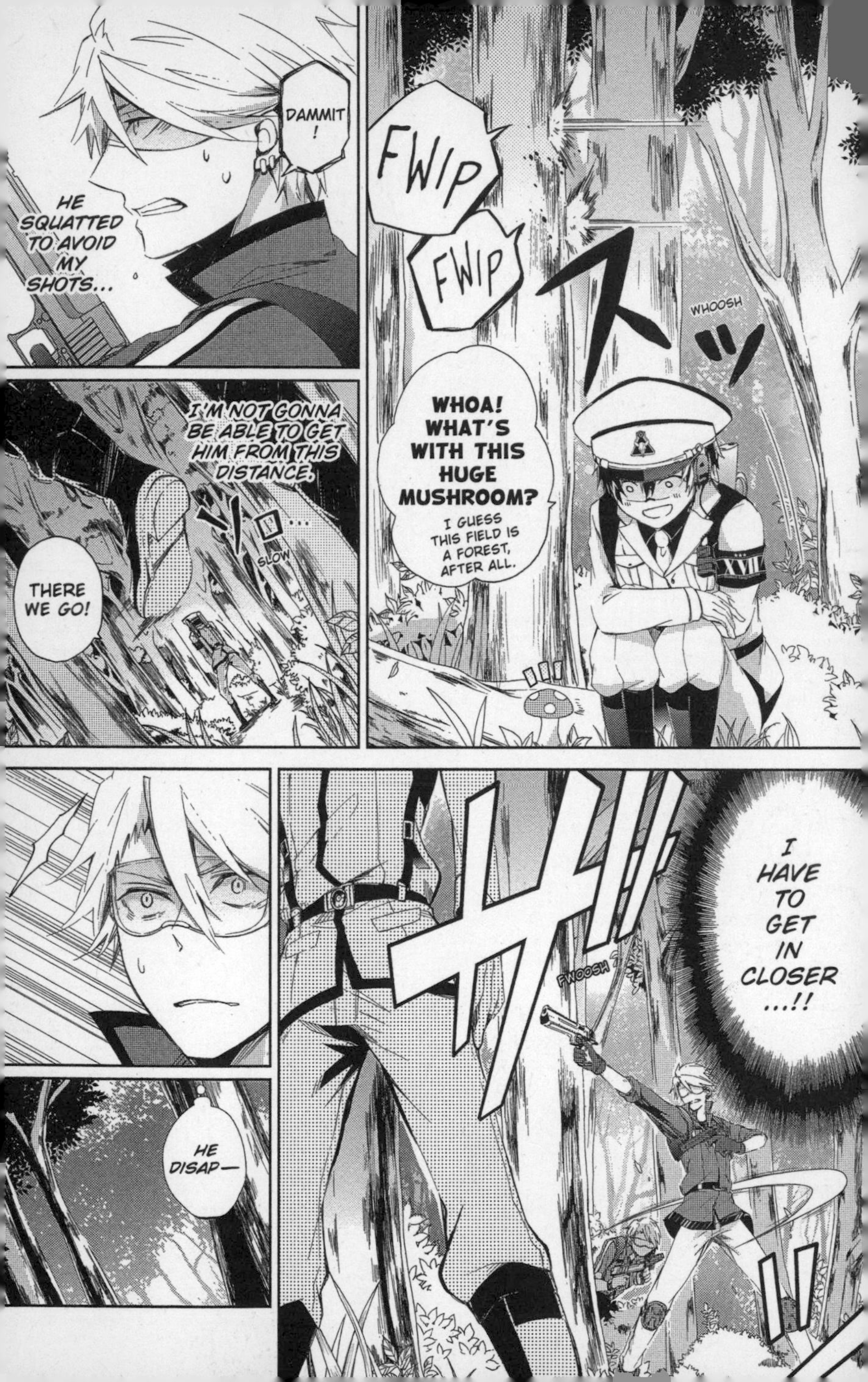
FWIP
FWIP
WHOOSH
WHOA! WHAT'S WITH THIS HUGE MUSHROOM?
I GUESS THIS FIELD IS A FOREST, AFTER ALL.
DAMMIT!
HE SQUATTED TO AVOID MY SHOTS...
I'M NOT GONNA BE ABLE TO GET HIM FROM THIS DISTANCE.
SLOW
THERE WE GO!
I HAVE TO GET IN CLOSER...!!
FWOOSH
HE DISAP—

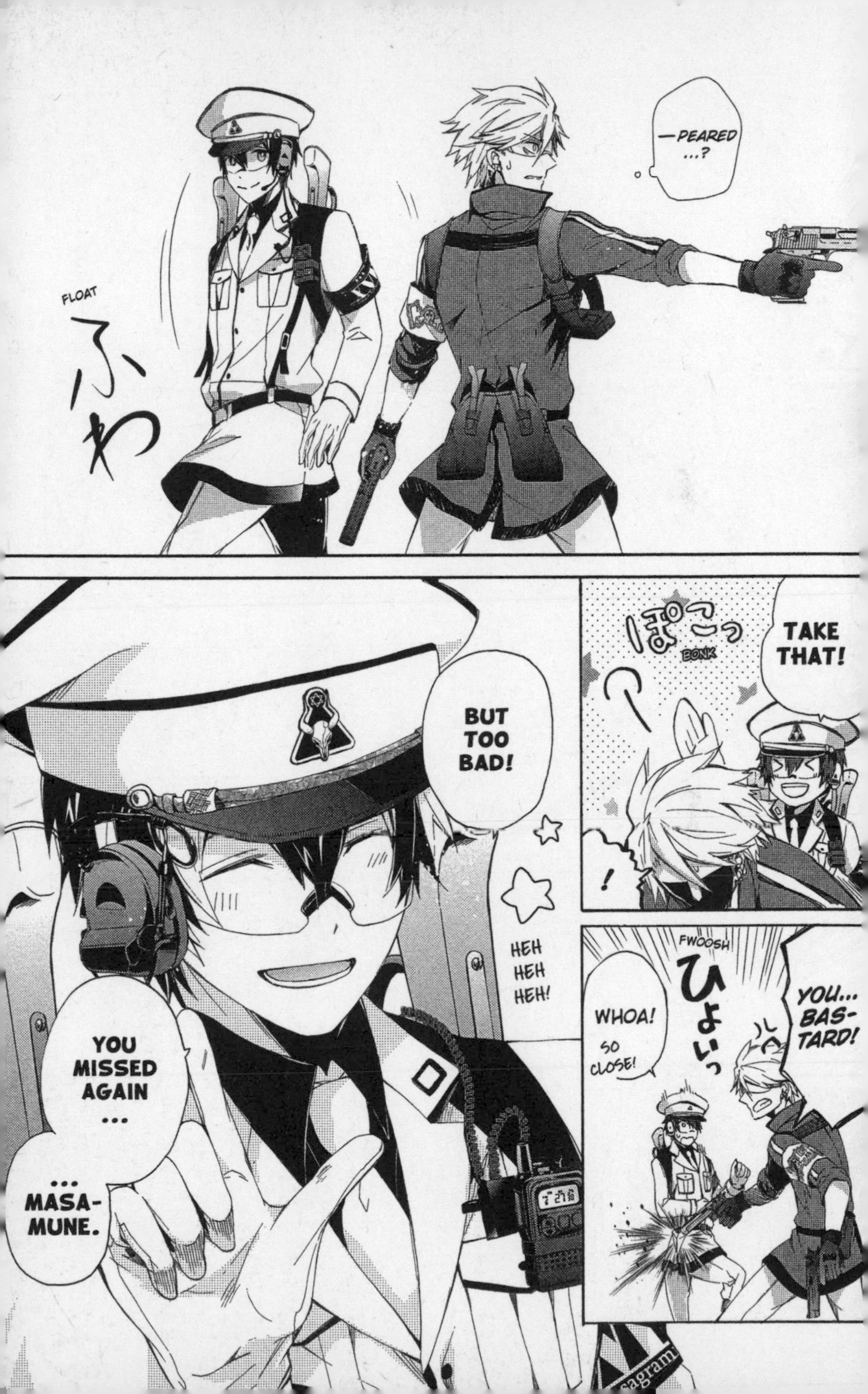
—PEARED ...?
FLOAT
ふわ
BUT TOO BAD!
HEH HEH HEH!
YOU MISSED AGAIN ...
... MASA-MUNE.
TAKE THAT!
ぽこっ
BONK
!
FWOOSH
ひょいっ
WHOA!
SO CLOSE!
YOU... BAS-TARD!

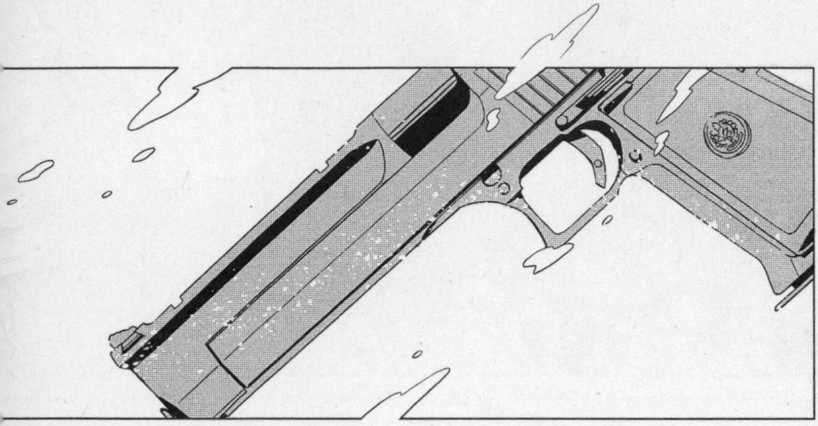

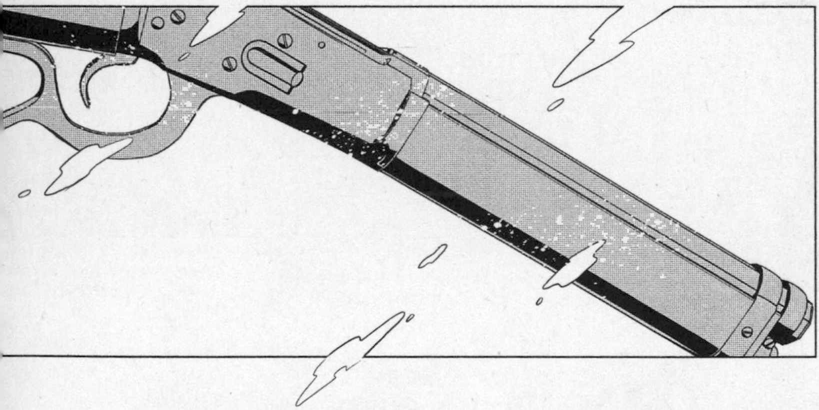

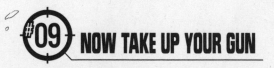

#09 NOW TAKE UP YOUR GUN

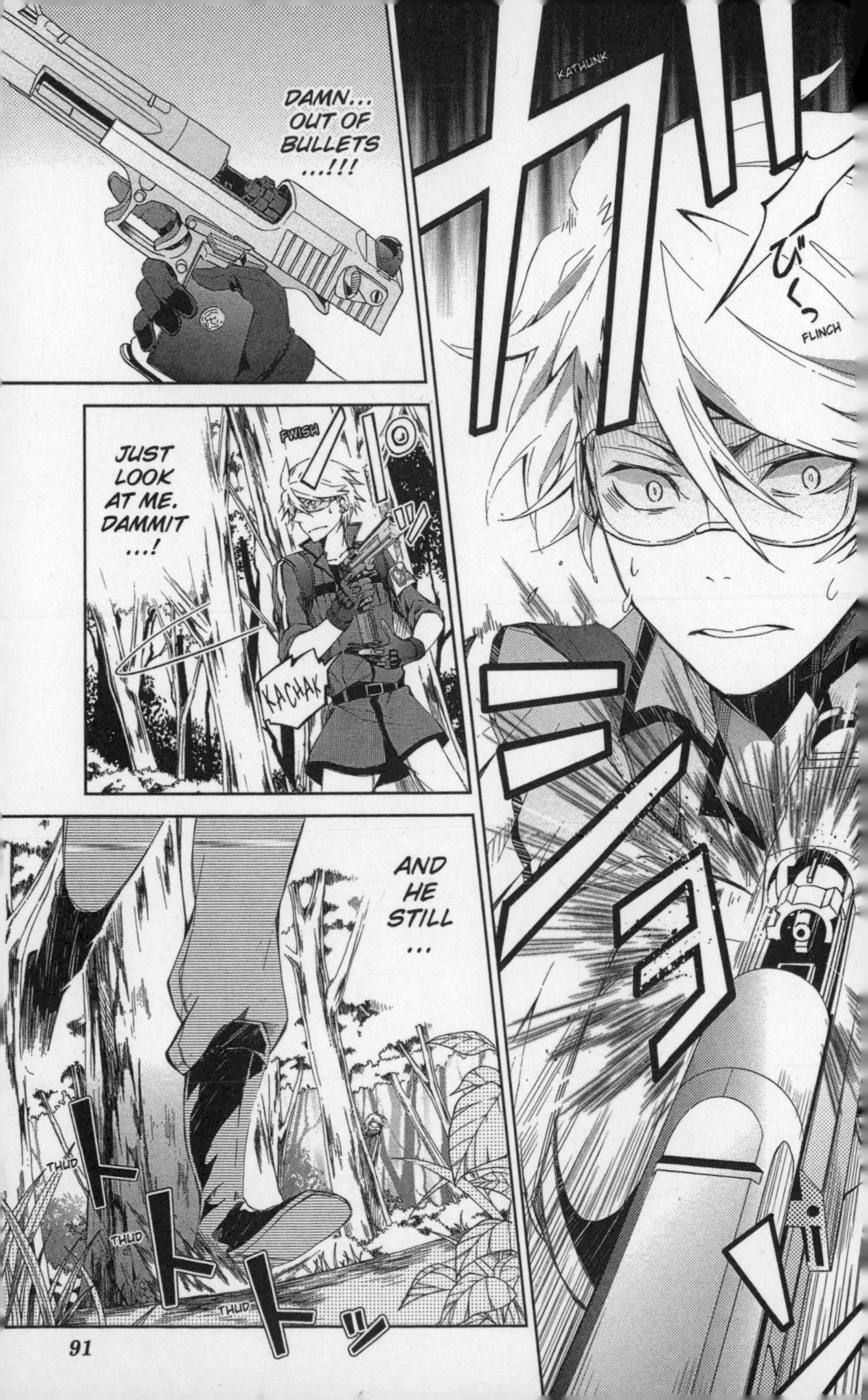
KATHUNK
びくっ
FLINCH
DAMN... OUT OF BULLETS ...!!!
FWISH
JUST LOOK AT ME. DAMMIT ...!
KACHAK
AND HE STILL ...
THUD
THUD
THUD

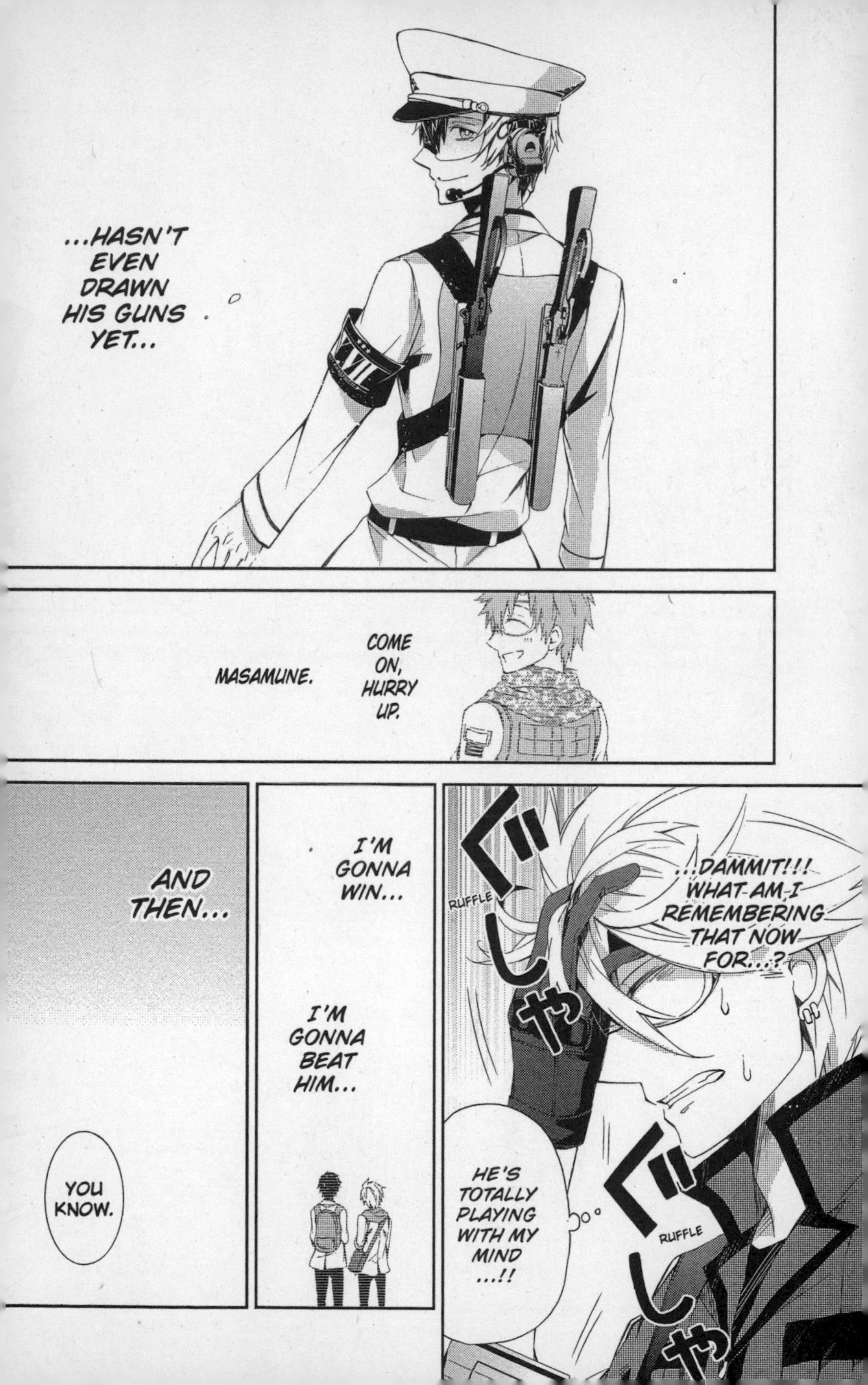
...HASN'T EVEN DRAWN HIS GUNS YET...
COME ON, HURRY UP.
MASAMUNE.
I'M GONNA WIN...
I'M GONNA BEAT HIM...
AND THEN...
YOU KNOW.
RUFFLE
...DAMMIT!!! WHAT AM I REMEMBERING THAT NOW FOR...?
HE'S TOTALLY PLAYING WITH MY MIND ...!!
RUFFLE

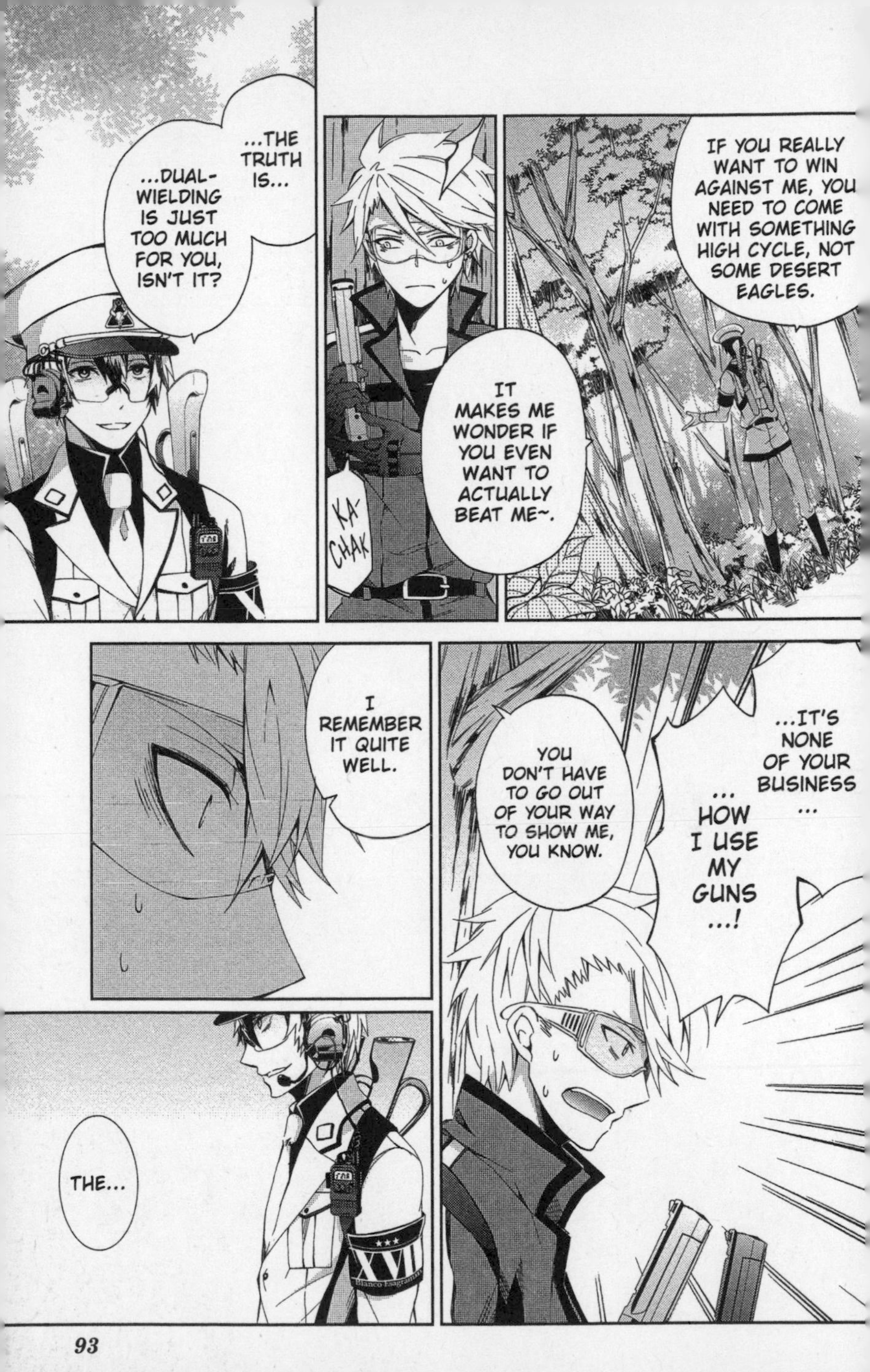
IF YOU REALLY WANT TO WIN AGAINST ME, YOU NEED TO COME WITH SOMETHING HIGH CYCLE, NOT SOME DESERT EAGLES.
IT MAKES ME WONDER IF YOU EVEN WANT TO ACTUALLY BEAT ME~.
KA-CHAK
...THE TRUTH IS...
...DUAL-WIELDING IS JUST TOO MUCH FOR YOU, ISN'T IT?
...IT'S NONE OF YOUR BUSINESS...
...HOW I USE MY GUNS...!
YOU DON'T HAVE TO GO OUT OF YOUR WAY TO SHOW ME, YOU KNOW.
I REMEMBER IT QUITE WELL.
THE...
XVII
Bianco Esagramma

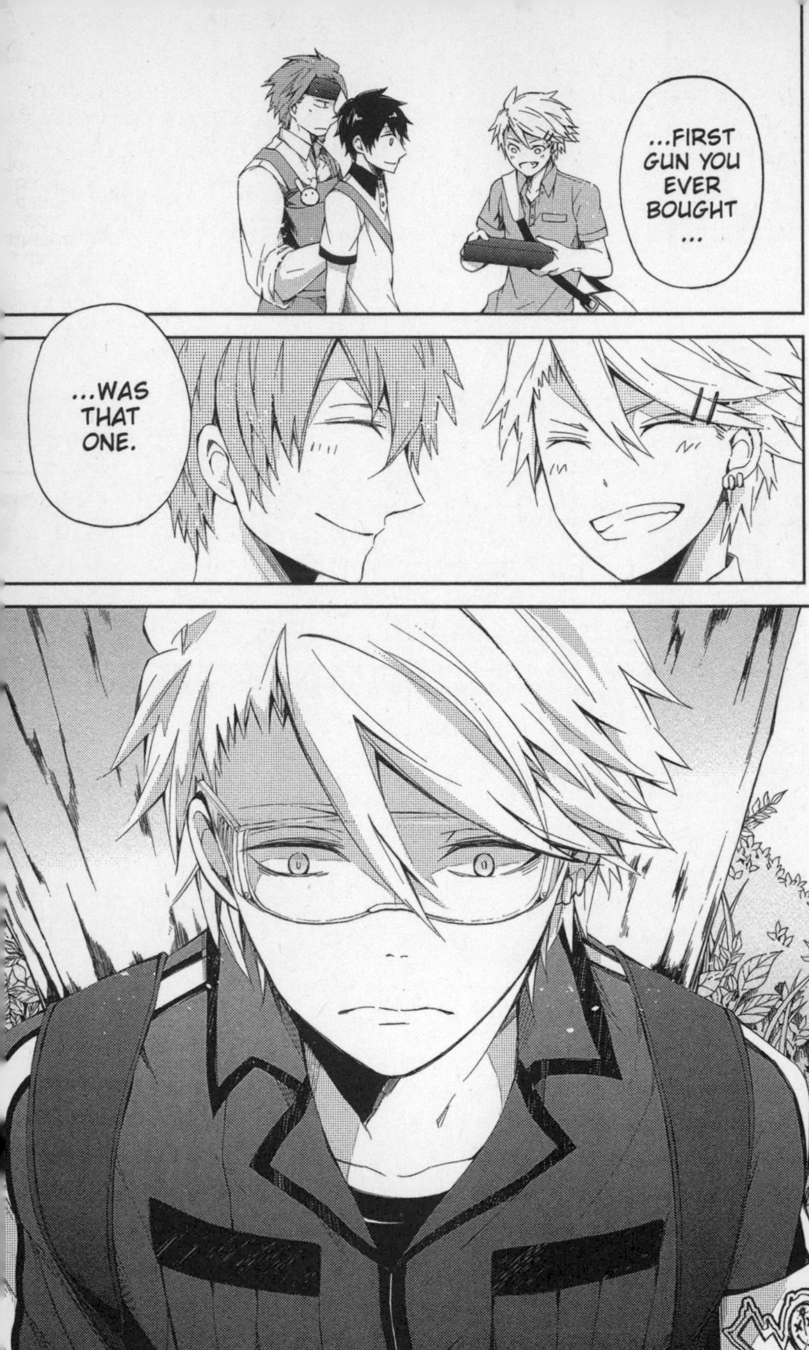
...FIRST GUN YOU EVER BOUGHT ...
...WAS THAT ONE.

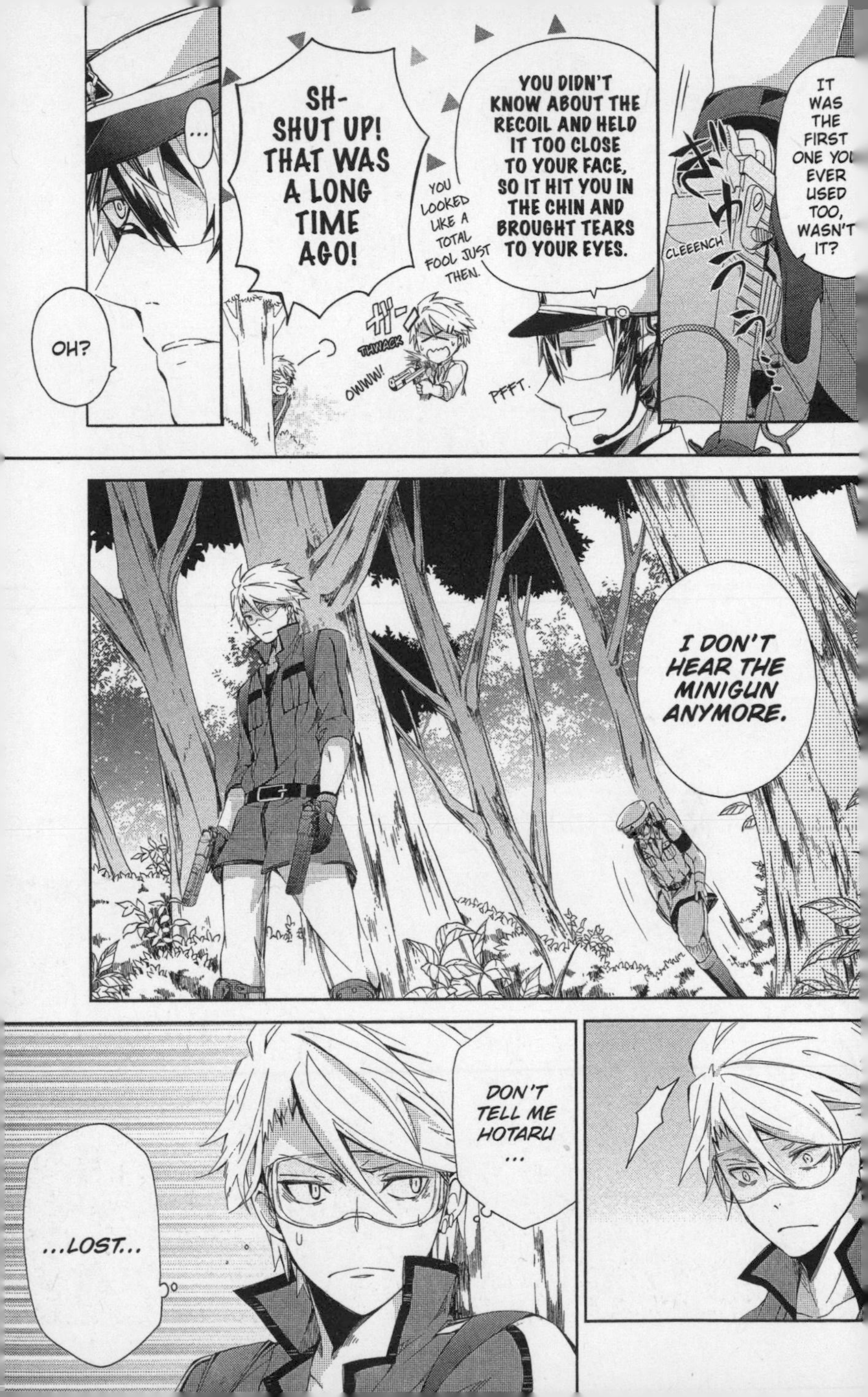
IT WAS THE FIRST ONE YOU EVER USED TOO, WASN'T IT?
CLEEENCH
YOU DIDN'T KNOW ABOUT THE RECOIL AND HELD IT TOO CLOSE TO YOUR FACE, SO IT HIT YOU IN THE CHIN AND BROUGHT TEARS TO YOUR EYES.
YOU LOOKED LIKE A TOTAL FOOL JUST THEN.
PFFT.
THWACK
OWWW!
SH-SHUT UP! THAT WAS A LONG TIME AGO!
...
OH?
I DON'T HEAR THE MINIGUN ANYMORE.
DON'T TELL ME HOTARU ...
...LOST...

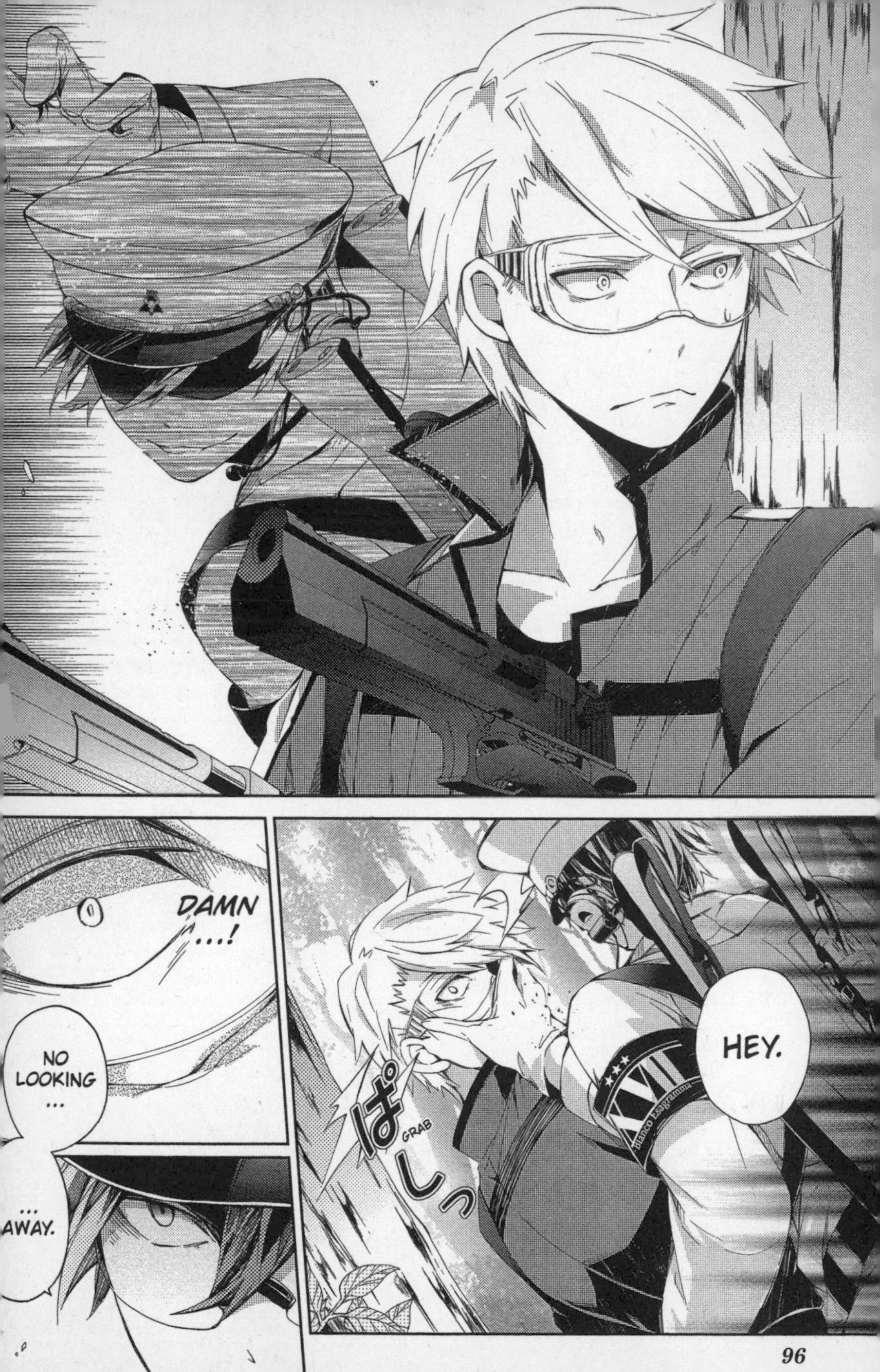
HEY.
ぱしっ
GRAB
DAMN ...!
NO LOOKING ...
... AWAY.

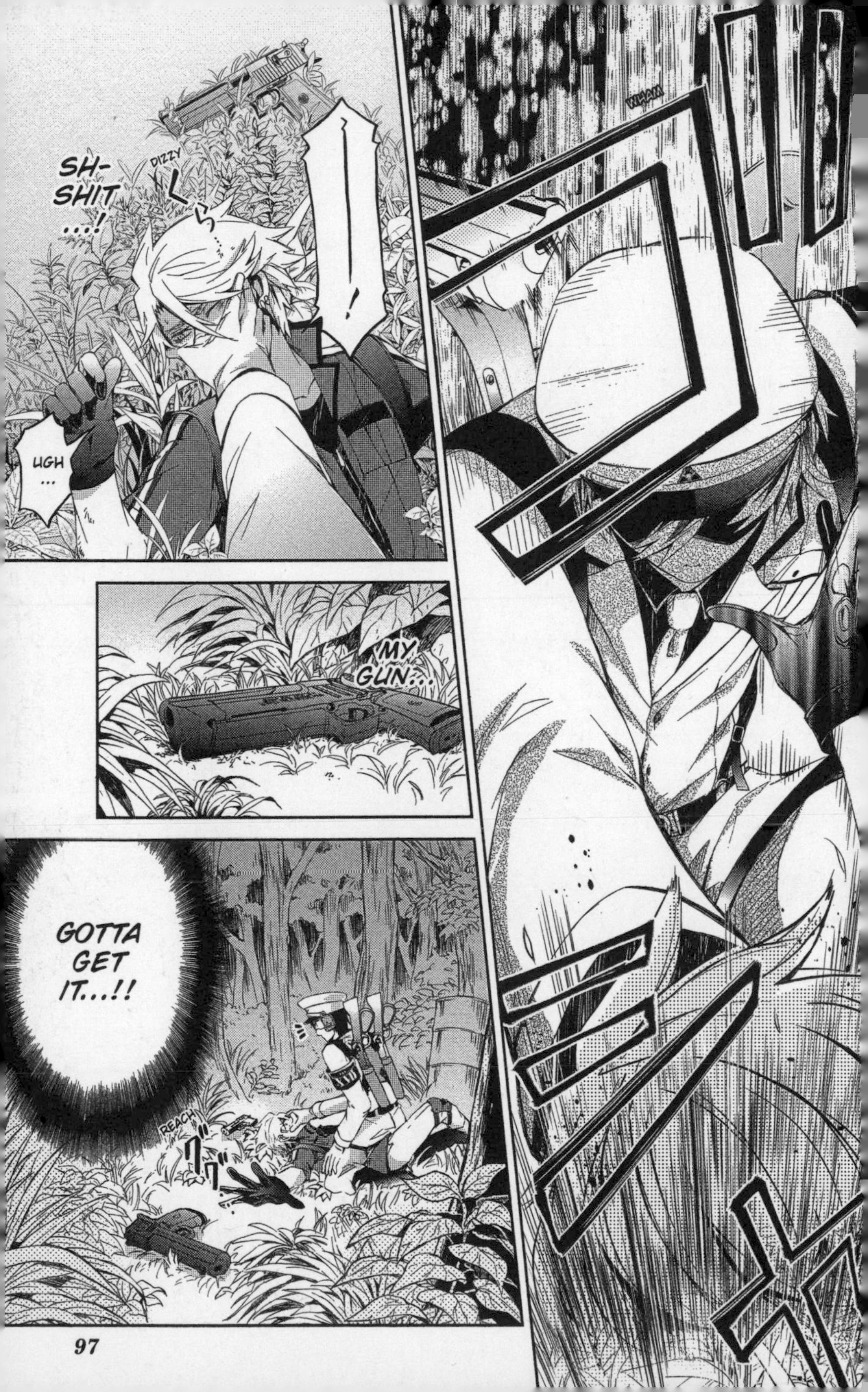
WHAM
DIZZY
SH-SHIT...!
UGH...
MY GUN...
GOTTA GET IT...!!
REACH

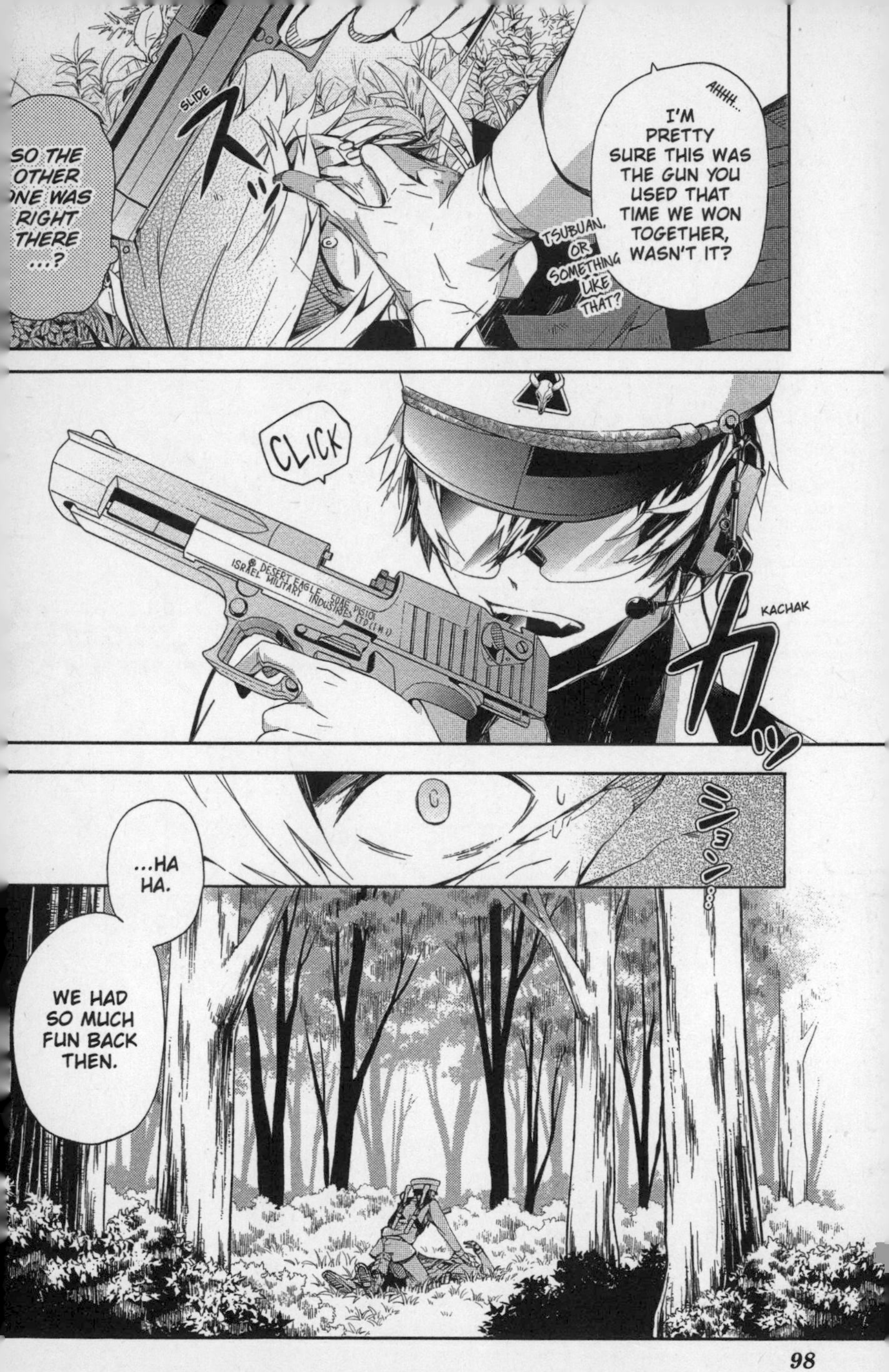
AHHH...
I'M PRETTY SURE THIS WAS THE GUN YOU USED THAT TIME WE WON TOGETHER, WASN'T IT?
TSUBUAN, OR SOMETHING LIKE THAT?
SLIDE
SO THE OTHER ONE WAS RIGHT THERE ...?
CLICK
KACHAK
...HA HA.
WE HAD SO MUCH FUN BACK THEN.

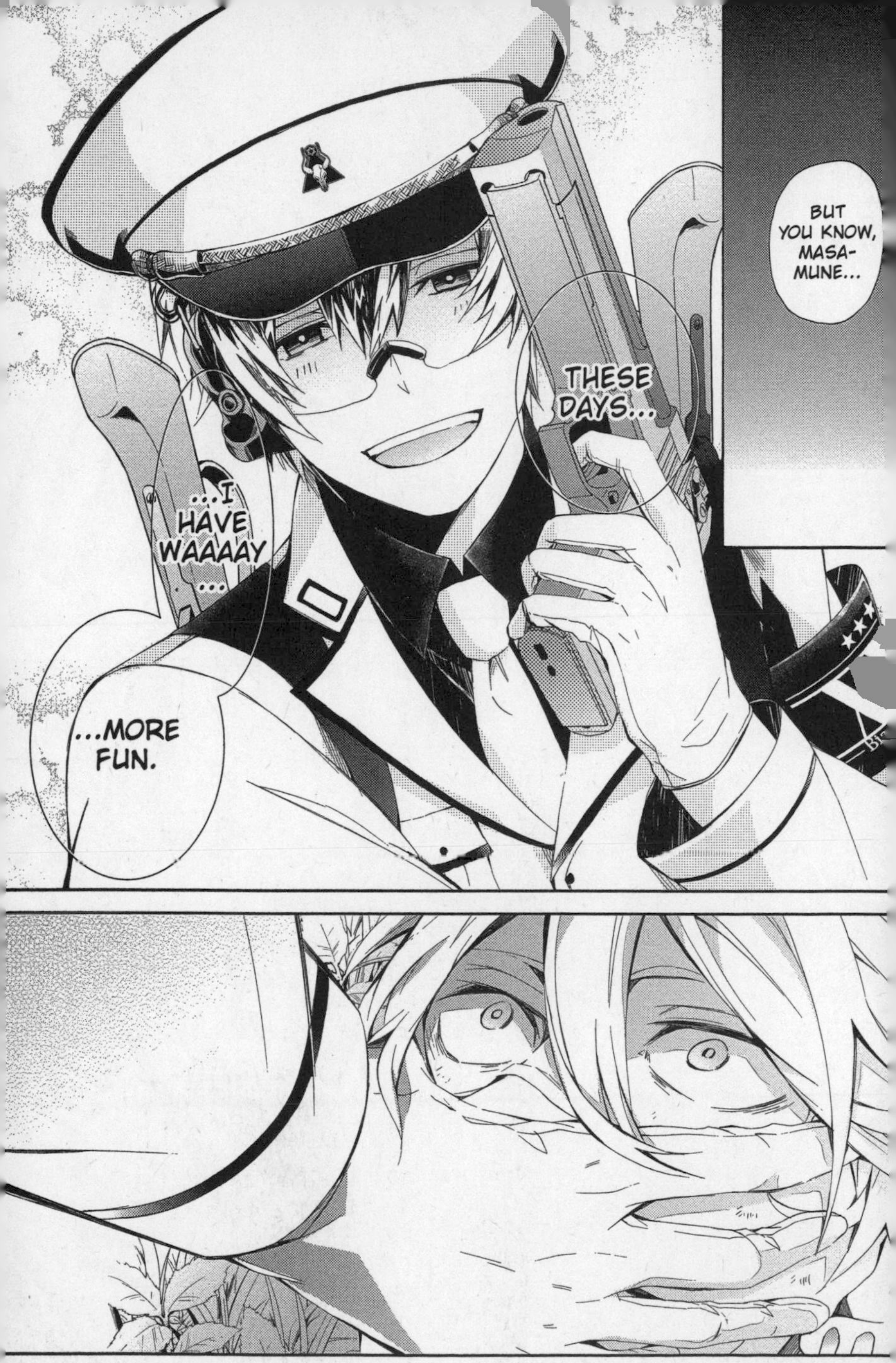
BUT YOU KNOW, MASA-MUNE...
THESE DAYS...
...I HAVE WAAAAY...
...MORE FUN.

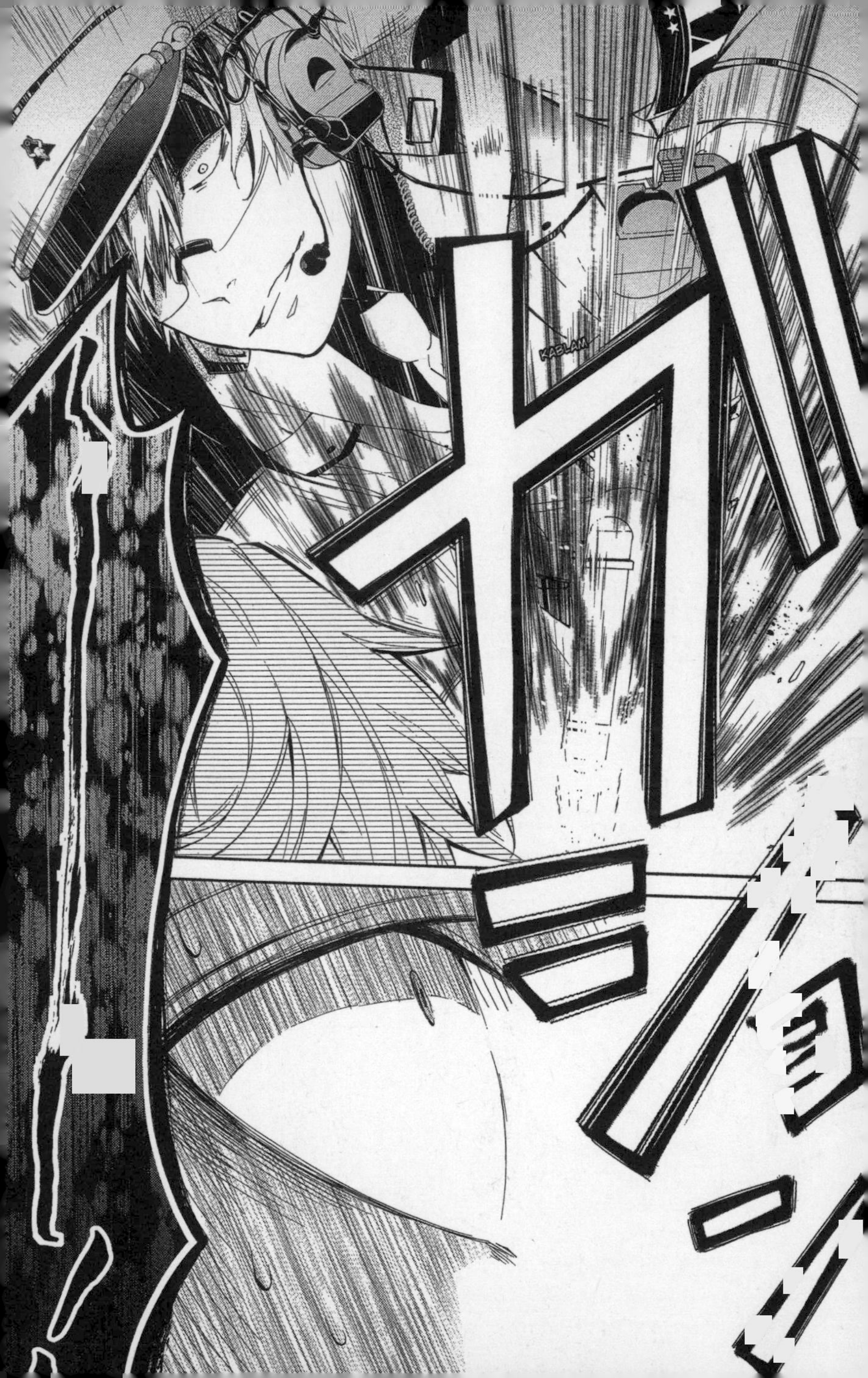
KABLAM

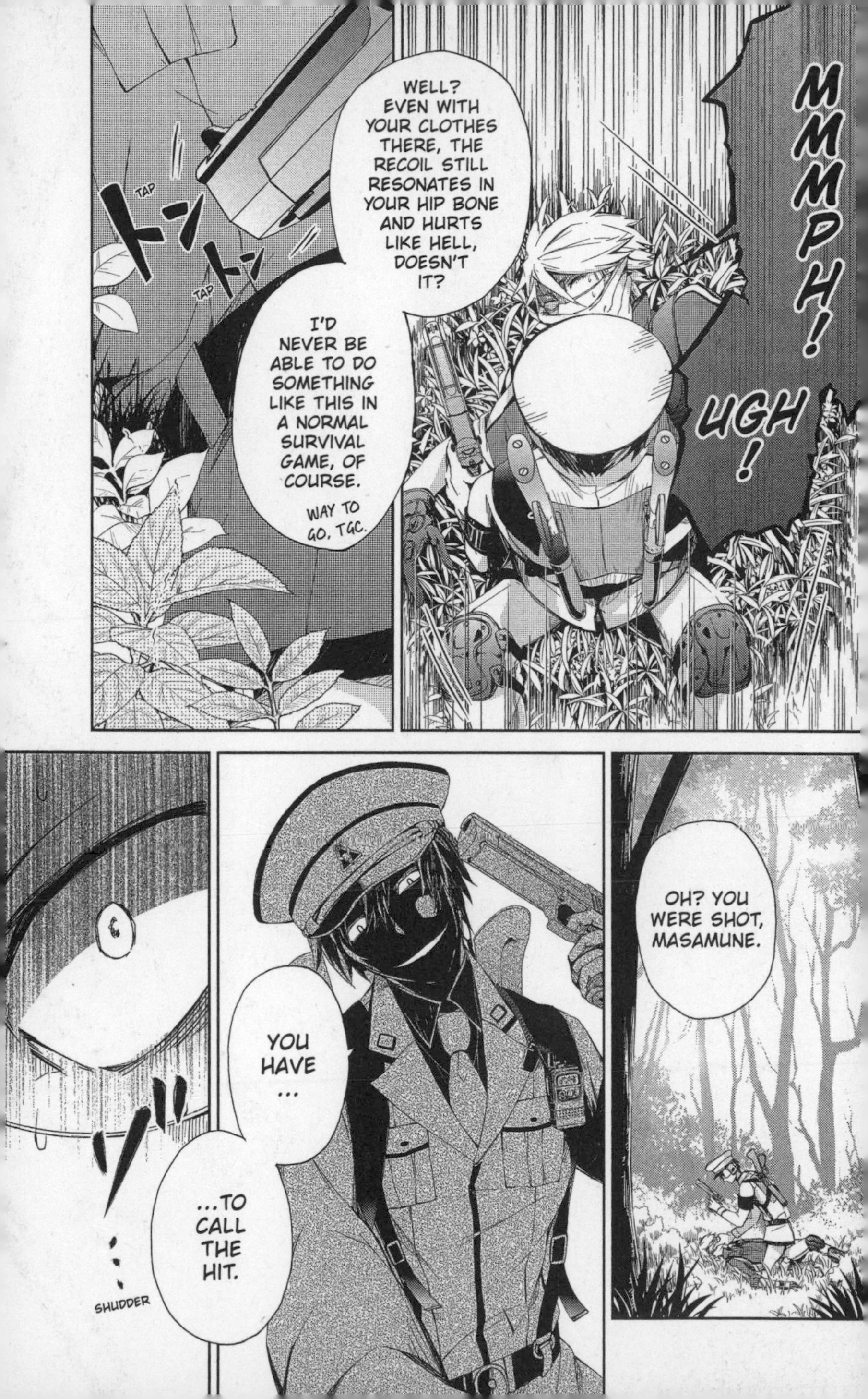
MMMMPH!
UGH!
WELL? EVEN WITH YOUR CLOTHES THERE, THE RECOIL STILL RESONATES IN YOUR HIP BONE AND HURTS LIKE HELL, DOESN'T IT?
TAP
TAP
I'D NEVER BE ABLE TO DO SOMETHING LIKE THIS IN A NORMAL SURVIVAL GAME, OF COURSE.
WAY TO GO, TGC.
OH? YOU WERE SHOT, MASAMUNE.
YOU HAVE...
...TO CALL THE HIT.
SHUDDER

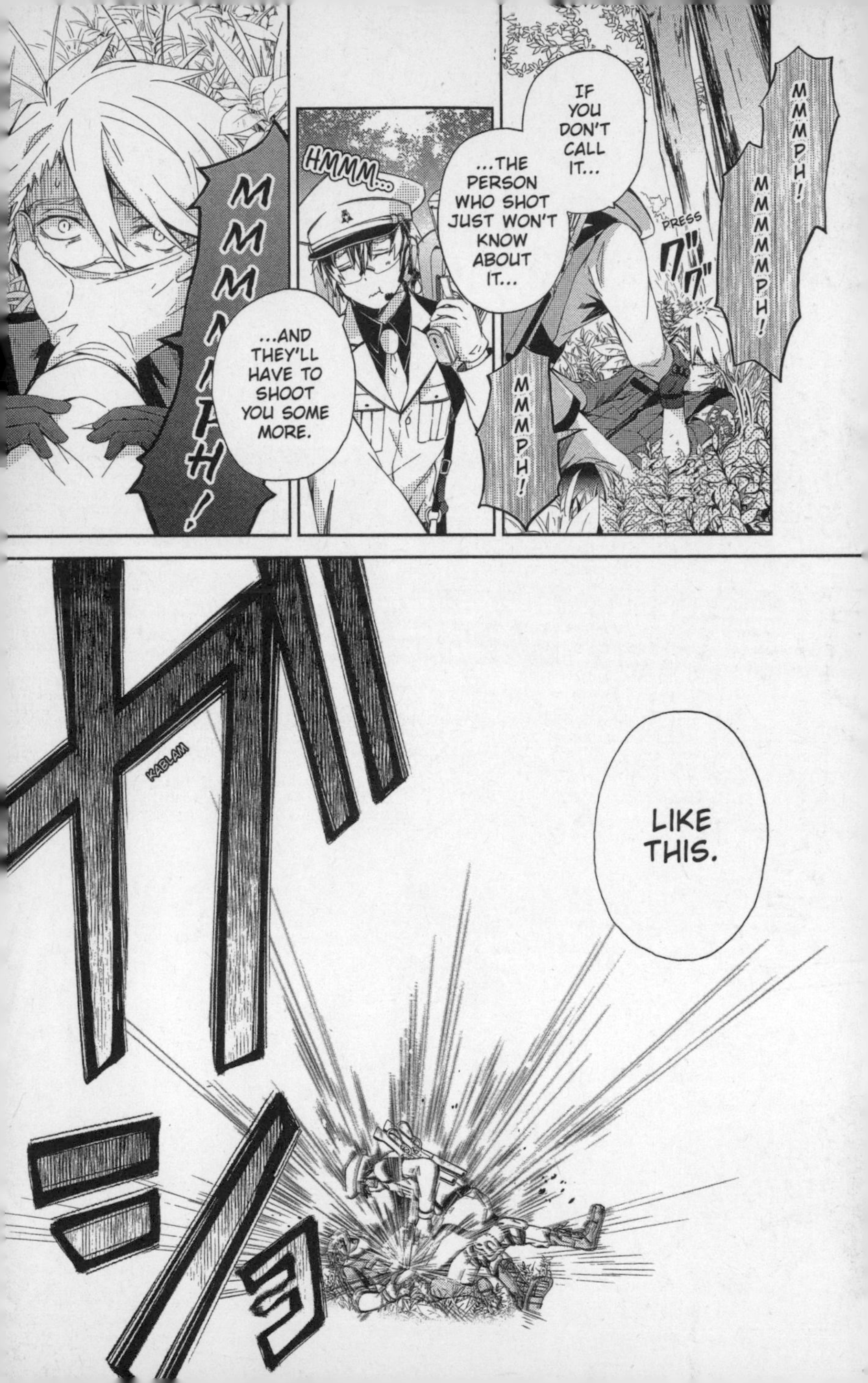
IF YOU DON'T CALL IT...
MMMPH! MMMMMPH!
PRESS
MMMPH!
...THE PERSON WHO SHOT JUST WON'T KNOW ABOUT IT...
HMMM...
...AND THEY'LL HAVE TO SHOOT YOU SOME MORE.
MMMMPH!
LIKE THIS.
KABLAM

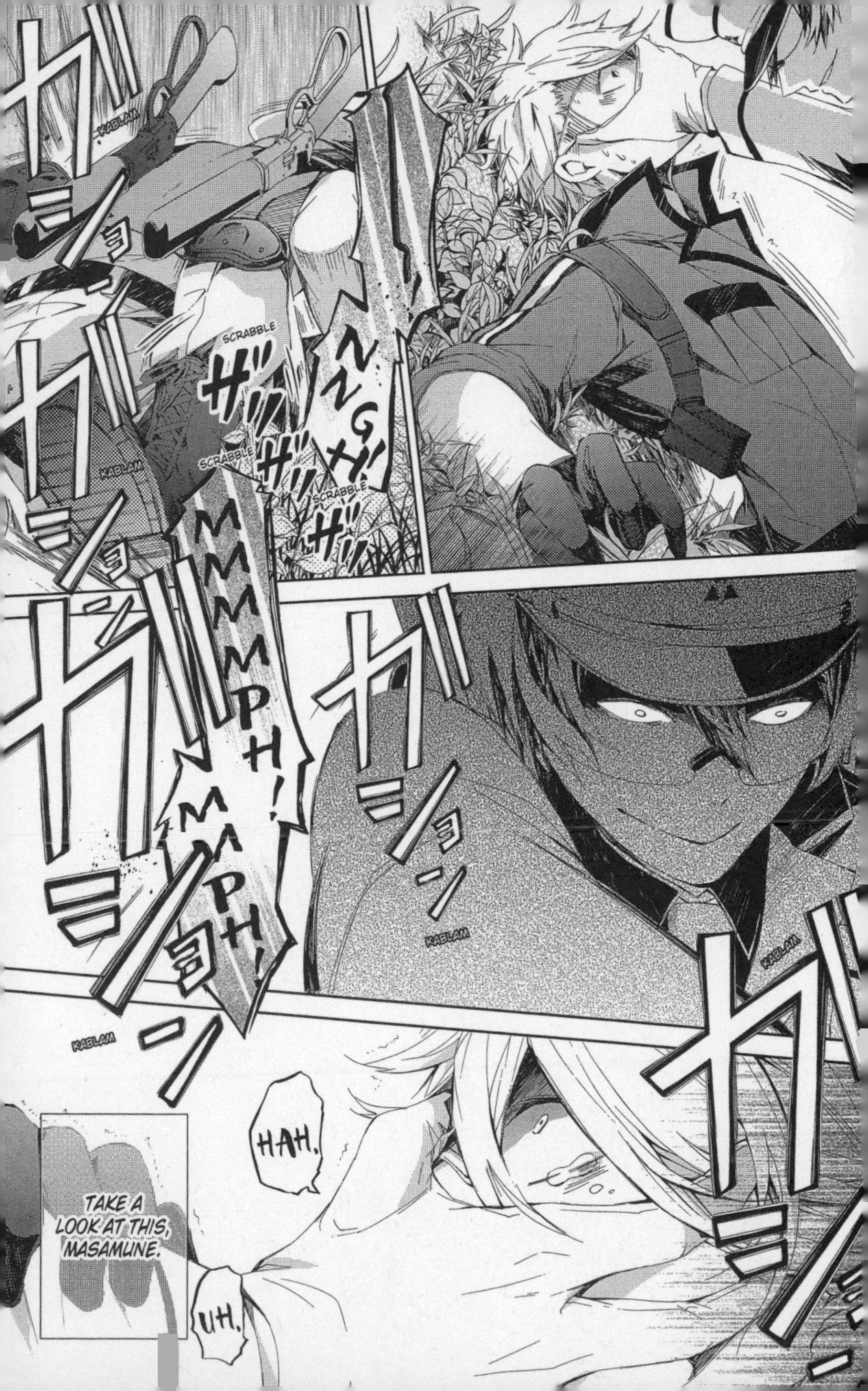

KABLAM
SCRABBLE
SCRABBLE
SCRABBLE
NNGH!
KABLAM
MMMMMMPH!
MMMPH!
KABLAM
KABLAM
KABLAM
HAH.
TAKE A LOOK AT THIS, MASAMUNE.
UH.

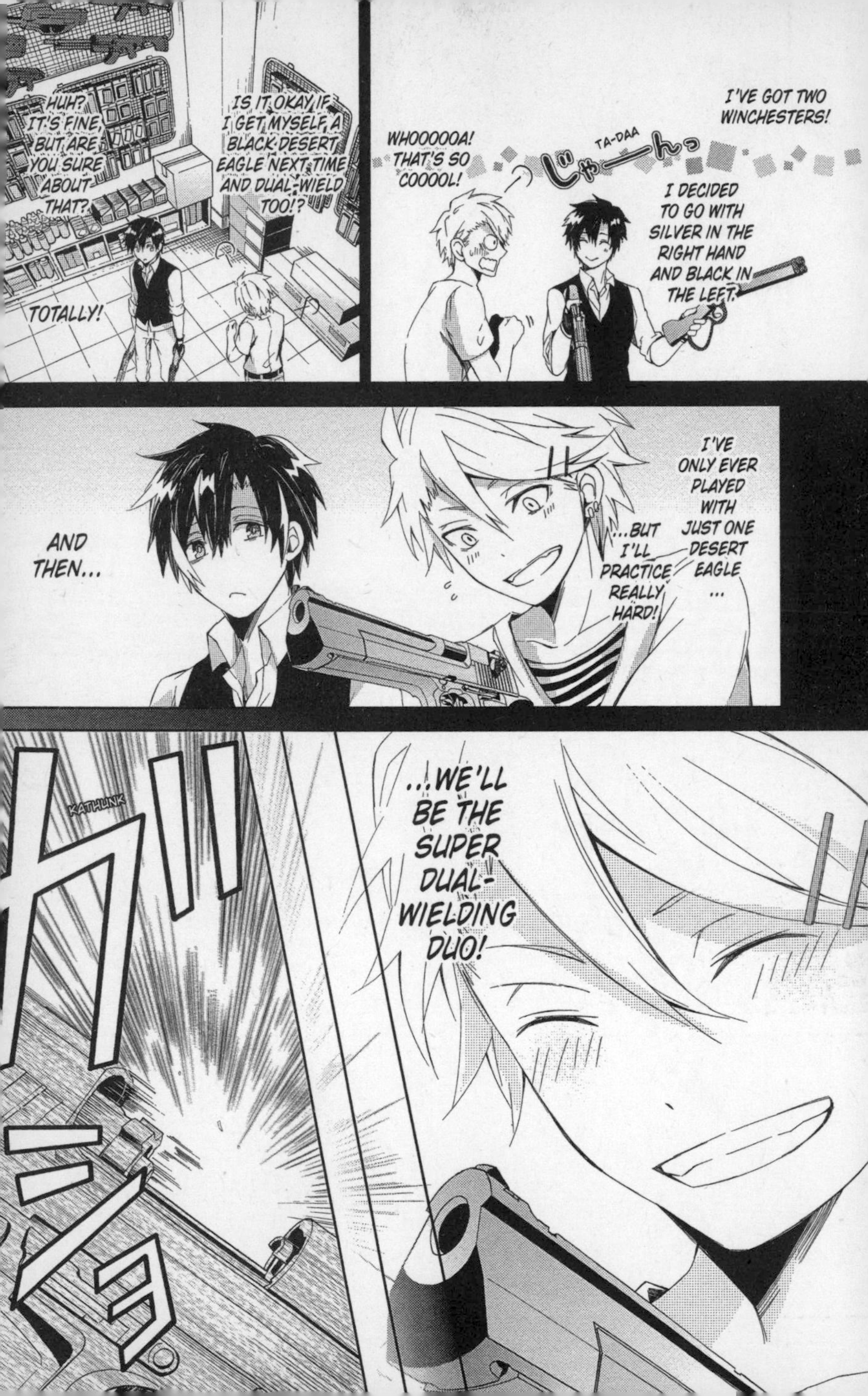
I'VE GOT TWO WINCHESTERS!
TA-DAA
じゃーんっ
I DECIDED TO GO WITH SILVER IN THE RIGHT HAND AND BLACK IN THE LEFT.
WHOOOOOA! THAT'S SO COOOOL!
IS IT OKAY IF I GET MYSELF A BLACK DESERT EAGLE NEXT TIME AND DUAL-WIELD TOO!?
HUH? IT'S FINE, BUT ARE YOU SURE ABOUT THAT?
TOTALLY!
I'VE ONLY EVER PLAYED WITH JUST ONE DESERT EAGLE ...
...BUT I'LL PRACTICE REALLY HARD!
AND THEN...
...WE'LL BE THE SUPER DUAL-WIELDING DUO!
KATHUNK

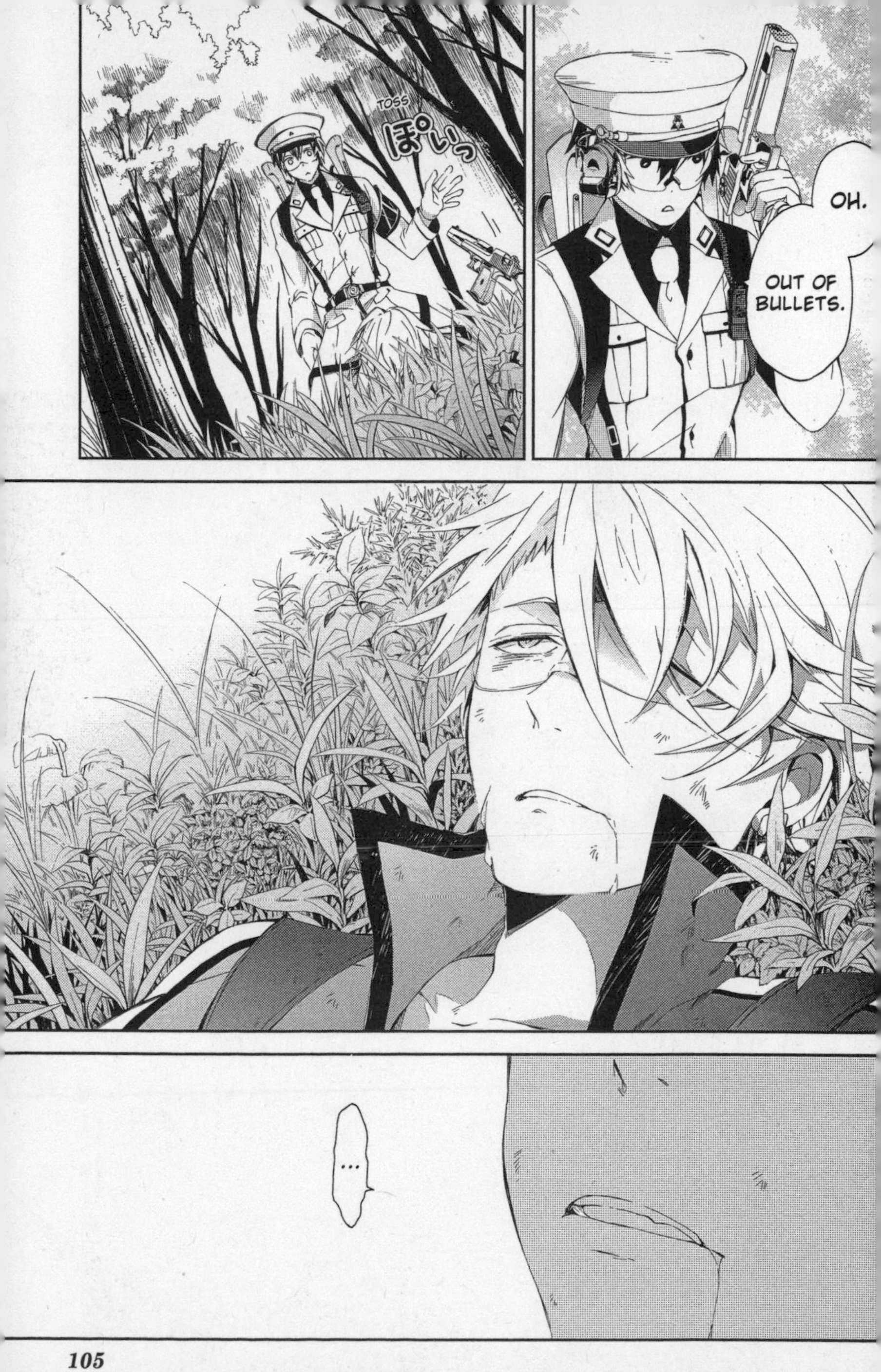
OH.
OUT OF BULLETS.
TOSS
ぽいっ
...

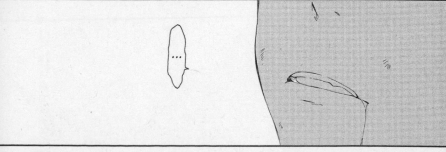

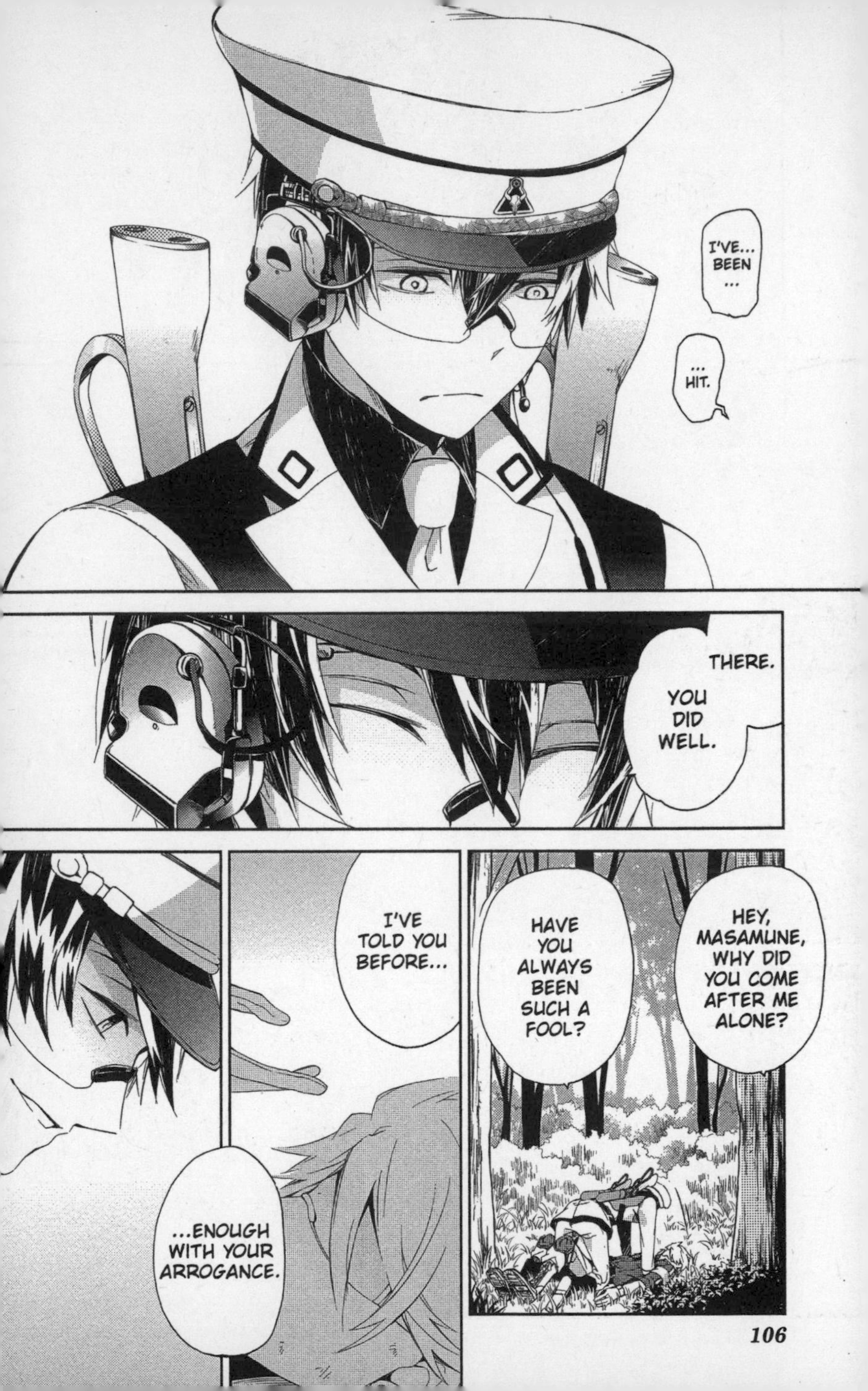
I'VE... BEEN ...
... HIT.
THERE. YOU DID WELL.
HEY, MASAMUNE, WHY DID YOU COME AFTER ME ALONE?
HAVE YOU ALWAYS BEEN SUCH A FOOL?
I'VE TOLD YOU BEFORE...
...ENOUGH WITH YOUR ARROGANCE.

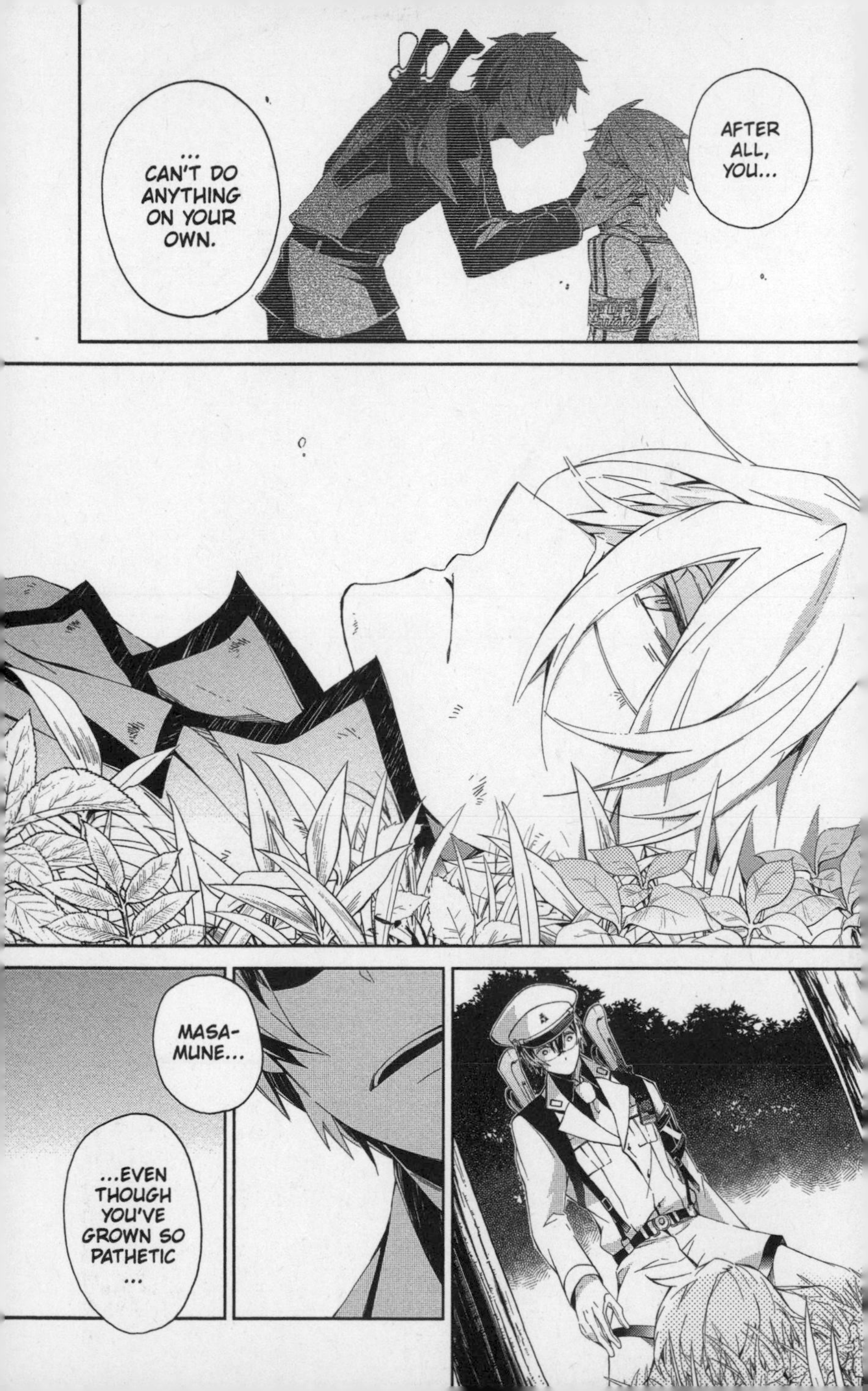

AFTER ALL, YOU...
... CAN'T DO ANYTHING ON YOUR OWN.
MASA-MUNE...
...EVEN THOUGH YOU'VE GROWN SO PATHETIC ...

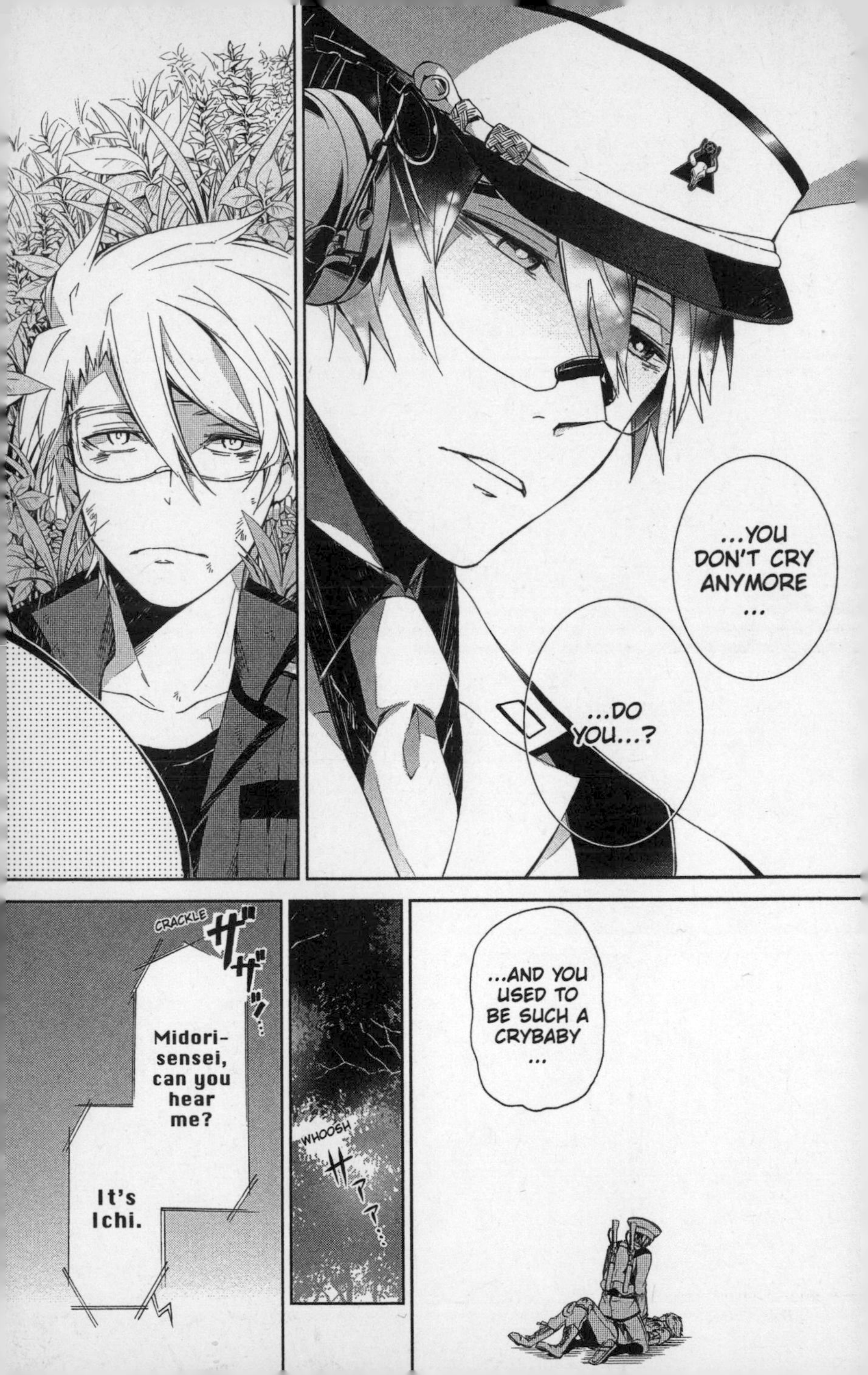
...YOU DON'T CRY ANYMORE ...
...DO YOU...?
...AND YOU USED TO BE SUCH A CRYBABY ...
WHOOSH
CRACKLE
Midori-sensei, can you hear me?
It's Ichi.

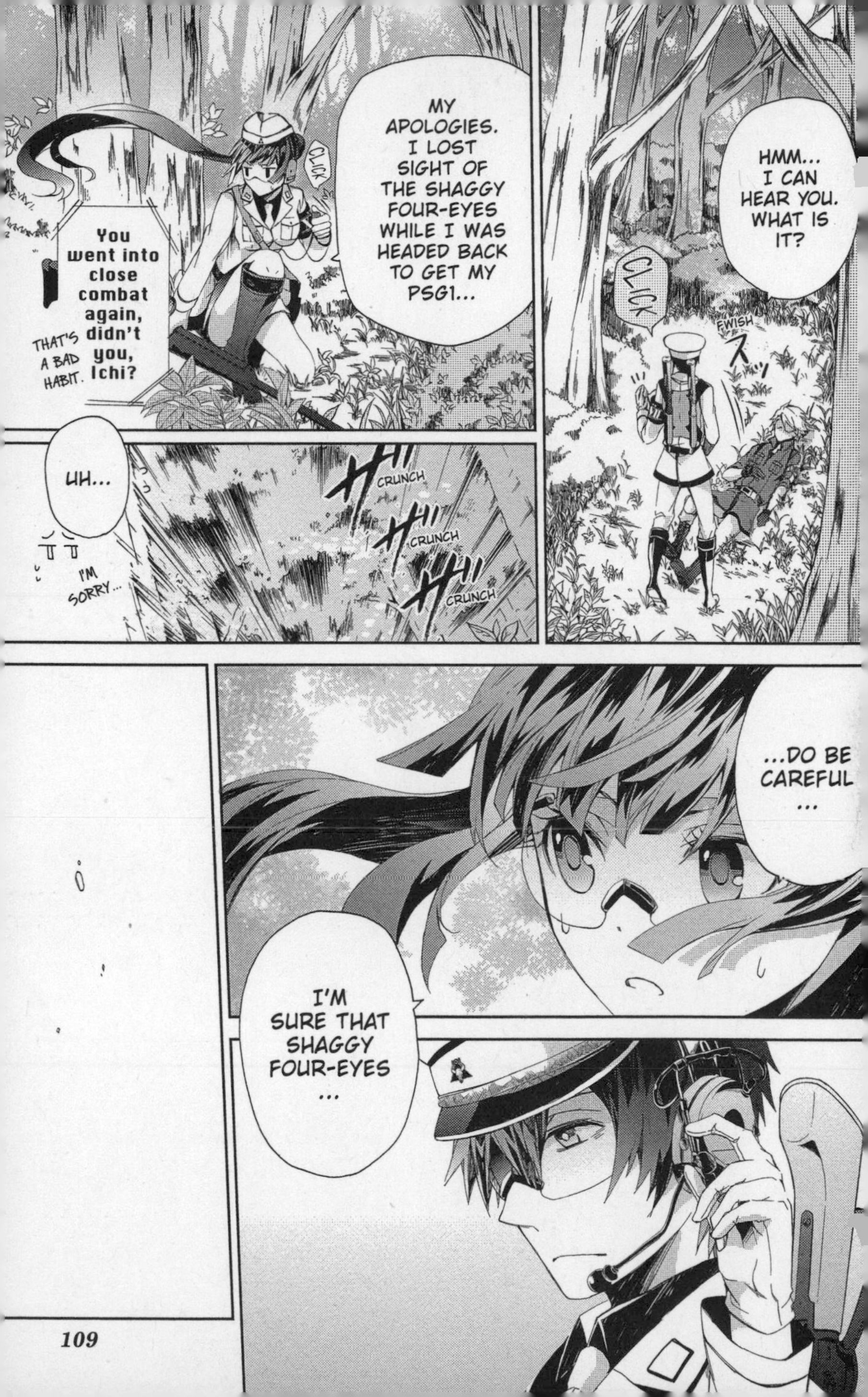
HMM... I CAN HEAR YOU. WHAT IS IT?
CLICK
FWISH
MY APOLOGIES. I LOST SIGHT OF THE SHAGGY FOUR-EYES WHILE I WAS HEADED BACK TO GET MY PSG1...
CLICK
You went into close combat again, didn't you, Ichi?
THAT'S A BAD HABIT.
CRUNCH
CRUNCH
CRUNCH
UH...
I'M SORRY...
...DO BE CAREFUL...
I'M SURE THAT SHAGGY FOUR-EYES...

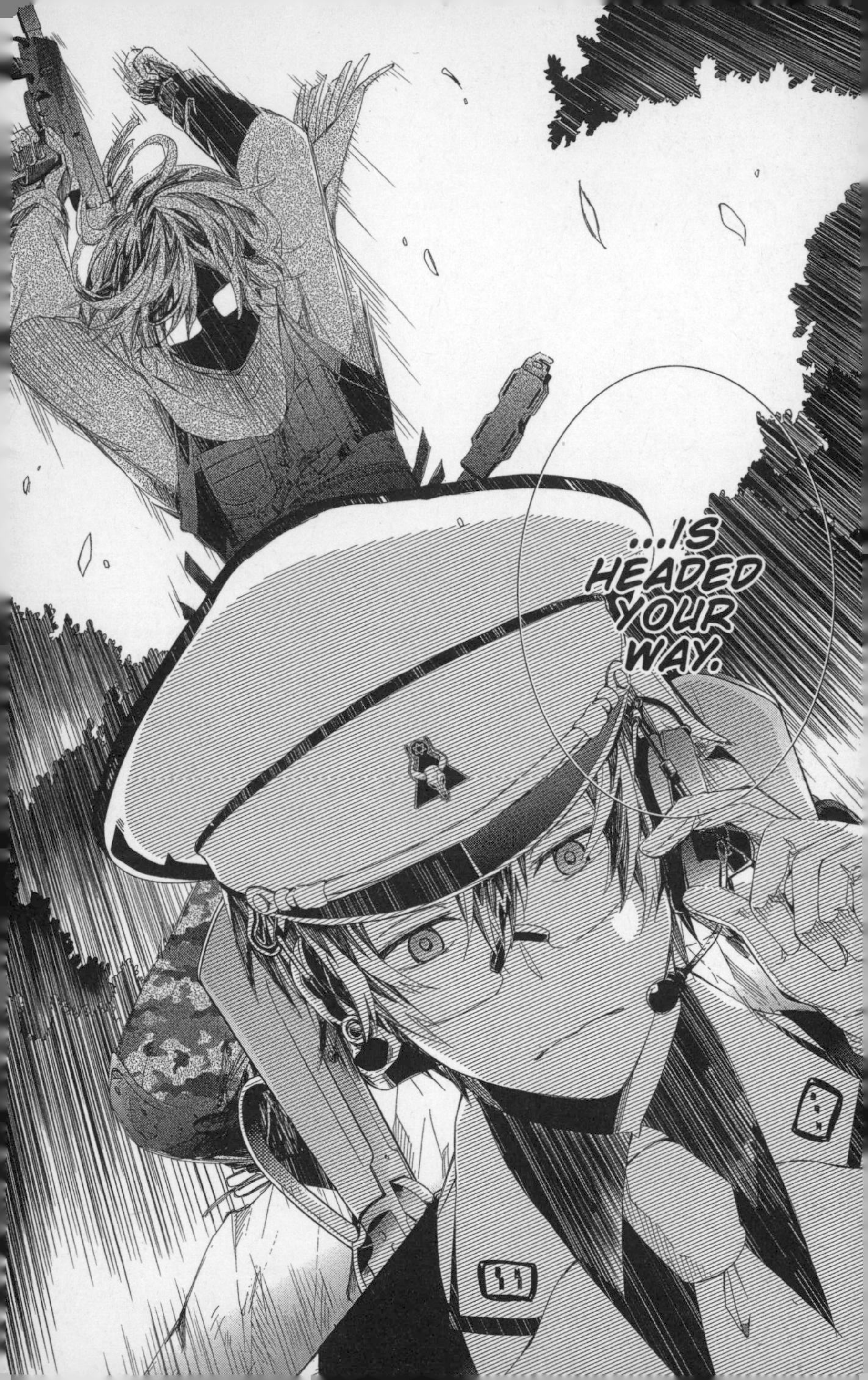
...IS HEADED YOUR WAY.

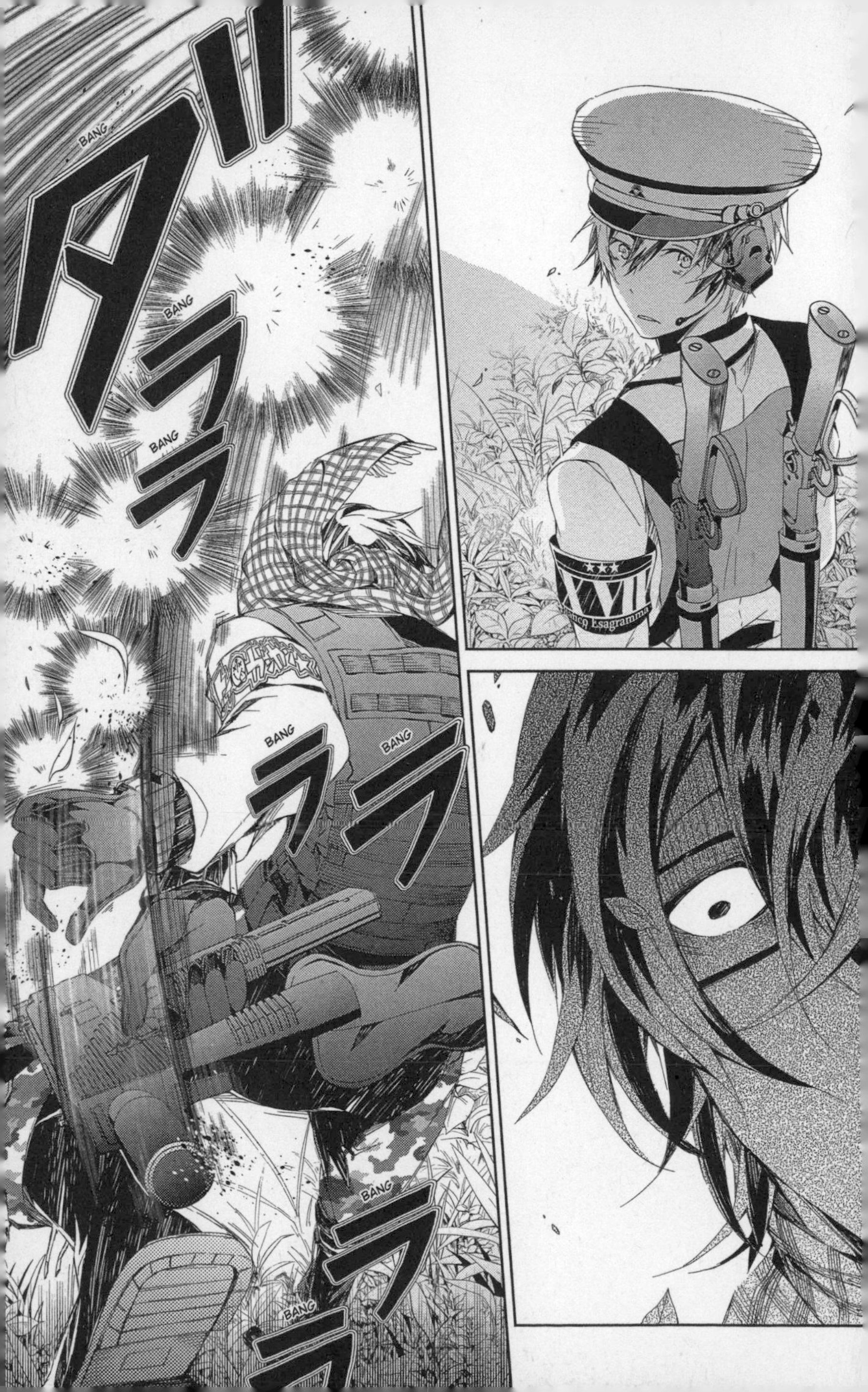
XVII
Esagramma
ダ
BANG
ラ
BANG
ラ
BANG
ラ
BANG
ラ
BANG
ラ
BANG
ラ
BANG

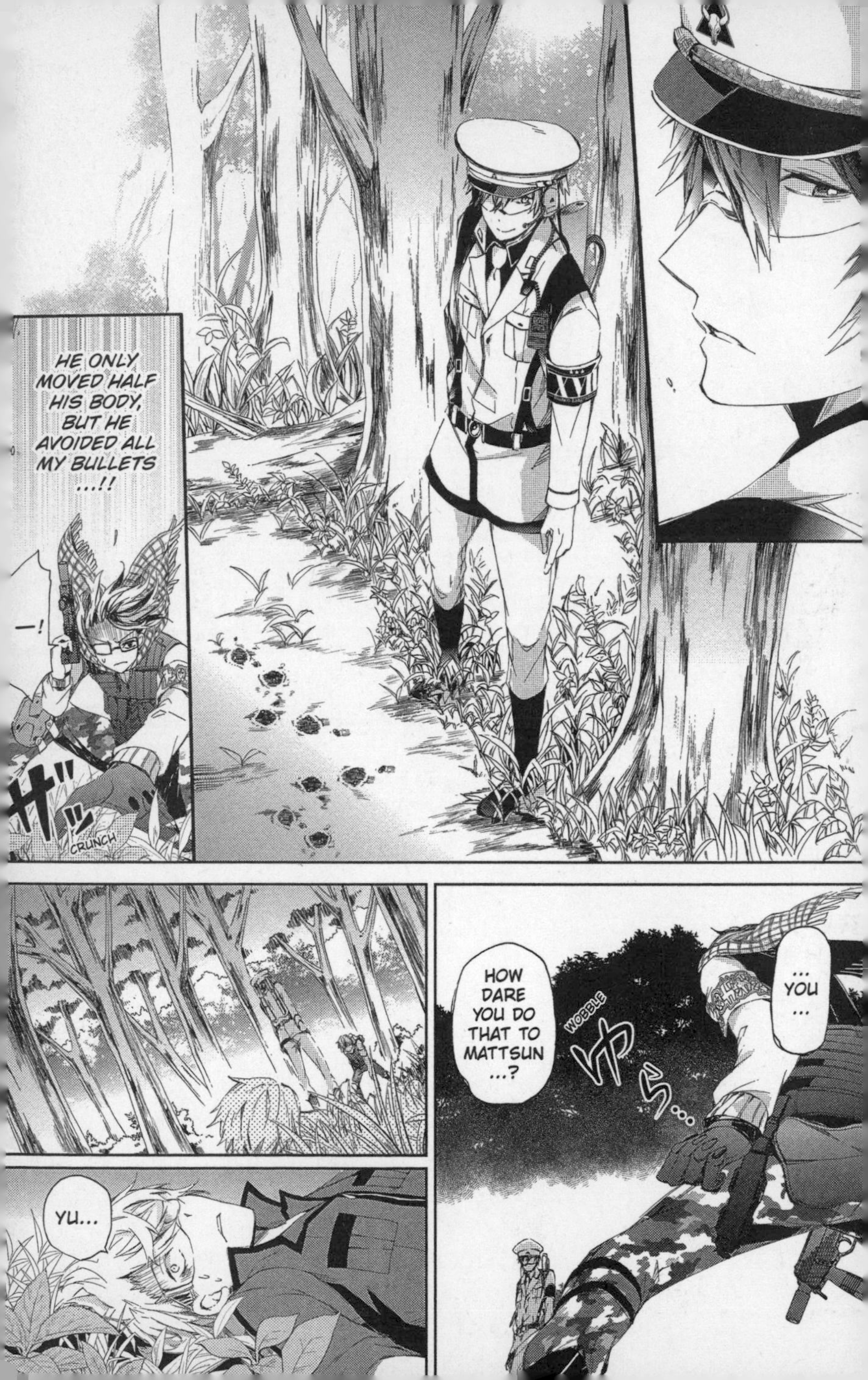
HE ONLY MOVED HALF HIS BODY, BUT HE AVOIDED ALL MY BULLETS ...!!
—!
CRUNCH
... YOU ...
WOBBLE
HOW DARE YOU DO THAT TO MATTSUN ...?
YU...

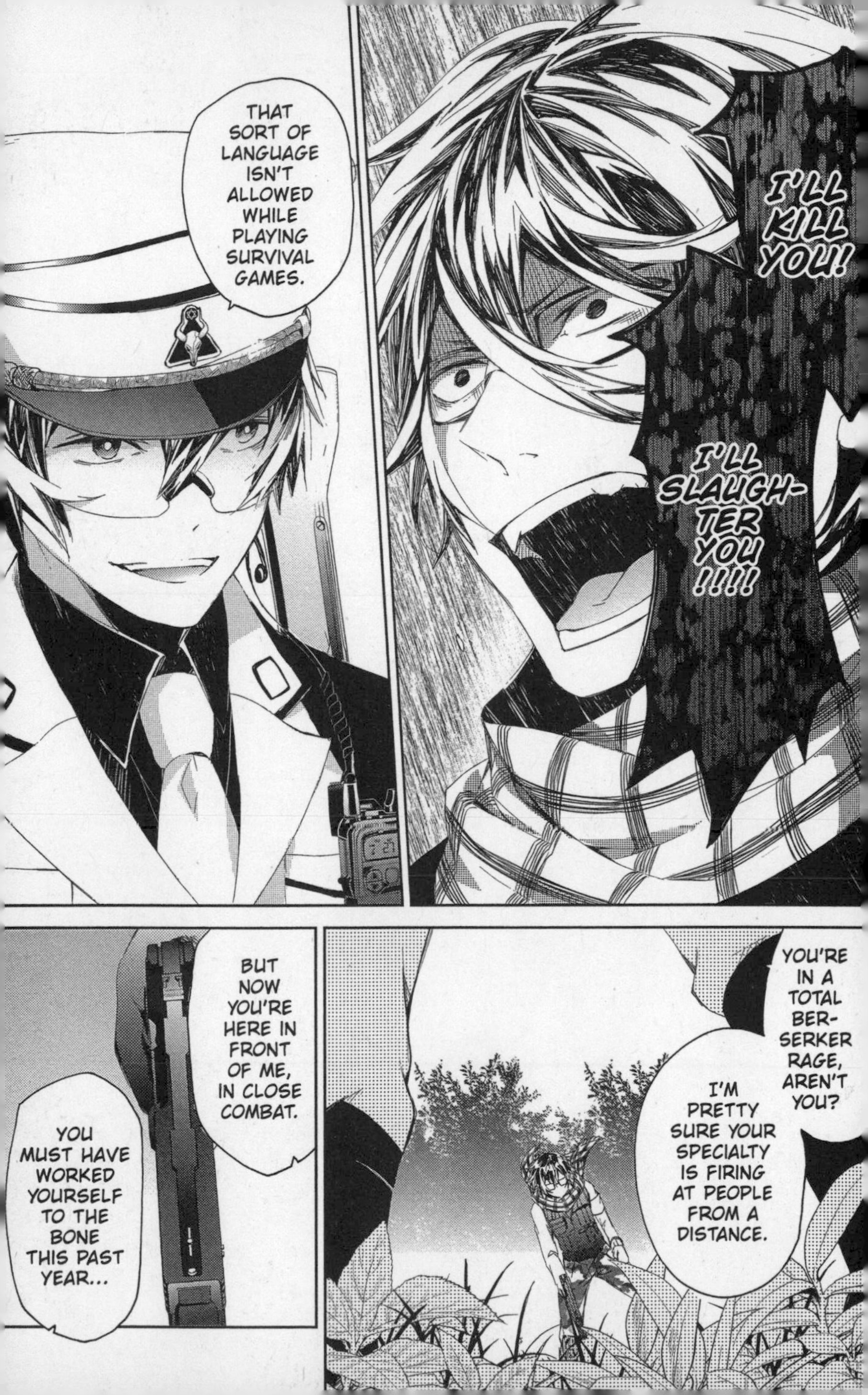
I'LL KILL YOU!
I'LL SLAUGHTER YOU!!!!
THAT SORT OF LANGUAGE ISN'T ALLOWED WHILE PLAYING SURVIVAL GAMES.
YOU'RE IN A TOTAL BERSERKER RAGE, AREN'T YOU?
I'M PRETTY SURE YOUR SPECIALTY IS FIRING AT PEOPLE FROM A DISTANCE.
BUT NOW YOU'RE HERE IN FRONT OF ME, IN CLOSE COMBAT.
YOU MUST HAVE WORKED YOURSELF TO THE BONE THIS PAST YEAR...

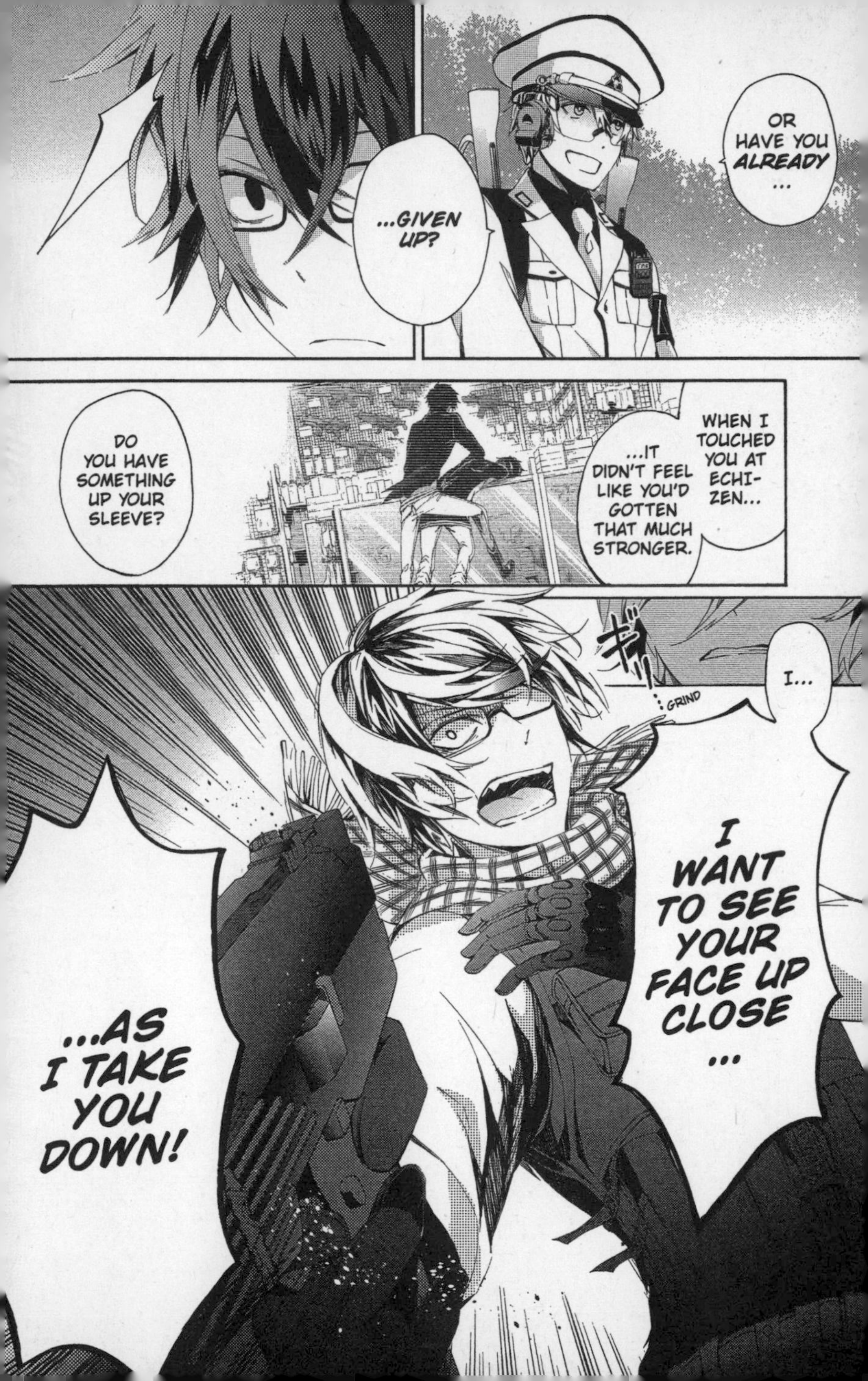
OR HAVE YOU ALREADY ...
...GIVEN UP?
WHEN I TOUCHED YOU AT ECHIZEN...
...IT DIDN'T FEEL LIKE YOU'D GOTTEN THAT MUCH STRONGER.
DO YOU HAVE SOMETHING UP YOUR SLEEVE?
GRIND
I...
I WANT TO SEE YOUR FACE UP CLOSE ...
...AS I TAKE YOU DOWN!

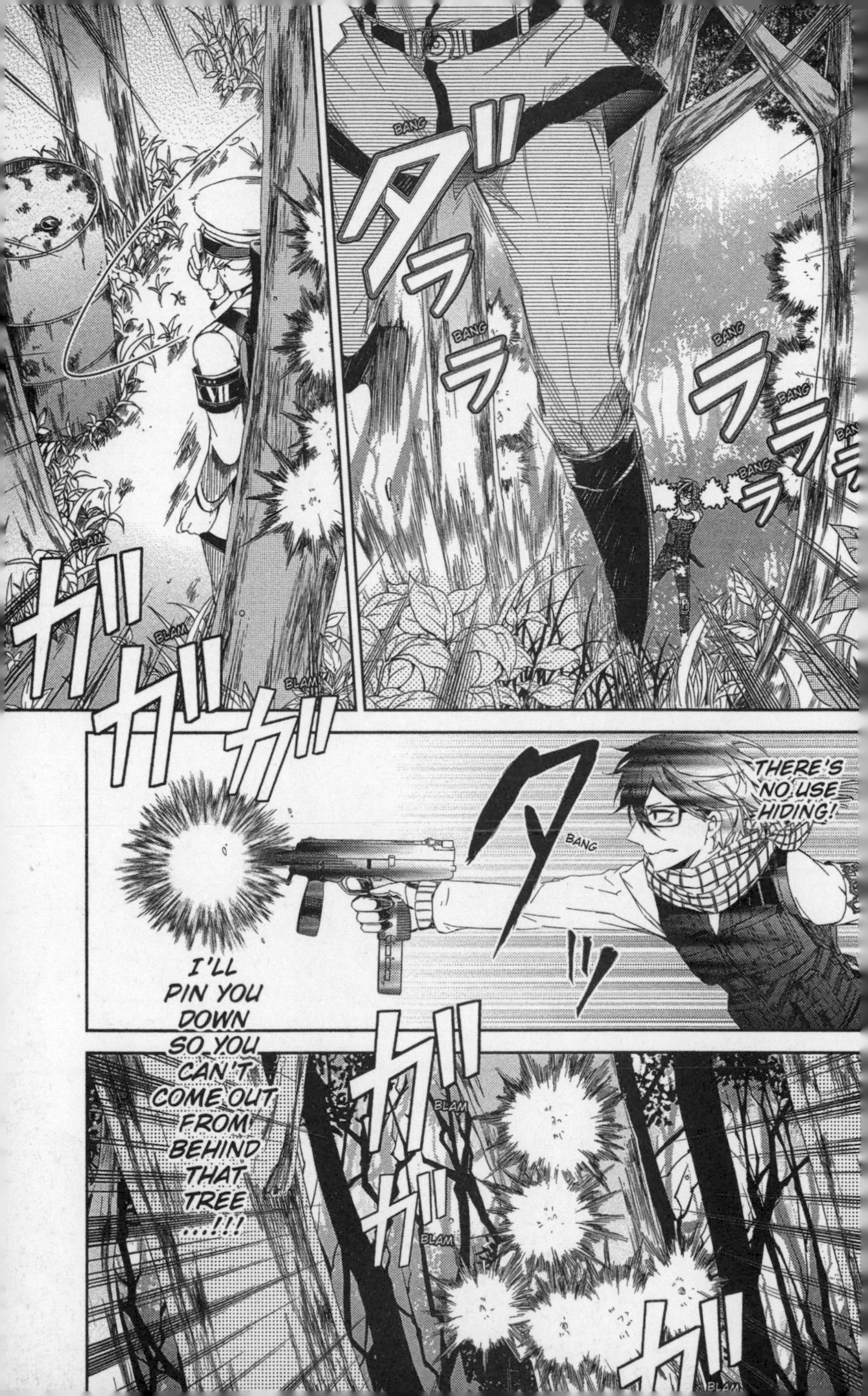

BANG
BANG
BANG
BANG
BANG
BANG
BLAM
BLAM
BLAM
THERE'S NO USE HIDING!
BANG
I'LL PIN YOU DOWN SO YOU CAN'T COME OUT FROM BEHIND THAT TREE ...!!!
BLAM
BLAM
BLAM

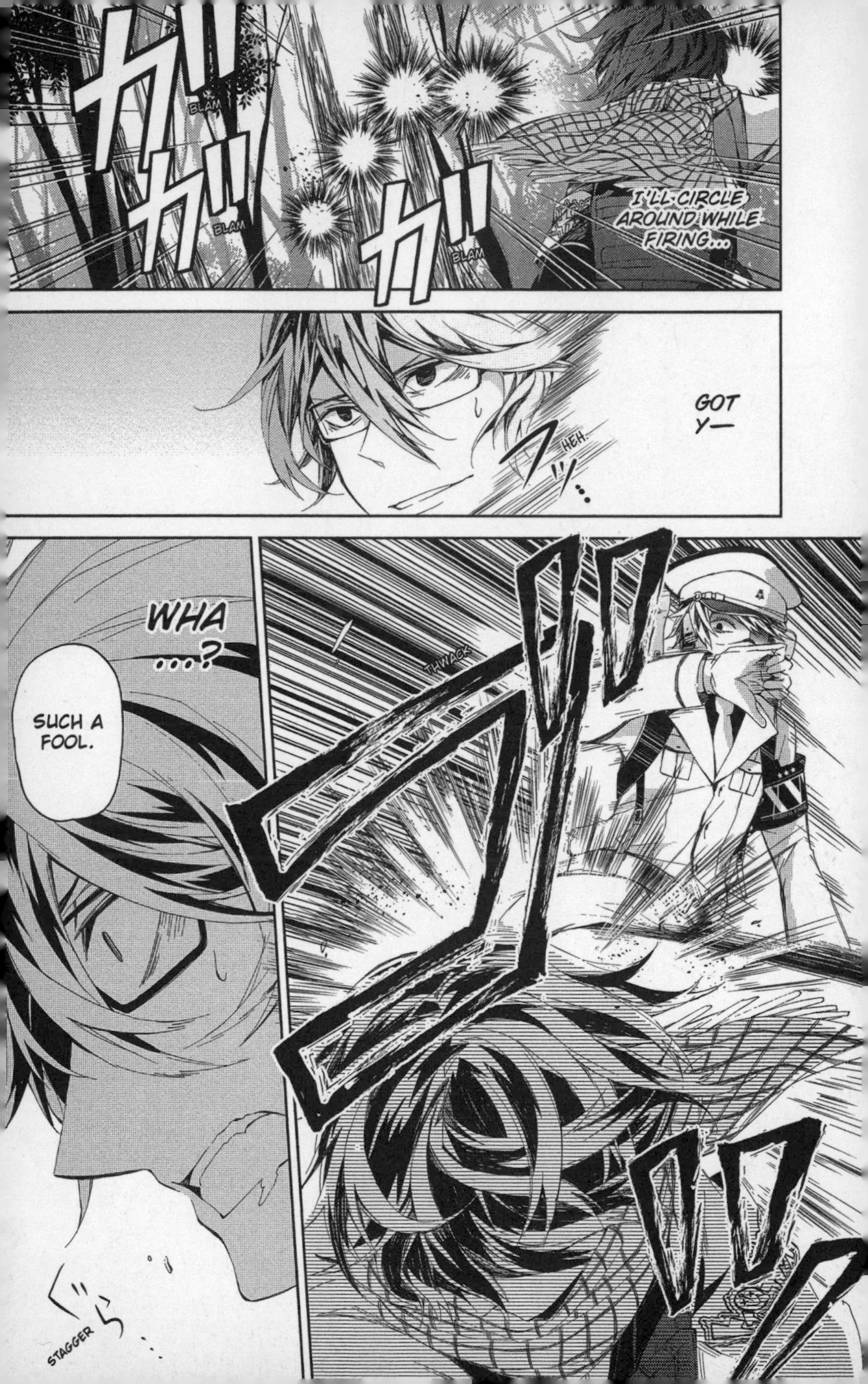
BLAM
BLAM
BLAM
I'LL CIRCLE AROUND WHILE FIRING...
GOT Y—
HEH.
THWACK
WHA ...?
SUCH A FOOL.
STAGGER

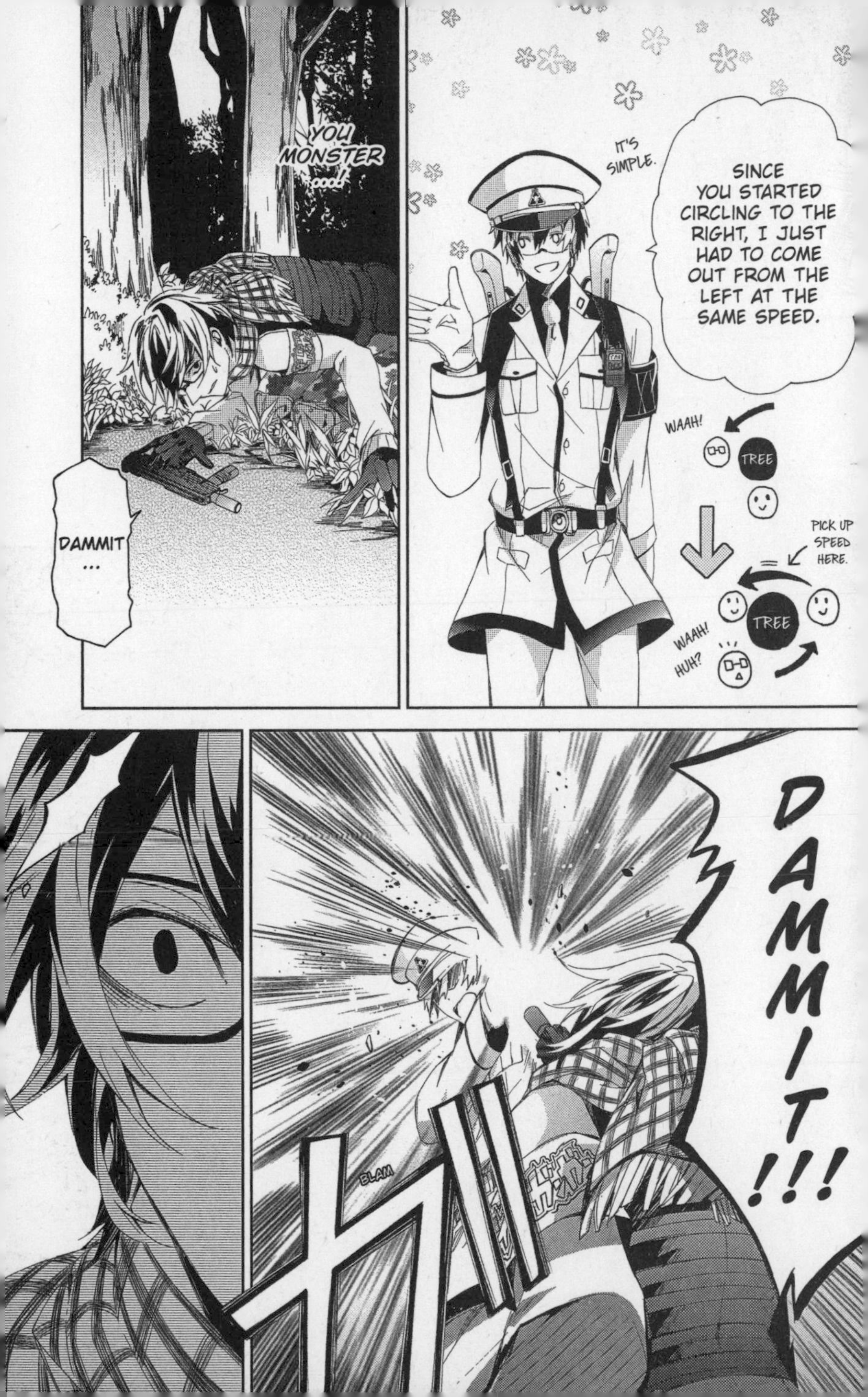
IT'S SIMPLE.
SINCE YOU STARTED CIRCLING TO THE RIGHT, I JUST HAD TO COME OUT FROM THE LEFT AT THE SAME SPEED.
WAAH!
TREE
PICK UP SPEED HERE.
TREE
WAAH!
HUH?
YOU MONSTER ...!
DAMMIT ...
DAMMIT!!!
BLAM

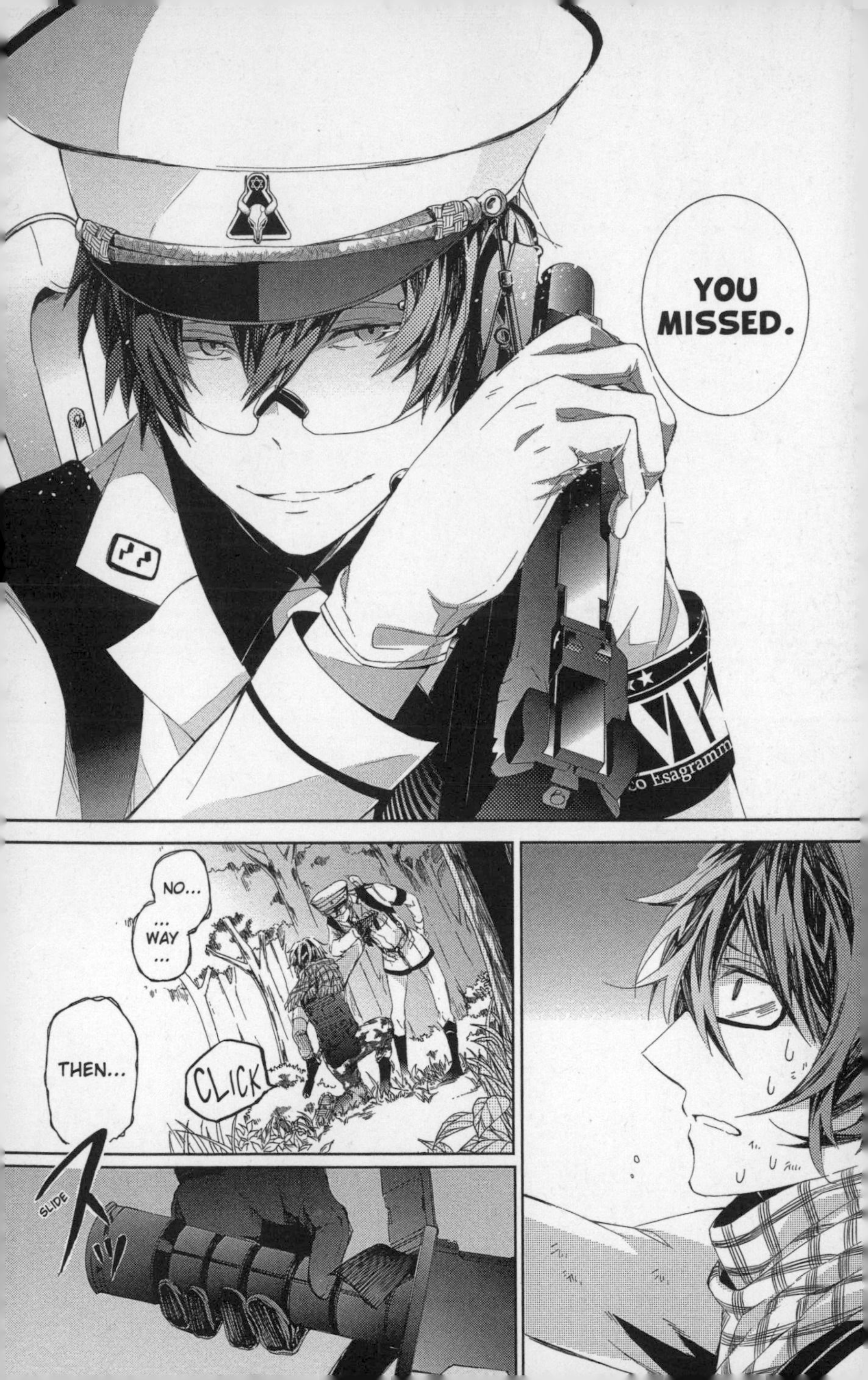
YOU MISSED.
NO...
... WAY ...
THEN...
CLICK
SLIDE

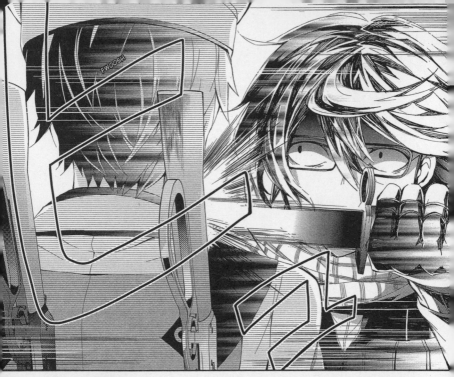

SO THE TMP WAS JUST A DECOY, AND YOU REALLY MEANT TO KILL ME WITH THE KNIFE?

YOU REALLY ARE A DETESTABLE LITTLE THING, AREN'T YOU?

A KNIFE, HUH?

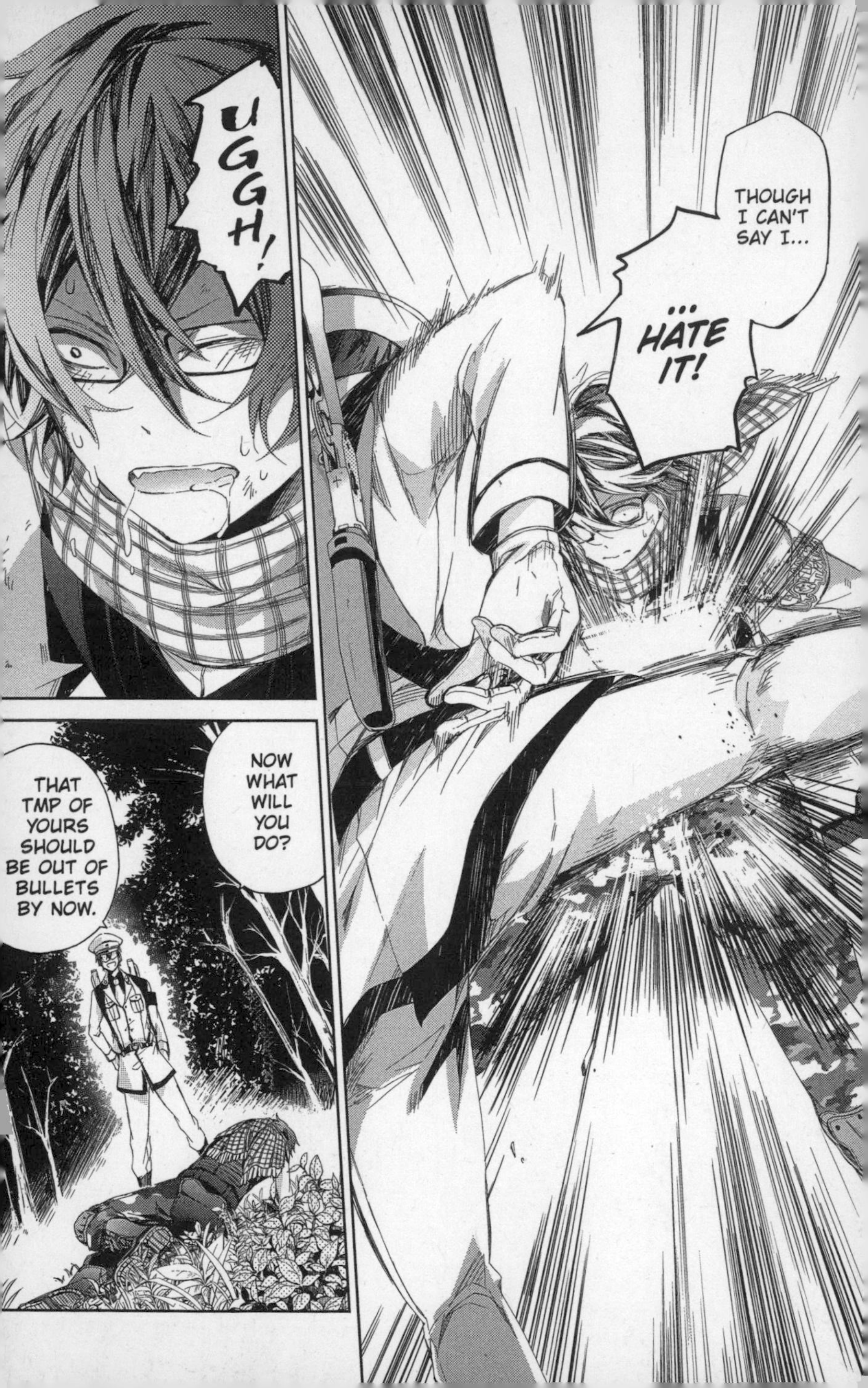
THOUGH I CAN'T SAY I...
...HÄTE IT!
UGGH!
NOW WHAT WILL YOU DO?
THAT TMP OF YOURS SHOULD BE OUT OF BULLETS BY NOW.

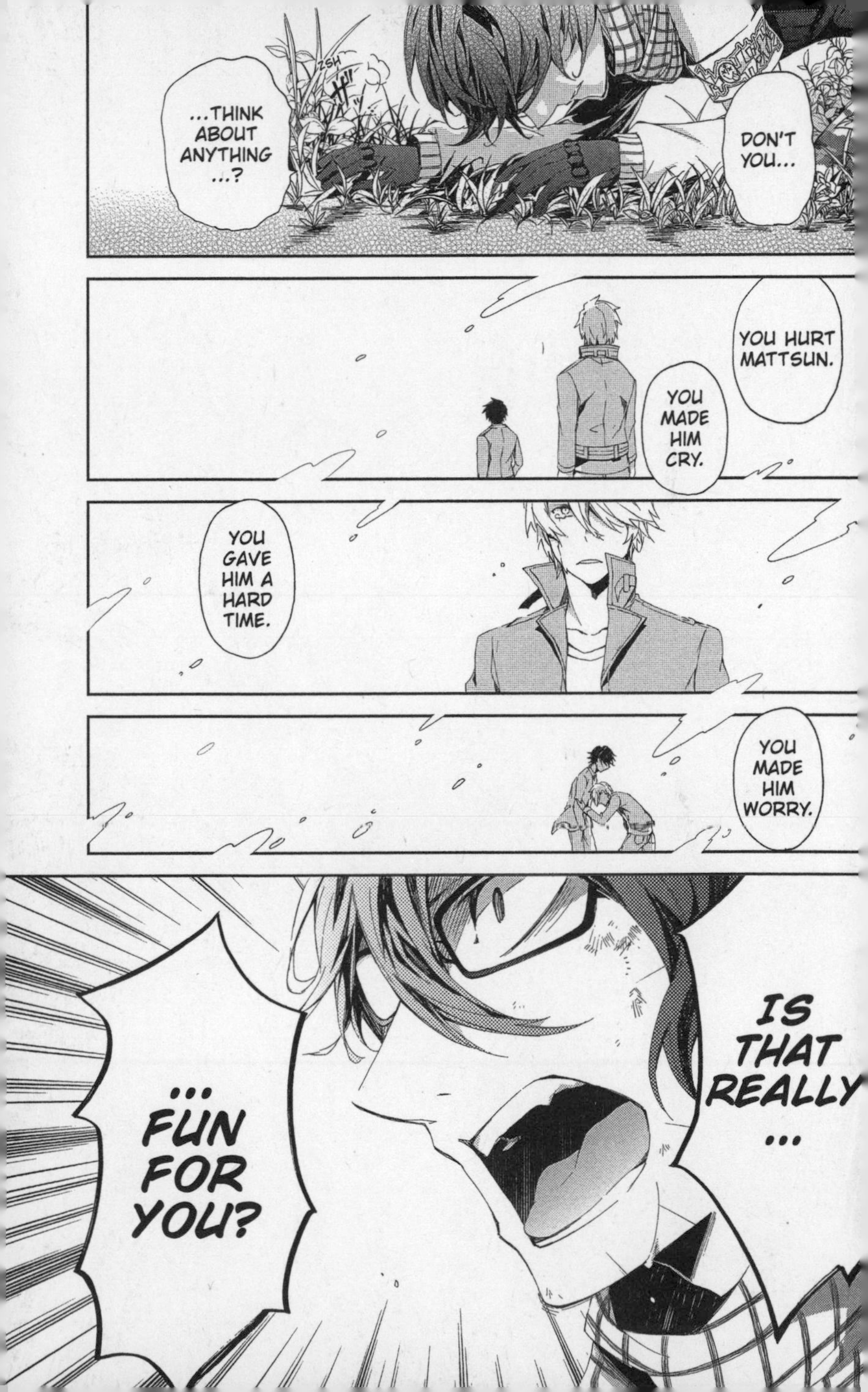
DON'T YOU...
ZSH
...THINK ABOUT ANYTHING ...?
YOU HURT MATTSUN.
YOU MADE HIM CRY.
YOU GAVE HIM A HARD TIME.
YOU MADE HIM WORRY.
IS THAT REALLY ...
... FUN FOR YOU?

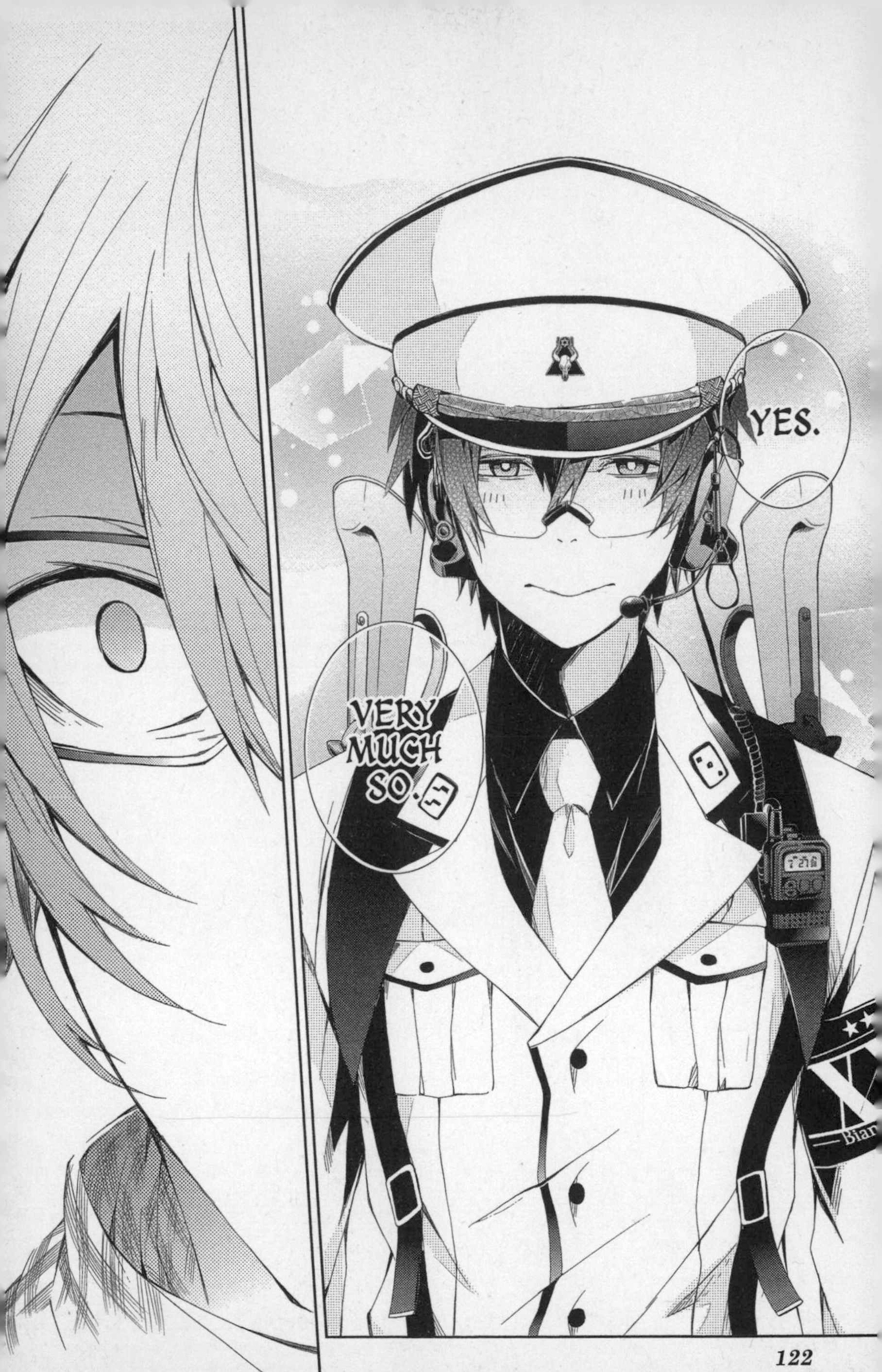
YES.
VERY MUCH SO.

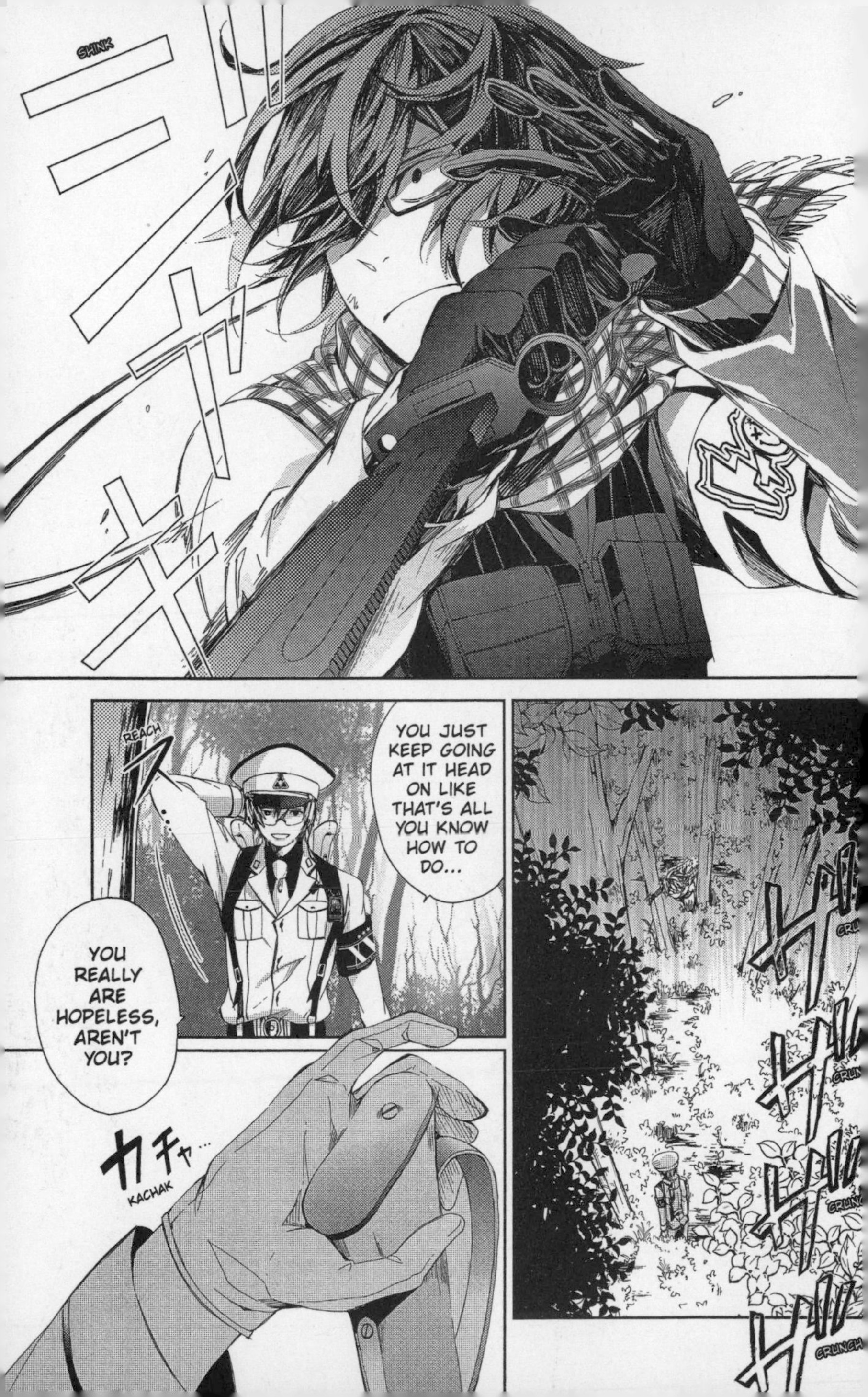
SHINK
REACH
YOU JUST KEEP GOING AT IT HEAD ON LIKE THAT'S ALL YOU KNOW HOW TO DO...
CRUNCH
CRUNCH
CRUNCH
CRUNCH
YOU REALLY ARE HOPELESS, AREN'T YOU?
カチャ…
KACHAK

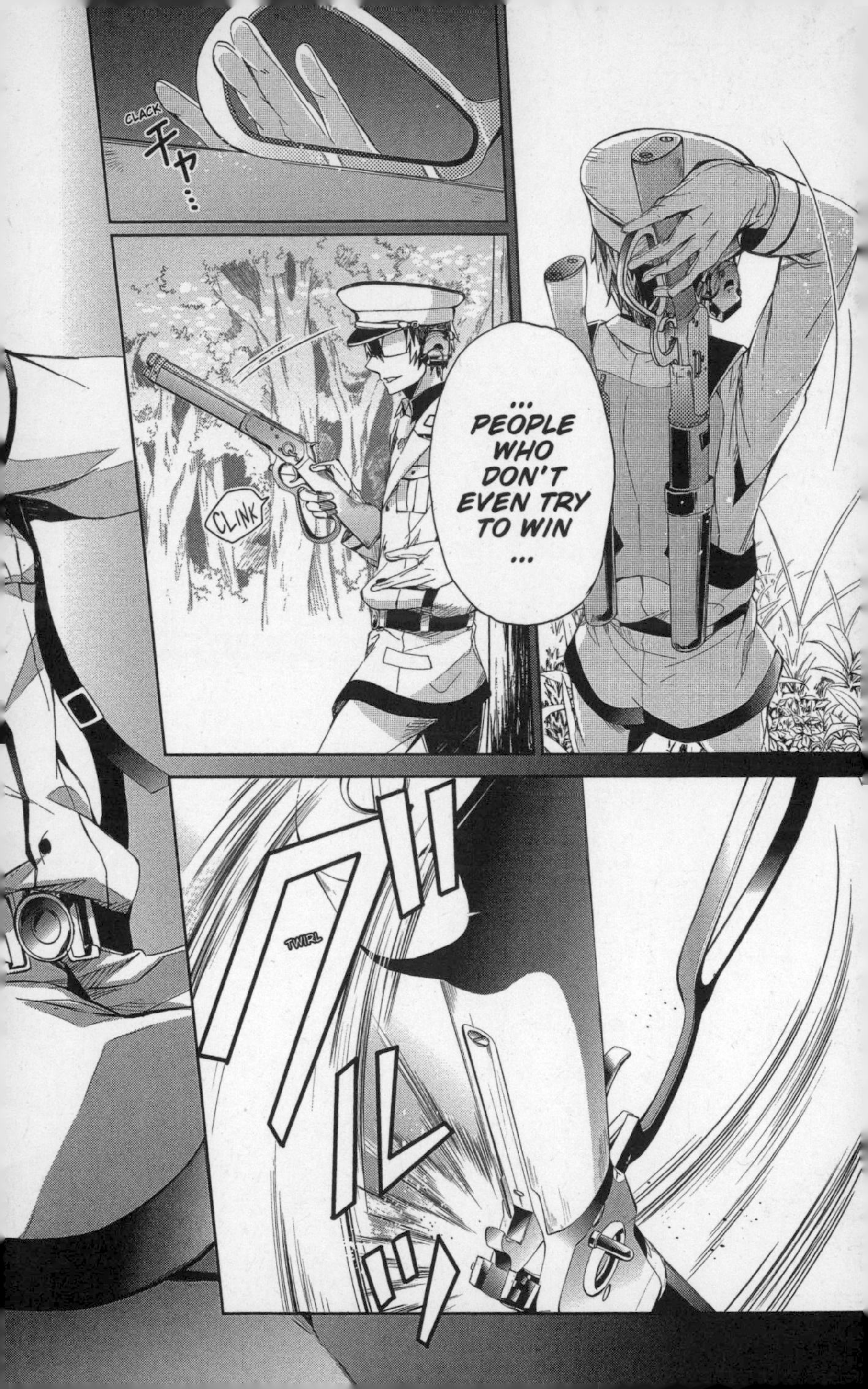
CLACK
チャ…
CLINK
... PEOPLE WHO DON'T EVEN TRY TO WIN ...
TWIRL

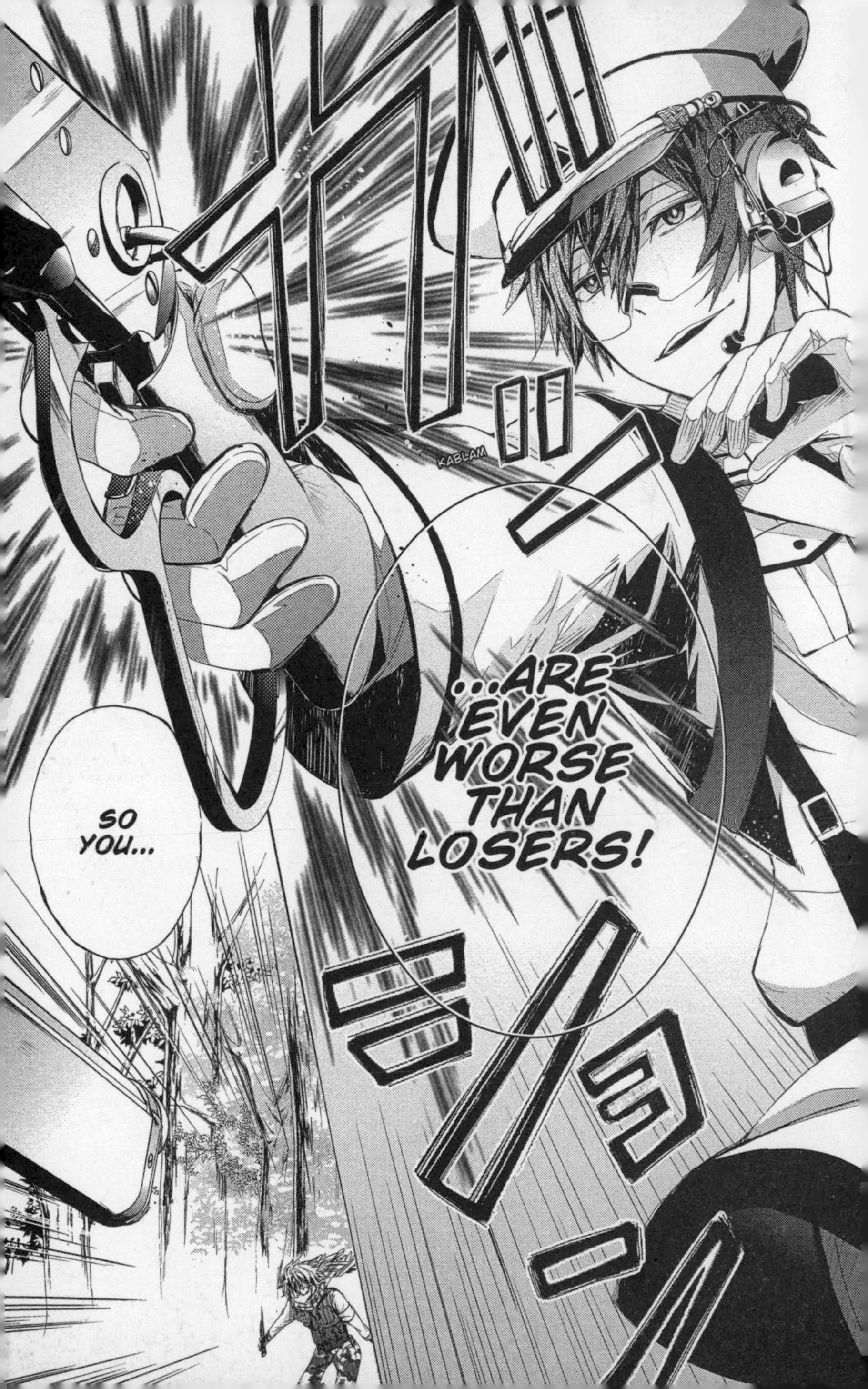
...ARE EVEN WORSE THAN LOSERS!
KABLAM
SO YOU...

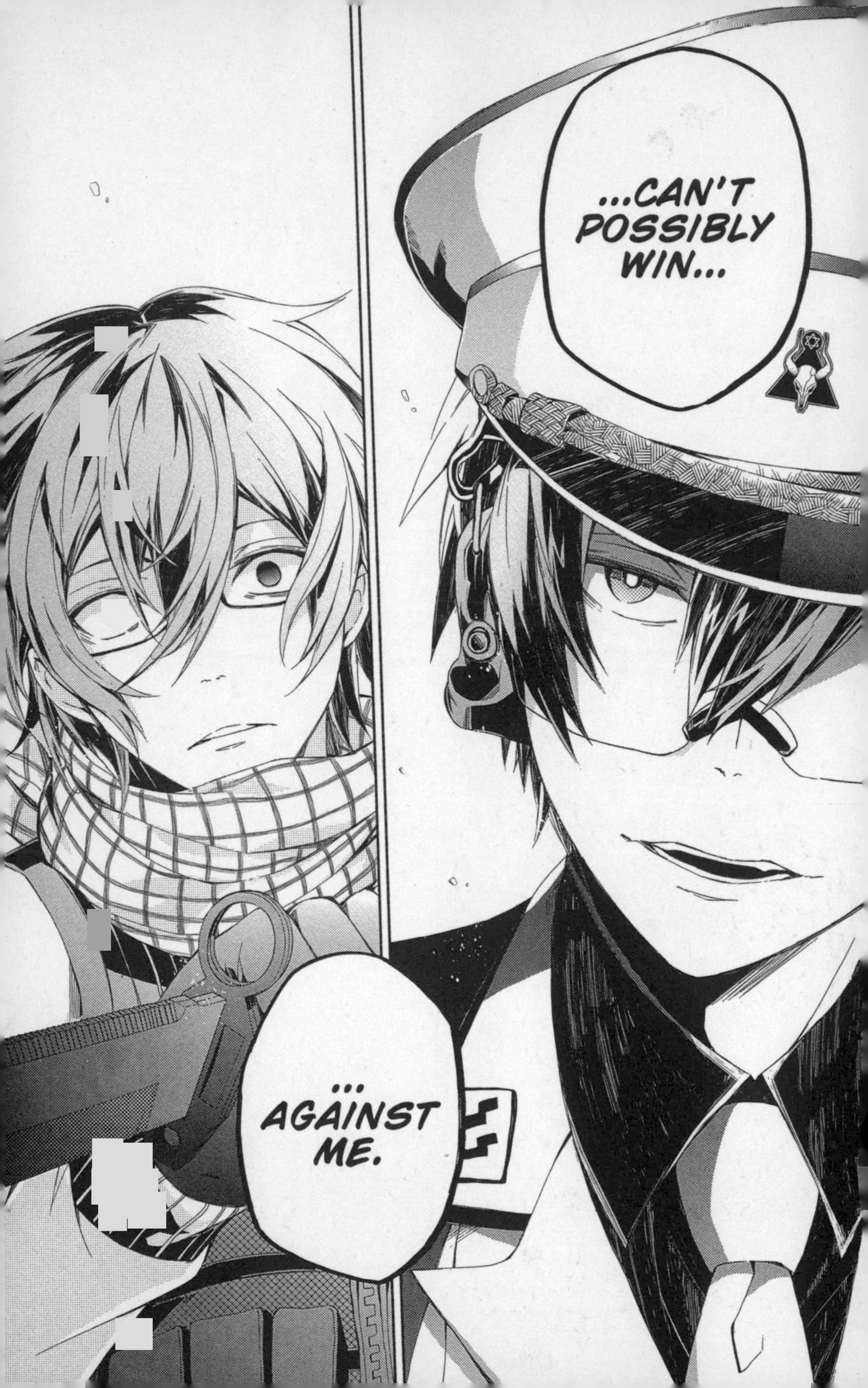
...CAN'T POSSIBLY WIN...
... AGAINST ME.

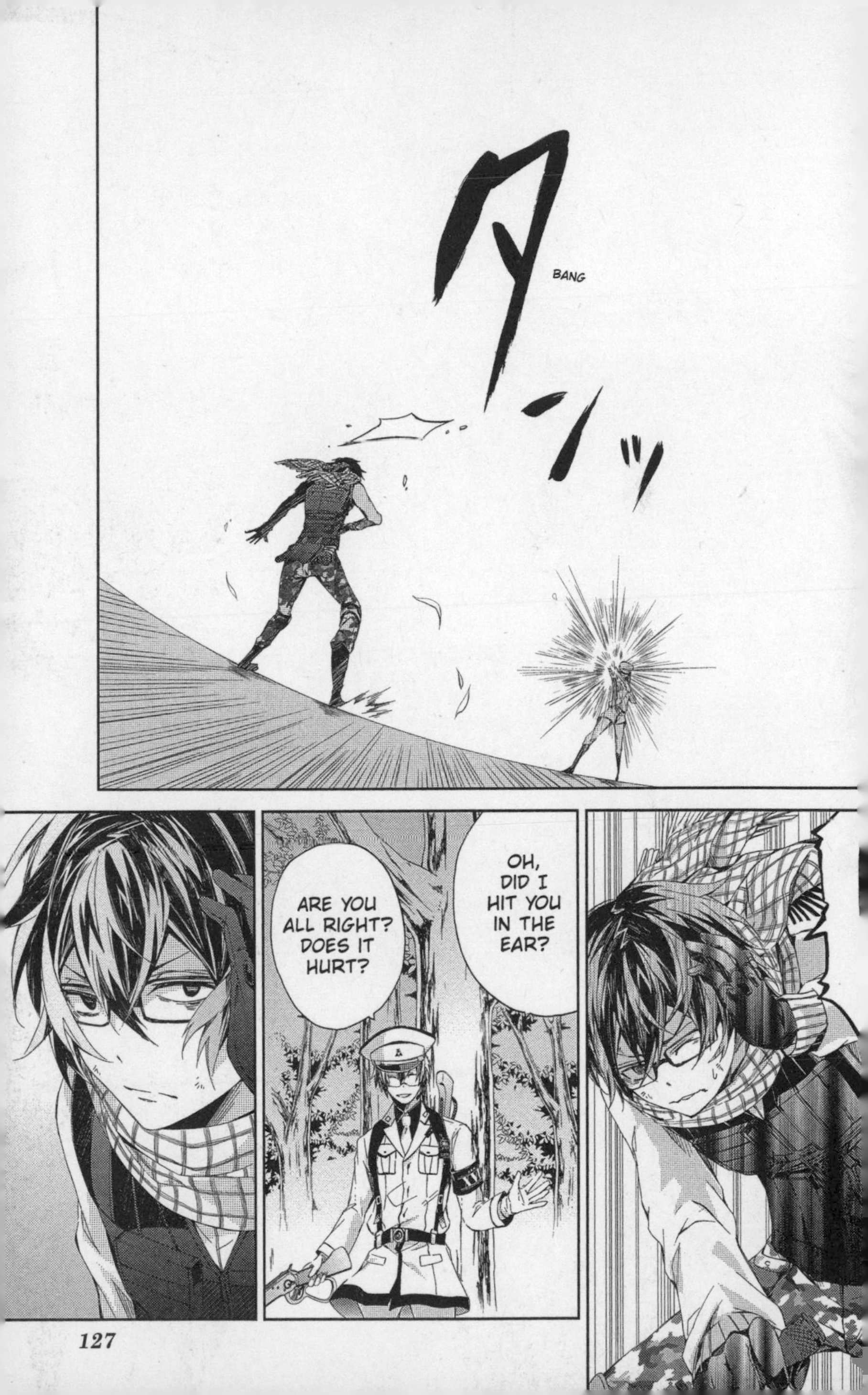
BANG
OH, DID I HIT YOU IN THE EAR?
ARE YOU ALL RIGHT? DOES IT HURT?

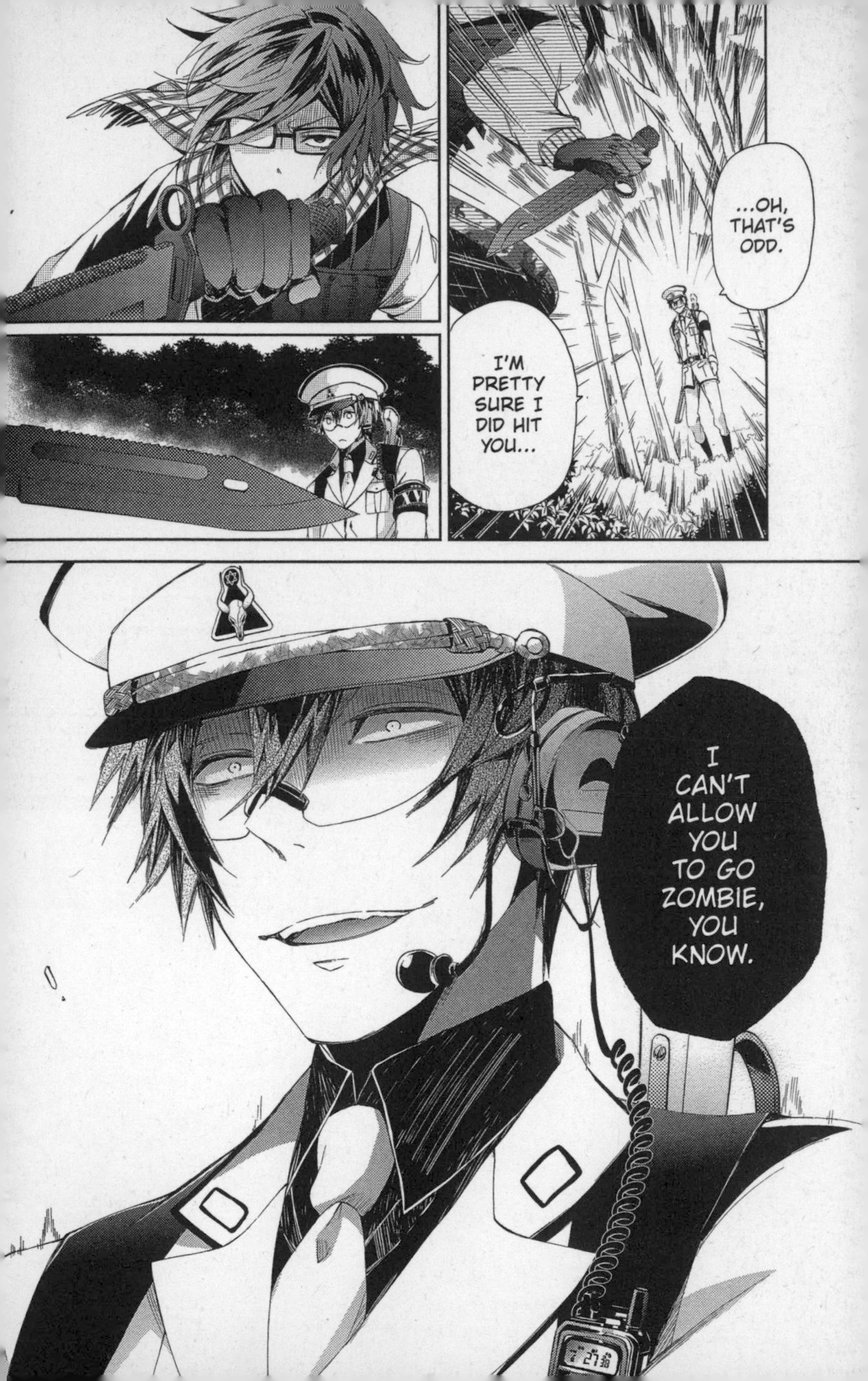
...OH, THAT'S ODD.
I'M PRETTY SURE I DID HIT YOU...
I CAN'T ALLOW YOU TO GO ZOMBIE, YOU KNOW.

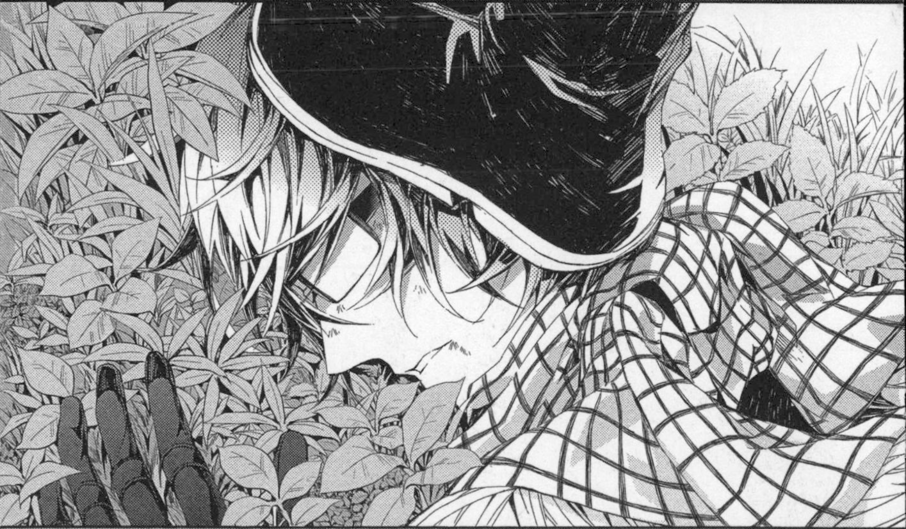

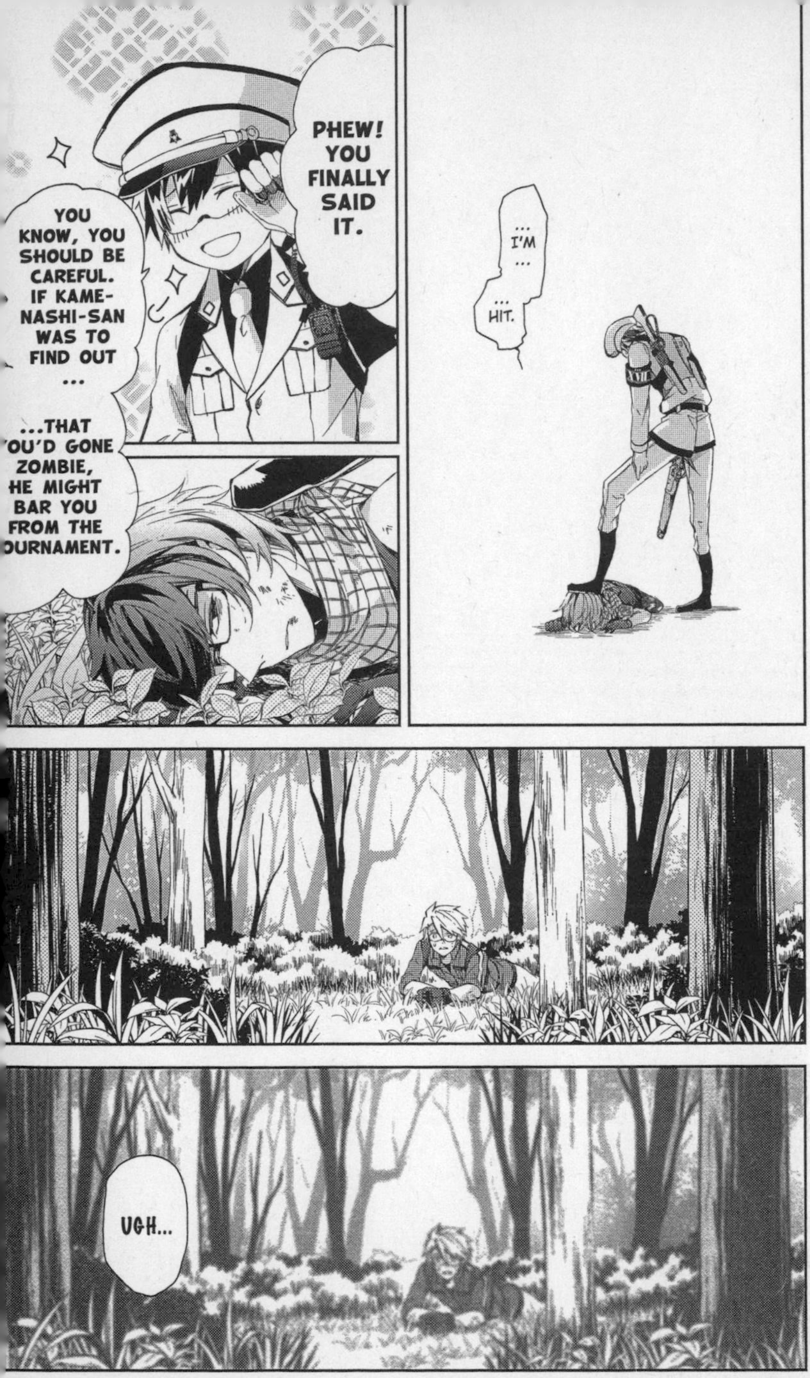
...I'M ...
...HIT.
PHEW! YOU FINALLY SAID IT.
YOU KNOW, YOU SHOULD BE CAREFUL. IF KAME-NASHI-SAN WAS TO FIND OUT ...
...THAT YOU'D GONE ZOMBIE, HE MIGHT BAR YOU FROM THE TOURNAMENT.
UGH...

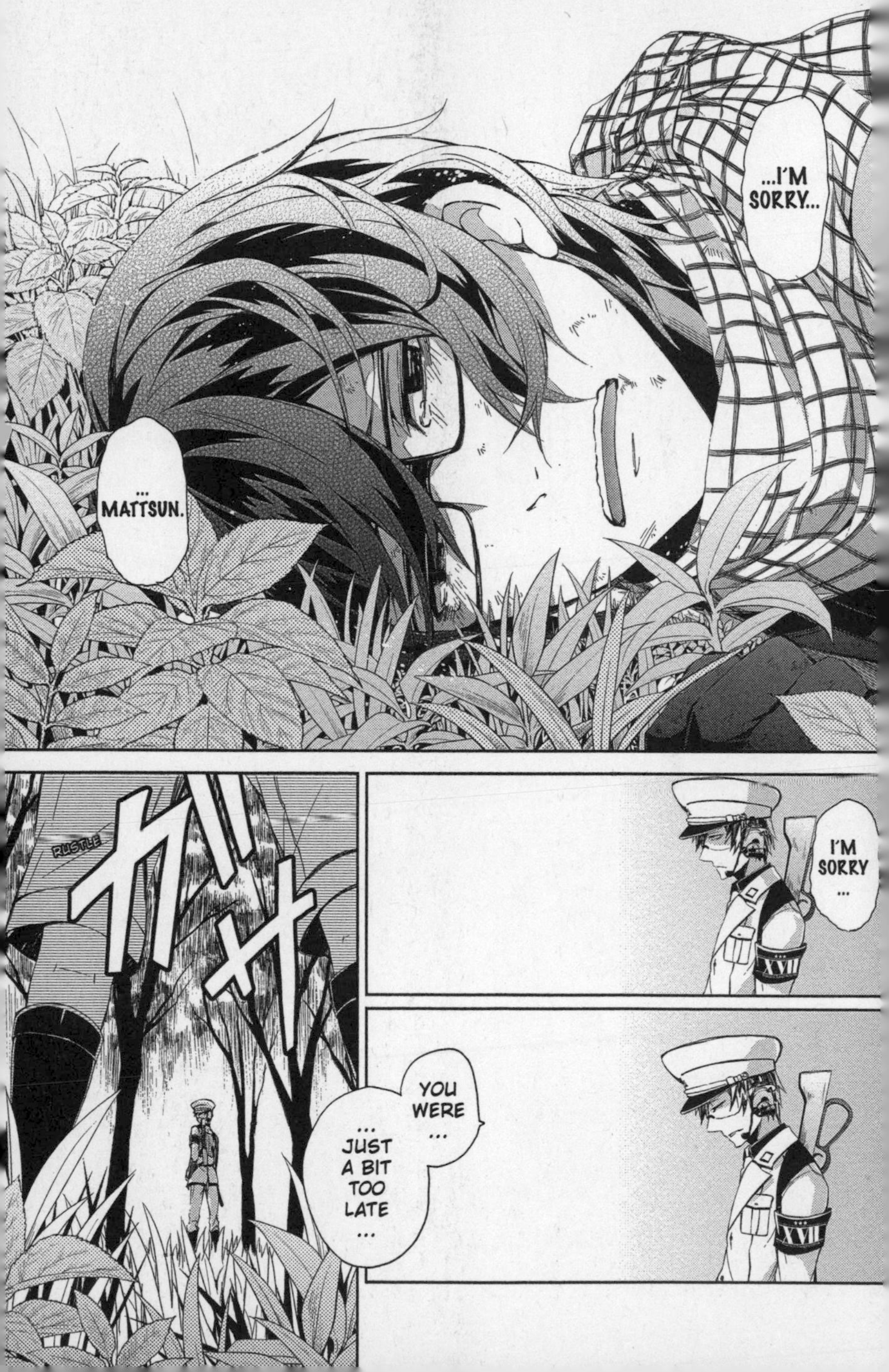
...I'M SORRY...
... MATTSUN.
RUSTLE
I'M SORRY ...
YOU WERE ... ... JUST A BIT TOO LATE ...

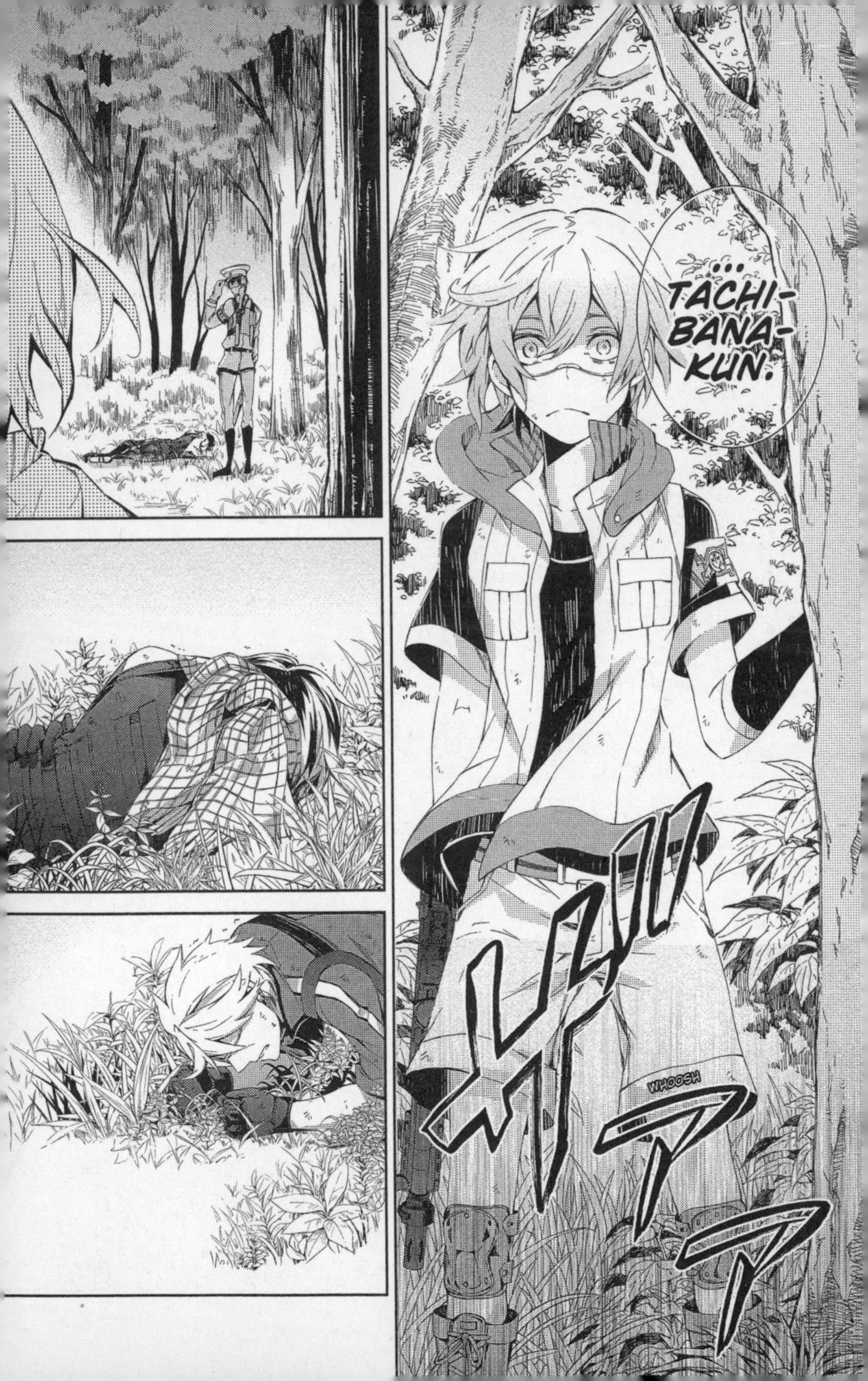
...TACHI-BANA-KUN.
WHOOSH

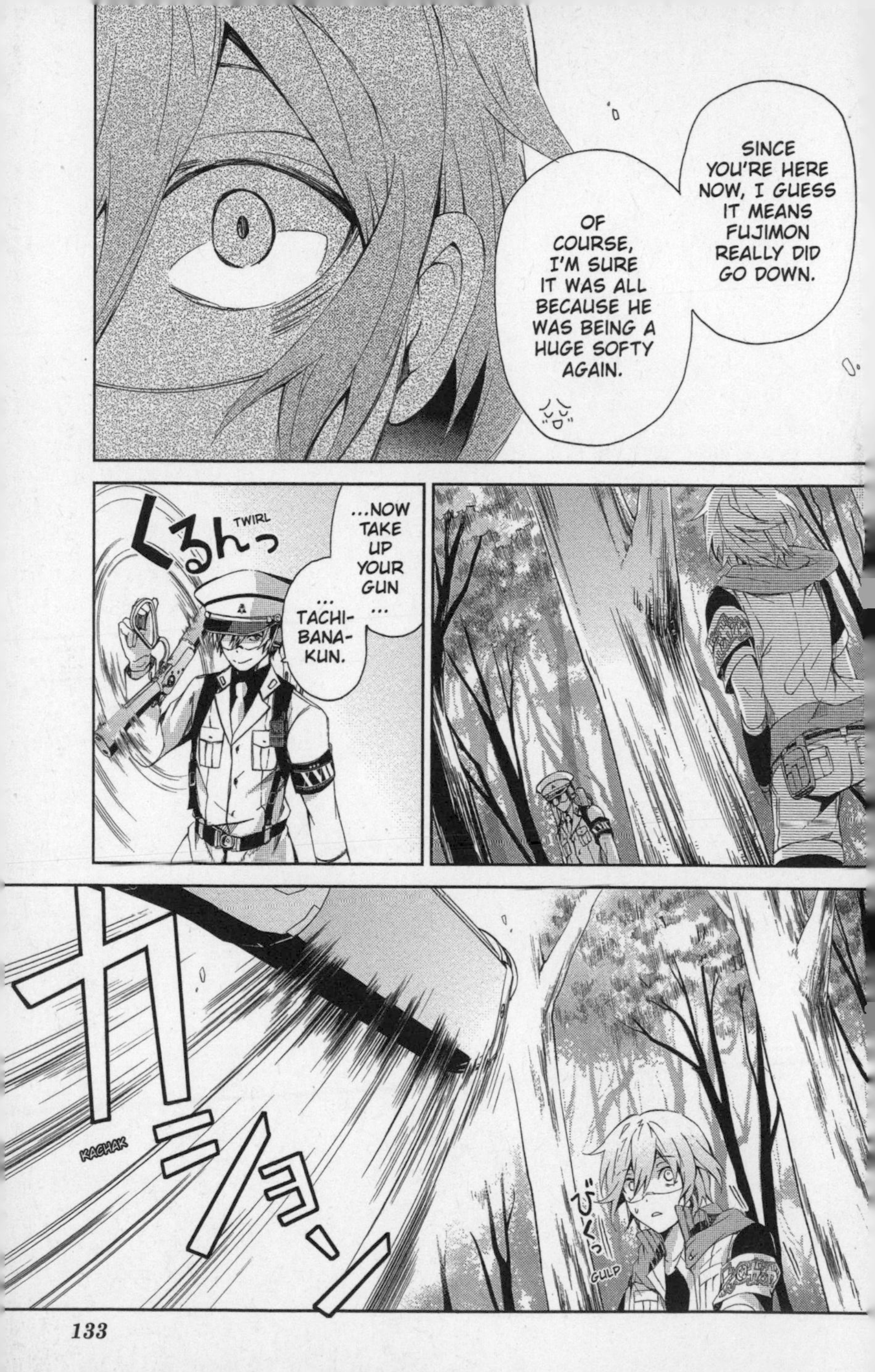
SINCE YOU'RE HERE NOW, I GUESS IT MEANS FUJIMON REALLY DID GO DOWN.
OF COURSE, I'M SURE IT WAS ALL BECAUSE HE WAS BEING A HUGE SOFTY AGAIN.
...NOW TAKE UP YOUR GUN ... ... TACHI-BANA-KUN.
くるんっ
TWIRL
ガチョン
KACHAK
びくっ
GULP

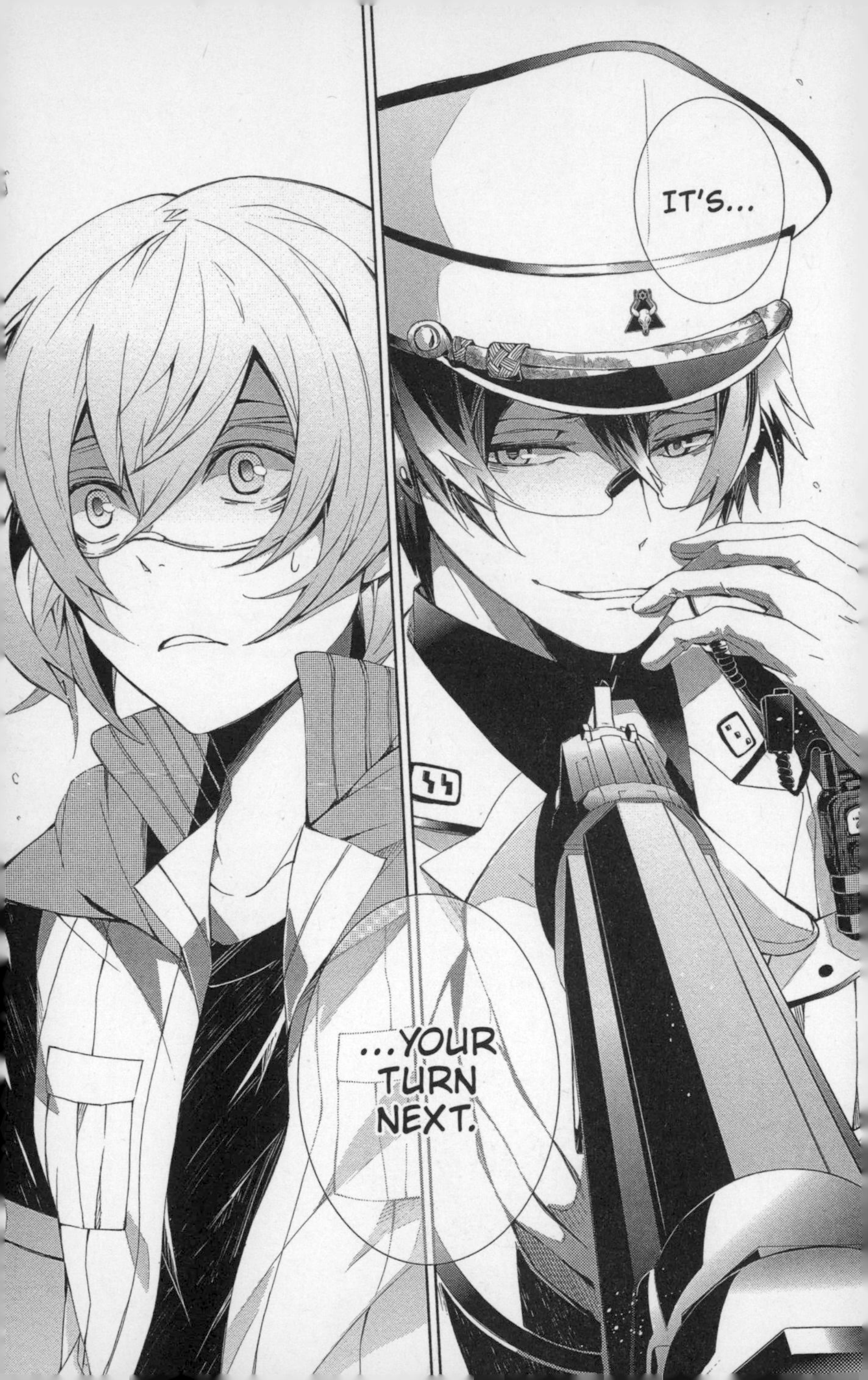
IT'S...
...YOUR TURN NEXT.

DEFINITELY DO NOT GO OVERKILL IN NORMAL SURVIVAL GAMES! IT'S THE CAUSE OF MANY INJURIES AND PROBLEMS.
YOU'RE ONE TO TALK.
A PROMISE TO MIDORI ♡

AOHARU×MACHINEGU

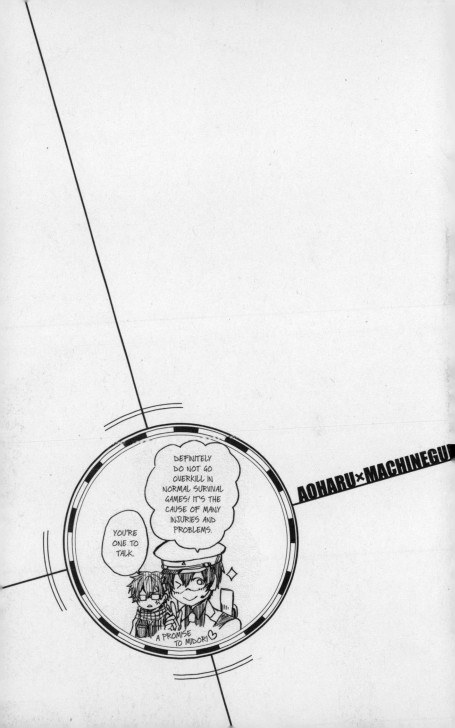

AOHARU

MACHINE GUN

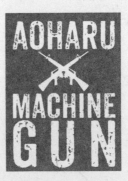

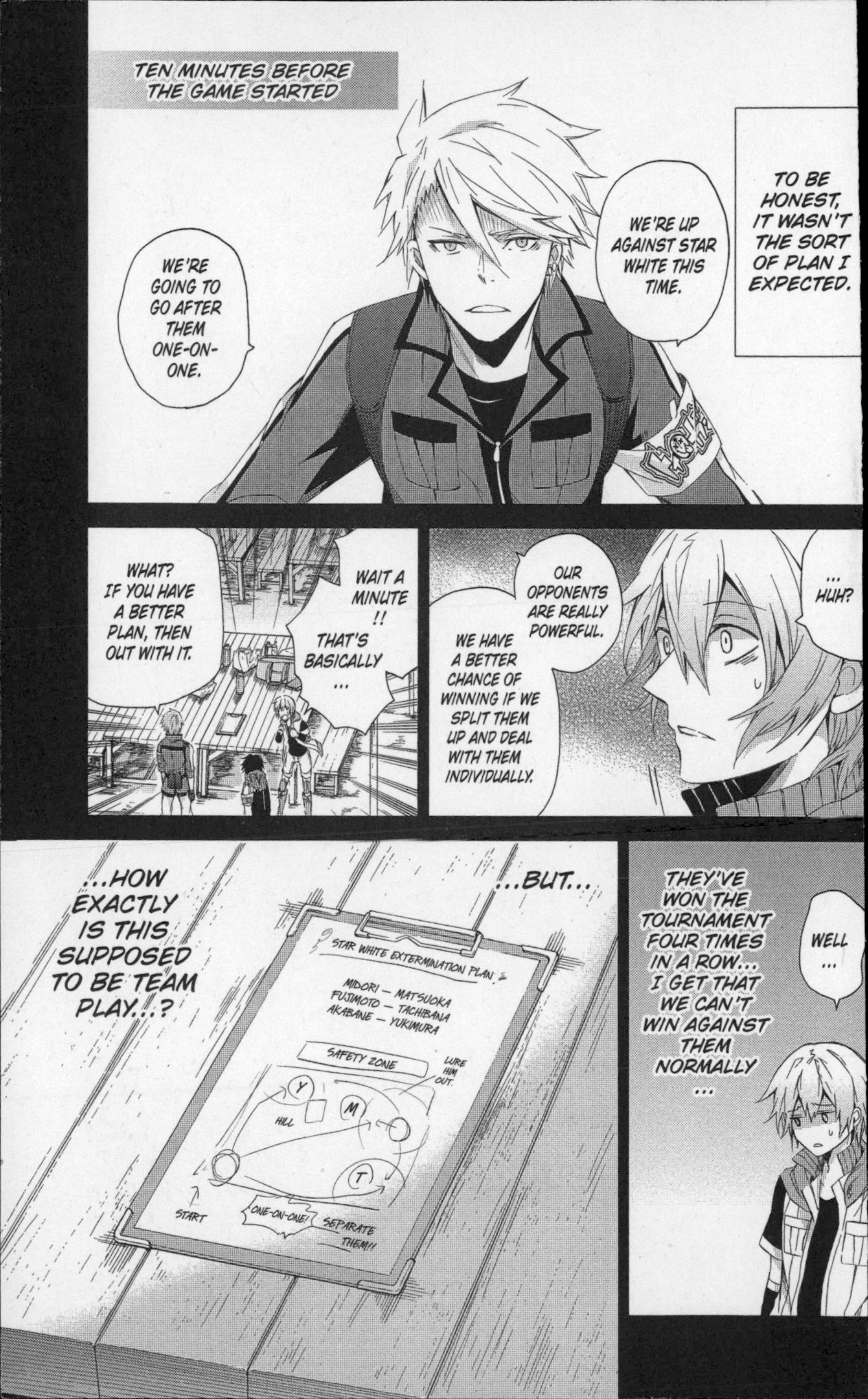
TEN MINUTES BEFORE THE GAME STARTED
TO BE HONEST, IT WASN'T THE SORT OF PLAN I EXPECTED.
WE'RE UP AGAINST STAR WHITE THIS TIME.
WE'RE GOING TO GO AFTER THEM ONE-ON-ONE.
... HUH?
OUR OPPONENTS ARE REALLY POWERFUL.
WE HAVE A BETTER CHANCE OF WINNING IF WE SPLIT THEM UP AND DEAL WITH THEM INDIVIDUALLY.
WAIT A MINUTE !! THAT'S BASICALLY ...
WHAT? IF YOU HAVE A BETTER PLAN, THEN OUT WITH IT.
WELL ...
THEY'VE WON THE TOURNAMENT FOUR TIMES IN A ROW... I GET THAT WE CAN'T WIN AGAINST THEM NORMALLY ...
...BUT...
...HOW EXACTLY IS THIS SUPPOSED TO BE TEAM PLAY...?
STAR WHITE EXTERMINATION PLAN
MIDORI — MATSUOKA
FUJIMOTO — TACHIBANA
AKABANE — YUKIMURA
SAFETY ZONE
LURE HIM OUT.
Y
M
HILL
T
START
ONE-ON-ONE!
SEPARATE THEM!!

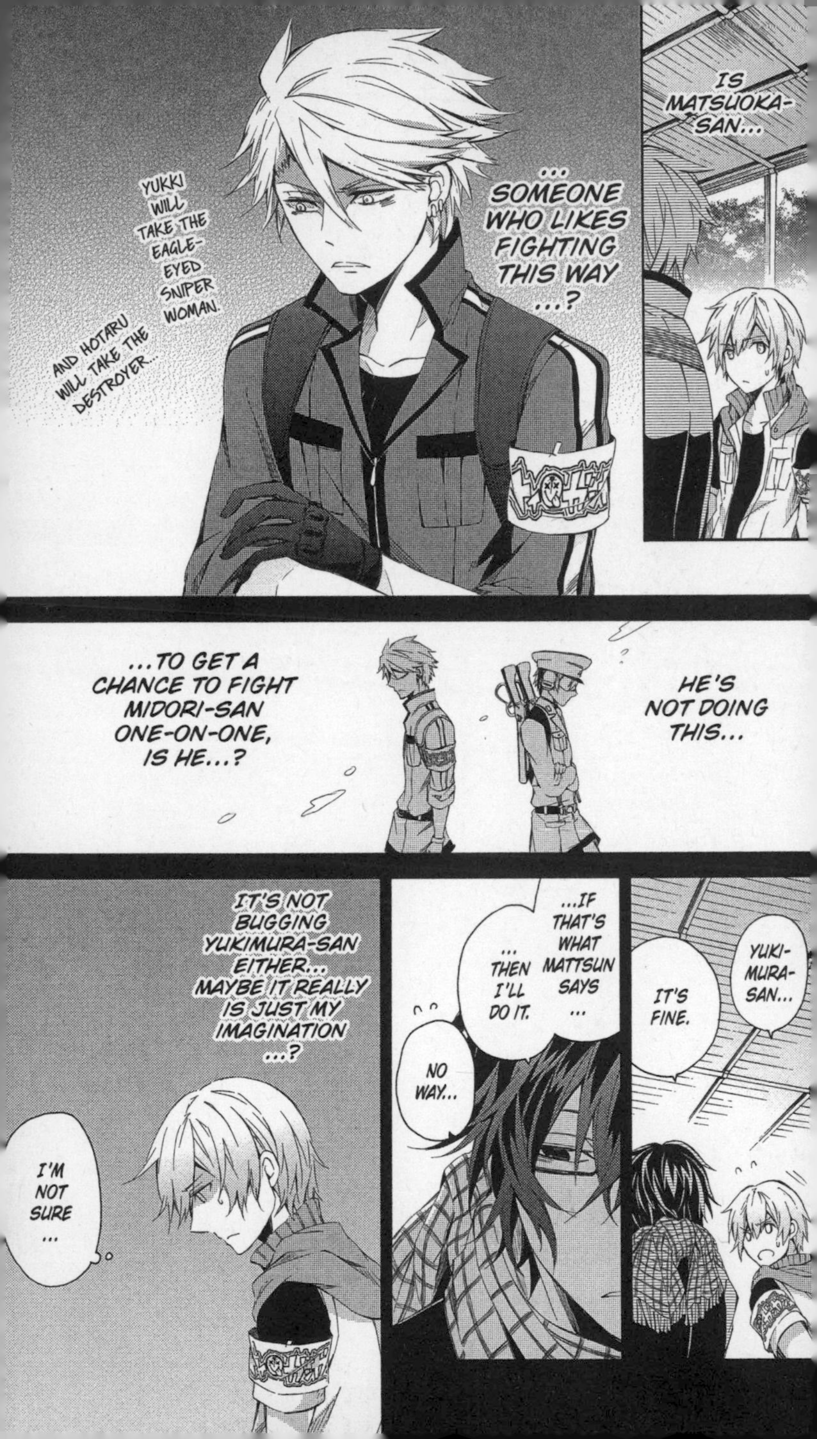
IS MATSUOKA-SAN...
...SOMEONE WHO LIKES FIGHTING THIS WAY...?
YUKKI WILL TAKE THE EAGLE-EYED SNIPER WOMAN.
AND HOTARU WILL TAKE THE DESTROYER...
HE'S NOT DOING THIS...
...TO GET A CHANCE TO FIGHT MIDORI-SAN ONE-ON-ONE, IS HE...?
YUKI-MURA-SAN...
IT'S FINE.
...IF THAT'S WHAT MATTSUN SAYS...
...THEN I'LL DO IT.
NO WAY...
IT'S NOT BUGGING YUKIMURA-SAN EITHER... MAYBE IT REALLY IS JUST MY IMAGINATION...?
I'M NOT SURE...

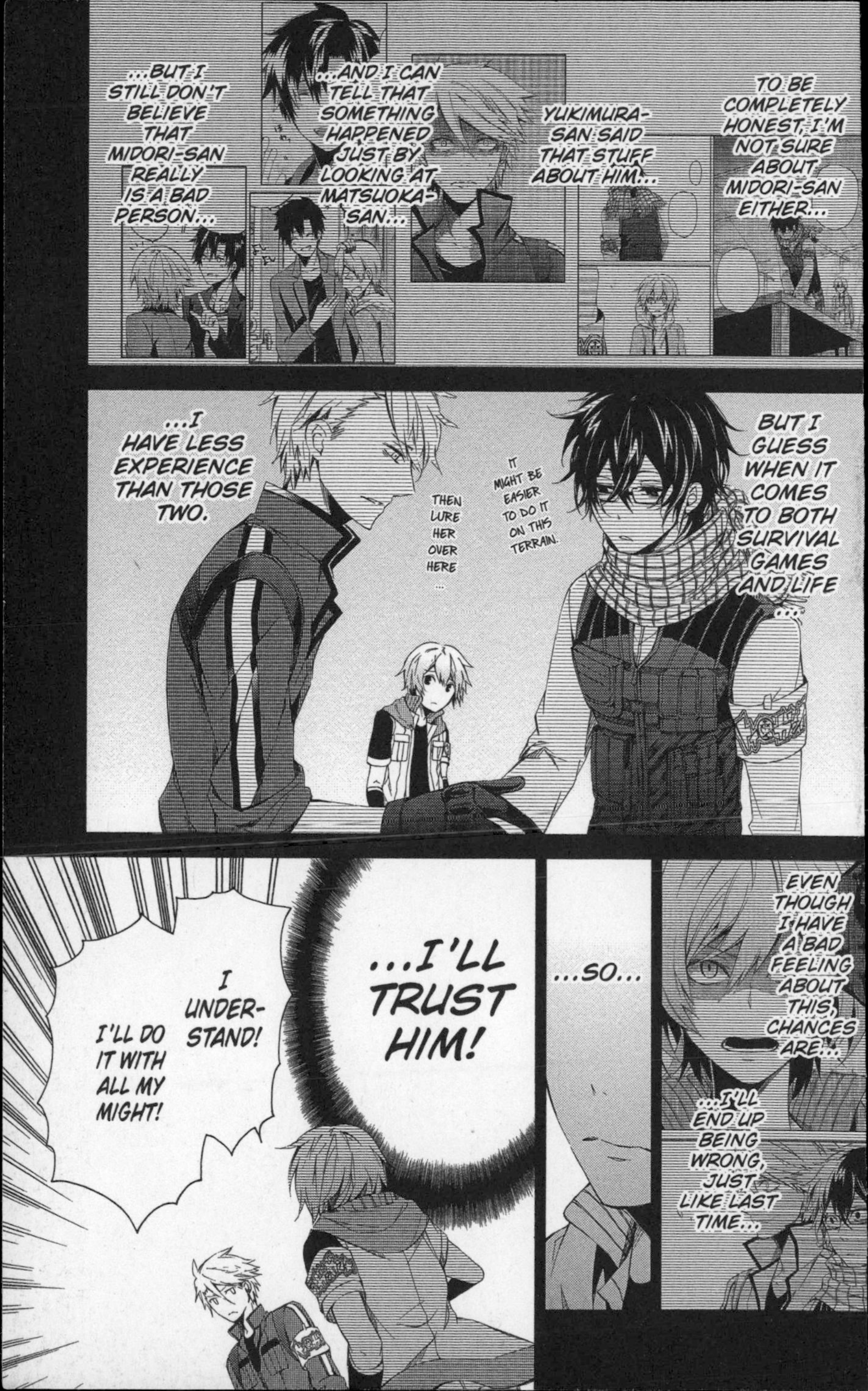
TO BE COMPLETELY HONEST, I'M NOT SURE ABOUT MIDORI-SAN EITHER...
YUKIMURA-SAN SAID THAT STUFF ABOUT HIM...
...AND I CAN TELL THAT SOMETHING HAPPENED JUST BY LOOKING AT MATSUOKA-SAN...
...BUT I STILL DON'T BELIEVE THAT MIDORI-SAN REALLY IS A BAD PERSON...
BUT I GUESS WHEN IT COMES TO BOTH SURVIVAL GAMES AND LIFE...
IT MIGHT BE EASIER TO DO IT ON THIS TERRAIN.
THEN LURE HER OVER HERE...
...I HAVE LESS EXPERIENCE THAN THOSE TWO.
EVEN THOUGH I HAVE A BAD FEELING ABOUT THIS, CHANCES ARE...
...I'LL END UP BEING WRONG, JUST LIKE LAST TIME...
...SO...
...I'LL TRUST HIM!
I UNDERSTAND!
I'LL DO IT WITH ALL MY MIGHT!

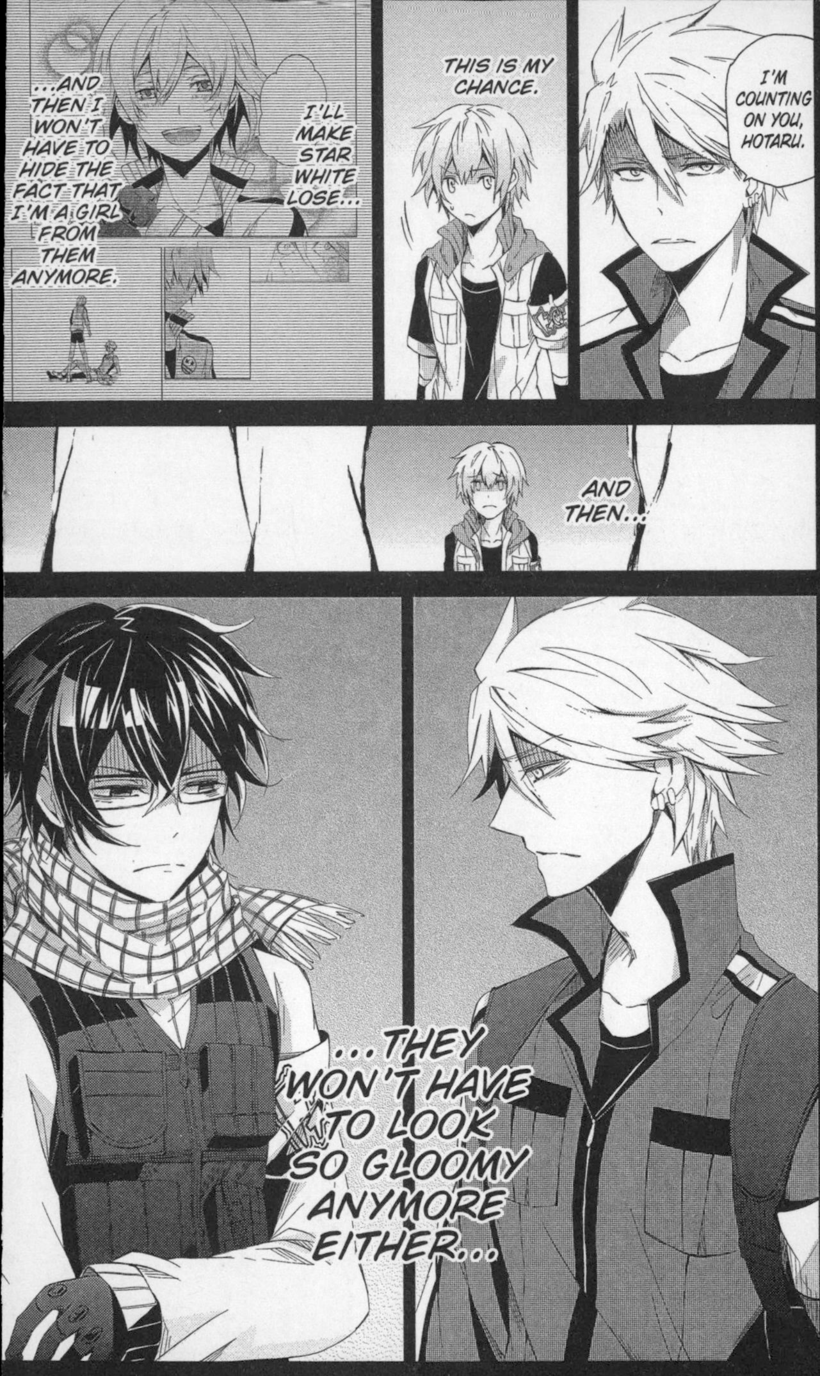
I'M COUNTING ON YOU, HOTARU.
THIS IS MY CHANCE.
I'LL MAKE STAR WHITE LOSE...
...AND THEN I WON'T HAVE TO HIDE THE FACT THAT I'M A GIRL FROM THEM ANYMORE.
AND THEN...
...THEY WON'T HAVE TO LOOK SO GLOOMY ANYMORE EITHER...

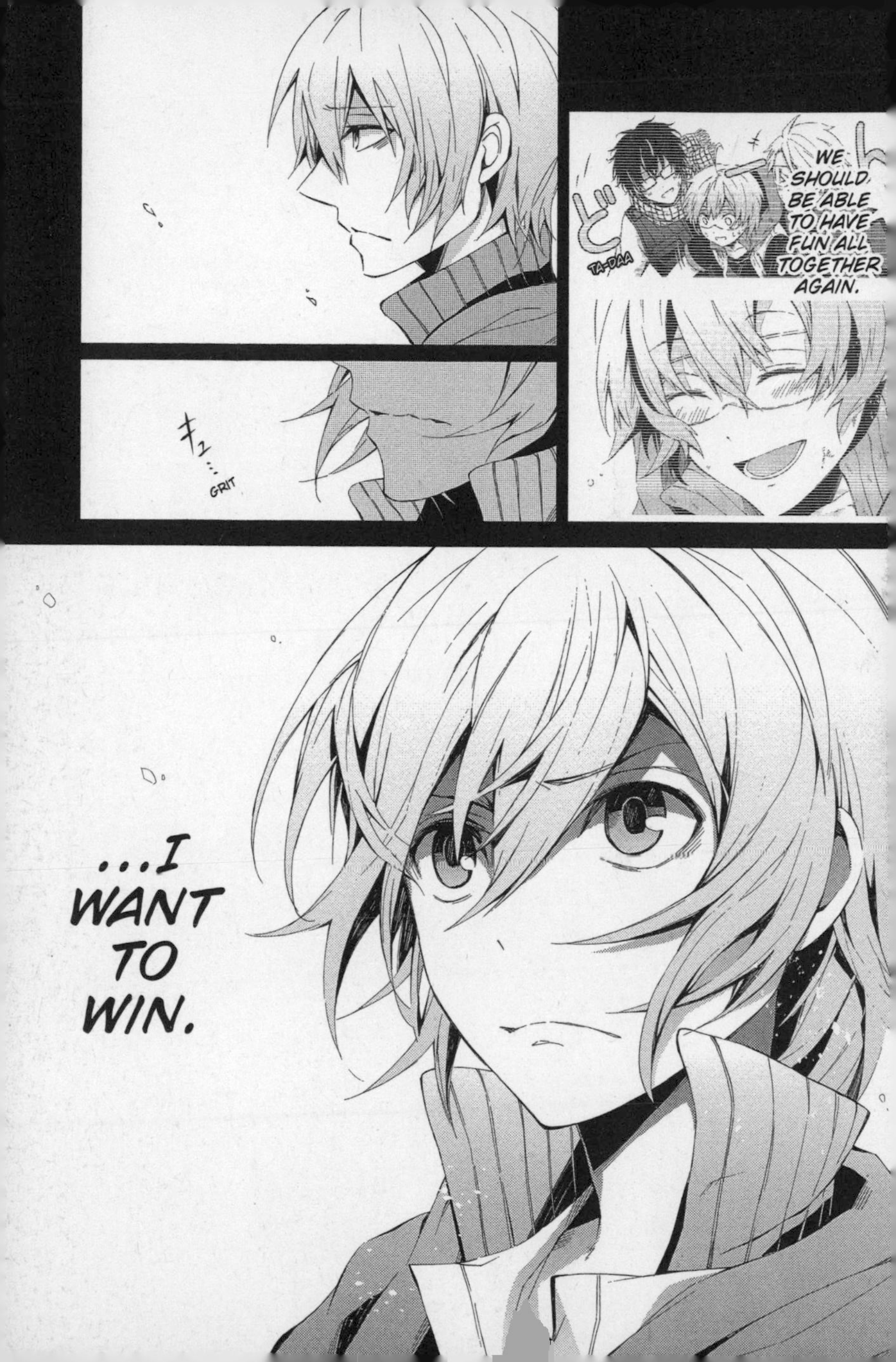

WE SHOULD BE ABLE TO HAVE FUN ALL TOGETHER AGAIN.
TA-DAA
GRIT
...I WANT TO WIN.

...FOR ME...
NOW TAKE UP YOUR GUN, TACHIBANA-KUN.
#10 WHAT'S RULING YOUR HEART RIGHT NOW

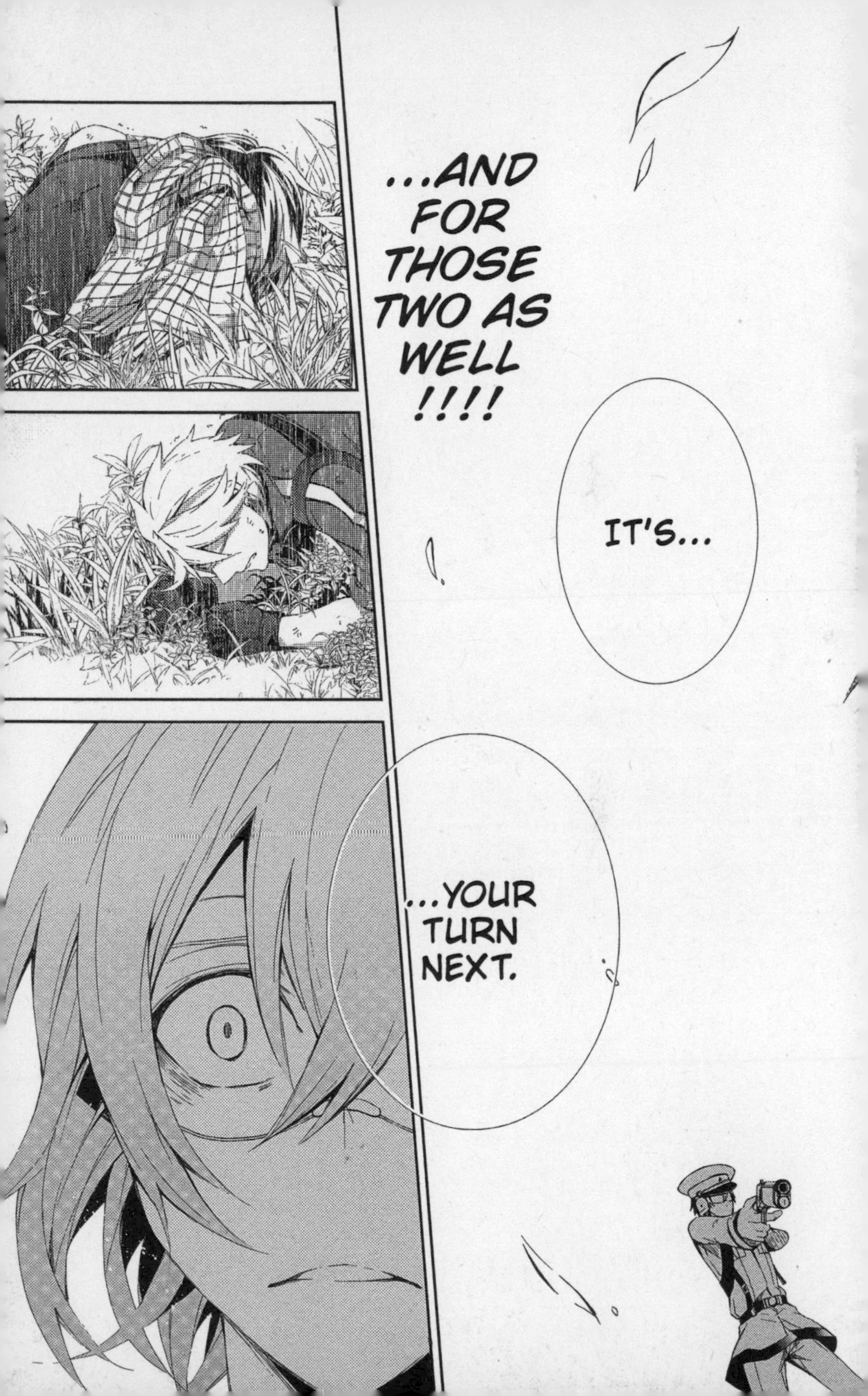
...AND FOR THOSE TWO AS WELL !!!!
IT'S...
...YOUR TURN NEXT.

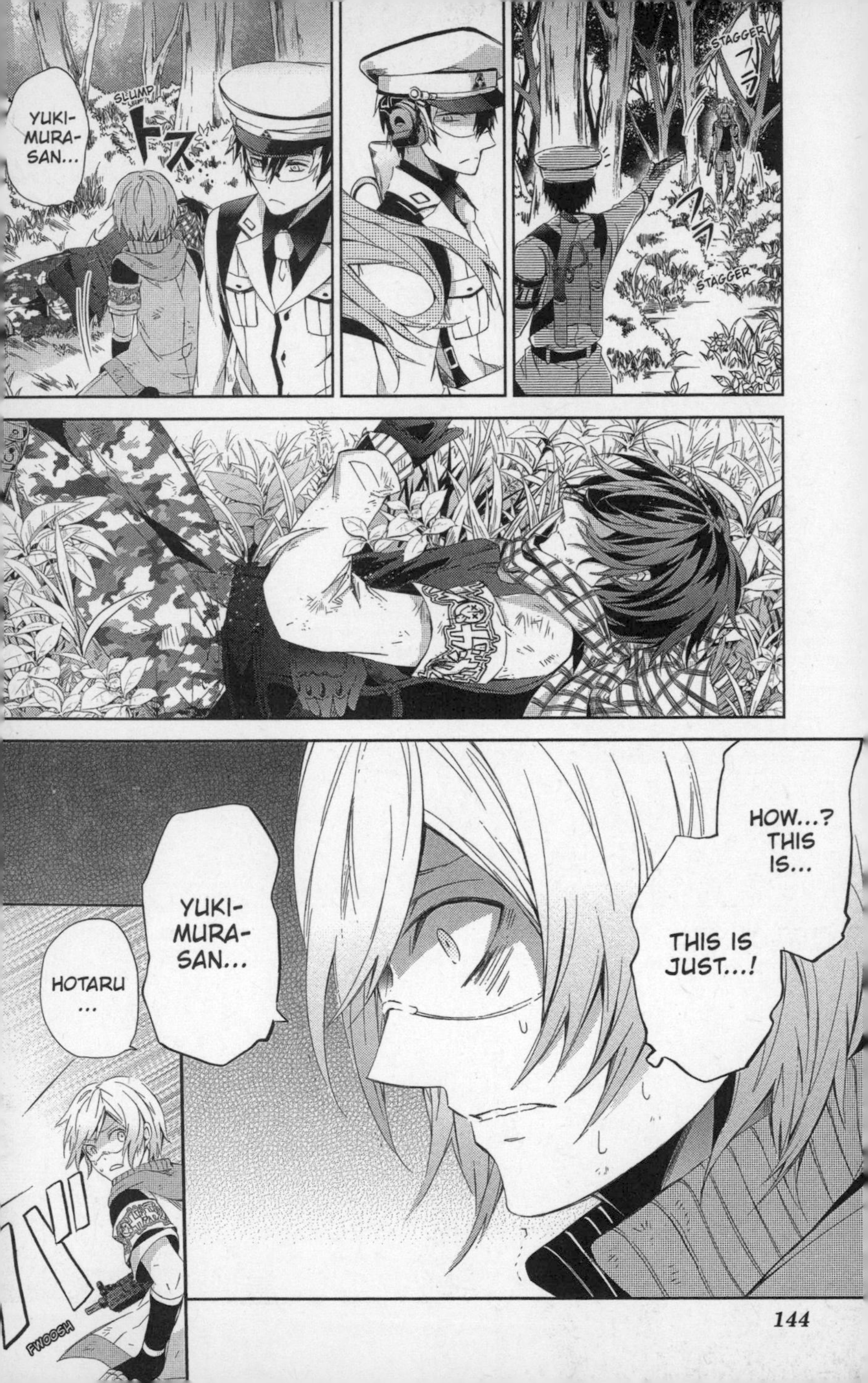
STAGGER
STAGGER
YUKI-MURA-SAN...
SLUMP
HOW...? THIS IS...
THIS IS JUST...!
YUKI-MURA-SAN...
HOTARU ...
FWOOSH

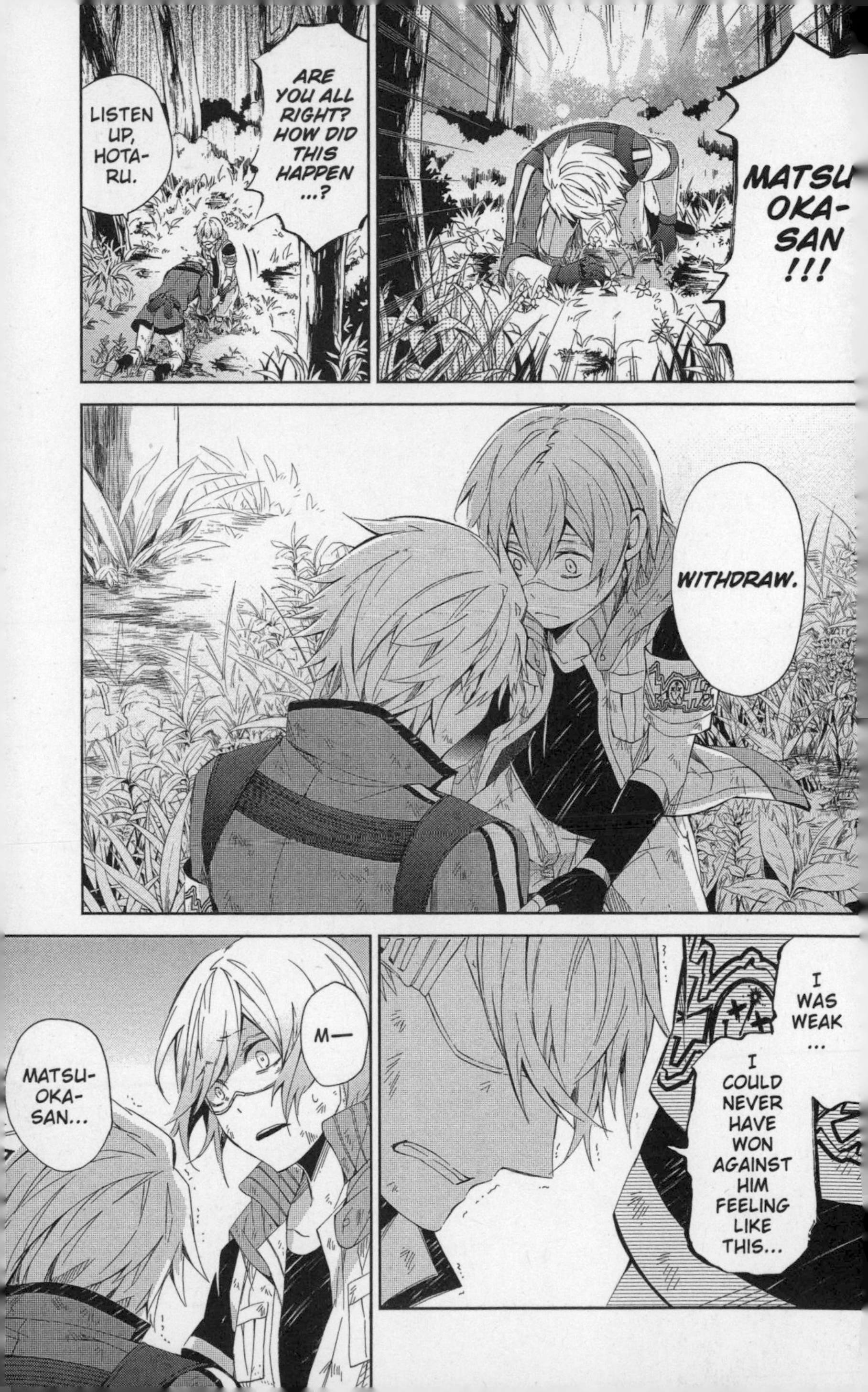
MATSU OKA-SAN !!!
ARE YOU ALL RIGHT? HOW DID THIS HAPPEN ...?
LISTEN UP, HOTA-RU.
WITHDRAW.
I WAS WEAK ...
I COULD NEVER HAVE WON AGAINST HIM FEELING LIKE THIS...
M—
MATSU-OKA-SAN...

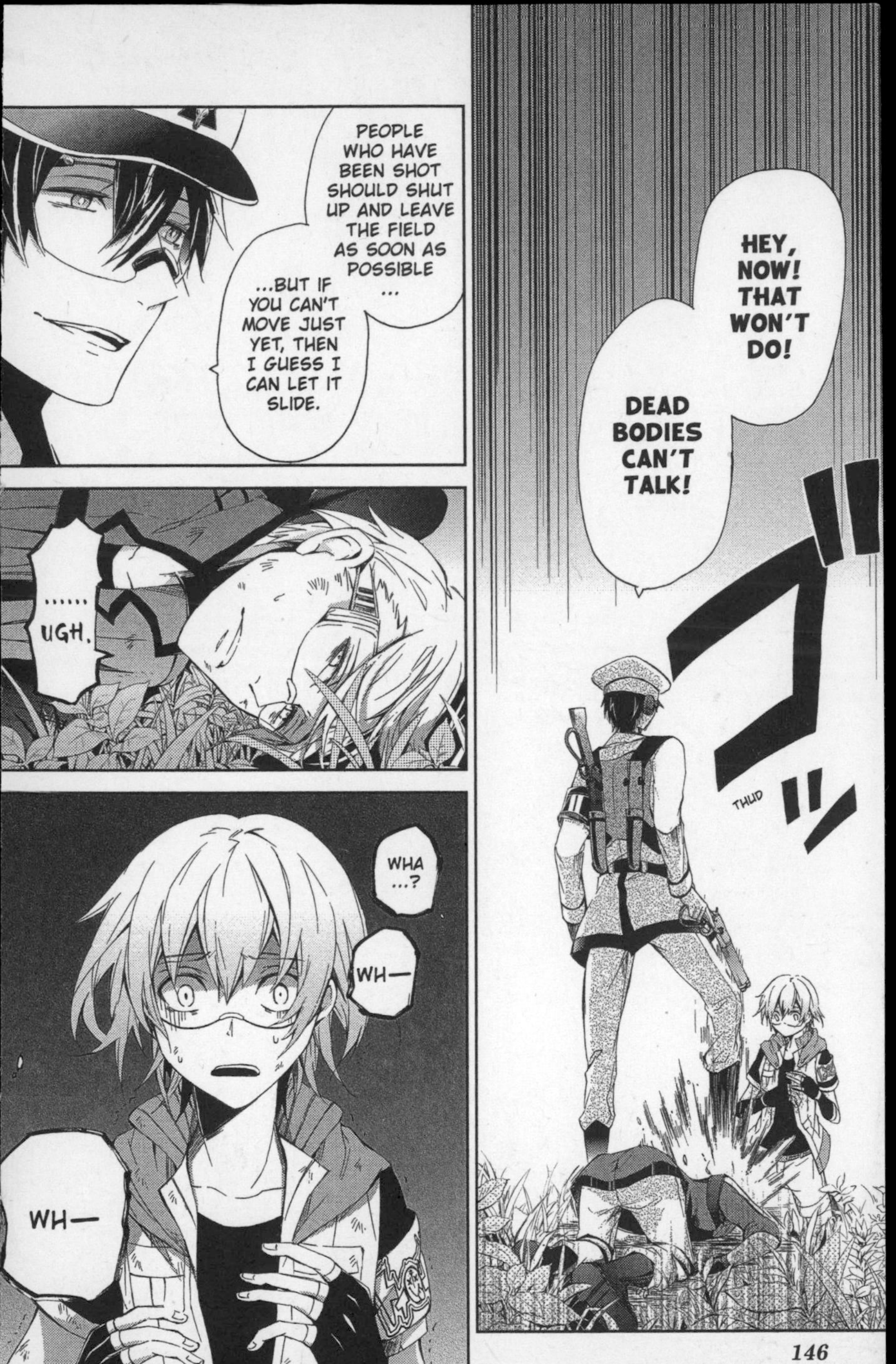
HEY, NOW! THAT WON'T DO!
DEAD BODIES CAN'T TALK!
THUD
PEOPLE WHO HAVE BEEN SHOT SHOULD SHUT UP AND LEAVE THE FIELD AS SOON AS POSSIBLE...
...BUT IF YOU CAN'T MOVE JUST YET, THEN I GUESS I CAN LET IT SLIDE.
...... UGH.
WHA...?
WH—
WH—

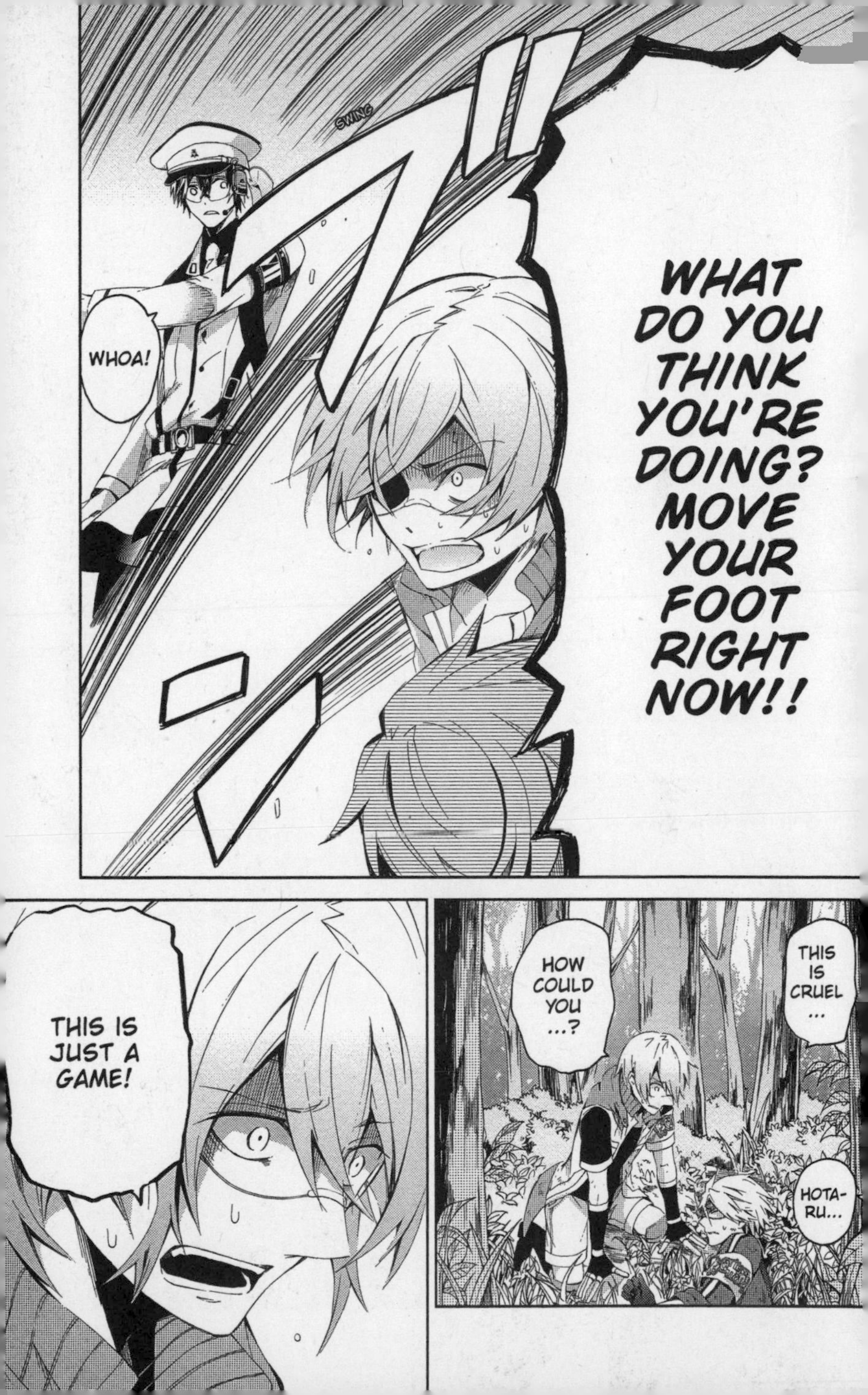
SWING
WHAT DO YOU THINK YOU'RE DOING? MOVE YOUR FOOT RIGHT NOW!!
WHOA!
THIS IS CRUEL...
HOW COULD YOU...?
HOTA-RU...
THIS IS JUST A GAME!

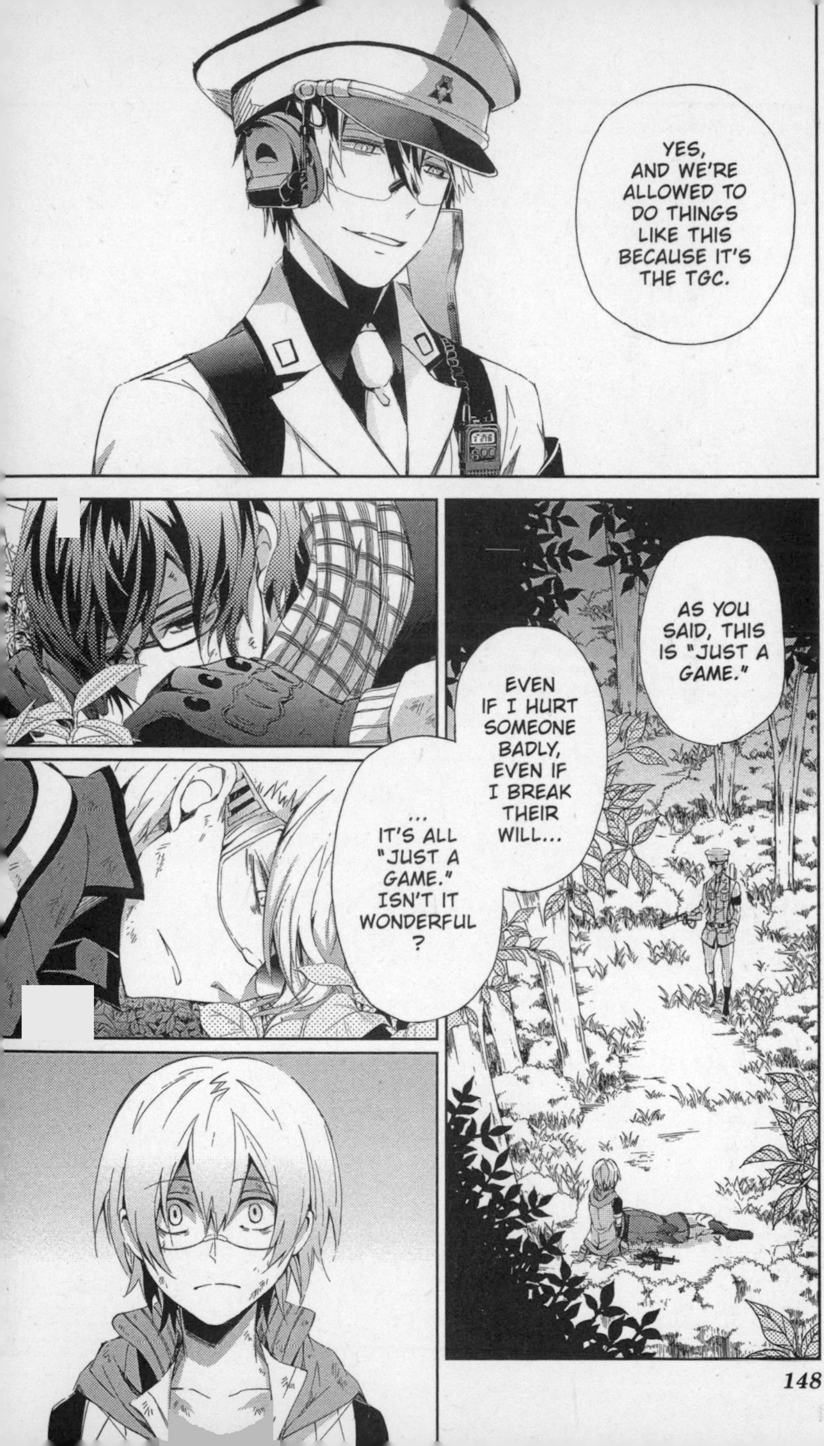
YES, AND WE'RE ALLOWED TO DO THINGS LIKE THIS BECAUSE IT'S THE TGC.
AS YOU SAID, THIS IS "JUST A GAME."
EVEN IF I HURT SOMEONE BADLY, EVEN IF I BREAK THEIR WILL...
... IT'S ALL "JUST A GAME." ISN'T IT WONDERFUL ?

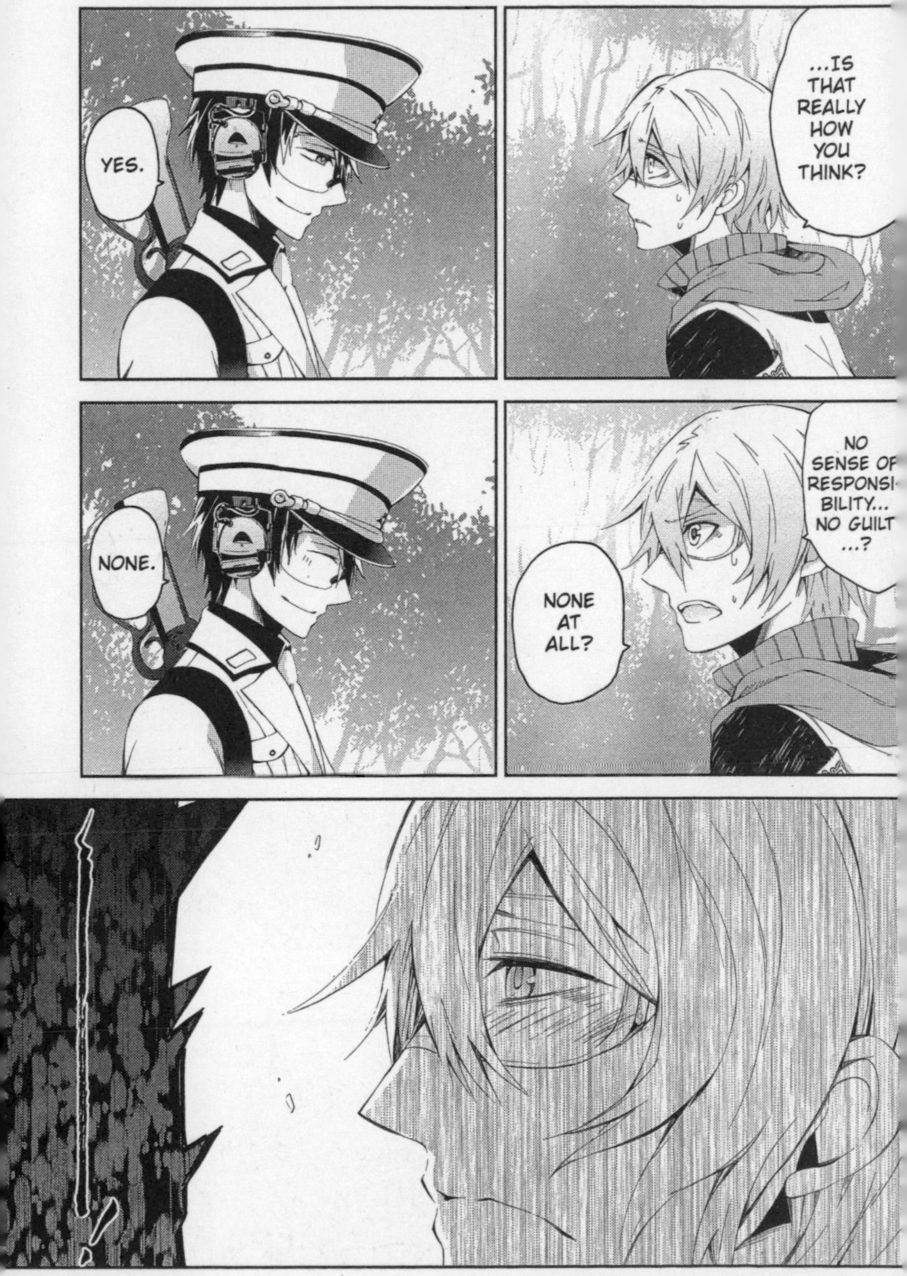
...IS THAT REALLY HOW YOU THINK?
YES.
NO SENSE OF RESPONSI-BILITY... NO GUILT ...?
NONE AT ALL?
NONE.

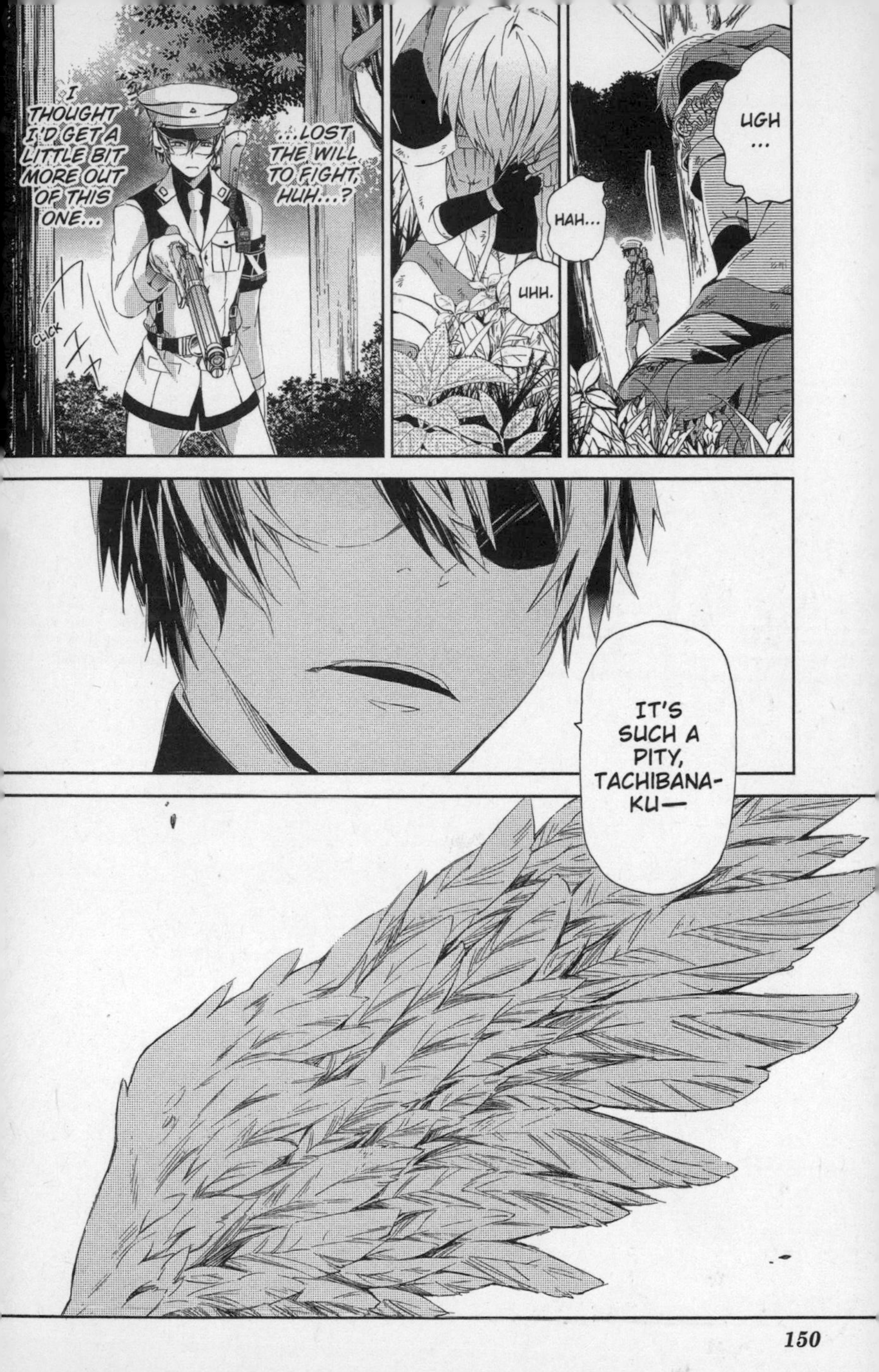
UGH ...
HAH...
UHH.
...LOST THE WILL TO FIGHT, HUH...?
I THOUGHT I'D GET A LITTLE BIT MORE OUT OF THIS ONE...
CLICK
IT'S SUCH A PITY, TACHIBANA-KU—

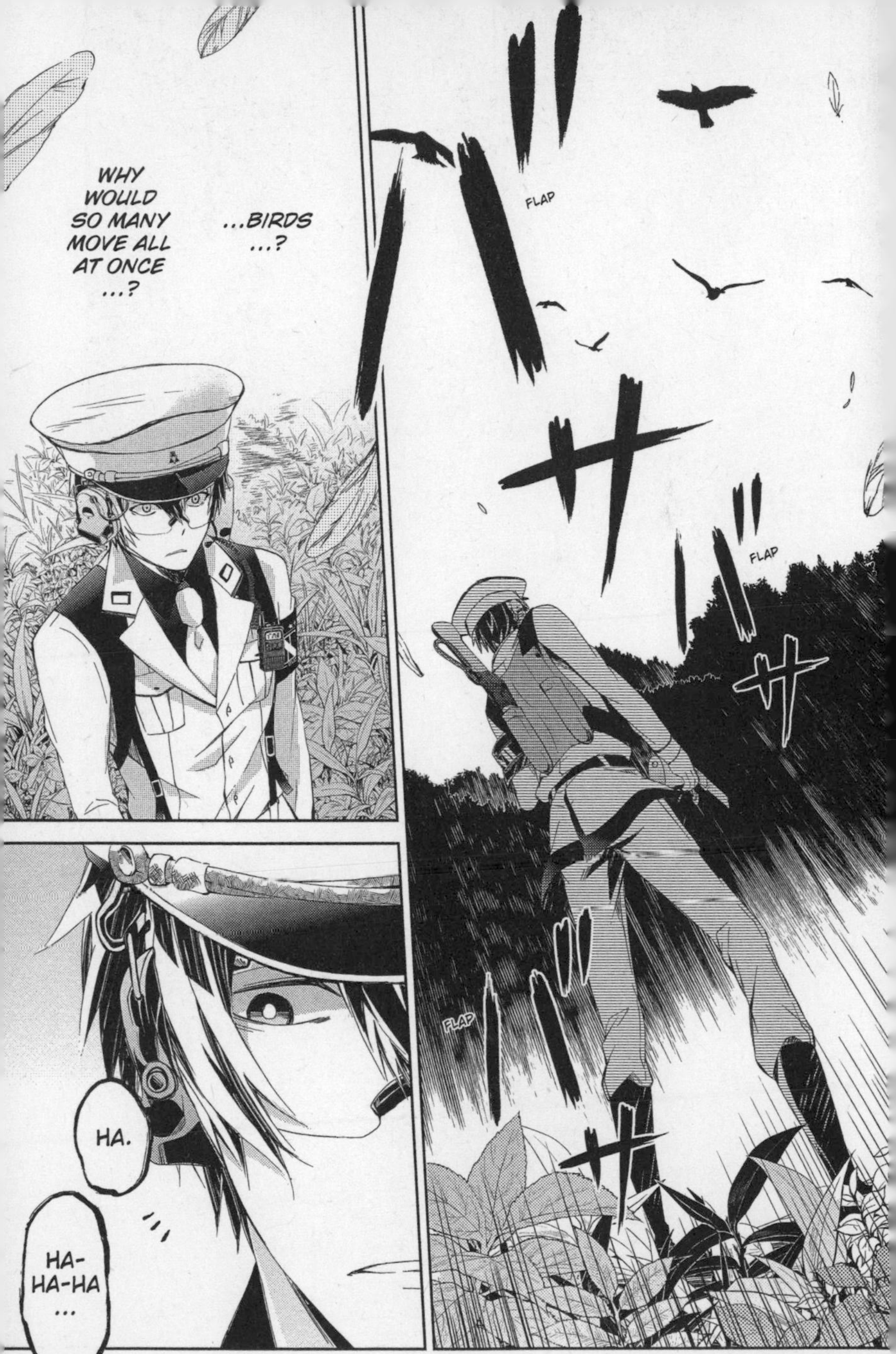
FLAP
FLAP
FLAP
...BIRDS ...?
WHY WOULD SO MANY MOVE ALL AT ONCE ...?
HA.
HA-HA-HA ...

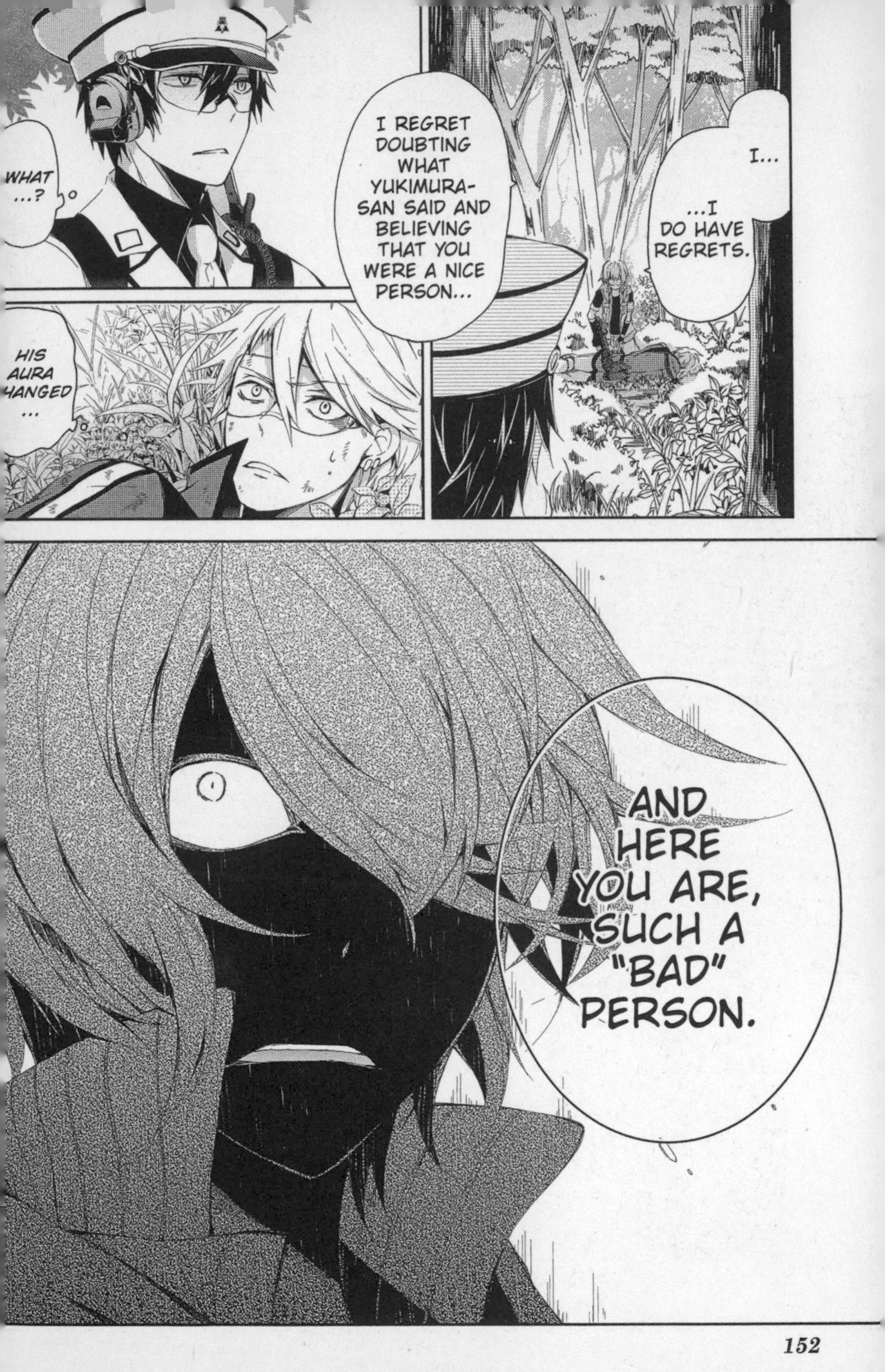
I...
...I DO HAVE REGRETS.
I REGRET DOUBTING WHAT YUKIMURA-SAN SAID AND BELIEVING THAT YOU WERE A NICE PERSON...
WHAT...?
HIS AURA HANGED...
AND HERE YOU ARE, SUCH A "BAD" PERSON.

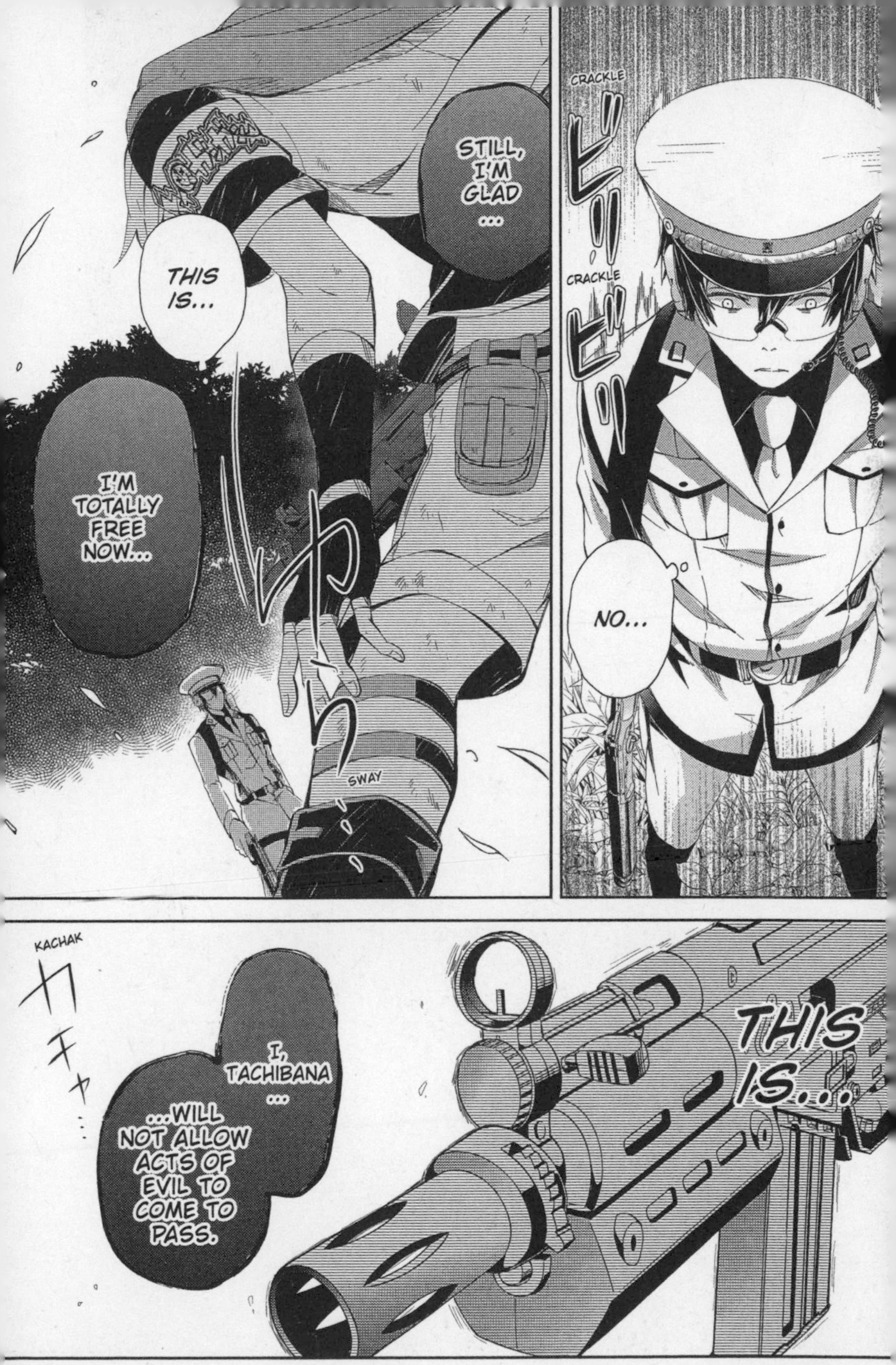
CRACKLE
CRACKLE
NO...
STILL, I'M GLAD...
THIS IS...
I'M TOTALLY FREE NOW...
SWAY
THIS IS...
I, TACHIBANA...
...WILL NOT ALLOW ACTS OF EVIL TO COME TO PASS.
KACHAK

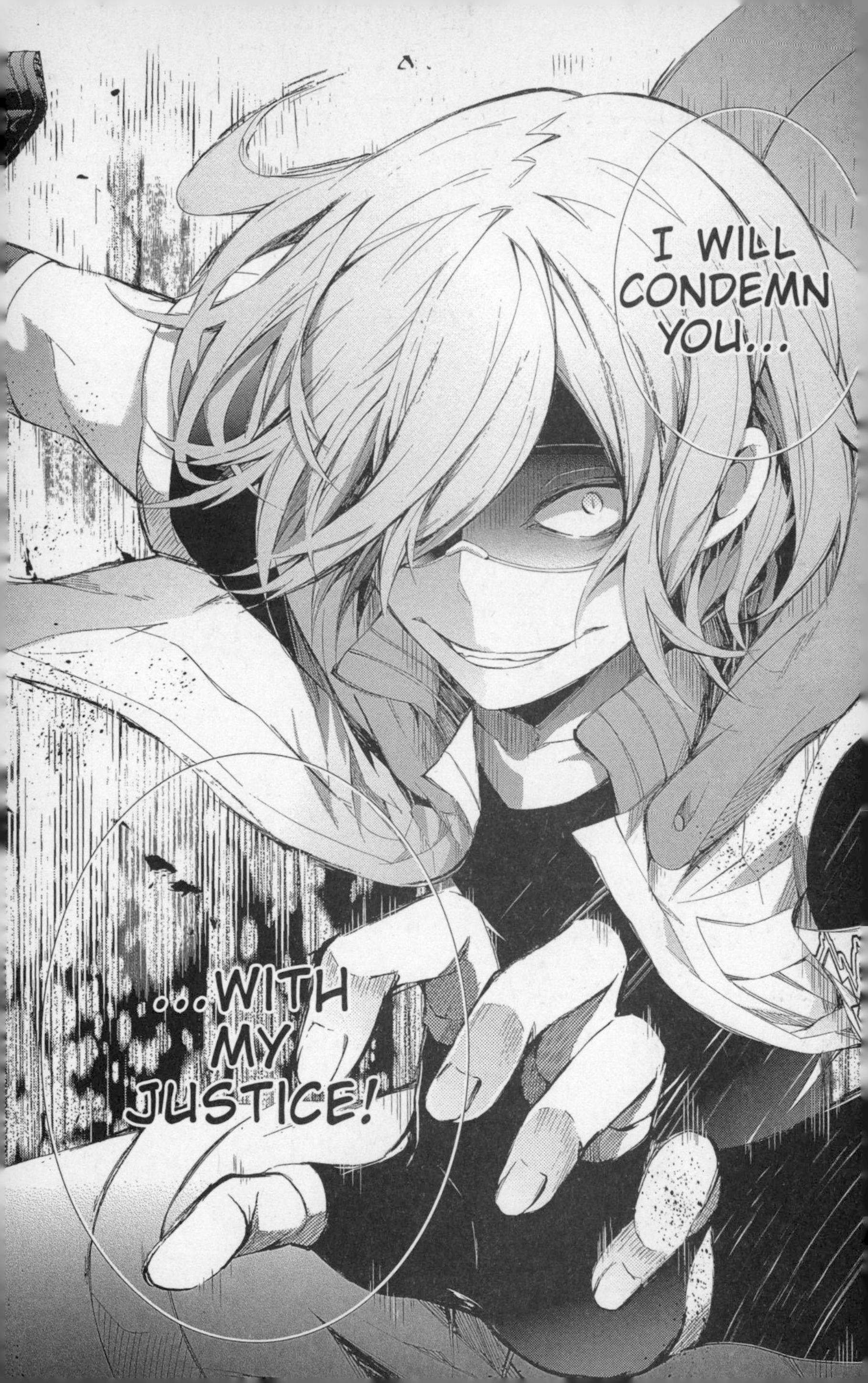
I WILL CONDEMN YOU...
...WITH MY JUSTICE!

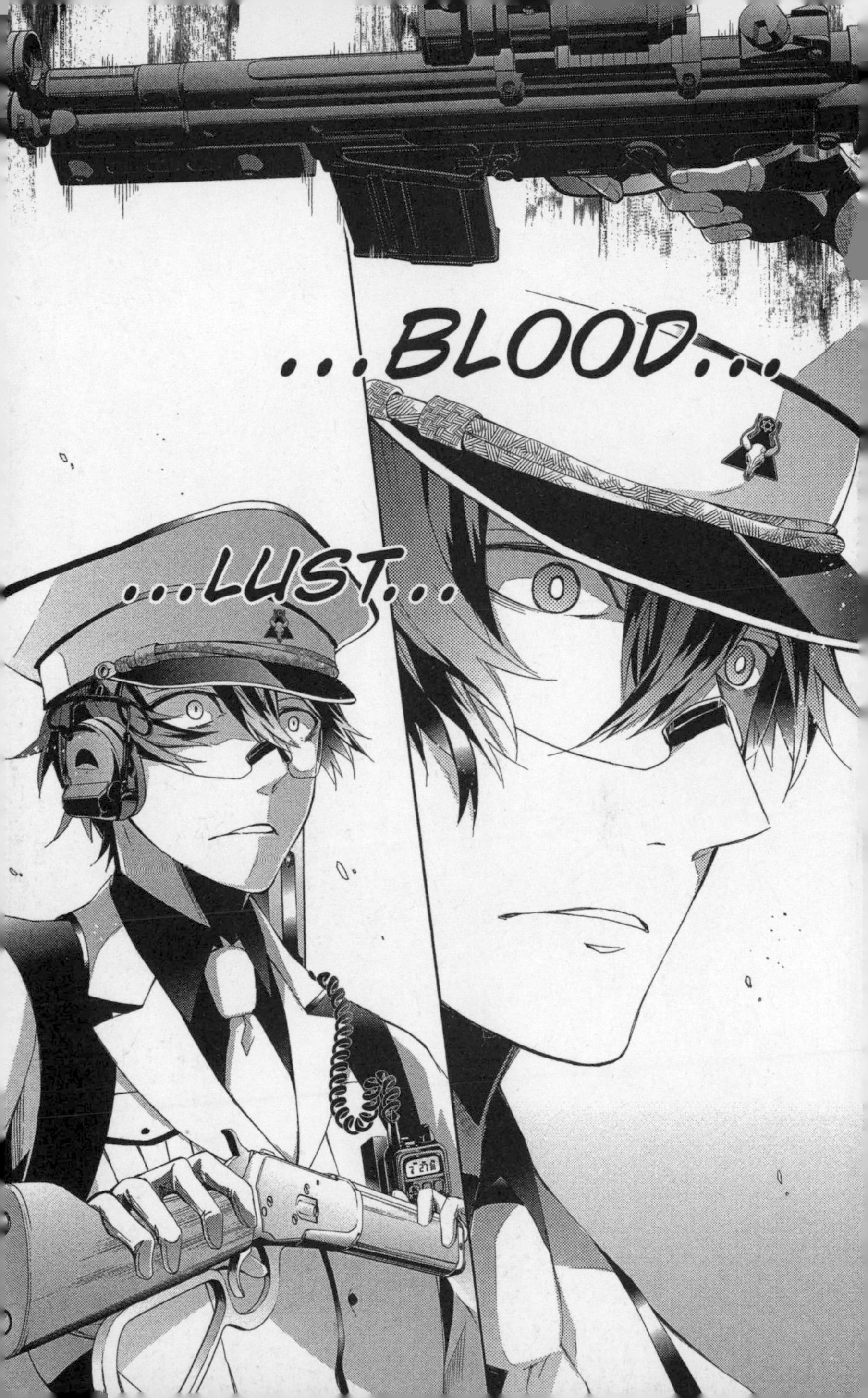
...BLOOD...
...LUST...

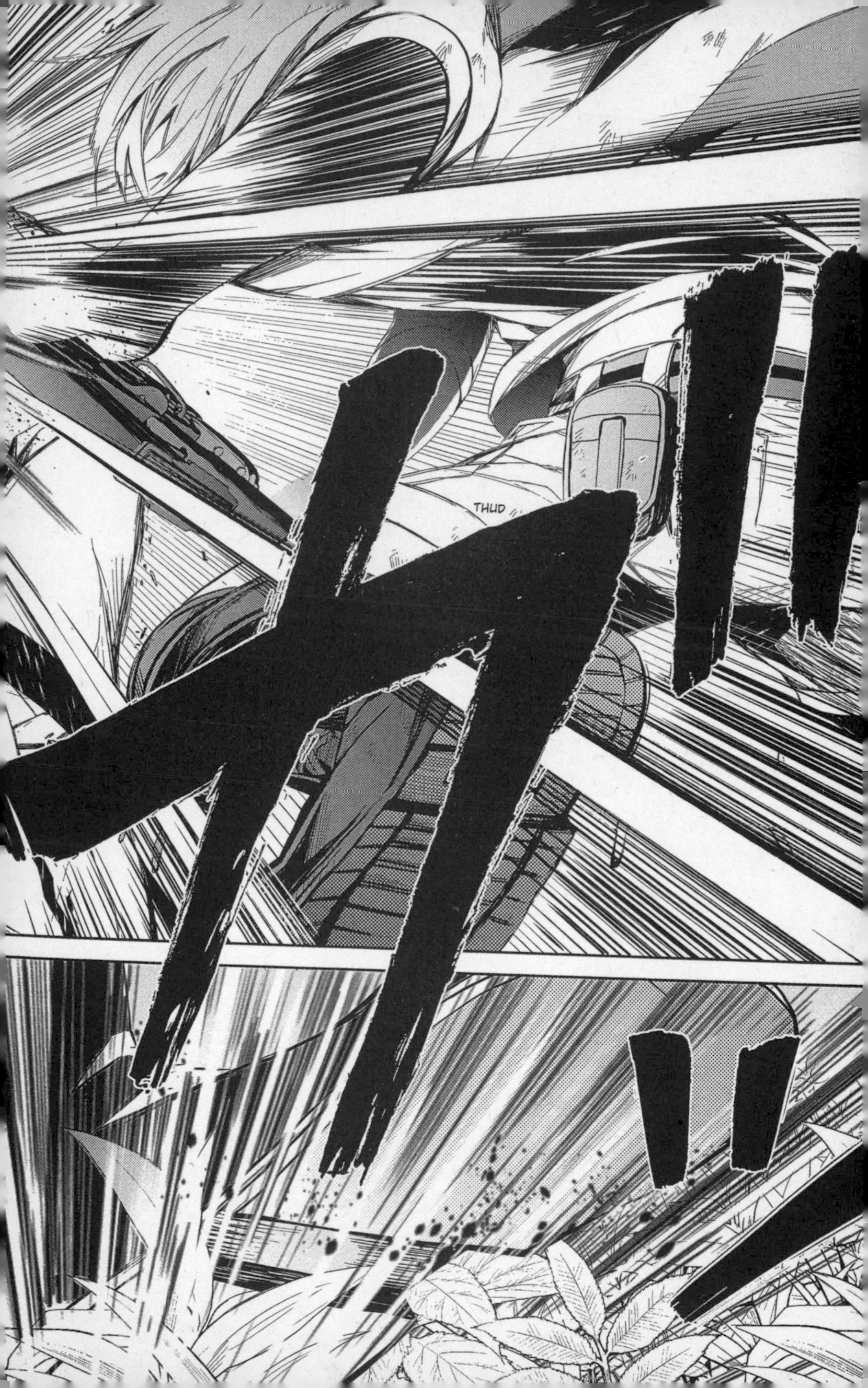
THUD

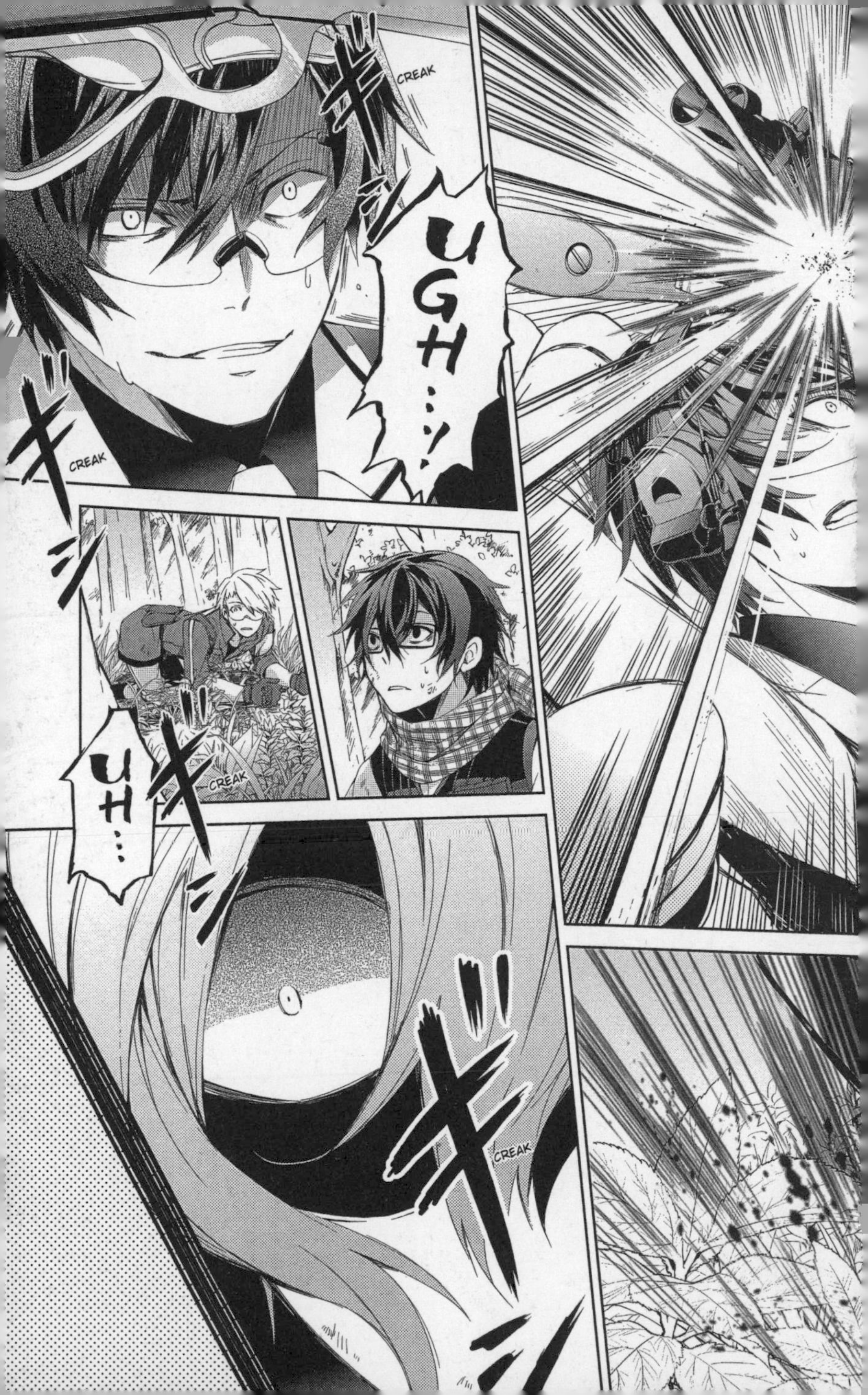
CREAK
UGH...!
CREAK
UH...
CREAK
CREAK

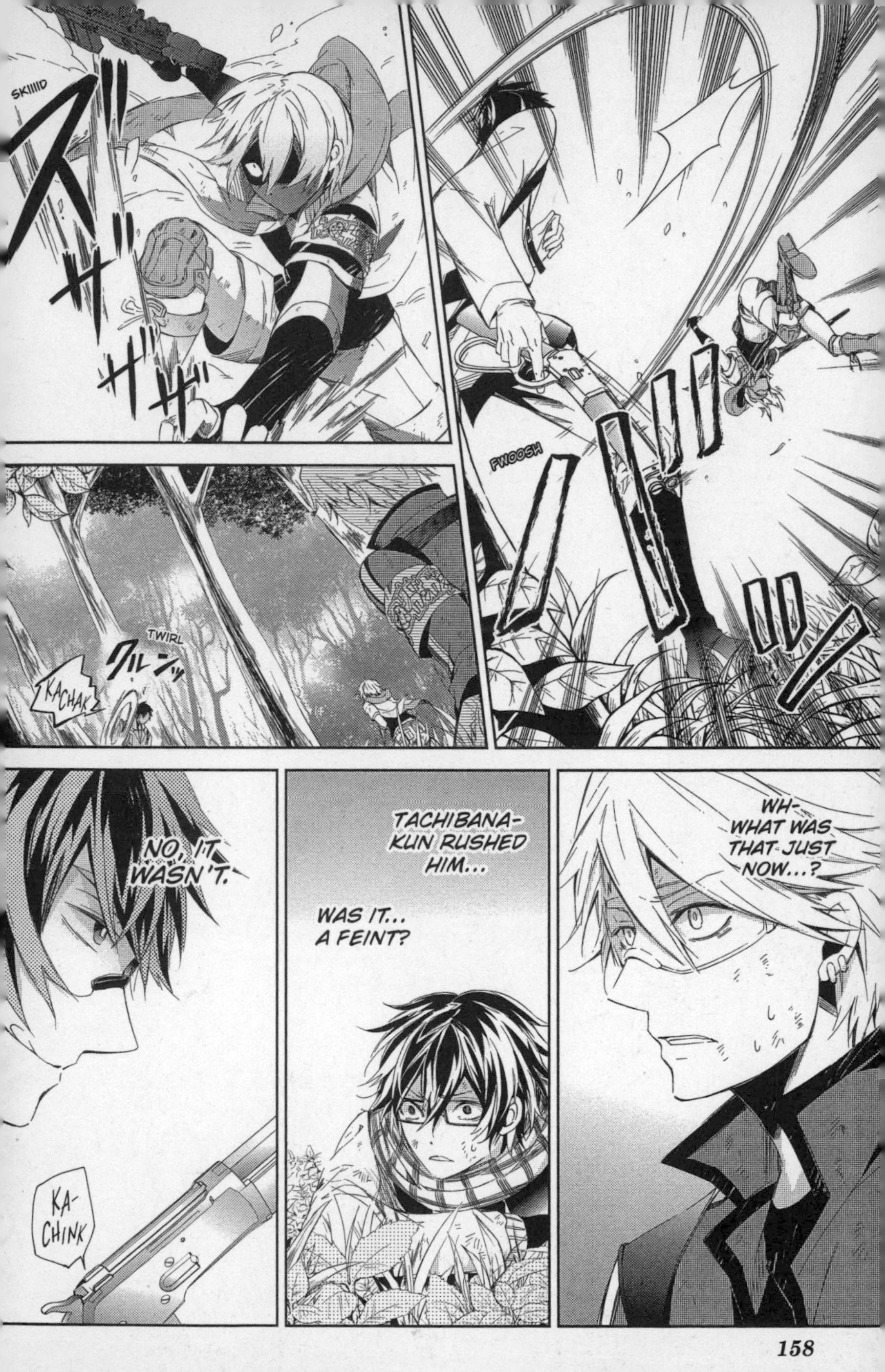

FWOOSH
SKIIIID
TWIRL
KACHAK
WH- WHAT WAS THAT JUST NOW...?
TACHIBANA-KUN RUSHED HIM...
WAS IT... A FEINT?
NO, IT WASN'T.
KA-CHINK

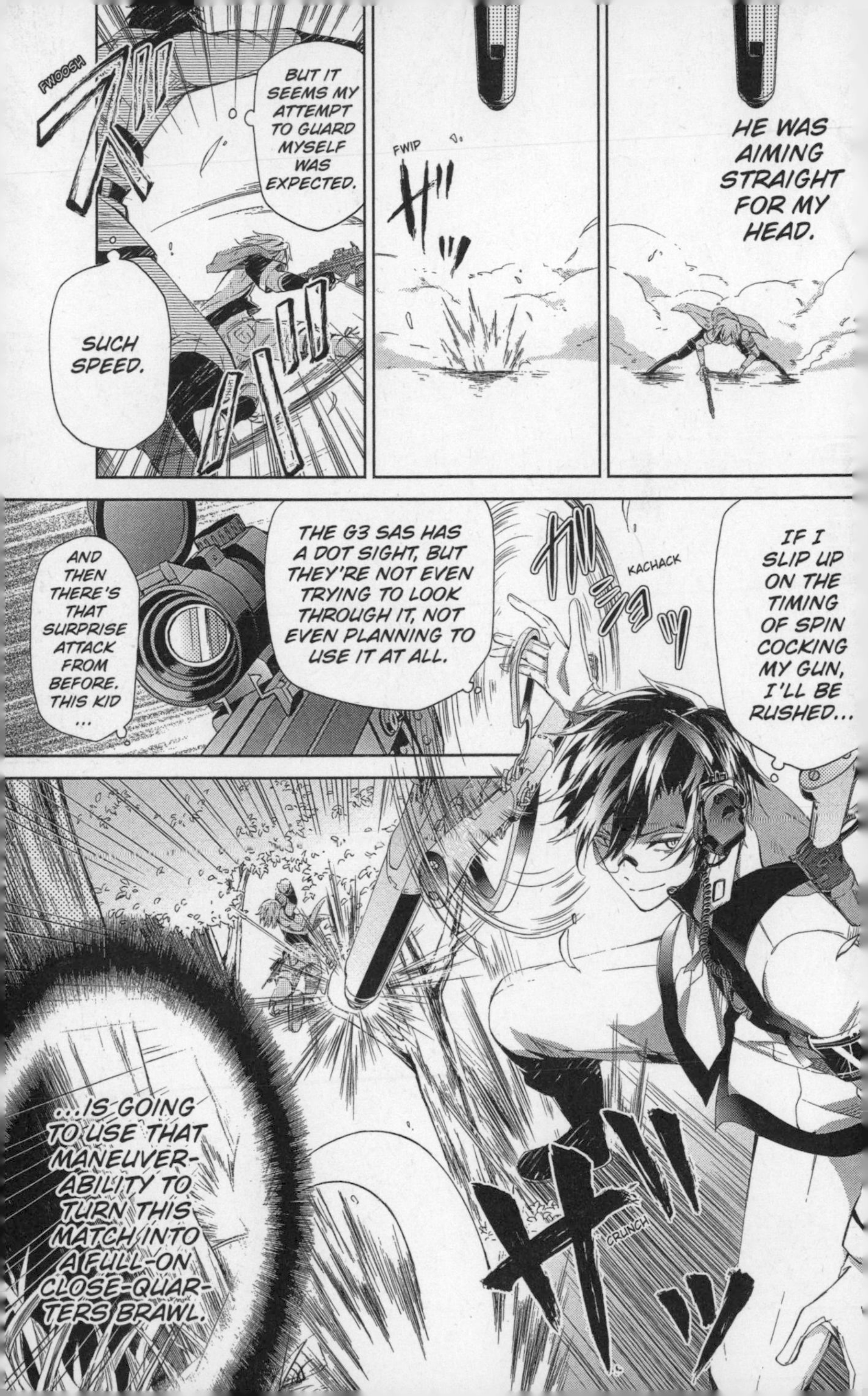
HE WAS AIMING STRAIGHT FOR MY HEAD.
FWIP
FWOOSH
BUT IT SEEMS MY ATTEMPT TO GUARD MYSELF WAS EXPECTED.
SUCH SPEED.
IF I SLIP UP ON THE TIMING OF SPIN COCKING MY GUN, I'LL BE RUSHED...
KACHACK
THE G3 SAS HAS A DOT SIGHT, BUT THEY'RE NOT EVEN TRYING TO LOOK THROUGH IT, NOT EVEN PLANNING TO USE IT AT ALL.
AND THEN THERE'S THAT SURPRISE ATTACK FROM BEFORE. THIS KID ...
...IS GOING TO USE THAT MANEUVER-ABILITY TO TURN THIS MATCH INTO A FULL-ON CLOSE-QUAR-TERS BRAWL.
CRUNCH

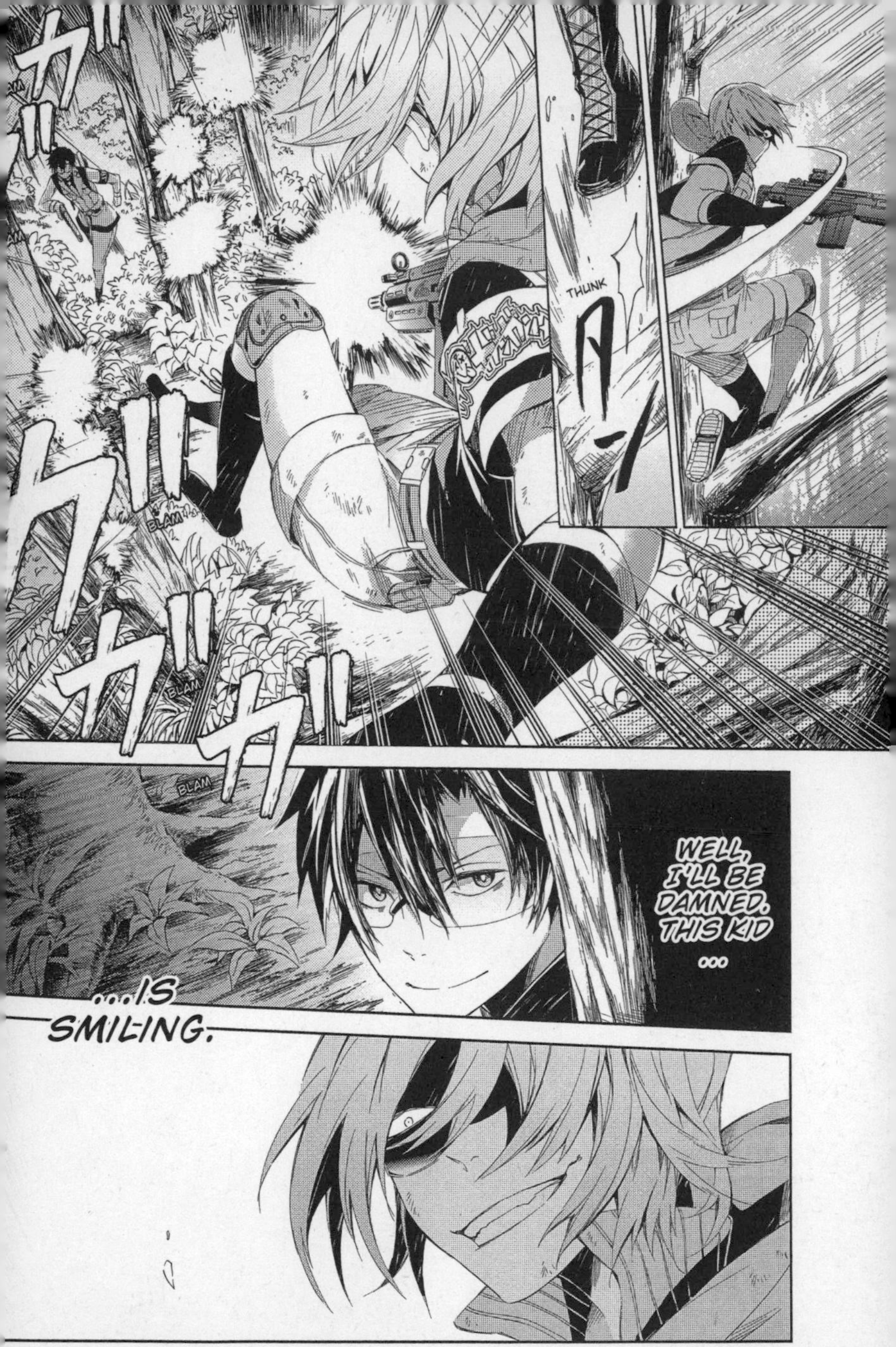
THUNK
BLAM
BLAM
BLAM
BLAM
WELL, I'LL BE DAMNED. THIS KID ...
...IS SMILING.

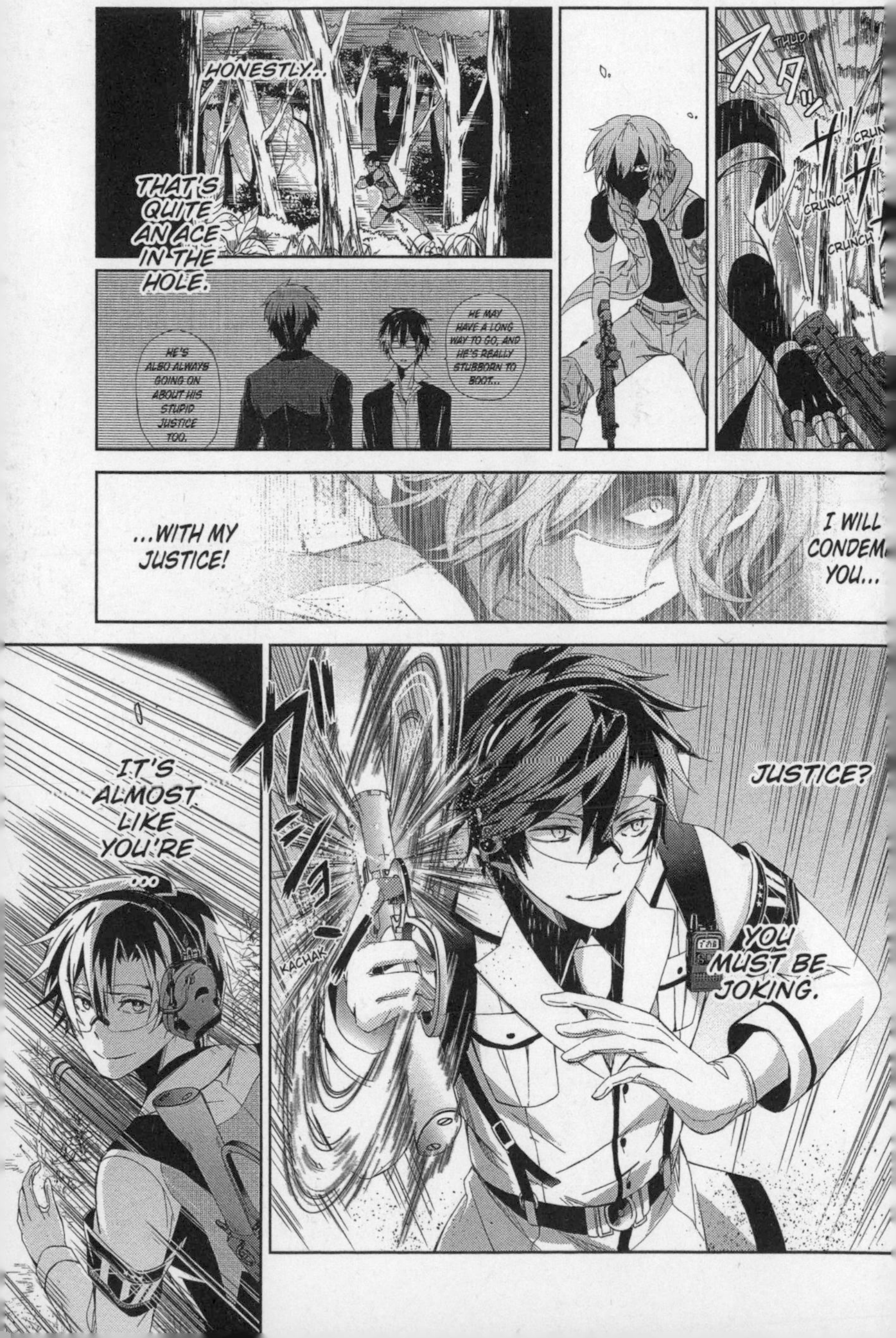
THUD
CRUNCH
CRUNCH
CRUNCH
HONESTLY...
HE MAY HAVE A LONG WAY TO GO, AND HE'S REALLY STUBBORN TO BOOT...
HE'S ALSO ALWAYS GOING ON ABOUT HIS STUPID JUSTICE TOO.
THAT'S QUITE AN ACE IN THE HOLE.
I WILL CONDEM YOU...
...WITH MY JUSTICE!
JUSTICE?
KACHAK
YOU MUST BE JOKING.
IT'S ALMOST LIKE YOU'RE ...

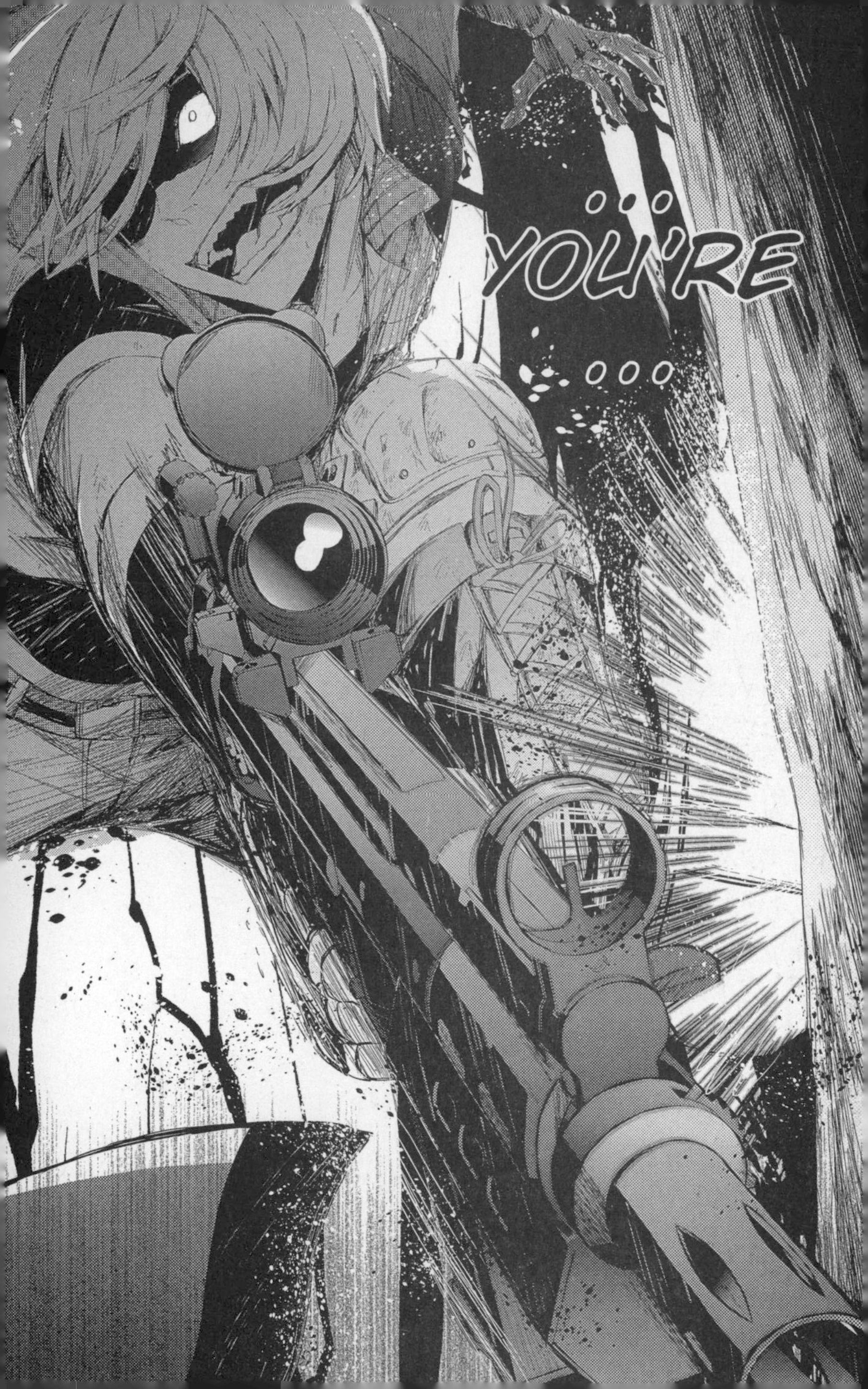
...YOU'RE
...

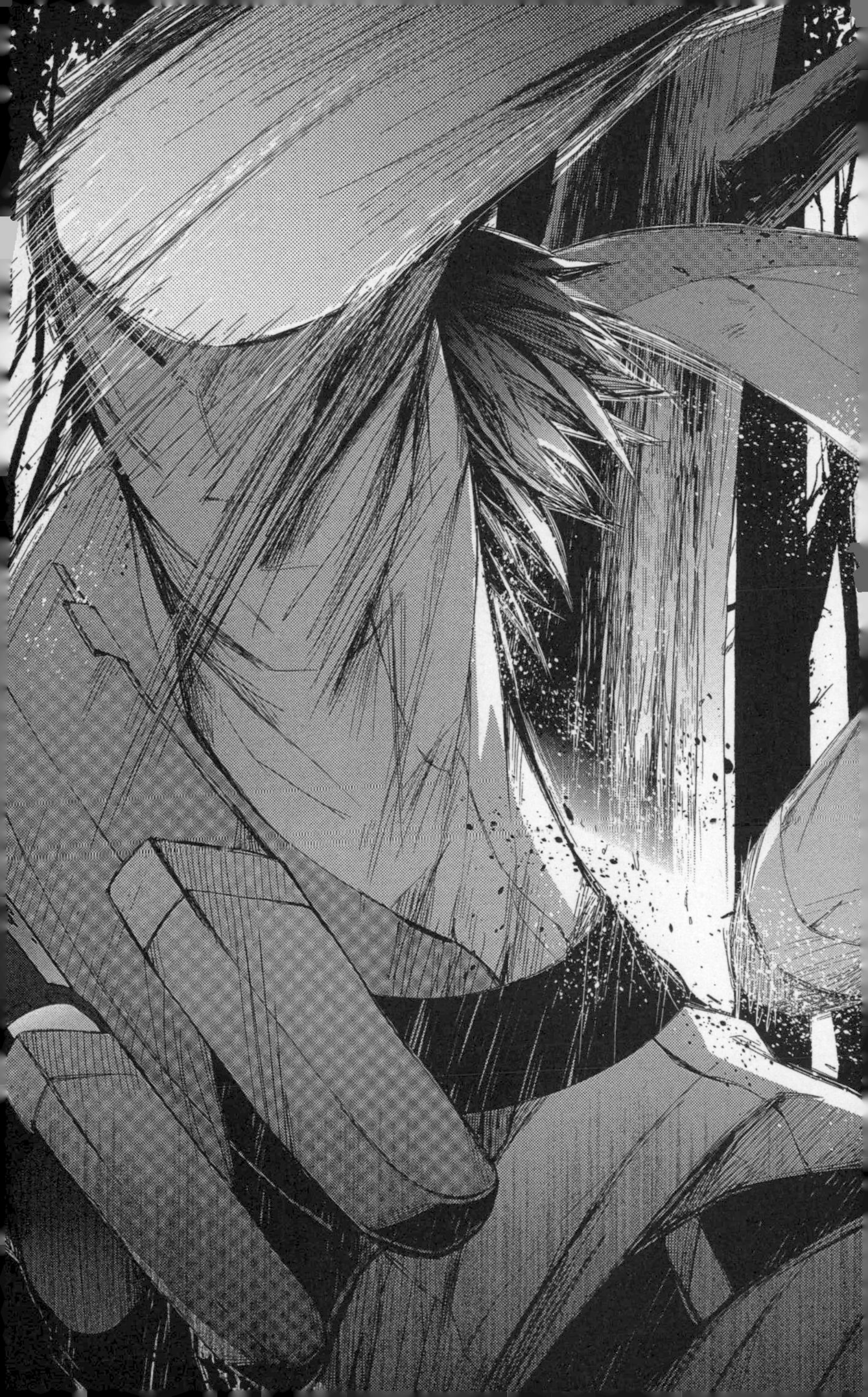

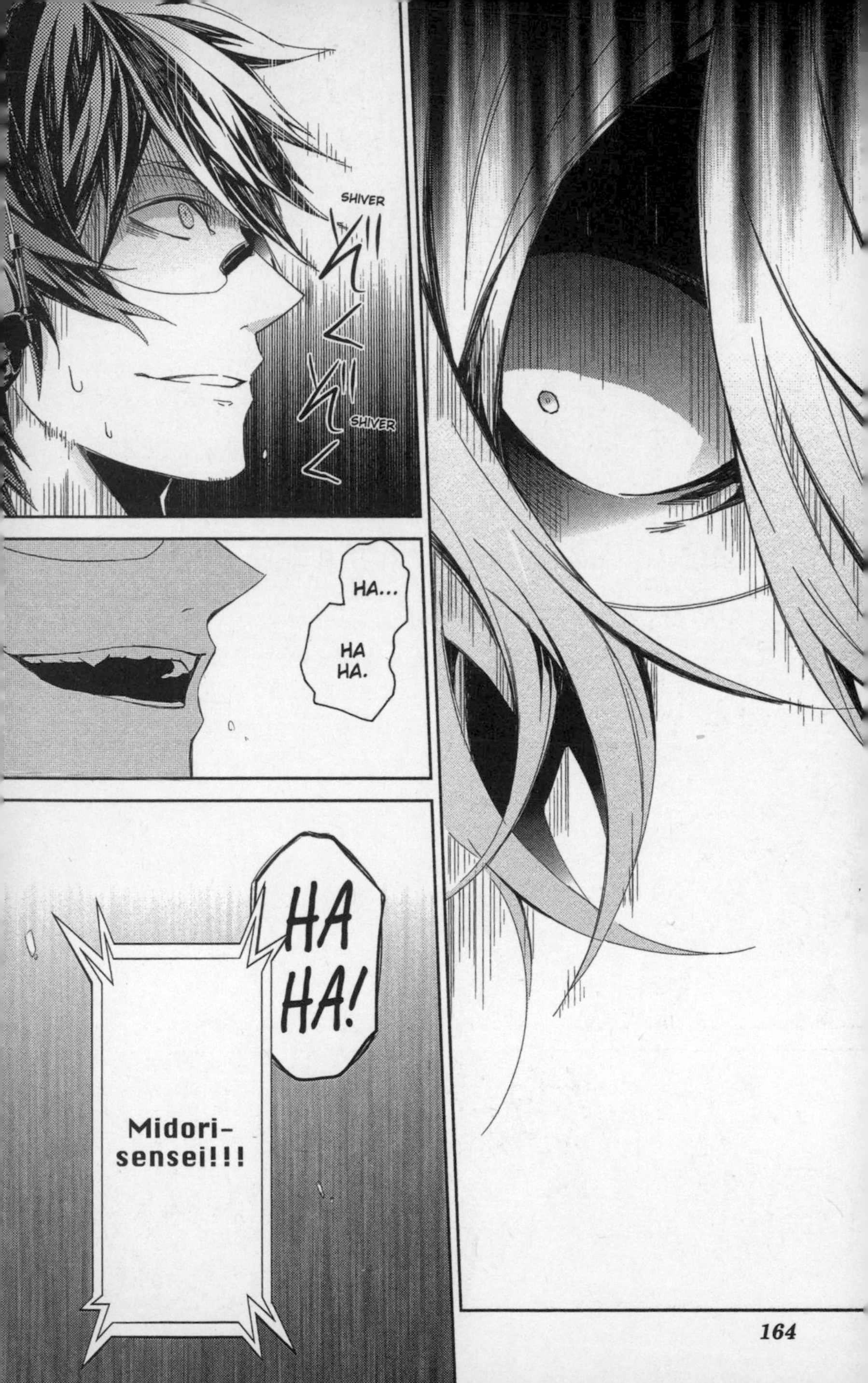
SHIVER
SHIVER
HA...
HA HA.
HA HA!
Midori-sensei!!!

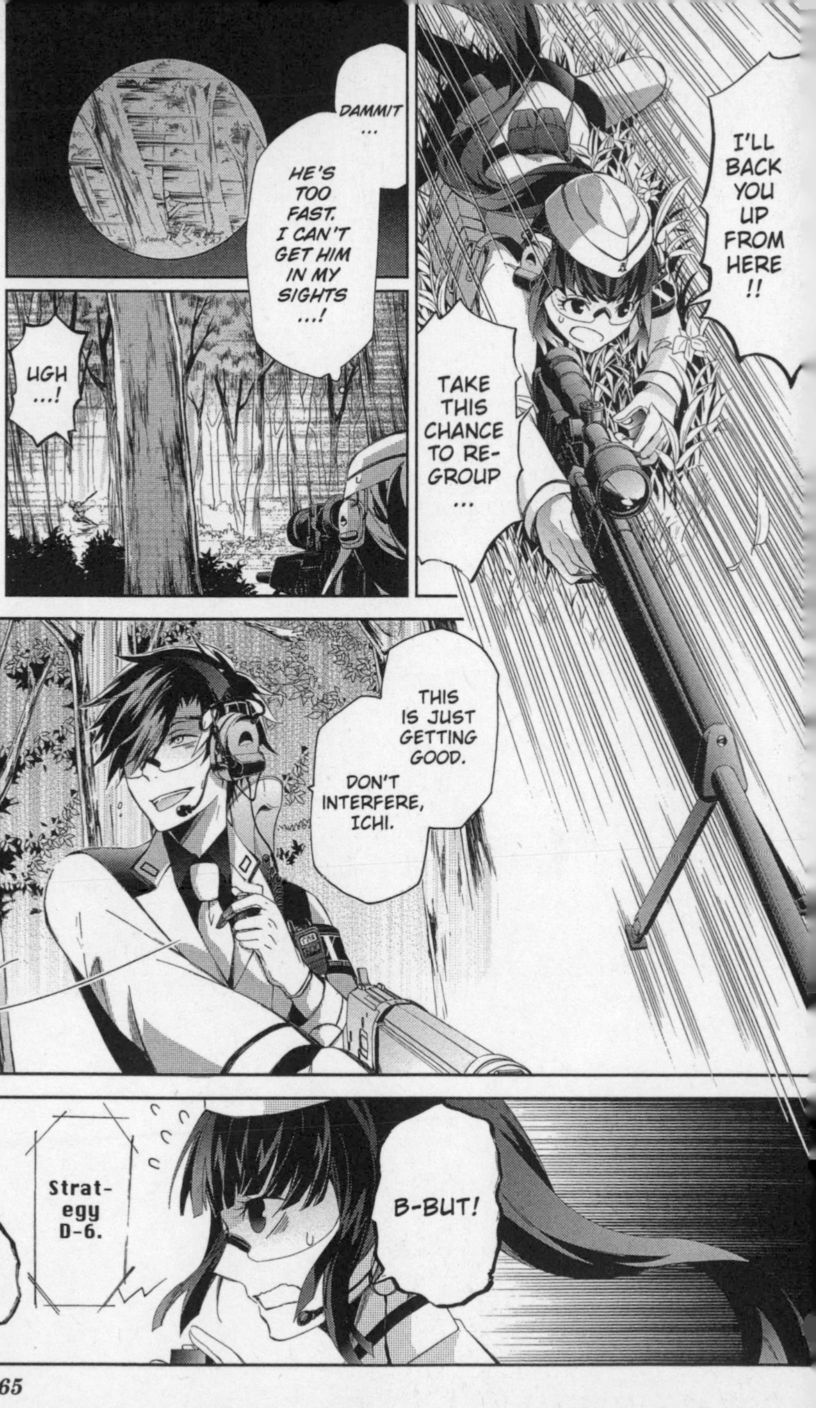
I'LL BACK YOU UP FROM HERE!!
TAKE THIS CHANCE TO RE-GROUP...
DAMMIT...
HE'S TOO FAST. I CAN'T GET HIM IN MY SIGHTS...!
UGH...!
THIS IS JUST GETTING GOOD.
DON'T INTERFERE, ICHI.
B-BUT!
Strat-egy D-6.
WHA—?

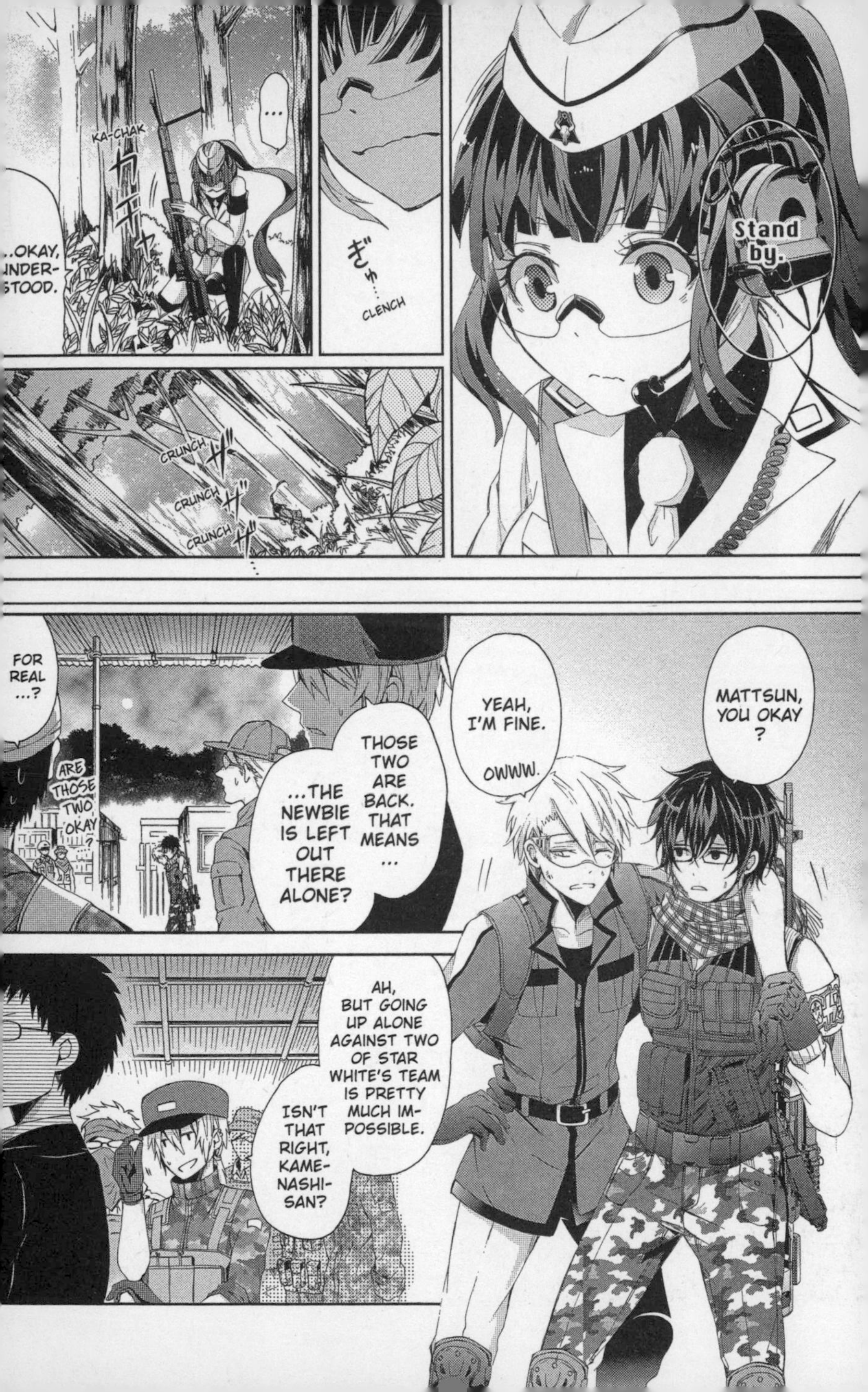
Stand by.
…
ぎゅ…
CLENCH
…OKAY, UNDER-STOOD.
KA-CHAK
CRUNCH
CRUNCH
CRUNCH
MATTSUN, YOU OKAY?
YEAH, I'M FINE.
OWWW.
THOSE TWO ARE BACK. THAT MEANS…
…THE NEWBIE IS LEFT OUT THERE ALONE?
ARE THOSE TWO OKAY…?
FOR REAL…?
AH, BUT GOING UP ALONE AGAINST TWO OF STAR WHITE'S TEAM IS PRETTY MUCH IM-POSSIBLE.
ISN'T THAT RIGHT, KAME-NASHI-SAN?

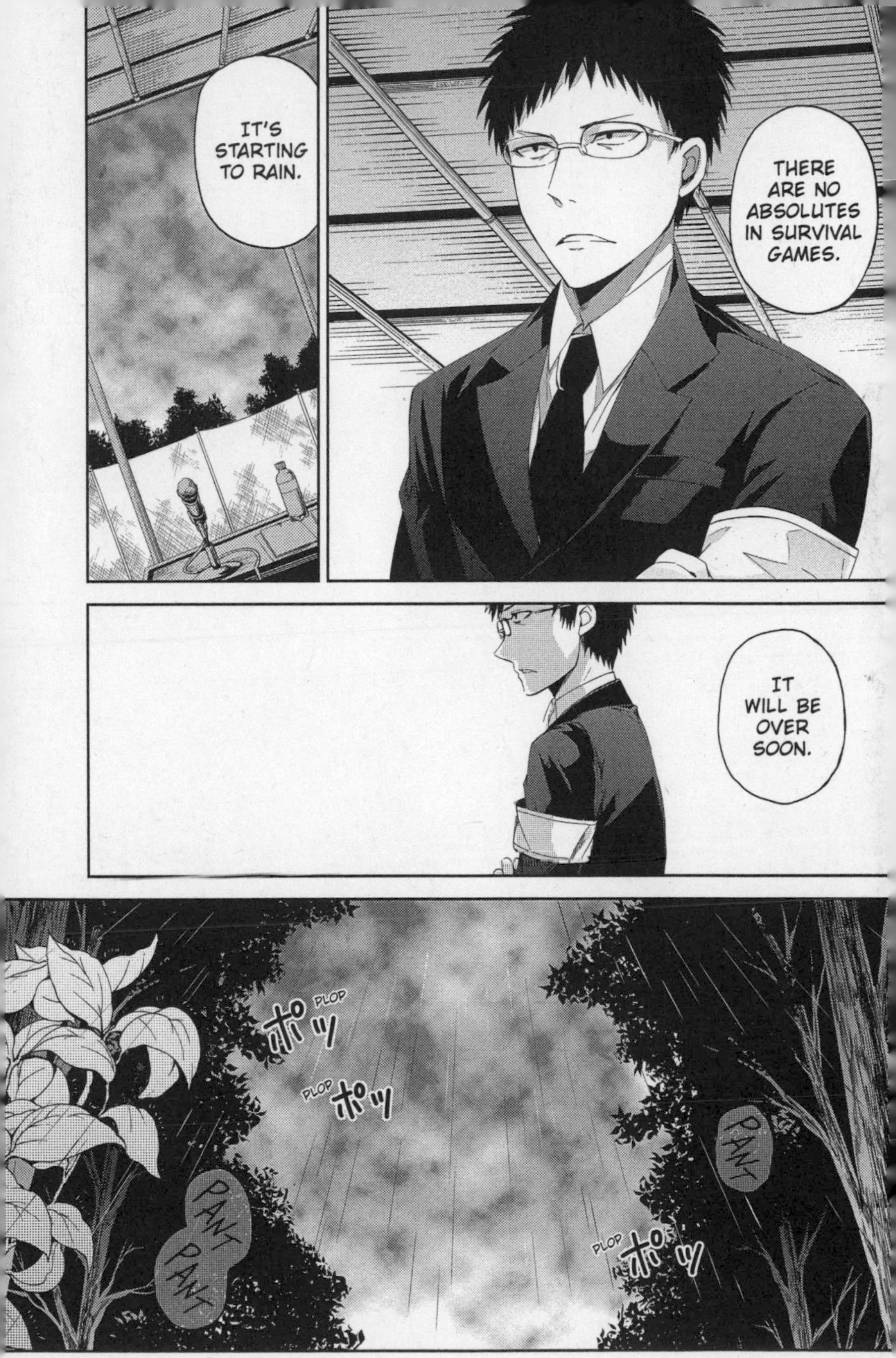
THERE ARE NO ABSOLUTES IN SURVIVAL GAMES.
IT'S STARTING TO RAIN.
IT WILL BE OVER SOON.
PANT
ポッ PLOP
ポッ PLOP
ポッ PLOP
PANT PANT

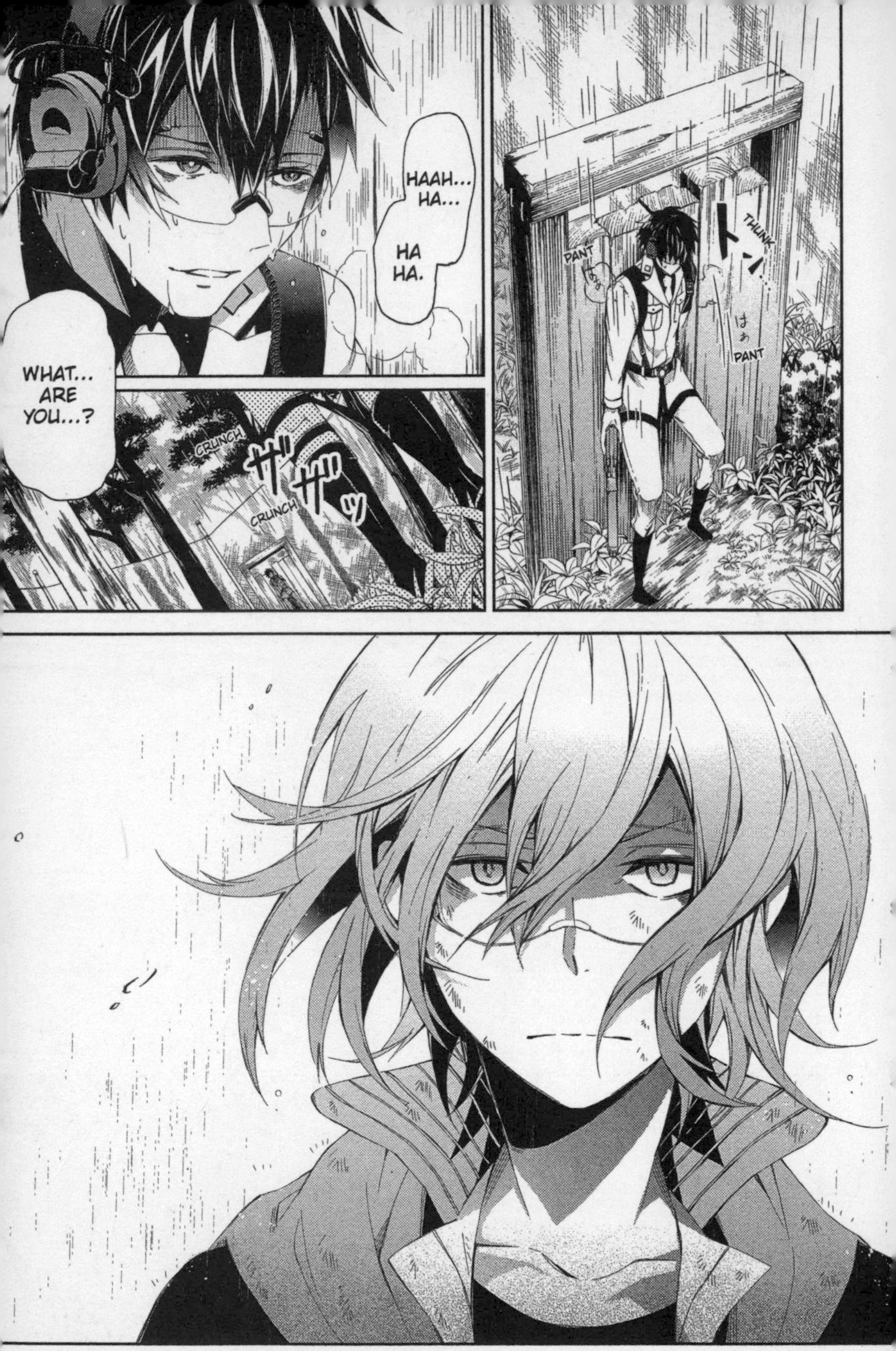
THUNK
PANT
PANT
HAAH... HA...
HA HA.
WHAT... ARE YOU...?
CRUNCH
ザザッ
CRUNCH

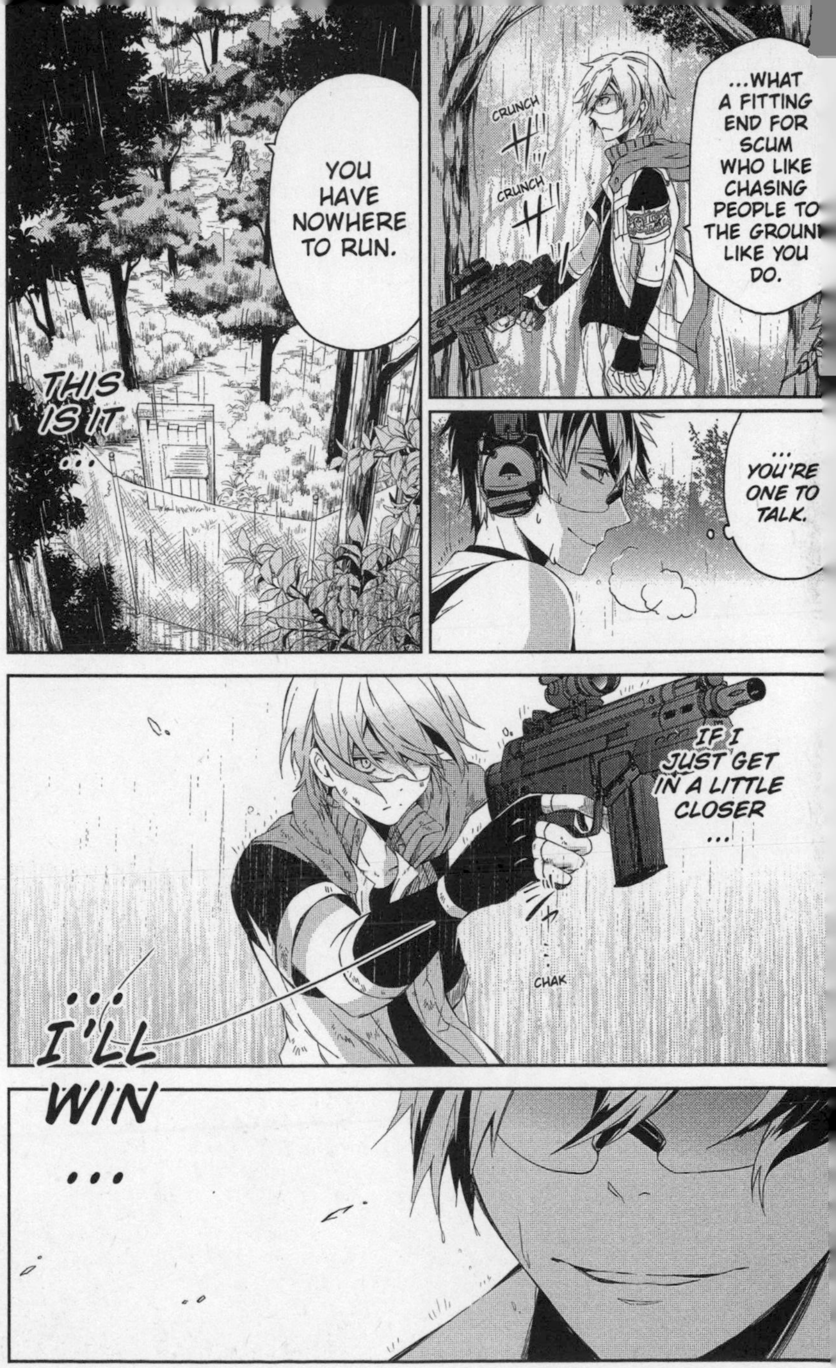
CRUNCH
CRUNCH
...WHAT A FITTING END FOR SCUM WHO LIKE CHASING PEOPLE TO THE GROUN LIKE YOU DO.
YOU HAVE NOWHERE TO RUN.
THIS IS IT ...
... YOU'RE ONE TO TALK.
IF I JUST GET IN A LITTLE CLOSER ...
CHAK
... I'LL WIN ...

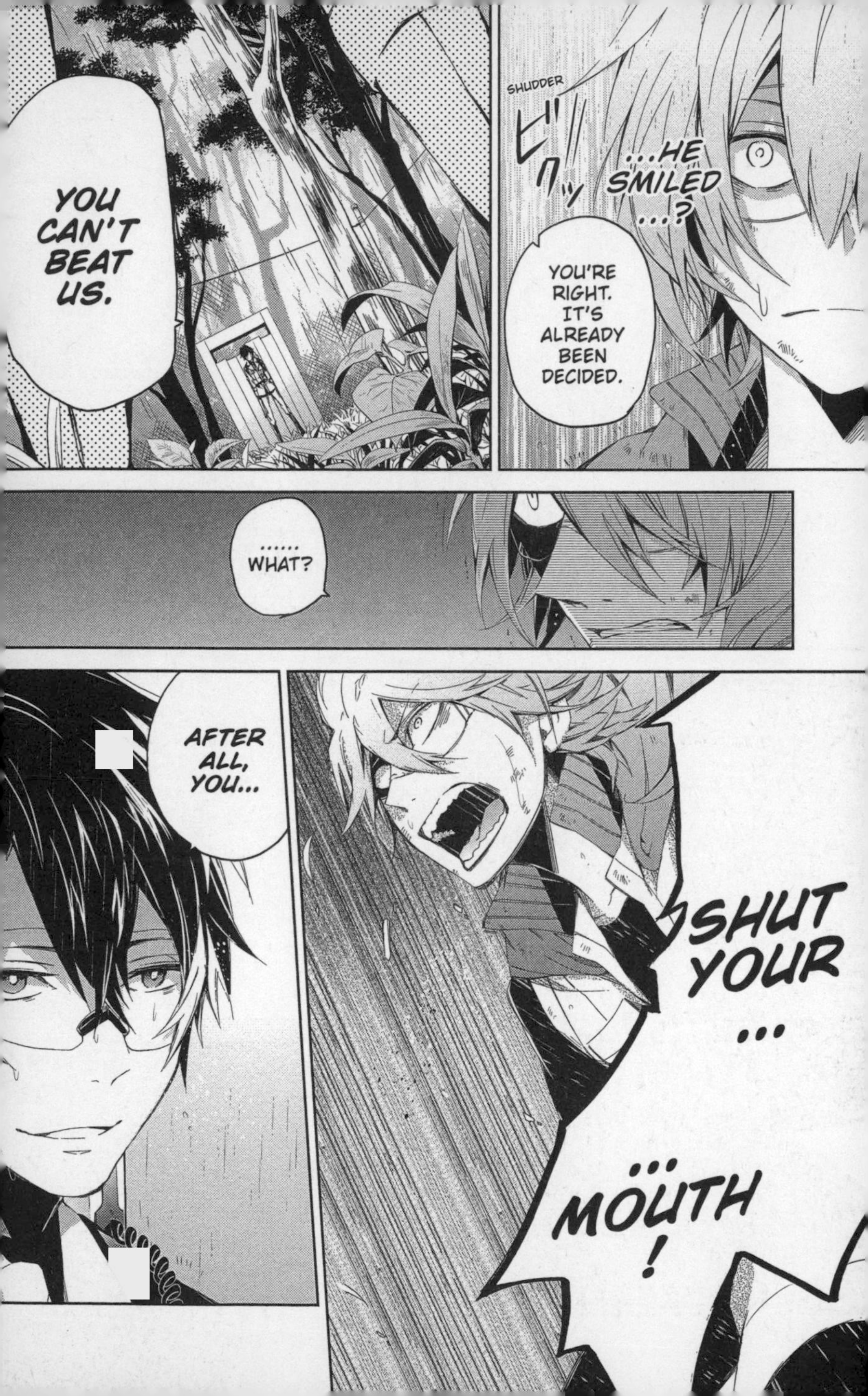
SHUDDER
ビクッ
...HE SMILED ...?
YOU'RE RIGHT. IT'S ALREADY BEEN DECIDED.
YOU CAN'T BEAT US.
...... WHAT?
AFTER ALL, YOU...
SHUT YOUR ...
... MOUTH !

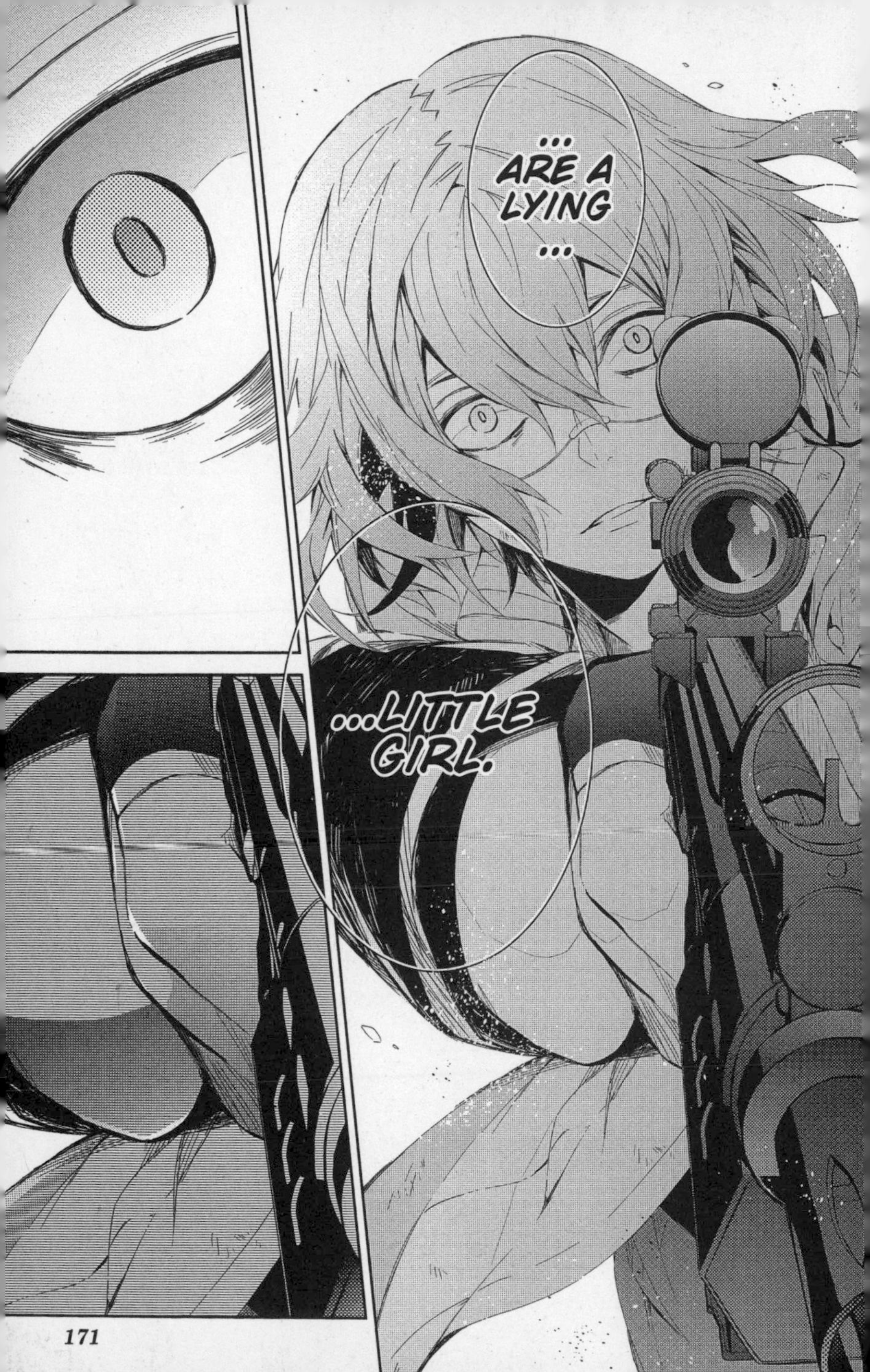
... ARE A LYING ...
...LITTLE GIRL.

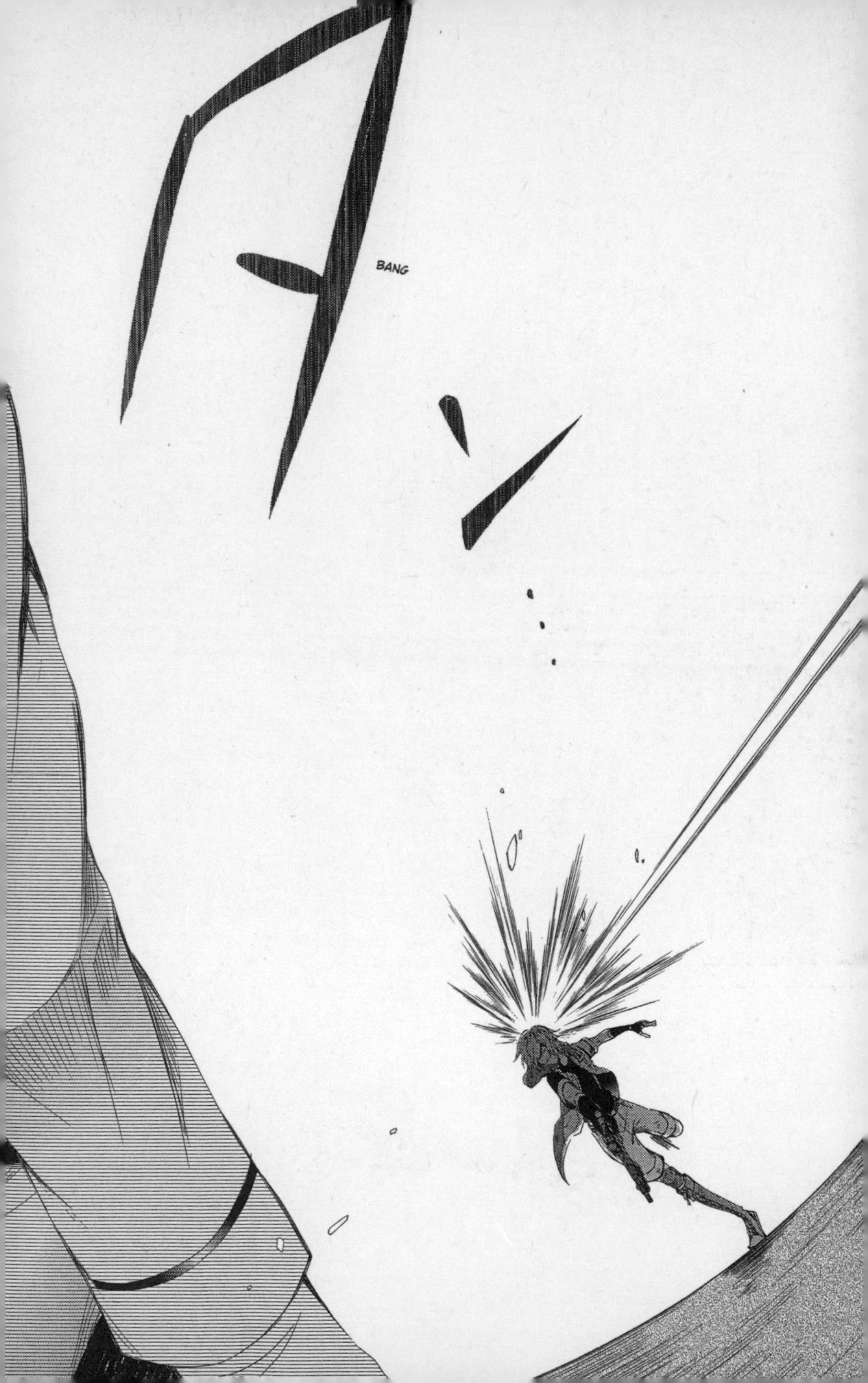
BANG

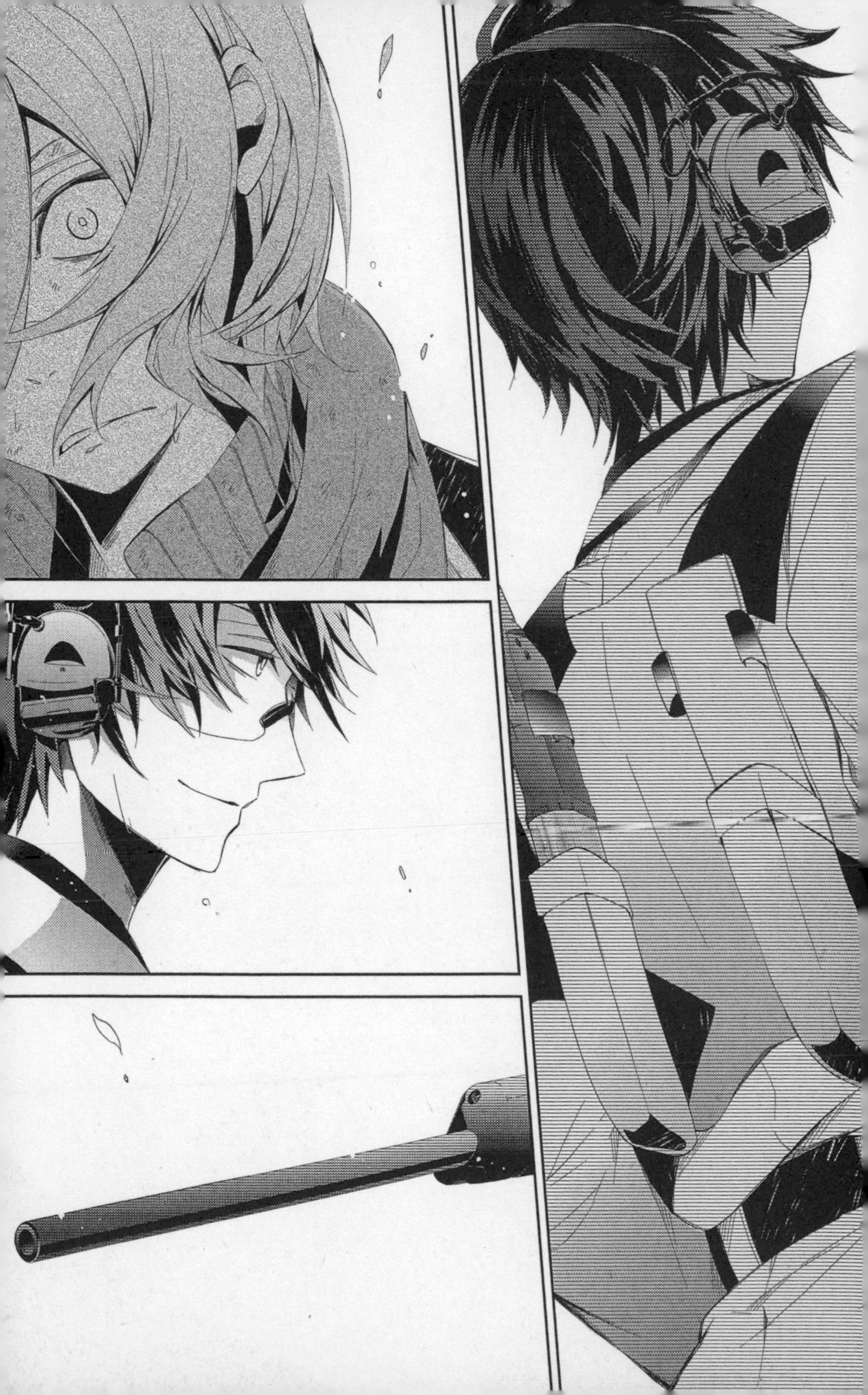

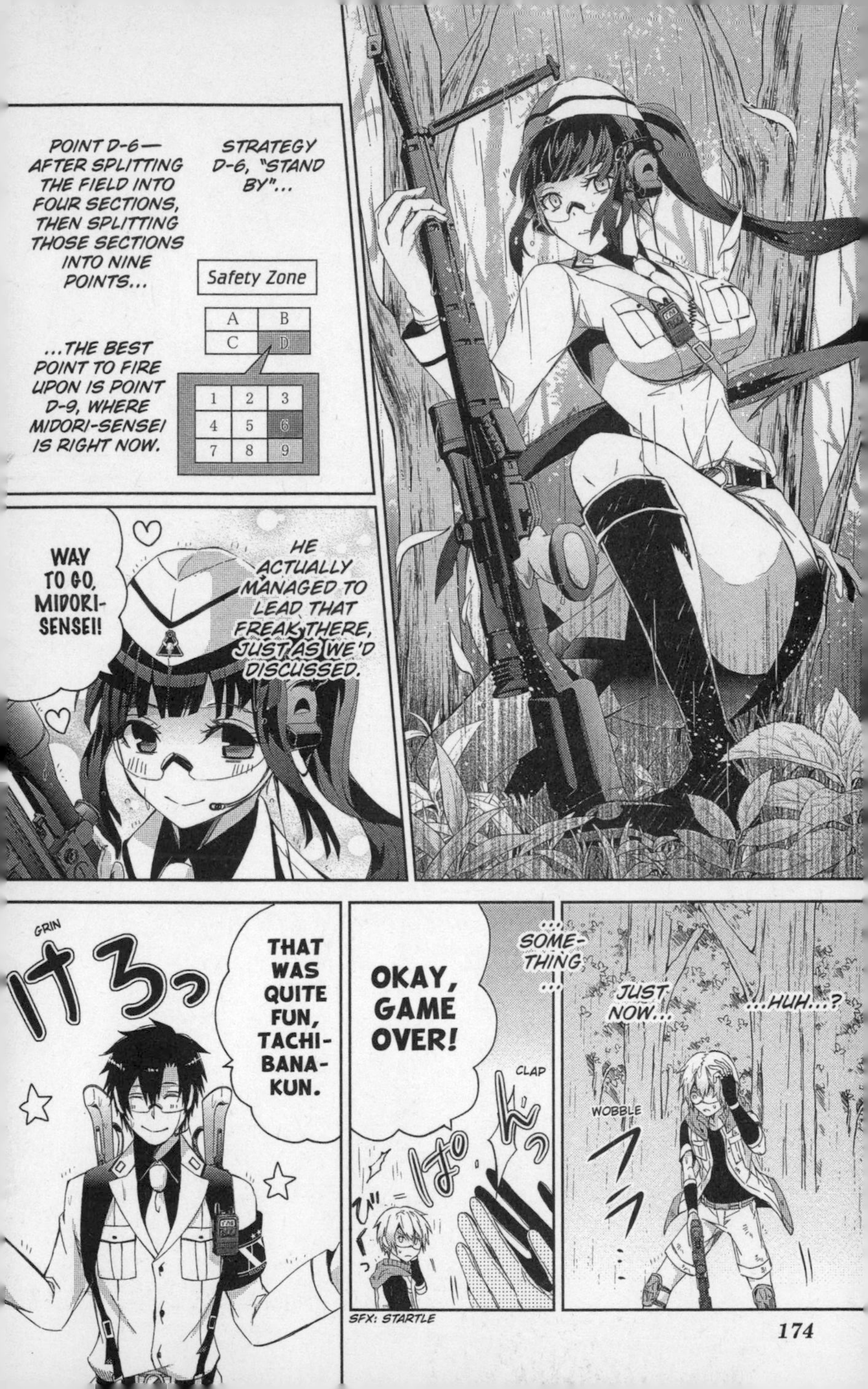

STRATEGY D-6, "STAND BY"...
POINT D-6— AFTER SPLITTING THE FIELD INTO FOUR SECTIONS, THEN SPLITTING THOSE SECTIONS INTO NINE POINTS...
Safety Zone
A B C D
1 2 3 4 5 6 7 8 9
...THE BEST POINT TO FIRE UPON IS POINT D-9, WHERE MIDORI-SENSEI IS RIGHT NOW.
HE ACTUALLY MANAGED TO LEAD THAT FREAK THERE, JUST AS WE'D DISCUSSED.
WAY TO GO, MIDORI-SENSEI!
...HUH...?
JUST NOW...
...SOME-THING, ...
WOBBLE
OKAY, GAME OVER!
CLAP
SFX: STARTLE
THAT WAS QUITE FUN, TACHI-BANA-KUN.
GRIN
けろっ

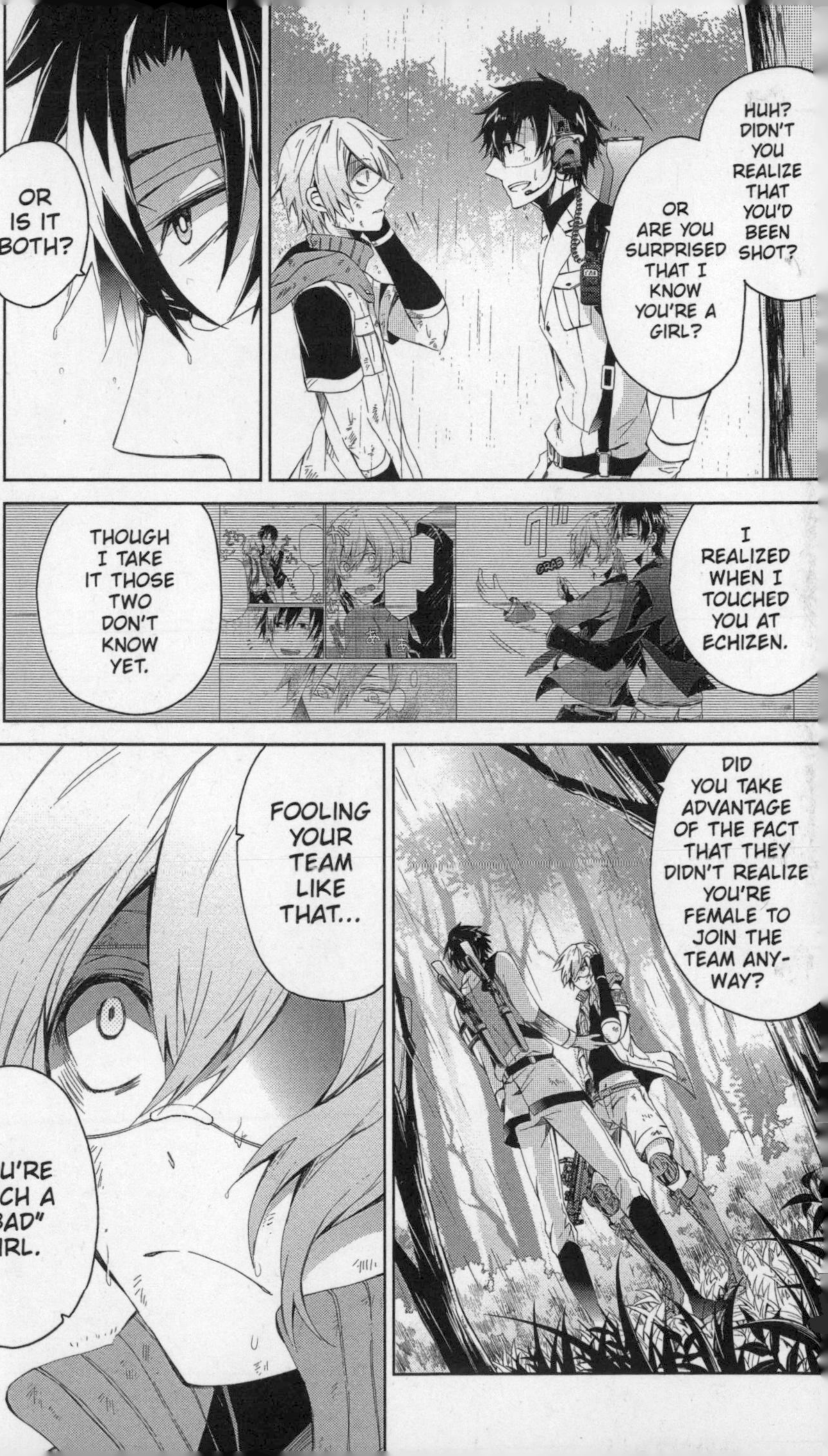
HUH? DIDN'T YOU REALIZE THAT YOU'D BEEN SHOT?
OR ARE YOU SURPRISED THAT I KNOW YOU'RE A GIRL?
OR IS IT BOTH?
I REALIZED WHEN I TOUCHED YOU AT ECHIZEN.
GRAB
THOUGH I TAKE IT THOSE TWO DON'T KNOW YET.
DID YOU TAKE ADVANTAGE OF THE FACT THAT THEY DIDN'T REALIZE YOU'RE FEMALE TO JOIN THE TEAM ANY-WAY?
FOOLING YOUR TEAM LIKE THAT...
YOU'RE SUCH A "BAD" GIRL.

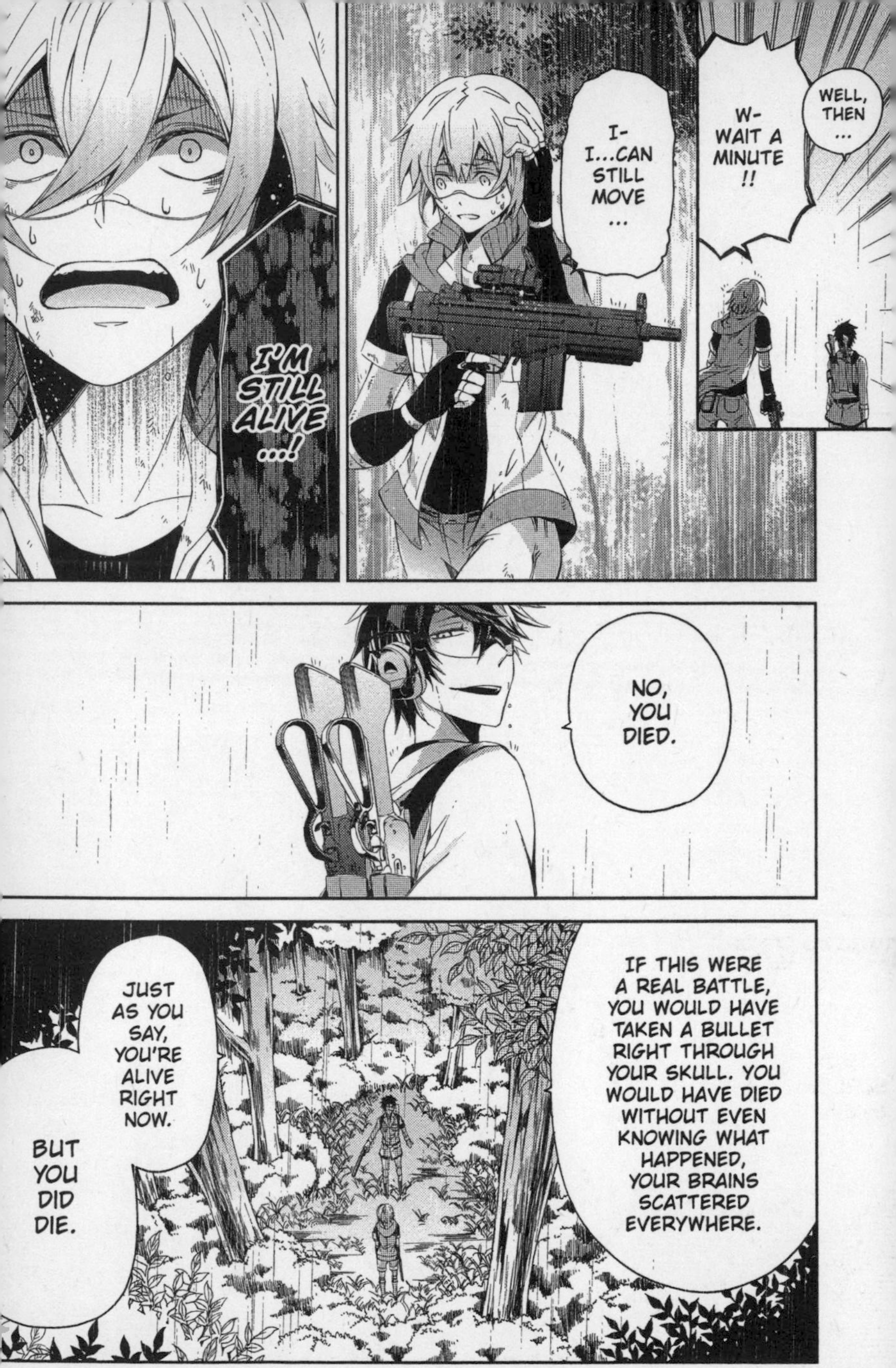
WELL, THEN ...
W- WAIT A MINUTE !!
I- I...CAN STILL MOVE ...
I'M STILL ALIVE ...!
NO, YOU DIED.
IF THIS WERE A REAL BATTLE, YOU WOULD HAVE TAKEN A BULLET RIGHT THROUGH YOUR SKULL. YOU WOULD HAVE DIED WITHOUT EVEN KNOWING WHAT HAPPENED, YOUR BRAINS SCATTERED EVERYWHERE.
JUST AS YOU SAY, YOU'RE ALIVE RIGHT NOW.
BUT YOU DID DIE.

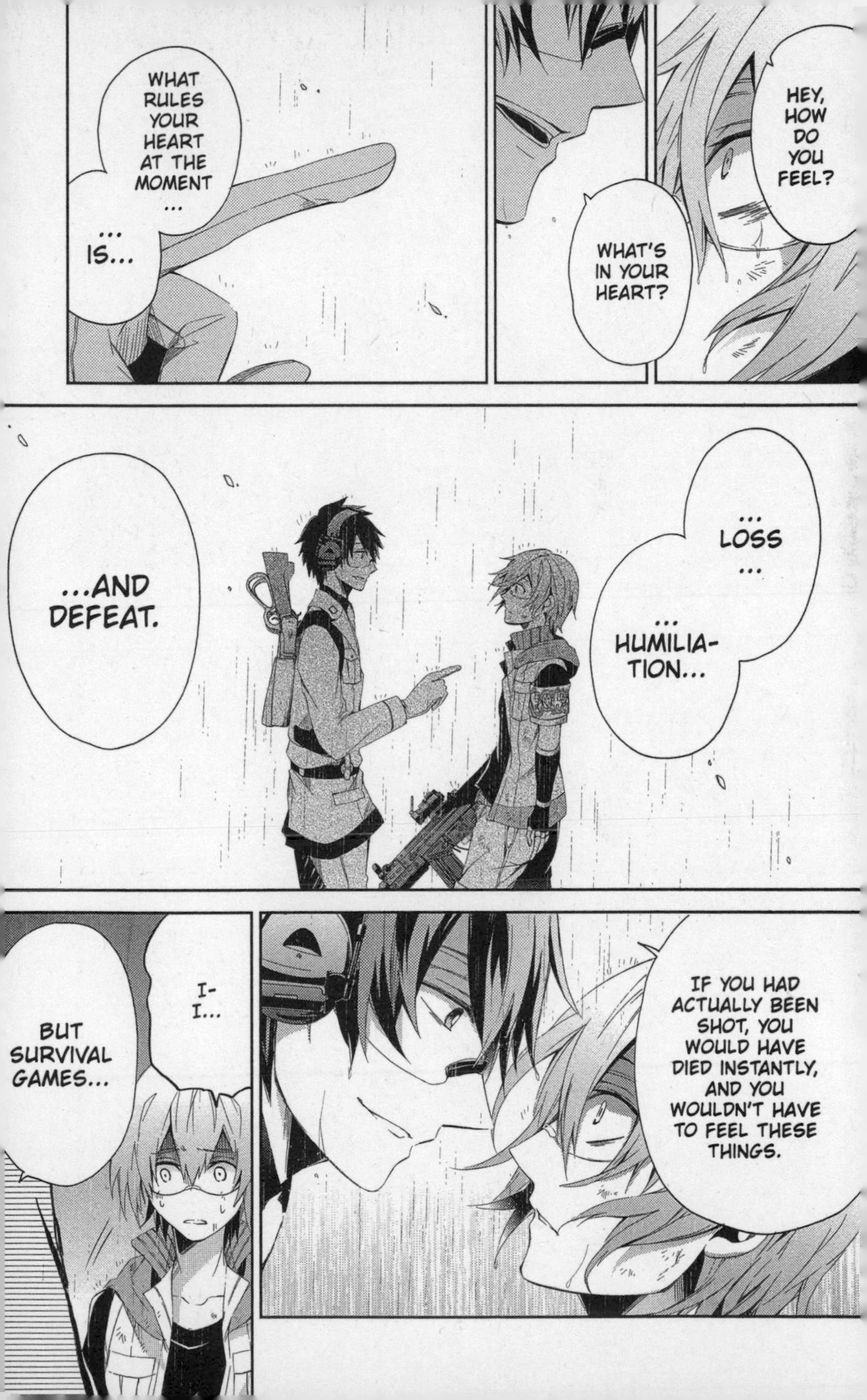
HEY, HOW DO YOU FEEL?
WHAT'S IN YOUR HEART?
WHAT RULES YOUR HEART AT THE MOMENT ...
... IS...
... LOSS ...
... HUMILIATION...
...AND DEFEAT.
IF YOU HAD ACTUALLY BEEN SHOT, YOU WOULD HAVE DIED INSTANTLY, AND YOU WOULDN'T HAVE TO FEEL THESE THINGS.
I- I...
BUT SURVIVAL GAMES...

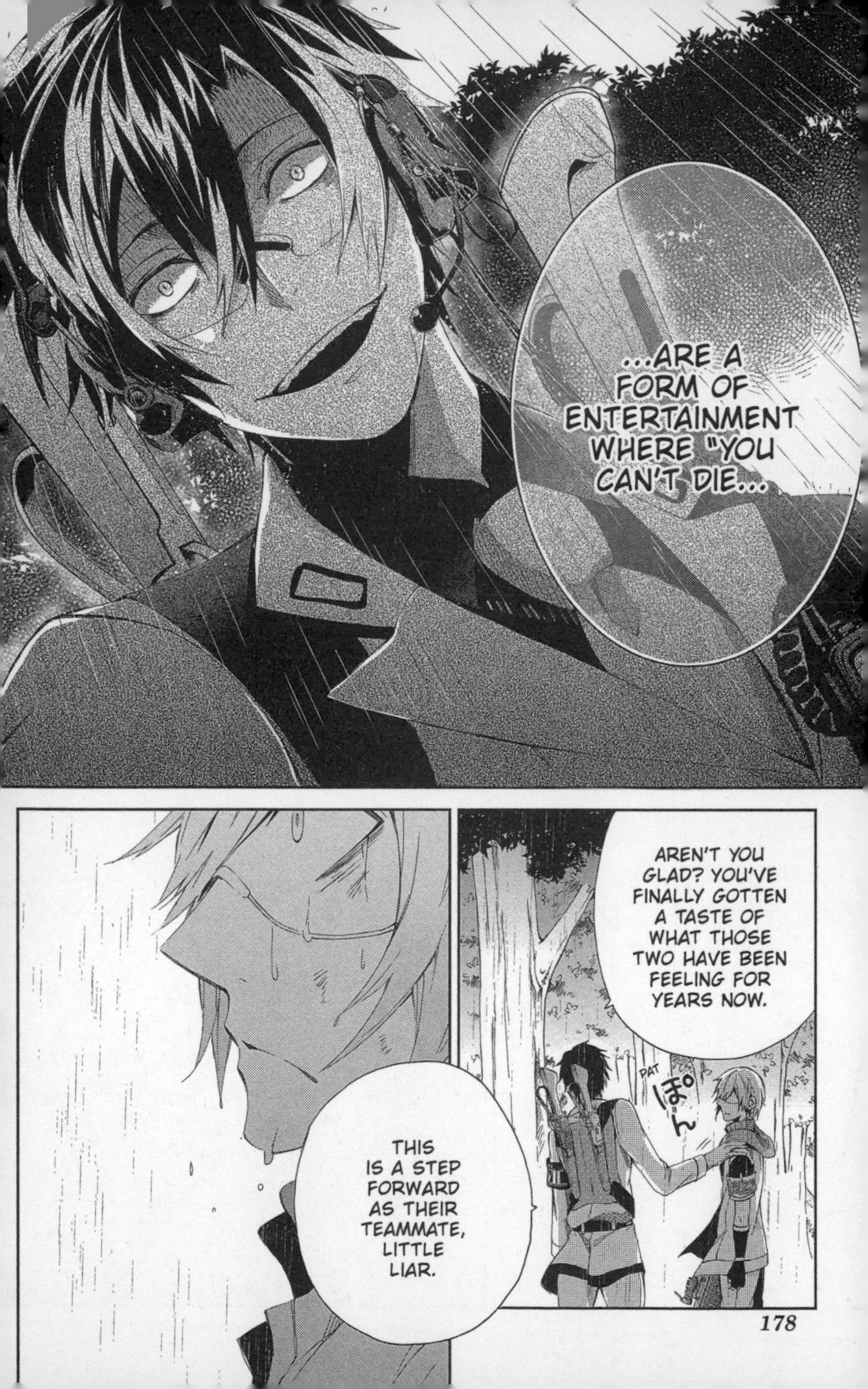
...ARE A FORM OF ENTERTAINMENT WHERE "YOU CAN'T DIE...
ARE'T YOU GLAD? YOU'VE FINALLY GOTTEN A TASTE OF WHAT THOSE TWO HAVE BEEN FEELING FOR YEARS NOW.
PAT
ぽん
THIS IS A STEP FORWARD AS THEIR TEAMMATE, LITTLE LIAR.

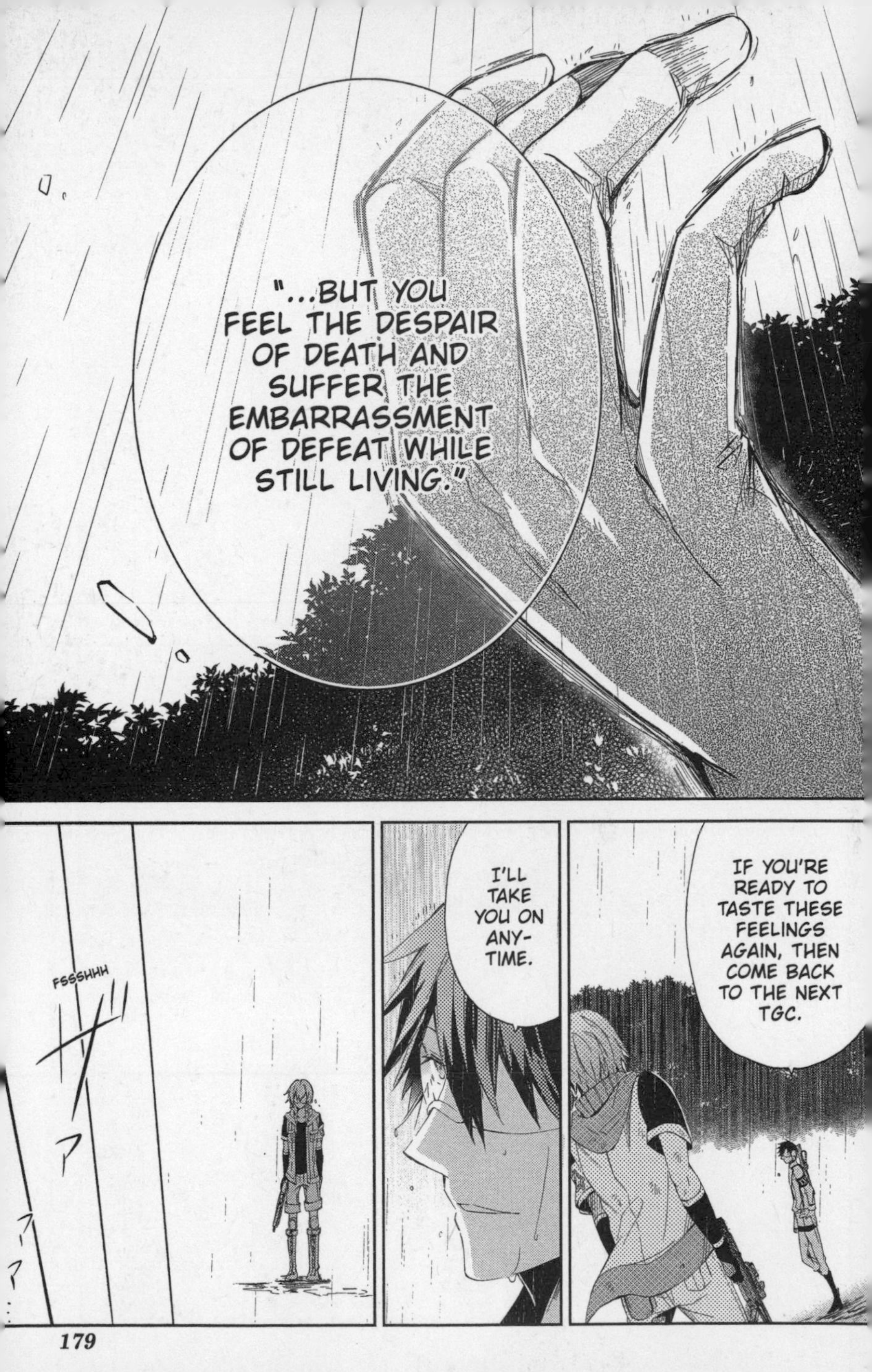
"...BUT YOU FEEL THE DESPAIR OF DEATH AND SUFFER THE EMBARRASSMENT OF DEFEAT WHILE STILL LIVING."
IF YOU'RE READY TO TASTE THESE FEELINGS AGAIN, THEN COME BACK TO THE NEXT TGC.
I'LL TAKE YOU ON ANY-TIME.
FSSSHHH

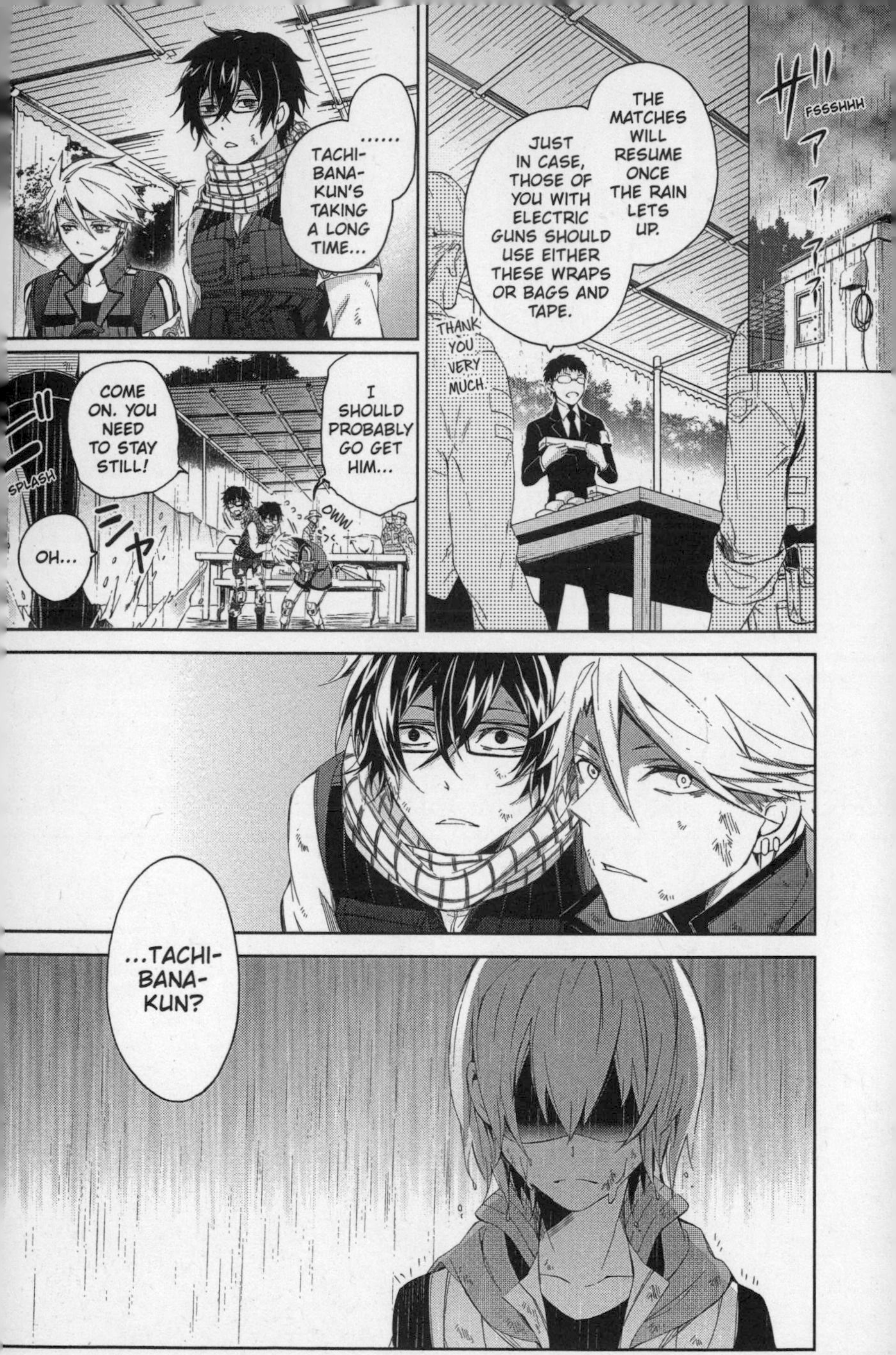
FSSSHHH
THE MATCHES WILL RESUME ONCE THE RAIN LETS UP.
JUST IN CASE, THOSE OF YOU WITH ELECTRIC GUNS SHOULD USE EITHER THESE WRAPS OR BAGS AND TAPE.
THANK YOU VERY MUCH.
...... TACHI-BANA-KUN'S TAKING A LONG TIME...
I SHOULD PROBABLY GO GET HIM...
OWW
COME ON. YOU NEED TO STAY STILL!
SPLASH
OH...
...TACHI-BANA-KUN?

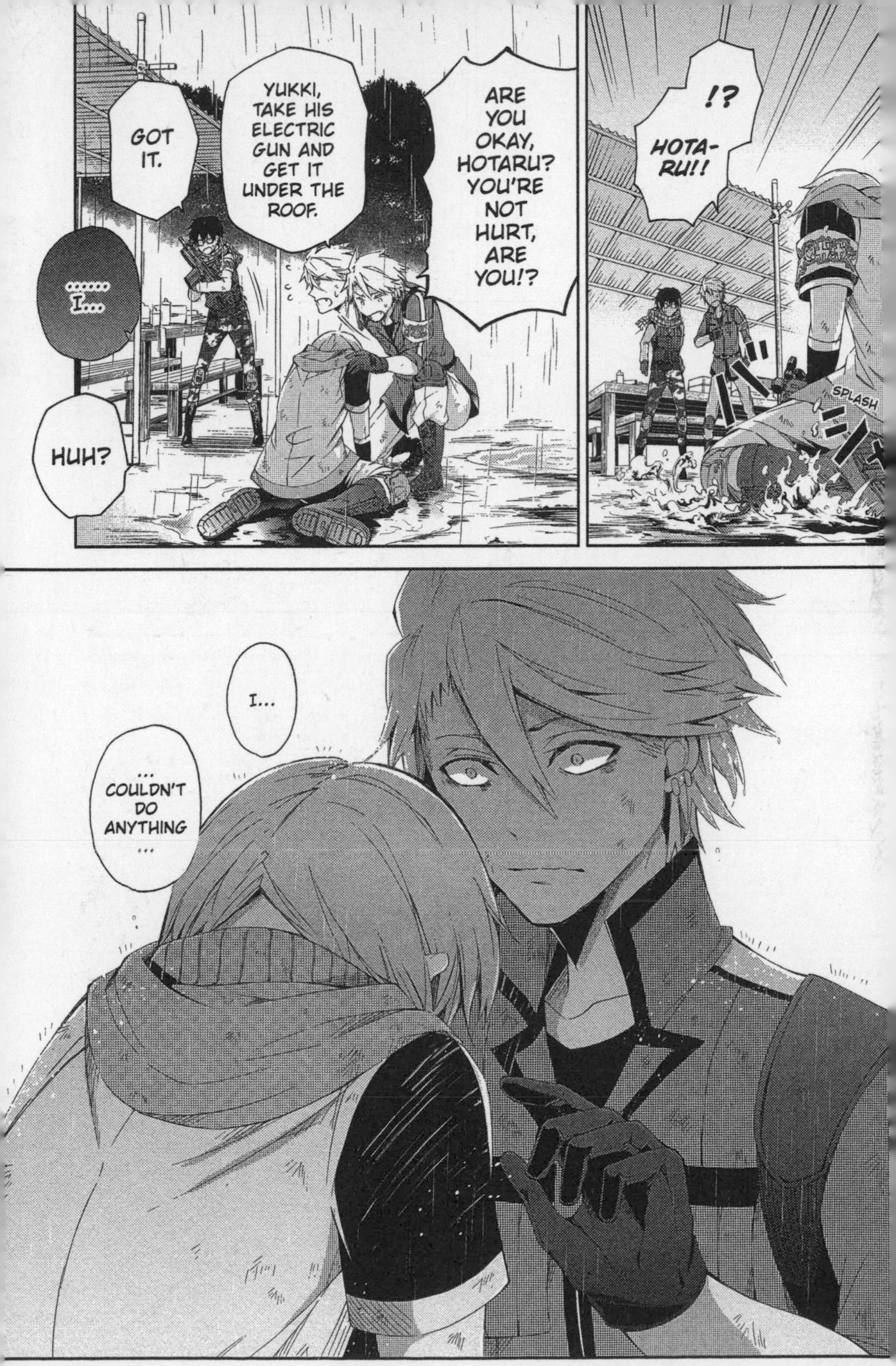
!?
HOTA-RU!!
SPLASH
ARE YOU OKAY, HOTARU? YOU'RE NOT HURT, ARE YOU!?
YUKKI, TAKE HIS ELECTRIC GUN AND GET IT UNDER THE ROOF.
GOT IT.
......I...
HUH?
I...
...COULDN'T DO ANYTHING...

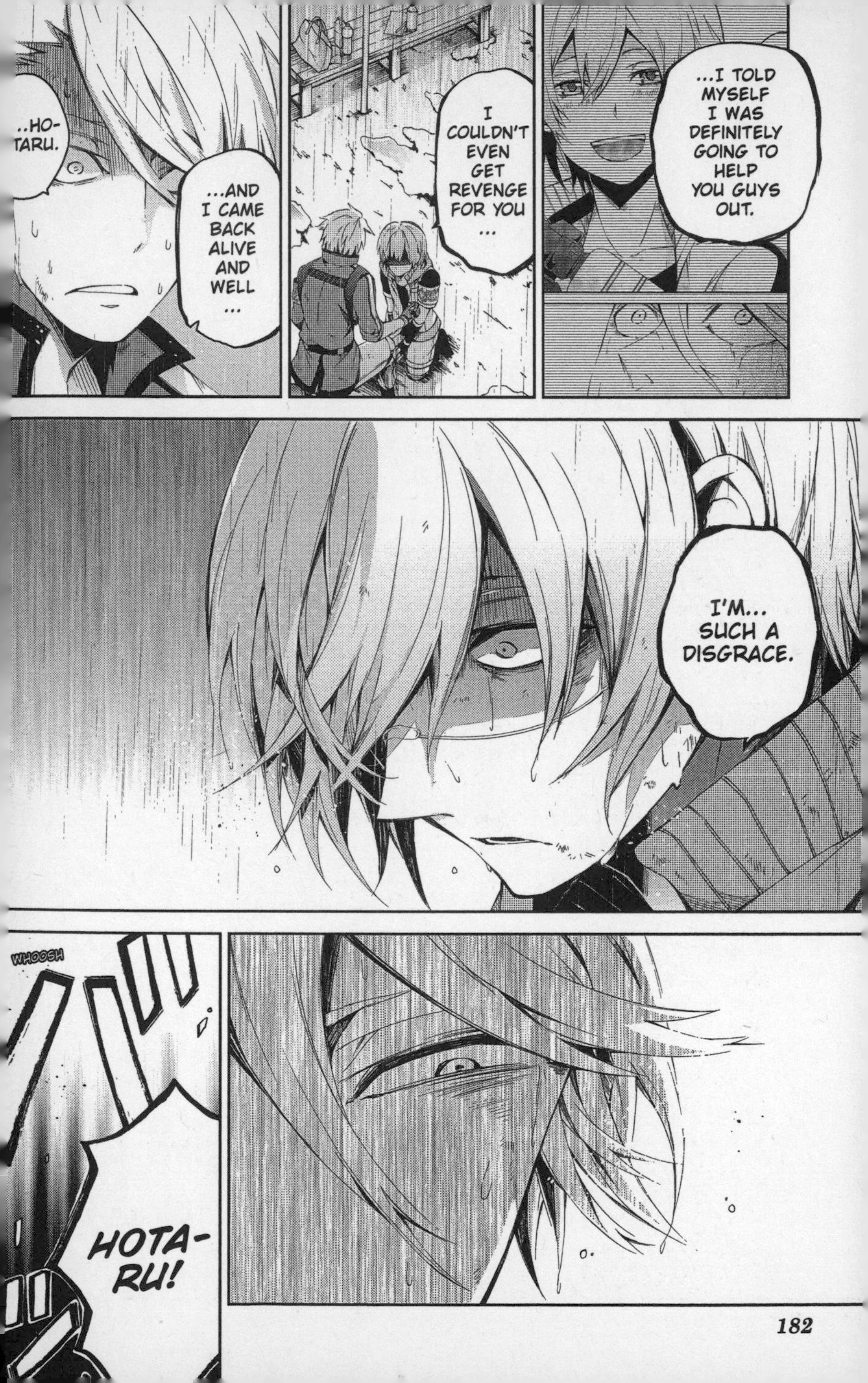
...I TOLD MYSELF I WAS DEFINITELY GOING TO HELP YOU GUYS OUT.
I COULDN'T EVEN GET REVENGE FOR YOU ...
...AND I CAME BACK ALIVE AND WELL ...
..HO-TARU.
I'M... SUCH A DISGRACE.
WHOOSH
HOTA-RU!

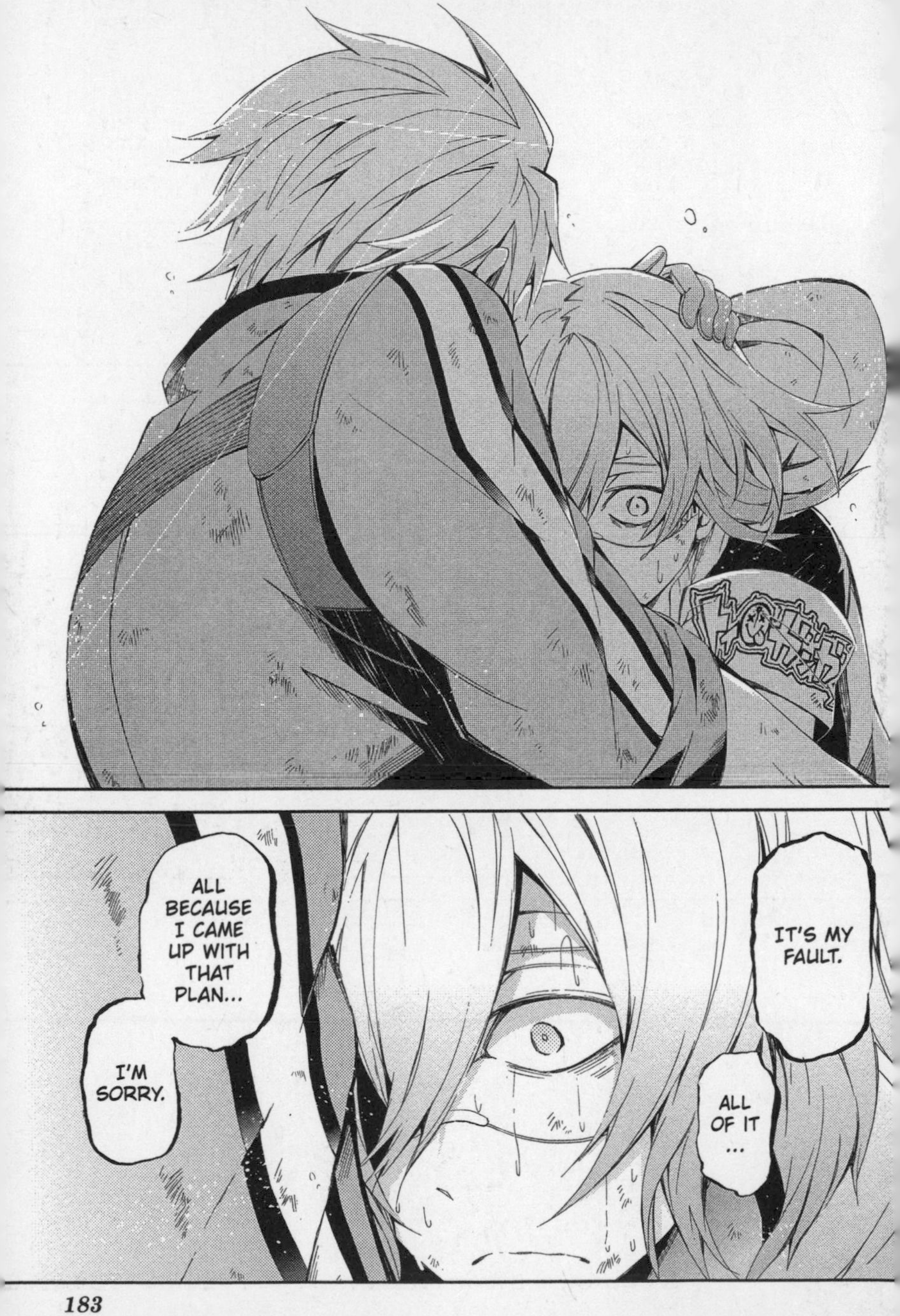
IT'S MY FAULT.
ALL OF IT ...
ALL BECAUSE I CAME UP WITH THAT PLAN...
I'M SORRY.

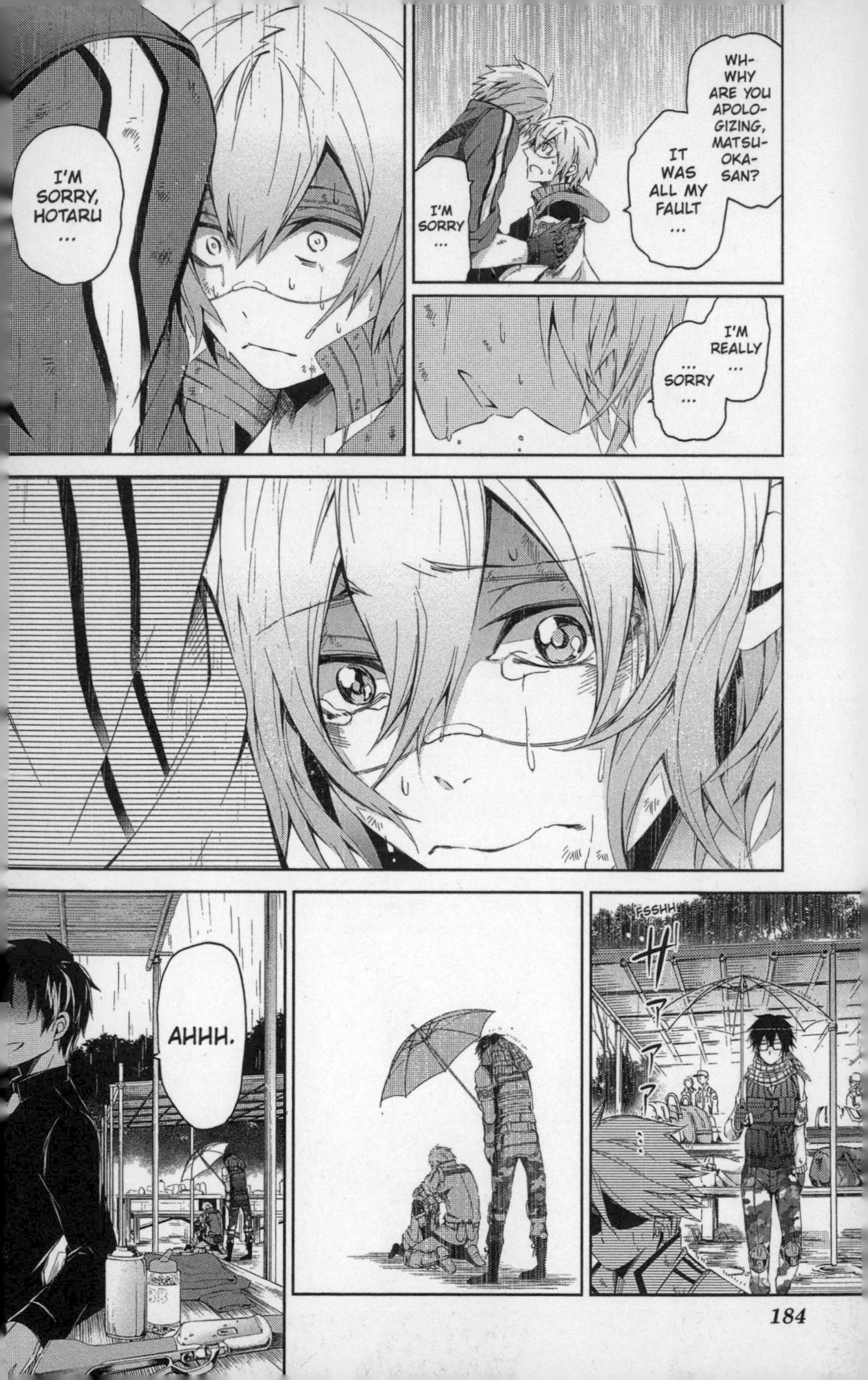
WH-WHY ARE YOU APOLOGIZING, MATSUOKA-SAN?
IT WAS ALL MY FAULT ...
I'M SORRY ...
I'M REALLY ... SORRY ...
I'M SORRY, HOTARU ...
FSSHH
...
AHHH.

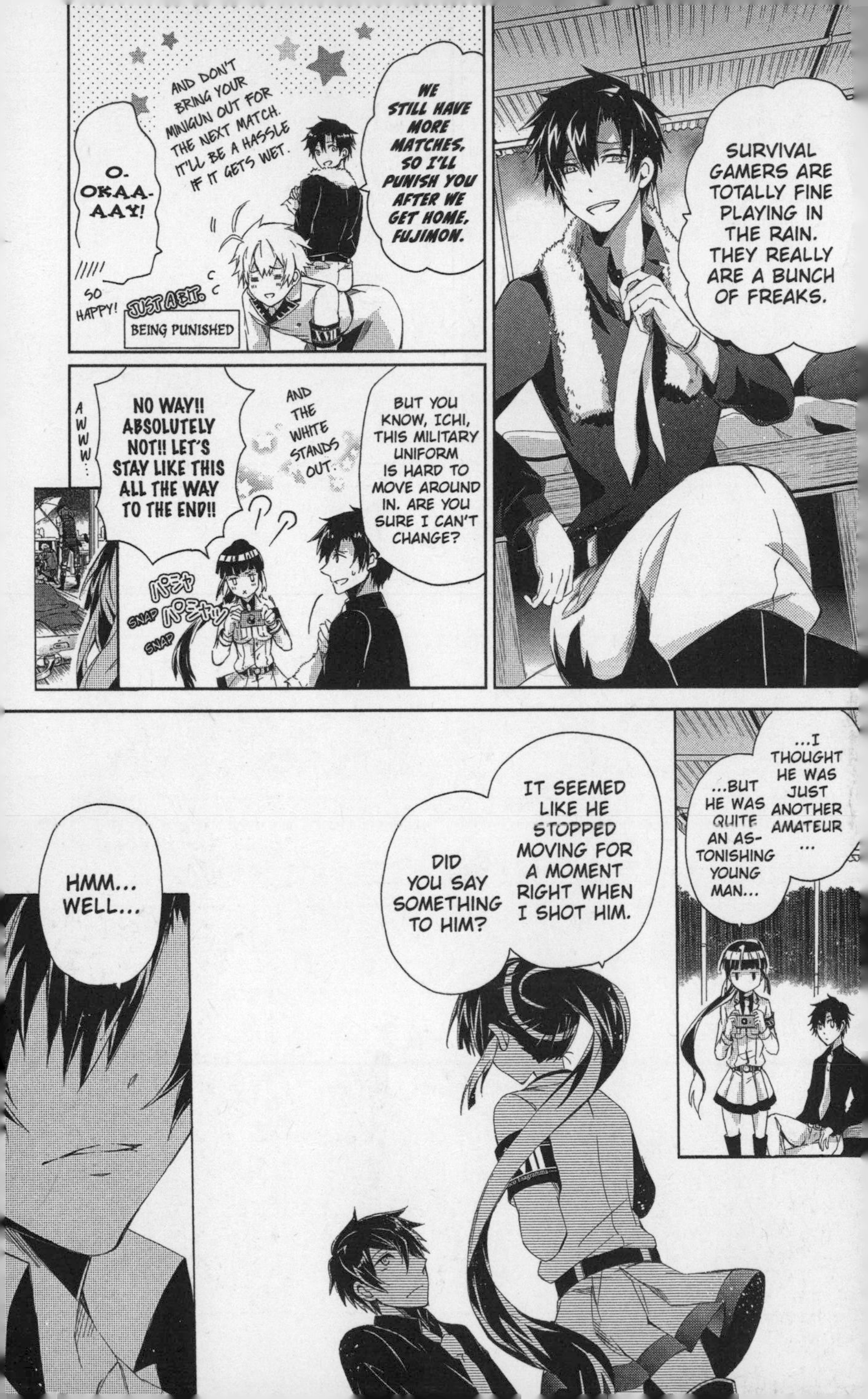

SURVIVAL GAMERS ARE TOTALLY FINE PLAYING IN THE RAIN. THEY REALLY ARE A BUNCH OF FREAKS.
WE STILL HAVE MORE MATCHES, SO I'LL PUNISH YOU AFTER WE GET HOME, FUJIMON.
AND DON'T BRING YOUR MINIGUN OUT FOR THE NEXT MATCH. IT'LL BE A HASSLE IF IT GETS WET.
O-OKAAAAY!
SO HAPPY!
JUST A BIT.
BEING PUNISHED
BUT YOU KNOW, ICHI, THIS MILITARY UNIFORM IS HARD TO MOVE AROUND IN. ARE YOU SURE I CAN'T CHANGE?
AND THE WHITE STANDS OUT.
NO WAY!! ABSOLUTELY NOT!! LET'S STAY LIKE THIS ALL THE WAY TO THE END!!
AWWW...
パシャ SNAP
パシャッ SNAP
...I THOUGHT HE WAS JUST ANOTHER AMATEUR...
...BUT HE WAS QUITE AN ASTONISHING YOUNG MAN...
IT SEEMED LIKE HE STOPPED MOVING FOR A MOMENT RIGHT WHEN I SHOT HIM.
DID YOU SAY SOMETHING TO HIM?
HMM... WELL...

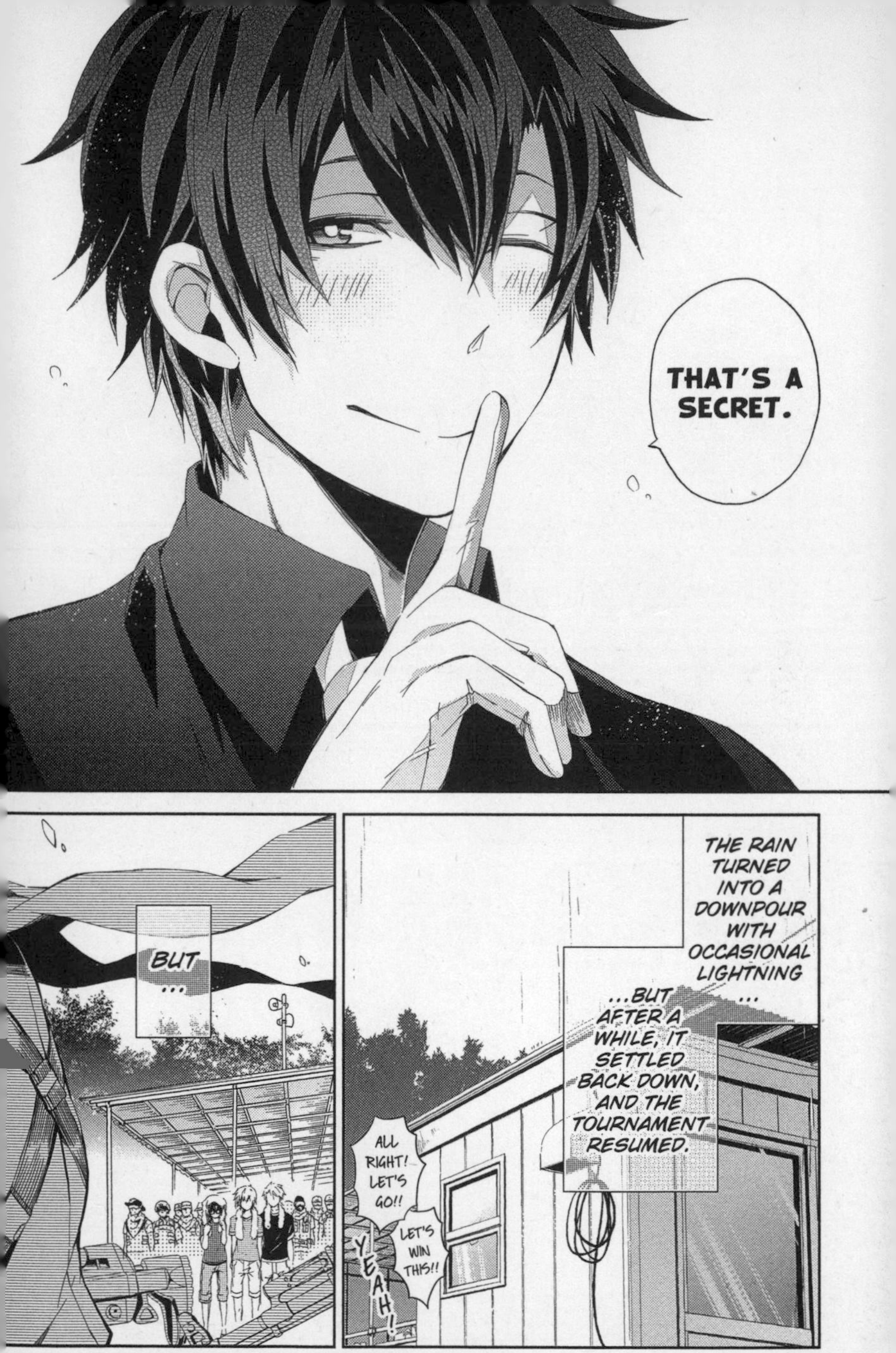
THAT'S A SECRET.
THE RAIN TURNED INTO A DOWNPOUR WITH OCCASIONAL LIGHTNING ...
...BUT AFTER A WHILE, IT SETTLED BACK DOWN, AND THE TOURNAMENT RESUMED.
ALL RIGHT! LET'S GO!!
LET'S WIN THIS!!
YEAH!
BUT ...

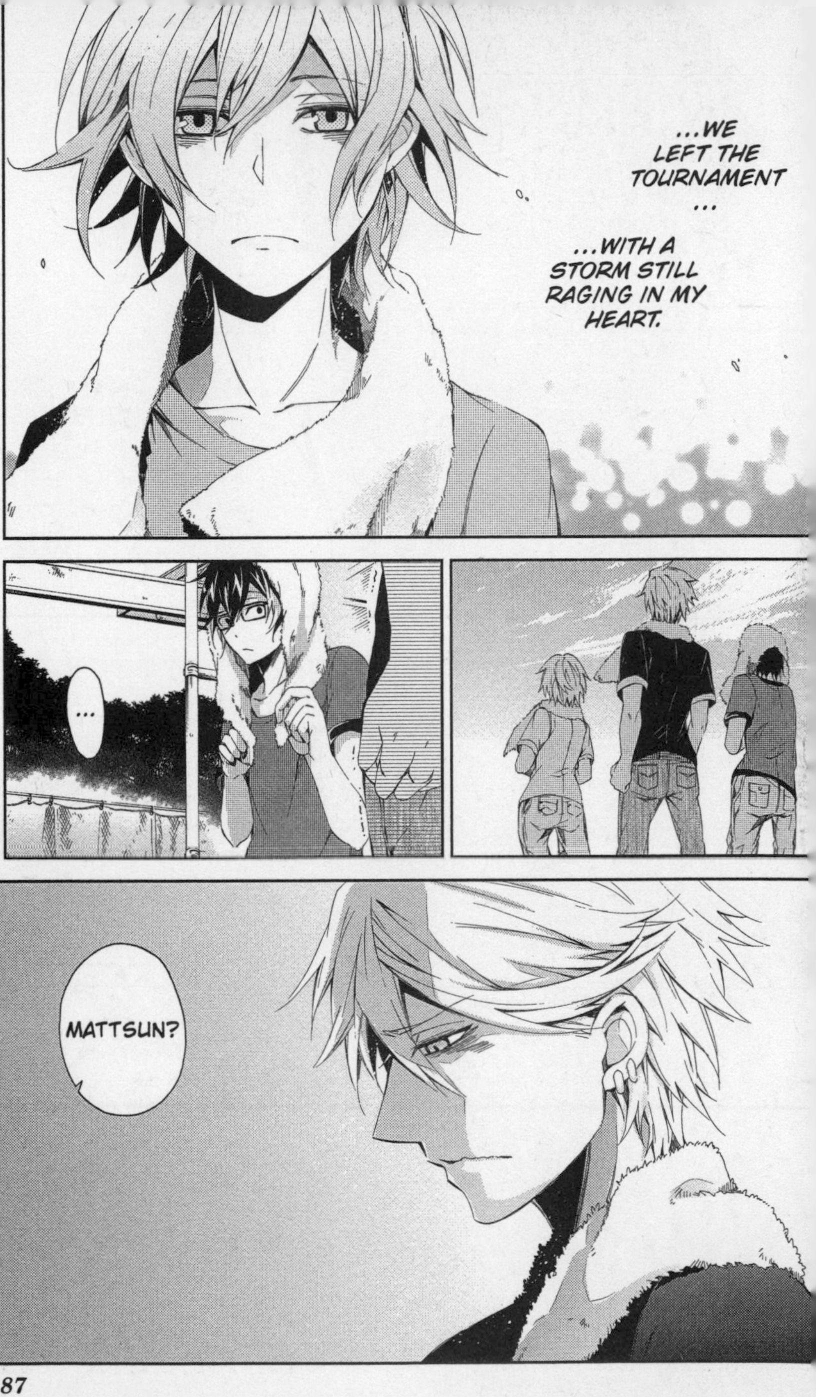
...WE LEFT THE TOURNAMENT ...
...WITH A STORM STILL RAGING IN MY HEART.
...
...
MATTSUN?

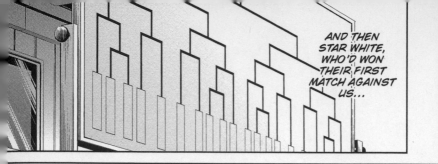

AND THEN STAR WHITE, WHO'D WON THEIR FIRST MATCH AGAINST US...

...
WENT ON TO BE KNOWN
...

...AS THE FIVE-TIME CONSECUTIVE CHAMPIONS.

AOHARU×MACHINE GUN ③ END

AOHARU × MACHINE GUN

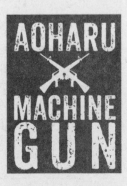

TACHIBANA AND THE OTHERS HAVE SUFFERED DEFEAT AT THE
HANDS OF TEAM STAR WHITE, AND NOW THEY HAVE RETURNED
TO THEIR EVERYDAY LIVES. HOWEVER, MIDORI'S WORDS HAVE
STABBED TACHIBANA'S HEART.

"FOOLING YOUR TEAM LIKE THAT...YOU'RE SUCH A 'BAD' GIRL."

BUT TACHIBANA REALIZES WHAT SHE NEEDS TO DO THANKS TO THE ADVICE OF HER FRIEND KANAE, AND SHE FINALLY DECIDES TO TELL MATSUOKA AND YUKIMURA THAT SHE'S A GIRL.

AT THE END OF THE DAY, WILL TACHIBANA BE ABLE TO PLAY SURVIVAL GAMES WITH THE OTHERS AGAIN?

WATCH FOR VOLUME 4 OF **AOHARU X MACHINEGUN** IN PRINT— APRIL 2017!

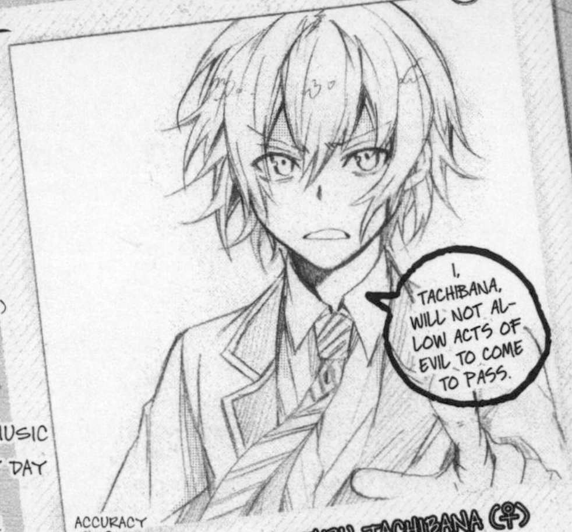
I, TACHIBANA, WILL NOT ALLOW ACTS OF EVIL TO COME TO PASS.

HOTARU TACHIBANA (♀)
OCCUPATION: STUDENT (HIGH SCHOOL 2ND-YEAR)

- BIRTHDAY: 4/1
- HEIGHT/WEIGHT: 5' 7"/121 LBS.
- BLOOD TYPE: A
- GUN USED: G3 SAS HC
- PLAYSTYLE: CLOSE-RANGE ATTACKER (BECAUSE HER BULLETS DON'T HIT)
- TEAM: TOY☆GUN GUN

- FAVORITE SUBJECT: GYM
- LEAST FAVORITE SUBJECTS: ENGLISH, MUSIC
- DAILY GOAL: ONE ACT OF JUSTICE EVERY DAY
- ABOUT HER UNIFORM: BECAUSE HER SCHOOL ALLOWS FEMALE STUDENTS TO CHOOSE BETWEEN PANTS AND SKIRTS, SHE WEARS PANTS. ALSO, SHE WEARS A BOY'S JACKET BECAUSE SHE HAS WIDE SHOULDERS.

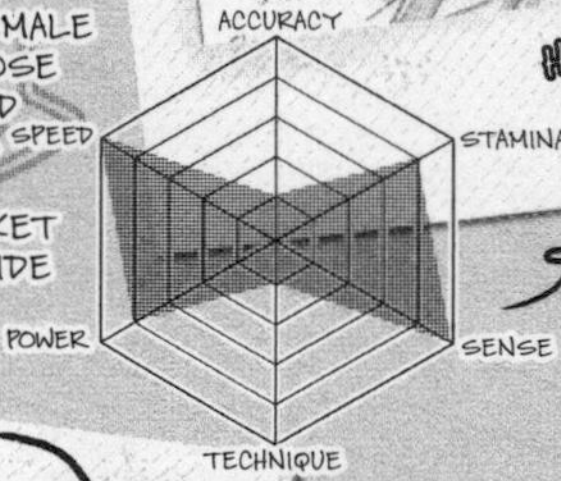
ACCURACY
STAMINA
SENSE
TECHNIQUE
POWER
SPEED

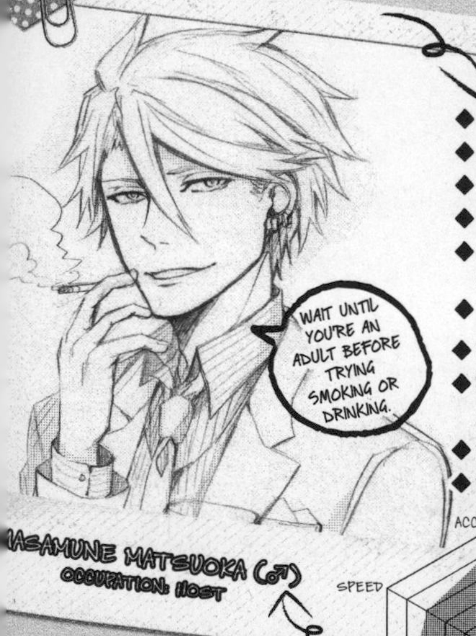
WAIT UNTIL YOU'RE AN ADULT BEFORE TRYING SMOKING OR DRINKING.

MASAMUNE MATSUOKA (♂)
OCCUPATION: HOST

- BIRTHDAY: 12/24
- HEIGHT/WEIGHT: 5' 11"/154 LBS.
- BLOOD TYPE: O
- GUN USED: DESERT EAGLE (SILVER AND BLACK)
- PLAYSTYLE: DUAL-WIELDING ALL-ROUNDER (OFTEN PLAYS COMMANDER BECAUSE OF HOW OBSERVANT HE IS)
- TEAM: TOY☆GUN GUN

- FAVORITE FOODS: STRING CHEESE, BEEF JERKY
- LEAST FAVORITE FOODS: SWEET THINGS, JAPANESE LIQUOR (BECAUSE IT AFFECTS HIM BADLY)
- BEST FOOD TO MAKE: ANYTHING STIR-FRIED
- BRAND OF CIGARETTES: MARLBORO
- SPECIAL SKILL: IDENTIFYING WOMEN'S PERFUMES

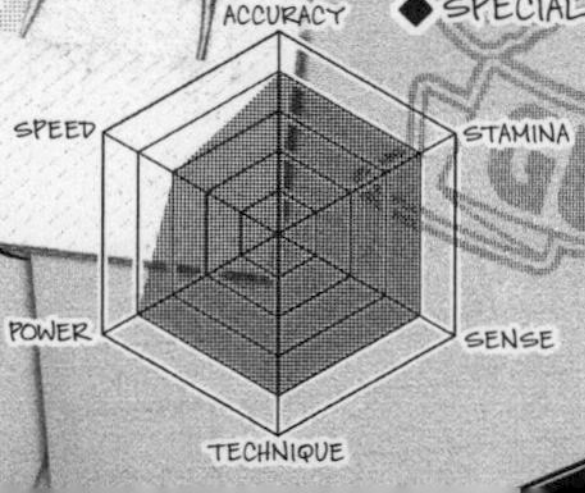
ACCURACY
STAMINA
SENSE
TECHNIQUE
POWER
SPEED

HELLO, I'M NAOE. I'VE DECIDED TO HAVE AN AUTHOR'S NOTE HERE. USUALLY I'M NATTERING AWAY ON TWITTER, SO WHEN THE TIME COMES, I CAN'T THINK OF ANYTHING TO SAY...ANYWAY, SINCE THIS IS MY FIRST TIME DOING THIS, I THINK I'LL TOUCH ON SURVIVAL GAMES AND SHARE SOME CHARACTER STORIES, SINCE THERE ARE BIOS ON THE FACING PAGE.

I'VE PLAYED SOME SURVIVAL GAMES MYSELF; IT'S ACTUALLY A VERY GENTLEMANLY SPORT. THERE'S A SPECIAL TOURNAMENT CALLED THE TGC IN THIS MANGA, AND IN THAT TOURNAMENT, COMPETING TEAMS CAN CHOOSE TO AGREE UPON ALLOWING PHYSICAL CONTACT, BUT USUALLY CONTACT IS FORBIDDEN. JUST IN CASE, IF READING THIS MANGA MAKES YOU INTERESTED IN TRYING SURVIVAL GAMES, PLEASE DO FAMILIARIZE YOURSELF WITH THE RULES. AND BE VERY CAREFUL NOT TO GET HURT. CHARACTERS' EXPRESSIONS ARE IMPORTANT IN MANGA, SO THEY'RE ONLY WEARING SHOOTING GLASSES, BUT FULL FACE PROTECTION IS BETTER!
I REALLY DO HOPE THAT YOU ENJOY YOURSELF PLAYING SURVIVAL GAMES.

THINGS GOT PRETTY SERIOUS THIS TIME, BUT IT'S USUALLY PRETTY LIGHT AND FLUFFY. AND NOW, I KNOW IT'S SUDDEN, BUT LET'S MOVE ON TO CHARACTER STORIES.

[HOTARU TACHIBANA] SHE'S THE CHARACTER WHO'S CHANGED THE MOST FROM THE ORIGINAL PLAN. AT FIRST, SHE WAS A LITTLE GIRL NAMED "KIIRO TACHIBANA." IT'S HARD TO HAVE A FEMALE PROTAGONIST IN G FANTASY. SHE HAS TO BE THE KIND OF GIRL WHO GIRLS LIKE. SO I TRIED ALL TYPES OF DIFFERENT APPROACHES, AND SHE TURNED INTO THE SORT OF CHARACTER YOU EITHER LOVE OR HATE. I FIGURED THAT IF NO ONE HATED HER, NO ONE WOULD REALLY LIKE HER EITHER...AND THAT WOULD MAKE HER KIND OF HALF-BAKED. HER NAME COMES FROM THE SENGOKU PERIOD WARLORD MUNESHIGE TACHIBANA. I THOUGHT ABOUT HAVING HER USE MALE PRONOUNS DESPITE BEING A GIRL, BUT I DECIDED TO HAVE HER USE HER LAST NAME INSTEAD. DURING THE TWO-SHOT PROLOGUE, I TRIED TO DIFFERENTIATE HER FROM MATSUOKA BY USING SOME TONE ON THE ENDS OF HER HAIR.
I WAVER BETWEEN TRYING TO DRAW HER CUTER OR COOLER, BUT I NEVER REALLY TRY TO DRAW HER FEMININE. ^^

[MASAMUNE MATSUOKA] HE WAS THE PROTAGONIST IN THE FRESH GANGAN SHORT STORY. AT FIRST, HE WORE HIS HAIR SLICKED BACK, BUT MY EDITOR TOLD ME "HE HAS TO HAVE BANGS," AND I REMEMBER FIGHTING OVER THAT. TO BE REBELLIOUS, I MADE HIS HAIRSTYLE HAVE JUST ONE SIDE SLICKED BACK. HE'S MEANT TO BE A HANDSOME CHARACTER, BUT I WONDER...WOULD GENERAL SOCIETY REALLY THINK A GUY WITH SUCH SLANTED EYES WAS HANDSOME? I PERSONALLY REALLY LOVE SLANTED EYES! I LOVE THEM, BUT I REALLY DO LIKE BLONDES WITH BLUE EYES TOO...HE MIGHT JUST BE THE CHARACTER WHO TIES TOGETHER ALL THE VISUALS THAT I LIKE THE MOST. HIS NAME COMES FROM THE SENGOKU WARLORD MASAMUNE DATE. I REALLY DO LIKE THE NAME MASAMUNE.

I WAS THINKING, "OH NO, AM I GOING TO BE ABLE TO FILL UP ALL THIS SPACE?" BUT IT TURNS OUT I DIDN'T HAVE ENOUGH SPACE.
I HOPE I SEE YOU AGAIN NEXT TIME...
THANK YOU VERY MUCH FOR READING ALL THE WAY UP TO THIS POINT!

Special thanks

MY EDITOR, THE EDITOR-IN-CHIEF, THE SALES STAFF, THE DESIGNERS, TOKYO MARUI, DEKA SHIMAMURA-SAMA, THE AKIHARABA BRANCH OF WILLYPEET, HIRANO-SAMA, KOMINA-SAMA, GA-SAMA, HAYATAROU SHINNOU-SAMA, MY ASSISTANT KURARA, URO (RASCAL), BUNJI-SAMA, WAKA SANADA-SAMA, MY FATHER, MY MOTHER, AND YOU!

by NAOE

Translation: Leighann Harvey
Lettering: Bianca Pistillo

AOHARU×KIKANJU Volume 3 ©2013 NAOE/SQUARE ENIX CO., LTD. First published in Japan in 2013 by SQUARE ENIX CO., LTD. English translation rights arranged with SQUARE ENIX CO., LTD. and Yen Press, LLC through Tuttle-Mori Agency, Inc., Tokyo.

English Translation ©2016 by SQUARE ENIX CO., LTD.

Yen Press
1290 Avenue of
New York, NY 1C

Visit us at yenpr
facebook.com/yu
twitter.com/yen
yenpress.tumblr.
instagram.com/y

First Yen Press Print Edition: February 2017
Originally published as an ebook in April 2016 by Yen Press.

Yen Press is an imprint of Yen Press, LLC.
The Yen Press name and logo are trademarks of Yen Press, LLC.

The publisher is not responsible for websites (or their content) that are not owned by the publisher.

Library of Congress Control Number: 2016946057

ISBN: 978-0-316-55335-3 (paperback)

10 9 8 7 6 5 4 3 2 1

BVG

Printed in the United States of America